BETWEEN THE LINES

Letters and Diaries from Elsie Inglis's Russian Unit

Elsie Inglis *(Edinburgh Central Library)*

BETWEEN THE LINES

Letters and Diaries from Elsie Inglis's Russian Unit

With best wishes

Audrey F. Cahill

Arranged and edited by
Audrey Fawcett Cahill

The Pentland Press Limited
Edinburgh Cambridge Durham

First published in 1999

369 Amberglen Close
P Bag X004
Howick
3290 South Africa
cahill@sai.co.za

ISBN 1 85821 630 3

CONTENTS

ILLUSTRATIONS

PREFACE AND ACKNOWLEDGMENTS

I owe the title and genesis of this book to some war papers which came into my hands some years back, and which were full of alarming details quite at odds with the matter-of-fact calm of the letters and diary entries. One read 'The actual Russian first line trenches are at the top of the hill behind the hospital – so that we are really in "No Man's Land".' Other hints suggested that the documents I was studying had been designed for reassuring family reading, and suppressed at least as much as they communicated. 'We always get orders to evacuate hours before there is any danger,' ran another letter, and I decided that part of an editor's job would be to find out more about these dangers so delicately suggested and so lightly dismissed.

So began a quest for information that would fill in the gaps in the manuscripts I had before me; and of the other letters and diaries that turned up from the same medical unit many were decidedly less reticent than those in my possession. What I had sought as background material propelled itself to the foreground, and I realised that I had found a complete story of dangers that were indeed dangers, and a corporate adventure much more exciting than any suggested by the clues in my own restrained records. Selecting and collating the extracts that would complement one another, and investigating what was left unwritten between *their* lines, became a major project, which has taken me into new fields and made me new friends.

I am indebted to the University of Natal for an Honorary Research Associateship which enabled me to use its libraries, technical equipment and personal expertise, and for funding the maps and some of the photographs in this book; to my friends and colleagues David Newmarch, Fidéla Fouché, Margery Moberly and Joan Reed, who have read and commented on the manuscript at various stages of its progress; to Glenda Robson for her skilled and willing help with the rapidly-changing problems of computer technology; and to Meg Ross, my very helpful Pentland editor.

For permission to use extensive quotation from their manuscript holdings I thank the trustees of the following institutions:

> the Fawcett Library for letters, diaries and photographs from its Scottish Women's Hospitals and Elsie Bowerman Collections; the Imperial War Museum for the papers of F.E. Rendel, the collected papers of Commander O.S. Locker Lampson, and the letter of L.J. Brown; the Leeds Russian Archive for the memoirs of Katherine North (née Hodges); the National Library of Scotland for the journals of Mary Lee Milne; the Edinburgh Central Library for the personal records of Lilias

Grant and Ethel Moir, and for some of Ethel Moir's photographs; the Mitchell Library in Glasgow for extracts from the minutes and official files of the Scottish Women's Hospitals and for permission to reproduce some of their photographs; the Lothian Health Services Archive for the letters of Yvonne Fitzroy; and the Public Records Office, for extracts from the Foreign Office Papers relating to the Scottish Women's Hospitals and the Serbian Divisions.

I must thank also the many archivists of these institutions who have gone to extra trouble to answer my questions and to suggest other sources. David Dougan and his staff at the Fawcett, Andrew Bethune at Edinburgh Central Library, and a great number of the staff of the Printed Books and Manuscripts Departments of the Imperial War Museum have been unfailingly helpful, often by fax or e-mail. In particular, Richard Davies of the Leeds Russian Archive has become something of a mentor, solving many of my puzzles about railway systems, place names, and Russian history and geography. Among the many historians whose published work provided both context and encouragement for my enterprise, Margot Lawrence, Leah Leneman and Alan Palmer have been generous in sharing their knowledge with me.

Another debt of gratitude extends to the relatives and friends holding the copyright and sometimes also the manuscripts of the records I have used: Margaret and the late Douglas Gordon Baxter for extracts and illustrations from Ysabel Birkbeck's diary; Felicity Blake for Lois Turner's diary and drawings; Roger and Patrick Cahill for the papers of Margaret Fawcett; John and Kathleen Orr for Margaret Marx's photograph album; Barbara Strachey Halpern for Elinor Rendel's letters to Ray Strachey; Michael Hodges for permission to quote from his aunt's memoirs; and Amy Maddox for permission to use Elsie Inglis's letters and reports from Russia. In spite of extensive efforts I have not been able to discover any other copyright holders, but if the publication of this book should reveal any more, I should be pleased to hear from them, and indeed from anyone with connections with Elsie Inglis's Russian Unit of the Scottish Women's Hospitals.

My greatest debt remains to the conscientious and articulate group of women who set down in such difficult circumstances and preserved so faithfully these first-hand accounts of their experience. I have many times wished that they could know how many of their records have survived, and could read the compelling tale to which they contributed.

Audrey Cahill
University of Natal, Durban

INTRODUCTION

(See maps 1 & 2)

Section 1: The Scottish Women's Hospitals

Shortly after the outbreak of the First World War, Dr Elsie Inglis offered her services as a surgeon to the Royal Army Medical Corps (RAMC).

> 'What did he say?' her niece asked her when she returned home from visiting the Edinburgh representative.
> He said, 'My good lady, go home and sit still.'[1]

This was probably the moment of the conception of the Scottish Women's Hospitals.[2]

Elsie Inglis was one of the second generation of woman doctors in Britain. She had qualified in 1892, and studied at Glasgow Royal Infirmary and Edinburgh University almost as soon as they admitted women. By 1914, at the age of fifty, she was a respected consultant physician and surgeon, a lecturer at Edinburgh University, and the founder of two hospitals in Edinburgh. Her own professional struggles had led her into the suffrage movement some years earlier, when the intransigence of many husbands in withholding consent for necessary operations on their wives had persuaded her that only when women had the vote would they be in a position to change the laws which gave men such power over their health and well-being.[3] From 1900 onwards she had spent much of her spare time and energy in building up the flagging suffrage movement in Scotland, and by 1914 she was honorary secretary of both the Edinburgh National Society for Women's Suffrage and the Scottish Federation of Women's Suffrage Societies (SFWSS).[4]

Over the years public support for women's suffrage had gradually increased, partly through the example of individual women who had made their way in the professional world in spite of great obstacles, partly through the publicity gained by the militant Women's Social and Political Union (WSPU, the suffragettes), and partly through the patient constitutional work of the National Union of Women's Suffrage Societies (NUWSS, the suffragists). In 1910 and 1911 two 'Conciliation Bills' designed to extend the franchise to women householders passed their second reading with a large majority, bringing the vote within close reach; but they were dropped in favour of the Liberal Government's Male Franchise Bill, with an assurance from the Prime Minister that it might be amended to include

1

women. In response to this disappointment, some members of the WSPU embarked on an arson campaign, attacked Members of Parliament and their property, and were in their turn treated with violence by the police. The Conciliation Bill of March 1912 was defeated in its second reading, and the promised amendments to the Franchise and Registration Bill of 1913 were declared out of order by the Speaker. It appeared that some public sympathy had been lost, and the constitutional suffrage societies believed that their militant colleagues had done them a disservice. Certainly the first half of 1914 was a year of crisis for the suffrage movement, which was now deeply divided between militants and constitutionalists.

With Britain's declaration of war on 4 August, a truce was agreed between the Government and both wings of the women's movement. Motivated mainly by patriotism and the widely-accepted belief that Britain was fighting a righteous war, the (English) National Union and the Scottish Federation of Women's Suffrage Societies were quick to act, but careful to choose a course that would advance the position of women. 'Let us prove ourselves worthy of citizenship, whether our claim is recognised or not,' wrote Millicent Fawcett, President of the NUWSS. Within the first week of the war, the suffrage societies had offered their services to the Local Relief Committees and to the Red Cross, and had established emergency workrooms and information centres to organise the many women anxious to serve their country.[5]

Being subject to the War Office, the Red Cross was at first unable to use the trained women doctors who came forward; apart from the conviction that women had no place at the front, it was also held that their proper work was with women and children, and that men would not like to be treated by a woman doctor. Undeterred, many joined privately-sponsored organisations and offered help to Britain's harder-pressed allies. First in the field were Elizabeth Garrett Anderson's daughter, Dr Louisa Anderson, and Dr Flora Murray, who with private subscriptions equipped a surgical hospital staffed entirely by women; by September 1914 they were hard at work in Paris.[6]

It was in the same spirit that Elsie Inglis responded to the rebuff of the RAMC. Instead of sitting still, she looked for a way of combining three major objectives – the service of her country, the opening up of professional opportunities for medical women, and the demonstration that women could be useful, even in wartime. On 12 August, at the first SFWSS committee meeting after the declaration of war, she proposed that they should offer to the Red Cross a fully equipped hospital, staffed completely by women, for service at home or abroad. The idea was welcomed with enthusiasm, and welcomed too by their English counterpart, the NUWSS, who agreed to co-

2

operate, although it was decided that in order to canvass as much support as possible, the contentious word 'suffrage' should not form part of the name of the organisation.[7]

Inglis was quite explicit about the value to be gained from the publicity of this new venture. Writing about the scheme to Millicent Fawcett, she said,

> I cannot think of anything more calculated to bring home to men the fact that women *can help* intelligently in any kind of work. So much of our work is done where they cannot see it. They'll see every bit of this.[8]

In the matter of organisation, the connection with the suffrage societies was an advantage. A great network of local societies was already efficiently organised: it had its own weekly paper, *The Common Cause,* and was used to raising funds. The initial executive committee consisted of members of the Scottish Federation's Organisation and Finance sub-committees, and, after an understandable objection from the English suffrage societies had been overruled, was named 'The Scottish Women's Hospitals for Foreign Service', soon shortened to 'SWH'. It later ran independently of the suffrage societies, and drew some of its members and supporters from outside their ranks. While Edinburgh always remained the headquarters, committees were also formed in Glasgow and London, to help with fund raising, and in London to interview applicants and select staff. In a remarkably short time the first hospital had been funded and equipped, and there was an enthusiastic response to the call for recruits. The Red Cross, though co-operative, was not free to act against the decree of the War Office, and so, like the Garrett Anderson hospital, the Scottish Women's Hospitals had to act independently. This gave them a freedom from external control which was to have significant consequences.

The First French Unit of the SWH crossed the channel on 4 December 1914, to form a base hospital at Royaumont Abbey, twenty-five miles from Paris. It was followed shortly by the first of several Serbian Units. By the end of the war fourteen Scottish Women's Hospitals, involving over a thousand women,[9] had worked in six different countries. Those who served in them came from all over Britain, and from Canada, Australia and New Zealand; not necessarily either Scottish or suffragists, they found in the Hospitals an opportunity for which they had been waiting. The evidence of their diaries suggests that they were willing, even proud, to be known as 'Scottish Women'.

A hospital unit was initially envisaged as comprising two senior doctors, ten trained nurses, an administrator, a clerk and two cooks, contracted for six months or a year at salaries ranging from £200 to £25 per annum, depending on the going rate for the jobs for which they were trained. They would be accompanied by an unpaid staff of two junior doctors and an unspecified number of orderlies, who would preferably have had the first aid training provided by the Voluntary Aid Detachments.[10] In practice, 'unit' became an ambiguous and confusing term, for apart from the fluctuation in numbers as staff were added or withdrawn, the original party was often divided into two or more smaller groups staffing different hospitals, and these were also sometimes spoken of as 'units', while the combined group retained in official records its initial name, e.g. 'Second Serbian Unit'. The first three units (in the original sense) went to France and Serbia, and when in April 1915 Eleanor Soltau, the doctor in charge of the First Serbian Unit at Kragujevac, fell ill, Inglis herself replaced her as chief medical officer.[11]

In October 1915, after a peaceful summer, Serbia was invaded simultaneously by a German-Austrian force in the north and by Bulgarians on her eastern border. The army, with some 30,000 boys between twelve and eighteen, retreated over the Albanian mountains to the Adriatic, and staff from some of the Scottish Women's Hospitals joined them. Inglis and her staff were then at Krusevac, but here she had patients who were seriously ill, and refused to leave them. As prisoners of war the women were allowed to continue working until their patients were well, when they were repatriated, reaching Britain in February 1916.[12]

When the repatriated women had been a few months in Britain – greatly in demand as speakers to raise funds for the SWH – a request came from the Prime Minister of Serbia, by then in exile. Two divisions of Southern Slavs, mostly Serbs,[13] had been recruited from Austrian conscripts who had deserted to the Russians; they were to be attached to the Russian Army, but had no medical support. The Prime Minister asked if the Scottish Women's Hospitals and the Serbian Relief Fund, which had also run hospitals in Serbia, could provide four 'flying field hospitals' – mobile medical units – to be attached to these divisions.[14] It was agreed that the two organisations should each be responsible for two hospitals.[15]

The Russian Unit of the SWH, whose life and adventures are told in this book, was therefore a sequel to the Hospitals' work in Serbia. It set sail for Archangel at the end of August 1916, with Inglis as its chief medical officer. The headquarters staff would pay the salaries, but as they were already busy enough running the existing units in France and Serbia, the equipment and maintenance of this one became the responsibility of the London Committee, to whom Inglis sent her regular reports.[16] In the official records, the Russian Unit was also known as the Fifth Serbian Unit, the Russo-Roumanian Unit, and the London Unit. Its members had only a vague idea of where they would be going in Russia, and probably no one could have told them much more than they knew, for the situation on the eastern front had been fluid from early in the war, and was changing rapidly even as they embarked.

Section 2: The War in 1916

1915 had been a bad year for the Entente, making nonsense of the 1914 predictions that the war would be over by Christmas. The two 'little nations', Belgium and Serbia, for whose protection Britain, France and Russia claimed to be fighting, were both under enemy occupation, and the great powers were no nearer accomplishing the promised rescue. Russia, after initial successes in East Prussia and Galicia in 1914, had lost all the ground she had gained. A shell shortage and the difficulty of moving supplies and equipment compounded the problems of her long front and vast distances. With Danube traffic impeded by Bulgaria's alliance with the Central Powers, and with Constantinople and the Dardanelles in Turkish hands, Russia's only viable ports were Archangel, icebound for five months of the year, Murmansk, the rail link for which was still under construction, and Vladivostok on the Sea of Japan, 5,787 miles from Moscow across the Siberian wastes.[17] Since railways within Russia were almost all single-track, more ammunition and other supplies accumulated at these ports than could be moved by the inadequate and inefficiently-run rail network. By contrast, Austria's conquest of Serbia had put the almost-completed Orient Line from Berlin to Baghdad entirely in the hands of the Central Powers, linking Germany with her ally Turkey, and threatening the Anglo-Persian oil installations in the Gulf.

On the western front, the Second Battle of Ypres had dragged on inconclusively from April to June, with heavy losses on both sides, the first exposure to poison gas, and apparently permanent and static entrenchment from the Channel to the Swiss border. In the Mediterranean a British force which had landed at Gallipoli in April in a costly and futile attempt to take control of the Dardanelles had withdrawn in December. Meanwhile a combined French-British force which had landed at the malaria-infested port of Salonica, in the dubious hope of reconquering Serbia from the south, had met with little success and much sickness. Farther east, in Mesopotamia, General Townshend's garrison at Kut was under protracted siege, while at home there had been Zeppelin raids on London, a coal strike, and severe political discord. The first Defence of the Realm Act, passed on 15 March 1915, had signalled the seriousness of Britain's position by giving wide powers of state intervention in the regulation of industry and agriculture.[18]

The substitution of women for men in many essential services now became government policy,[19] opening up many new opportunities for women, but causing industrial disputes with the trade unions.

The beginning of 1916 brought neither the promised military breakthrough nor peace at home: Townshend and the Kut garrison surrendered in the spring, Irish Nationalist anger at the deferment of the granting of Home Rule came to a head (with German support) in the Easter Rising in Dublin, and the divisions of opinion over conscription and war strategy threatened to topple the already shaky Coalition Government. Introduced in March, conscription was another sign that the initial optimism about the duration of the war had dissipated. The inconclusive Battle of Jutland on 31 May failed to establish Britain's control of the seas, and shipping losses by mines and submarines continued to increase. On 5 June Lord Kitchener and his staff drowned on their way to Russia, when HMS *Hampshire* struck a mine west of the Orkneys. Lloyd George, as Secretary of State for War in Kitchener's place, began to talk about giving the enemy 'a knock-out blow'. The Somme Offensive, opening on 1 July, was meant to be such a blow, but British losses on the first day alone were 57,470; and of these 20,000 were killed or subsequently died of wounds.[20] This battle was to drag on until mid-November, with enormous casualties on both sides, and little ground gained.

The Russian front gave more hope: in May and June, in an offensive calculated to draw Austro-German forces from the west, General Brusilov led an advance into Galicia, recapturing much of the territory already won once and lost again in 1915. This limited success encouraged Roumania, which had so far remained neutral, to enter the war on the side of the Entente, with far-reaching consequences both for the Scottish Women's Hospitals and for the subsequent course of the war.

Roumania occupied a strategic, if vulnerable, position between Austria and the Black Sea coast, and had for some time been wooed by both sides. One of the incentives offered by the Entente was the promise (made on the supposition of victory) of the addition of large tracts of Austria-Hungary, including Transylvania. Since Transylvania contained many ethnic Roumanians, this was a powerful inducement, and when Brusilov's success seemed to portend a general victory, Roumania decided to declare war on the Central Powers.[21] For the strategists in the west, this seemed a triumph.

Generals on the eastern front were more sceptical. The Russian chief-of-staff, General Alekseev, contended that the addition of a small and comparatively untrained army was insufficient compensation for the cost of defending the long extension to the front which Roumania's participation in the war would bring.[22] Russia's western front had previously stretched from the Baltic to the northern tip of Roumania. It was now considerably lengthened and complicated, for in 1916 Roumania was an awkward shape: roughly like a top-boot in outline, only its sole touched Russian territory, the other three-quarters of its boundary being contiguous to Austria-Hungary, Bulgaria, and Occupied Serbia. Even its Black Sea coast was at risk from the Turkish fleet, augmented as this was by the two German warships, the *Goeben* and the *Breslau*.[23] While Roumanian rail communication westward was good, eastward with Russia it was poor, and movements of troops and supplies were much easier for the Central Powers than for the new alliance. Believing Roumania to be a liability rather than an asset, Alekseev was reluctant to supply more than the bare minimum of Russian troops to defend it: he agreed to provide only two infantry divisions and one cavalry division – 50,000 men in all, amongst whom were the 14,000 Southern Slavs of the First Serbian Division to which the Scottish Women were to be attached.[24] So it was that when they arrived in Russia, Elsie Inglis and her field hospitals were sent to the far south-west, and into Roumania.

Section 3: The Sources

To the majority of the unit, the unfamiliar experience of going to the front was intensified by the vastness of Russia and its distance and difference from home. Many seem to have made a deliberate effort to record their impressions, if at first out of normal traveller's curiosity, certainly later from a recognition of the importance of the events to which they became witnesses. Inglis's brief as chief medical officer was to inform her committees of the work of the hospitals for which they were ultimately responsible, and to provide them with the information they would need for their unremitting fund-raising. Her regular reports and delightful letters to the London Committee achieved this admirably, and were widely publicised in *The Common Cause* and, in truncated and often garbled form, in local newspapers. Those serving under her had no such obligation, and yet a remarkable number not only made careful notes of persons and events, but kept and preserved their diaries and letters long after they had discarded all their other writings. Scattered across Britain, in various archives and libraries and in private hands, are memoirs, articles, diaries, letters and photograph albums: 33 substantial items of personal history, involving 17 different authors. In their diaries and their letters home the orderlies, ambulance drivers, and other members of the unit wrote parallel histories, supplementary to Inglis's reports and concerned with the same broad military and historical events and with many of the same people, seen from different points of view.

In several cases secondary intentions were added to the original one, some of the writers leaving records in more than one genre, with diary or letter material being trimmed or expanded and reworked into a more presentable or more public form. The committees at home were always anxious for first-hand accounts from returning members, and as the events of 1916 and 1917 gathered momentum, many of the unit must have recognised that the notes they had made to prompt their own memories and the letters they had written to their families and friends would have a wider interest. From the care that has been given to their preservation, it is reasonable to infer that the authors came to regard these writings as in some sense a contribution to history: most of the thirty-three major sources, and many of the minor ones, were given to libraries and archives for safe-keeping, and the few manuscripts still in private hands have been transcribed by the relatives who inherited them.

Together these records form a corpus in which there is a remarkable care and consistency about events and dates, suggesting that the few published articles and memoirs which followed are based on letters or diaries, and that behind the letters themselves is a detailed diarising of events and impressions. Because Russia followed the Julian calendar, thirteen days behind the Gregorian one, the women had to make a deliberate effort to remember where they were in the western time-scheme, and the careful dating of entries was no doubt a necessary aid to their own orientation. This, with the fact that the actual working groups were small, makes it possible to check one account against another, and to reconstruct many of the movements of individuals and much of the daily life of the hospitals. While the points of view, attitudes and opinions of the writers differ, and indeed go through a series of changes, the recording of what we may call 'fact' is verifiable, and reveals an almost scholarly degree of care.

Since three of the seven major diaries begin at Archangel, it would appear that there was either some suggestion, perhaps by Dr Inglis, that the unit was involved in a venture that might be worth recording, or some agreement amongst a group of orderlies that they would keep diaries. The six orderlies who left the most substantial personal records had in common a good education and a strong sense of duty, and formed a closely-knit group: Elsie Bowerman and Yvonne Fitzroy met each other on the train to Liverpool, and remained close friends until Bowerman's departure in January 1917; Margaret Fawcett and Lois Turner made friends on the ship; and Ethel Moir and Lilias Grant joined the unit together. On board ship and in Russia, these six contrived to share accommodation and to work together when they could, and no doubt their communal enterprise contributed to their conscientious recording. (Moir's Letter-book, though substantially a collection of her letters home, has obviously been augmented from a detailed diary as well as from guide books and other sources.) Other important personal records are the letter collections of Elinor Rendel, a final-year medical student, an unpublished memoir by the driver Katherine Hodges, and the diaries of Mary Milne, cook, and Ysabel Birkbeck, ambulance driver.

Almost all the original letters and diaries were written in pencil, and the rare use of ink in a letter called for comment. There must also have been a shortage of notepaper and books, for letters were often written on pages torn from notebooks, and some diaries cease abruptly when the books are full. The strict censorship exercised on the western front was not applied to the women in this unit; they were told at an early stage that their letters, which went in the consular mail-bag, would not be censored. While cables sent through the Consulate arrived with the place names encoded and quite unidentifiable, battlefields and army positions were identified freely in both letters and diaries, and retreats described in all their awful confusion. Only in mid-1917 when the popularity of British allies in Russia gave way to resentment and suspicion, did the diarists begin to exercise any caution.

Section 4: Records and Memories

The prevailing impression created by the extant diaries and letters is that the writers were from the first stimulated by the responsibilities thrust upon them, and that even at the end of their service, with all its disillusionments and frustrations, they would not have chosen to forego the experience. For the first time, they had been expected to venture out on their own in a foreign country, where even the lettering on the notices was unintelligible, and to make themselves not only understood, but obeyed. Mere orderlies on paper, they behaved like officers in Russia and Roumania, commandeering vehicles and labour, cajoling or threatening station masters into co-operation, enlisting when necessary the support of admirals and generals, and insisting on getting what the unit needed. There was a certain anomaly in their position. When they went to parties and concerts given by the officers of the Serbian or Russian regiments, they were chaperoned: Dr Inglis or another senior doctor accompanied them. When any duty was to be performed, they were sent off alone, to brave the perils of crowded troop trains and desperate peasantry. Fawcett's solitary trip to Bolgrad to fetch the unit's money, Bowerman's and Brown's pursuit through Roumania of the lost equipment, Butler's shepherding of the last detachment of nurses through revolutionary

Russia, and the detailing of solitary women to guard equipment and vehicles, are just a few of the recorded exploits which would be disturbing even today, and unthinkable in 1913.

'I knew I could trust you to do it,' seems to have been Inglis's response to those who executed the least reasonable of her orders. Most appear to have accepted without demur her assumption that to a British woman with courage and determination nothing was impossible. Believing that the members of her unit were capable of any feat, she almost persuaded them to believe this about themselves. The diaries manifest a growing confidence, caught by infection from Inglis herself, that where anything had to be done, determination and resourcefulness would find a way.

Yet while the cumulative impression given by the surviving records is that for the writers their time in Russia was an affirmative experience which they wanted to remember, this was evidently not true for everyone. We know from references in the diaries and in some cases from the official sources, that there were a few members of the unit who did not respond so favourably to the challenges, and who were invalided home or who left in panic or dudgeon before their contracts were up. The most serious case was the breakdown of one of the drivers, the recently-widowed Angela Bell, whose insistence on leaving the unit in the fraught days just before the first retreat caused her friends much distress and anxiety, and created a dilemma about how to ensure her safety.

Perhaps the first to react against Mrs Haverfield's discipline, she resigned some days before the October retreat, and is reported to have wandered about the villages and towns staging noisy scenes about her grievances, and flourishing her whip and loaded revolver threateningly.[25] She was clearly ill, but refused to go home, and after many consultations between Inglis and the British Consul, the Roumanian authorities had her certified so that she might be sent out of danger. Inglis attributed her instability to the shock sustained in India a few months previously when she had seen her husband killed by a tiger; internal evidence in the diaries suggests that her current condition might have been precipitated by the additional shock of her exposure to the bombing of Medgidia, where, as Milne records in her entry for 14 October, she conducted herself with exemplary courage and presence of mind when everyone around was panicking.

There were possibly other less conspicuous instances of psychological disorder which went unrecognised, or were dismissed as cases of 'funk'. One orderly, who broke her contract and incurred the wrath of her fellows by exaggerating her exploits during the Dobrudga retreat, met with scant sympathy when she wrote that she had had a nervous breakdown. Birkbeck mentions a driver whom she found crying by her car in the early stages of the work in the Dobrudga, and another who cried all the time in the days after the retreat. At a time when 'shell-shock' or 'battle fatigue' was only beginning to be distinguished from cowardice and malingering, there was little sympathy for any but the most obvious mental disorientation, and most of the women were more tolerant of the bizarre behaviour of some of their patients than of symptoms of weakness in their fellow workers. The few accounts of such failures of nerve are a useful reminder of the conditions which most of the diarists and letter-writers underplayed. The casualties, although they must at least have written letters, do not appear to have thought them worth preserving: we know about their reactions only through their colleagues' discreet mention in the most confidential of the diaries, and through Inglis's necessary communications with the committees.

It seems probable that in the minds of those who did wish to remember, a contributing factor was their sense of having successfully endured an ordeal that initiated them into a more serious and more demanding world than any they had known before. Few of the letters or diaries betray much initial consciousness that they were embarked on a major contribution to women's history: although the officers were all active members of one or other of the suffrage societies, and used the voyage and long train journey to educate their subordinates where necessary, the prevailing response of the younger women seems to have been an upsurge of patriotic delight at being allowed to serve their country. For them the primary importance of the enterprise probably lay less in its contribution to the public demonstration of women's capabilities than in the change it wrought to the way they thought of themselves. The doctors had already made their way into a profession against a prejudice that was strong when they began practising, and still persistent in 1914; they had, in a sense, arrived, and were believed in by enough people to give them confidence in themselves. The younger orderlies and drivers were a different case: although some had worked for a year or two as teachers or secretaries, most had had more education than they could hope to apply in any direct way and, but for the war, might have lived humdrum or unproductive lives. Their enlistment in the Scottish Women's Hospitals wrought a radical change in their self-assurance, and therefore in their prospects.

The chance to prove themselves, and to share the risks and hardships of the soldiers, was in itself to be a privileged sharing in an experience denied to most women. Even more important was the development of sober realism that followed; a necessary process of maturation which the protective pre-war society would have denied them. They needed to discard their illusions about war, just as men needed to shed their sentimentality about women. The diaries and letters reflect this process of growth: after the initial euphoria of knowing that they are going to the front, and the imitative masculine swaggering of the youthful and adventurous Transport, the women's sentimentality and excitement give way to a more realistic assessment of the enterprise they are engaged in. They see the waste and the horror of war, and begin to be doubtful of the result, and even of the value. The excitement is replaced by a recognition of duty, and this is combined with an awareness of the complexity of the problem of continued fighting in the face of such tremendous loss, and the incompatibility of a foreign war with revolution and civil war. While a few keep strictly to their six months' contract, others opt to continue serving or agree to stay until replacements arrive; the glamour has gone, and the impetus comes from a sense of duty, a desire to 'see the matter out', and the recognition that there is no one to take their places.

Like a number of other privately-organised women's units that took themselves across the forbidden frontiers in the First World War, the Scottish Women's Hospitals established, not only that women could work as hard as men, but also that they could be brave 'under fire', and could meet the unexpected and unforeseen disaster with enterprise and aplomb. Their success was more than the public demonstration of a latent power that needed recognition; for the younger women it also in some measure created that power, and their intense and rapid learning experience is reflected in their writings.

CHAPTER 1
Getting Acquainted

As August 1916 drew to a close, dozens of young women converged on Liverpool to join Elsie Inglis's unit of the Scottish Women's Hospitals, known to its friends and members as the SWH. In spite of the name of the organisation, only thirteen members of this unit came from Scotland: of the rest, five were from Ireland, three from Wales, and fifty from England. In the party were some professional nurses, trained cooks and laundresses, employed at salaries of between £30 and £50 a year, and four doctors at a much higher salary; but most of the women were voluntary workers, who until 1917 were prohibited by International Red Cross regulations from receiving payment. They brought with them small amounts of pocket-money, mostly about £10, which they handed to Miss Henderson, the administrator, for safe-keeping.

A few of the young women already knew others in the unit: Ethel Moir and Lilias Grant, both from Inverness, had joined up together, and among the Transport were several veterans who had served in Serbia the previous year. Most, however, found themselves entirely among strangers, and as they assembled at the Western Hotel to await embarkation orders, they regarded one another with curiosity and some anxiety. Many had recently had their hair cut short, and were not yet used to their own appearance. They felt strange in their wide-brimmed felt hats and their new uniforms of lightweight grey serge, and were no doubt rather hot in the British overcoats which were to prove so inadequate in a Russian winter. They carried small haversacks, rugs and water bottles, and handed over to porters their bed-bundles and the larger kit-bags which contained their kettles, spirit stoves, canvas basins for personal use, and all the clothing they would have for the next six months. One of them, Elsie Bowerman, had her kit in a Wolseley valise, a remarkable type of hold-all designed to double as a warm and weatherproof outdoor sleeping bag, and recently marketed in the Army and Navy Stores; and Margaret Fawcett was proud of a down sleeping bag given her by her brother, who had been in Canada and who knew what mid-continental winters could be like; but most simply had a few blankets which they unrolled at bed time. Their list of requirements included 'two pairs of knickers, serge'; these were not undergarments but breeches, designed to be

13

worn under the mid-calf-length skirt when the wearers were engaged in any physical activity, and found to be more and more useful without the skirt as they toiled away at pitching tents, scrubbing floors and driving ambulances. Their breeches, their workman-like boots and their short hair often caused the Scottish Women to be taken for boys, and occasionally even for spies. At the outset, however, the 'knickers' were part of the general strangeness of the new life on which they had embarked.

The uniform of members of the Transport was khaki, which led to their being nicknamed 'The Buffs'; they looked smarter than the hospital staff, 'The Greys', some of whom greatly envied them. The Transport Section, though in theory a part of the same London Unit and ultimately under Dr Inglis's authority, was run more or less independently. Its commandant was the Honourable Mrs Evelina Haverfield, a heroic and glamorous person who had served as hospital administrator with Dr Inglis in Serbia. The Buffs had assembled for a final inspection near the Florence Nightingale statue in Waterloo Place in London,[1] and had then driven to Liverpool, to wait at the Western Hotel until their ship was ready. Among them were Katherine Hodges, very young, and excited to be going to war; Frances Donisthorpe, a veteran of the Serbian campaign and the second-in-command; Ysabel Birkbeck, officially designated as 'driving instructor'; Edith Faithfull, who as driver of one of the heavy lorries was to be in constant danger of being bogged down and left behind; and Hester Mackenzie-Edwards, who had already worked as a motor mechanic in the newly-acceptable substitution of women in men's jobs.

Dr Inglis reported that there were seventy-five persons, including four doctors, the unit being two doctors short.[2] The other three doctors were Lilian Chesney, Catherine Corbett and Lina Potter, all of whom had served in Serbia. Elinor Rendel had enlisted as an X-ray operator, but being in her final year of medical training, was soon to be entrusted with much of the responsibility of a fully qualified doctor. Accompanying them were three Serbian officers and thirty-two non-commissioned officers who had come from Corfu,[3] where the remnant of the Serbian army had reassembled and recuperated after their 1915 retreat over the Montenegrin mountains; they and the hospitals were going to join the First Serbian Division, which was now attached to the Russian army. To travel from Corfu to Odessa via England was a very long way round, but since the entry of Turkey and Bulgaria into the war on the side of the Central Powers, the shorter route through the Mediterranean and Black Sea was blocked to the Entente. Even so, the route taken by the *Huntspill* was far to the west and north of the normal peace-time route to the White Sea, and the ship followed a zig-zag course well into the Arctic Circle and within sight of Bear Island before turning south again to the small White Sea port of Archangel. There were mines in the Channel and the North Sea, but the greater danger lay in the highly mobile submarines, with which Germany had already sunk many British ships – fifty-one merchant vessels in July and August alone.[4]

Although Roumania entered the war on 27 August, when the *Huntspill* was still anchored in the Mersey, the Scottish Women do not seem to have known this until they reached Archangel. It was a fact that was to become very important to them, for it determined how they would be used, and where. Even as they tried to prepare themselves for the work they expected to do, plans about where to employ them were in a state of fluidity matched only by that of the eastern front itself. Since popular sentiment favoured the liberation of Transylvania from the Austro-Hungarian yoke, Roumania's first action was to send most of her small army and her best general to the weakly defended passes in the Transylvanian Alps, where their sudden incursions met with misleading initial success. A small force was left to hold the Dobrudga border with Bulgaria, to which, after its initial reversals in early September, the First Serbian Division was added among the reinforcements. Since the London Unit had come expressly to help this division, it was to the Dobrudga front that they were sent.

For all their conscientious study of Russian and Serbian during the voyage, the language that turned out to be most useful to them in 1916 was German, spoken as a second language by the Austrian Slavs in the Serbian Division with which they were to work, and by many of the Roumanians with whom they would have to deal. But on the journey, they knew little of what they might expect, except that they were needed, and they spent their time preparing for their work, and getting to know one another.

London

Katherine Hodges, Ambulance Driver.[5]

It all began in the dressing room of the British School of Motoring in July 1916. I had arranged to take a course of mechanics in order to help me to get a motor job on one of the fronts, if possible, and while I was washing some grease off after my second lesson, a girl dashed in in a terrible rage, the gist of her complaint being that she had had everything fixed up to go to Russia as an ambulance driver with the Scottish Women's Hospitals Unit, when they discovered that she was under age and refused to take her.

I pricked up my ears at this, as a friend of mine and I had long been trying unsuccessfully to enrol as drivers in anything for anywhere; I asked where the Headquarters of the SWH were to be found. 'Whitehall,' was the answer. I hurried out, took a taxi to the address given, rushed in, and breathless with excitement asked if any drivers were required. 'Yes.' I was delighted. I was then taken in to see the Honourable Mrs Evelina Haverfield, who commanded the Transport Section of this particular unit, and in a few minutes the whole thing was fixed up.

I tore out, wired my friend C, wired my father, and then the rush began, for we were to leave England in less than ten days' time. Fittings for uniforms, boots, stocks of khaki clothes of all descriptions, medicines, tinned foods, and goodness knows what else were got together...

The amazing thing to me, as I look back, is the frame of mind in which we most of us started off. It really amounted to an intense excitement, the feeling of 'We're going to the war, isn't it marvellous? We're going to the war.' Those of us who were quite new to it all certainly were in this state, and hadn't the faintest conception of what 'war' actually meant. We were young and to us it was going to be a wonderful adventure – just that. Well, it was a wonderful adventure, but not in the sense which we had imagined it.

Huntspill **Liverpool to Archangel**

Lilias Grant, Hospital Orderly. *Diary Wednesday 30 August*

Had an opportunity of seeing something of our shipmates this morning; think we are going to be a jolly crowd. Mrs Haverfield's Transport Unit is very smart; they have nearly all got their hair cut short, and bar the shorts, they might be men. Indeed, when talking to them, one wonders what sex they are. After lunch we were all photographed in a group, and were then told we were sailing in the afternoon. So we got all our kit put on the transport waggons, and ourselves in two big brakes, and started off for the docks. Many quaint remarks came to us from the crowd in the street on our way, one man saying, 'Now I shouldn't mind joining that lot.' Another in a very scathing voice said, 'They are not going into danger at all.' We finally got on board and I think we all got a bit of a shock on seeing the boat. We heard that we were not expected on board for a week, so nothing was ready for us. However, we are all here to make the best of things, and we just have to. Moir, Mackenzie, and I are sharing a cabin: we had many difficulties to cope with, and the lack of washing materials was the worst, but we finally got into our bunks, having sprinkled them well with sulphur first!

Dr Elsie Inglis, Chief Medical Officer. *Letter*[6]

You never in your life saw such a filthy boat as this was when we came aboard. The captain had been taken off an American liner the day before.

The only officer who had been on this boat before was the engineer officer. All the rest were new. The crew were drunk to a man, and, as the Transport officer said to me, 'The only way to get this ship right, is to get her *out*.' So we got out. I must say we got into shape very quickly. We cleaned up, and now we are painting. They won't know her when she gets back. She is an Austrian Lloyd captured at the beginning of the war, and she has been trooping in the Mediterranean since...

This is quite a tiny little boat. She has all our equipment, fourteen of our cars. For passengers, there are ourselves – seventy-five people – and three Serbian officers, the mother and sister of one of them, and thirty-two Serbian non-commissioned officers. They are going to our division...

Lois Turner, Mess Orderly. *Diary Wednesday 30 August*
After supper we stayed on the top deck – there is not much deck on this old bus – waiting to start. They only towed us into the river then, when we again dropped anchor for the night. The crew was drunk, and we had to wait for them to be brought on. Our cabin we found occupied by two men.

Friday 1 September
We began military drill this morning with no great success, as it was getting stormier as we got towards the north of Ireland, and not only did we find it difficult to keep our balance, but people began to retire from public life p.d.q. I survived till lunch, when I retired below, and thank heavens was not sick.

Saturday 2 September
We have just had boat drill. Dr Inglis is in our boat, and as I am the only decent swimmer, I am to have charge of her if anything happens. Thank goodness she is small.

Sailing north-east now, somewhere not far off Iceland, they say. This morning we picked up long wireless messages about Zepp raids on London. The bloodthirsty cheers of some people at hearing about the charred remains at Enfield were simply sickening.

Ysabel Birkbeck, Driving Instructor. *Diary 1-3 September*
My lecture on a Ford ambulance was thinly attended first time, but the audiences grew. Yesterday Mrs Haverfield came, and we skimmed through everything: care, ignition, carburettor, in theory. Today I shall take down a carburettor. Some know nothing at all, others I dare say more than I do. It makes me smile when I think how lately I met my first Ford ambulance; some of the others have been on them for months, and all

listen open-mouthed to my teaching. I wish I had got to lecture on the lorries – I could talk about them for ever.

Not a thing has been seen since we left the coast of Ireland, except an enemy submarine last night, which meant boat drill. Three blasts of the siren and we all leap into life belts and gallop to our respective boats. I have a sheepskin waistcoat which affords a lot of amusement on these occasions. Usually after dinner we collect in a music salon and sing party songs. Then one or two Serbian officers join us, and sometimes bring some of their men with them. One, with a wonderful voice, sits and sings on and on, his men accompanying him with chords. It has a depth and richness that makes the other songs cheap to theirs. How sad their songs are.

Ethel Moir, Hospital Orderly. *Tuesday 5 September*
It has been one of those voyages which produce the deeply-sworn 'never again' of suffering passengers. One regrets living on an island, and the only comforting verse of Scripture that suggests itself for one's tombstone is 'There shall be no more sea'! I want one more voyage only, as long as life lasts, and that is 'back to Blighty' again.

...I'm writing this 'standing at attention' at my bunk, waiting for 'cabin inspection'. We do have to undergo such a lot of nonsense in the way of drills, saluting, etc. – talk about soldiers!

Margaret Fawcett, Mess Orderly. *Letter Thursday 7 September*
We have been extraordinarily lucky in our journey. The first two days on the sea were very choppy, and we were mostly deadly sick. This is a rhyme of Turner's. Turner is quite a friend of mine – we have arranged to share tents at the other end.

> I am hanging o'er the rail
> Am I looking for a sail?
> No, I'm not.
> I am papa's only daughter
> Casting bread upon the water
> In a way I didn't orter,
> That's what.

She thought of it when she was sitting on the deck feeling particularly green.

It seems ages since we left England, although the days do not hang heavily on our hands; we are kept much too busy. We have breakfast at 8.30, cabin inspection and roll call at 9.30, military drill, which I take for part of the staff at 10.30, and Swedish drill at 11.00. During the rest of the day there are various classes in Serbian, French, and Russian. I am taking Serbian.

As far as I can remember, our hospital staff consists of four doctors, a matron, an assistant matron, a secretary, an administrator, a sanitary inspector, an X-ray operator, sixteen sisters, and sixteen orderlies. When we arrive we are supposed to be going to divide into two hospitals, one for either end of the Serbian front.

The first Friday morning was splendid. We came quite close to the east coast of Ireland. It was a lovely morning, although the wind was getting rough, and the scenery was perfect. On Sunday a German submarine was sighted. We took a zig-zag course for about twenty minutes, but the brute did not appear again. Unfortunately it was early in the morning before any of us were up, so we missed the thrill.

Yvonne Fitzroy, Hospital Orderly. *Letter 3-6 September*

This beautiful paper is the result of a few kind words to the purser. It might be cleaner, I allow. The picture at the top isn't the least like us. We are old and grubby and grey – as I said before, Austrian – and hitherto used as a troopship in the Mediterranean. Our escort left us as she found the weather rather depressing – but we've got a 4-inch gun mounted aft in the charge of three delightful bluejackets. They possess a refreshing contempt for the merchantmen who form the rest of the crew, and I must say, the difference is apparent, and not much in the latter's favour.

I've only been laid up one day. We started in beautiful weather and retraced the steps of Medusa as far as the Giant's Causeway – then turning west, steamed out into the Atlantic where we met a heavy sea. To avoid the submarine area we made a big detour and did not turn north till we had reached a point two hundred miles west of the Mull of Kintyre. Now we are steaming north-east and should reach the Arctic Circle tomorrow... The sea looks very cold and grey and Arctic! We have not seen a sail for three days.

There are about thirty Serbian soldiers on board, and three officers. Very nice they seem, and long-suffering, for we practise our Serbian on them frenziedly.

As far as I can make out, the great majority of my fellow workers are professionals – teachers, very largely. Bowerman, the girl I travelled up with from Euston, was at Girton, and as she survived the *Titanic* is, I feel, proof against all lesser disasters. The Transport leader, Mrs Haverfield, is a very attractive and charming person, but she has the most amazing effect on her followers. They would, I believe, be quite, *quite* happy if she condescended to wipe her boots on them once a day. And she is so very different in appearance to her short-haired masculine unit. They all look very smart, though. *We* are not so smart to look at, but the captain says he would back the Greys all along the line; and the head steward says our drill is beautiful!

Elsie Bowerman, Orderly. *Letter 3-7 September*[7]

There's lots to tell you about the people, much too long to write, but they are a ripping lot. It is so nice to get with a set of people who are all keen, all see the funny side of things, all prepared to face anything. Of course I only see Mrs Haverfield from a distance, as she is one of the *very* exalted, but she is a dear whenever our paths happen to cross. Her second in command is Donisthorpe, who's like a man; Mother saw her off, and will tell you of her, but she is, I believe, splendid. I don't know her, but am very frightened of her; she's extremely efficient, quite an old campaigner, and knows all the tricks of the trade. Our officers are Dr Inglis, Dr Chesney, Dr Corbett, and Dr Potter, who have all been out before; sanitary inspector a girl called Pleister, X-ray operator Rendel, and matron Miss Fox – and very nice, Irish, tall and imposing. Among the orderlies I think the nicest are Fawcett, a ripping kid who belongs to the Women's Reserve Ambulance, and drills us when physically able, Grant – Scotch, who has been in a VAD hospital – Brown, Mackenzie, ...but they are all nice. The least interesting at present are the sisters, but doubtless we shan't think this later on when we tremble before them.

I don't think I told you we sighted one submarine, but it was 6 a.m. so none of us were up, which was rather a swiz. They think she might have been the *Deutschland*,[8] as she was very large, and made no attempt to pursue us. We saw her when she was four miles away, but apparently she didn't notice us till about ten miles off. We made off with our stern towards her so as to give her as small a target as possible. The only other things we have sighted are a solitary tramp and one battleship.

Have just heard I'm to be in Dr Inglis's hospital when we divide into two, so I shall have to mind my Ps and Qs. Fitzroy is to be in it too, I am glad to say; I think her father has something to do with the Foreign Office,[9] so have to be careful how I air my views!...

We have sports in the afternoon. I'm afraid I was a slacker as far as they were concerned, except for the tug of war between the Scots Greys (us) and the Buffs (the Transport). I regret to say the Transport won owing to their colossal weight.

Inglis *Letter Friday 6 September*[10]

The voyage has been a pleasant one in every way. As soon as sea-sickness was over, the unit developed a tremendous amount of energy, and we have had games on deck, and concerts, and sports, and a fancy-dress competition! All this in addition to drill every morning, which was compulsory.

Some of the dresses at the fancy dress competition were most clever. There was Napoleon – the last phase, in the captain's long coat and somebody's epaulettes, and one of our grey hats, side to front, excellent; and Tweedledum and Tweedledee, in saucepans and life belts. One of them got herself up as a 'greaser', and went down to the engine-room to get properly dirty, with such successful result that, when she was coming up to the saloon with her little oiling can in her hand, one of the officers stopped her with, 'Now where are you going to, my lad?'

Elinor Rendel, X-ray operator. *Letter Thursday 7 September*[11]

This is a wild adventure I am on. It reminds me in some ways of the WS and WCC[12] and our camp life at Studland. So many of the women here have belonged to semi-military organisations such as the Women's Reserve Corps, etc., in which they do a lot of saluting, that the military spirit has crept in – much to the annoyance of the sisters, who have already begun to rebel.

Dr Inglis likes a good deal of deference paid to her as head of the unit, and she goes in for roll-calls, cabin inspection, etc. We have to stand to attention, and at roll-call she has given the order that we are to say 'Here, Ma'am'. Some of the unit are already rather upset by this and there are one or two grumblers. The officers, i.e. the doctors, matron and administrator, are accused of being too much on their dignity. You can imagine the kind of thing. The secretary, sanitary inspector and myself feel secretly that our claims to authority have been a little overlooked. Otherwise we loyally and wisely uphold the higher command. Anyway we have deck cabins to ourselves, which is something. Some of the criticism is true, I think. Some of our leaders have been bitten with the military craze and they love saluting, giving orders, etc. without having grappled with the essentials. They rather like making us salute them for example without dreaming of returning the salute. However I think it's all been rather a game to pass the time and make us forget submarines.

Vera Holme is here and much to the fore. She is here as a chauffeur. She used to drive Mrs Pankhurst's car, and left the WSPU when they took to burning houses.

Fawcett *Letter Friday 8 September*

Turner and I slept in a life-boat last night. It did not get dark all night. We have been travelling well within the Arctic Circle, but are going south now, and hope to see land either tonight or tomorrow morning. We hope to reach Archangel on Sunday. Last night we saw the Northern Lights, and there was a splendid sunrise this morning... Some of us saw a whale's waterspout the other day, and we saw several schools of porpoises, but we are too far north for them now.

We have arrived safely in the White Sea, the opening of which we passed in the night. I saw two seals this morning.

Archangel

Mary Milne, Chief Cook. *Diary Sunday 10 September*[13]

A launch came alongside, with three very attractive naval officers...the girls are hanging over the edges of the ship. The poor Greys are very much in the background – our uniforms are simply hideous – very unbecoming, and the Buffs are so smart, hence we look awful frights beside them, and no one looks at us when they are about. It is rather a shame to turn us out like charity school girls; we have no respect for ourselves – can't have.

Tuesday 12 September

In the morning the great news was that I had my hair cut off by the ship's barber. Three of us had it done, as a seven days' journey in a dirty Russian train is not a thing to look forward to with long hair. Most of the girls already had theirs cut. Of course I felt miserable about it to begin with, and I look jolly plain, but all the same it is a great joy to know one is quite tidy.

Fawcett *Diary Monday 11 September*[14]

Visited a village about a mile from the quay. Houses and everything made of logs. We found a pretty little wayside shrine. The Russians are very friendly and we have great fun trying to understand them – they are a great deal quicker at grasping what we mean than we are what they mean. We went into a tiny shop to buy cigarettes, and in the living room we found a darling baby in a swinging cradle. Every house in Russia has its ikon, including the shops.

In the afternoon the entire unit paraded in Archangel. We visited the Cathedral and Peter the Great's house (1694). When we had finished sightseeing, we went to tea with the Vice-consul. Coming back in the launch Bowerman and Fitzroy managed to tumble into the river, but luckily they were not hurt, beyond a few bruises, which have left them very stiff. They were quite the right people to tumble in if someone had to, as they made so little fuss about it.

Bowerman *Diary Monday 11 September*
Glorious sail down the river 'home' to the *Huntspill* – wonderful sky – brilliant sunset – grey banks of clouds hanging over Archangel – the golden dome of the cathedral shining above – induced in us a mood of silence and pleasant drowsiness. Fitzroy and I were to be rudely roused from our reveries, though. As we were crossing the gang planks between the wharf and our boat, one of them (with Fitzroy on it) slipped off at one end and she fell into the water, carrying me with her. Fortunately neither of us went under as F managed to catch hold of a cross-bar on the wharf and I, after treading water for a few seconds, found also something to hold on to until someone dragged me up into safety. F was more difficult to rescue as there was a space of water between her and the ship, but Vera Holme, with great promptitude, got a man to fetch a plank which was placed across the space and she and the sailor hauled Fitzroy on to *terra firma*. Our first thoughts were of our clothes – our one and only suits – which we were wearing – also our greatcoats and hats – all now of course soaked through. However we were hustled off to bed after hot baths, almost intoxicated with hot toddy – and were none the worse the next day save for a few bruises and some stiffness. Even our clothes survived wonderfully, owing to the good offices of the stewardess who pressed them all for us.

Tuesday 12 September
Owing to the efforts of the British naval men, all the hospital stores, motor cars, etc. were unloaded and entrained. We were ready to start for our journey south by evening. We are to go straight through to Odessa – urgent messages have come through from the Serbs that they are badly in need of hospital assistance.

Train Archangel to Moscow

Grant *Diary Tuesday 12 September*
We have left the *Huntspill*, alas, although many of us at the time wished to get on shore. We had a roll-call in the saloon after we were all packed, and a funny-looking crew we were with our water bottles and knapsacks hung over us, and some with rucksacks as well. We waited in this condition for hours: some of the girls went to the piano, and we all sang popular songs to pass the time. At last we got the order to go, and we all marched down in twos to the deck, where we formed up and then marched

in threes headed by the ship's band – a scratch affair the crew had got up for our benefit. We went in this way to the train just across from the boat. The Russian troops were formed up into two lines of two deep, and we marched through them, and how they cheered us. We got into our different compartments and chucked down our things, and then came to the door of our corridor. Fawcett and I stayed there and watched everything, and I don't think I'll ever forget that sight: a gorgeous moonlight night, clear and frosty, and all the Russian troops now singing. Hundreds of voices all together, and in the background our good old friend the *Huntspill*, which really felt quite like home to us now that we were leaving her.

Fawcett *Diary Tuesday 12 September*
Splendid send-off by about 400 Russian troops. They all sang the various national anthems and cheered each of the Allies in turn about three times each. After each cheer, they caught hold of one of the officers of the Ally they were cheering, and tossed him five or six times into the air. They had cheers for our hospital unit and tossed Dr Inglis; she fled to the British Consul for protection, but he only laughed. Then one of the Russian officials made a little speech about the captain of the *Huntspill*, our transport, telling the men how he had brought us from England to help the *Serbke soldats*. They then cheered him vigorously and tossed him in the air, and as he is the fattest little man imaginable, it was a really funny sight. After everybody had been cheered about ten times, the Russians and the Serbians sang some of their national songs, and we had a fine display of Russian dancing. We finally got off at about 1.30.

Bowerman *Diary Tuesday 12 September*
Women seem to do most of the heavy work on the railways – fill up the water tanks on the trains, and load up with wood. Engines burn wood – there is also a wood fire at the end of each coach, which heats the pipes for warming the coach. We also saw gangs of women at work digging trenches and banking up the lines. The trains are lighted (at least ours was) merely by candles, so it is impossible to see to read after sunset. We amused ourselves though by talking and singing songs – our quartette (Fitzroy, Fawcett, Turner and I) very happy together, fitted in splendidly. We had spirit stoves and made frequent cups of tea, Russian fashion, with lemon.

Inglis *Letter Thursday 14 September*[15]
Here we are, well on our way to Moscow, having got through Archangel in two and a half days – a feat, for we were told at home that it might be

24

six weeks. They did not know that there is a party of our naval men here helping the Russians, and Archangel is magnificently organised now. When one realises that the population was 5,000 before the war, and is now 20,000, it is quite clear there was bound to be some disorganisation at first.

I never met a kinder set of people than are collected at Archangel just now. They simply did everything for us, and sent us off on a train with a berth for each person, and gave us a wonderful send-off. The Russian admiral gave us a letter which acts as a kind of magic ring whenever it is produced. The first time it was really quite startling. We were longing for Nyandoma where we were to get dinner. We were told we should be there at four o'clock, then at five, and at six o'clock we pulled up at a place unknown, and rumours began to spread that our engine was off, and sure enough it was, and was shunting trucks. Miss Little, one of our Russian-speaking people, and I got out. We tried our united eloquence, she in fluent Russian, and I saying, '*Shechaz*,' which means 'immediately', at intervals, and still they looked helpless and said, 'Two hours and a half.' Then I produced my letter, and you never saw such a change. They said, 'Five minutes,' and we were off in three. We tried it all along the line after that; my own belief is that we should still be at the unknown place, without that letter, shunting trucks...

This is a special train for us and the Serbian officers and non-coms. We broke a coupling after we left Nyandoma, and they sent out another carriage from there, but it had not top berths, so they had another sleeper ready when we reached Vologda. They gave us another and stronger engine at Nyandoma, because we asked for it, and they have repaired cisterns, and given us chickens and eggs; and when we thank them, they say, 'It is for our friends.'

Rendel *Letter*[16]

At every station that we stop at Dr Inglis jumps out and waves a letter given her by some official at Archangel. She talks in English and very bad French and stamps her foot and shakes her fist. All the railway officials come and shake their heads and our interpreters are kept hard at work. The result is that they promise that the train shall go on in fifteen minutes and it invariably stays two or three times as long. This morning we were kept for five hours in a station. We couldn't go for a walk or do anything because we were told all the time that we were going off in ten minutes... It is a very odd life, and we are all getting a little tired of it...

Supper is handed round by the orderlies. It consists of rolls and butter, baby chickens (cold) and cheese sometimes.

Moscow

Fawcett *Diary Saturday 16 September*

Due to arrive at Moscow early in the morning. We reached the outskirts of the town at about 8 o'clock, but were kept hanging about for hours just outside. We eventually reached the station at about 2.30. The station was just being made at the beginning of the war – it is now turned into a Red Cross hospital. It made one realise what it is like to have war in one's own country, to see the wounded coming and going. Grant had a sick headache, so one of the Russian sisters came right out to the train to fetch her into the hospital. They kept her there all the afternoon whilst we were fed and taken to see the sights, and were perfectly sweet to her. I had to march the hospital staff down to the waiting room. Oh! why can't the sisters march in step! The orderlies have been told that they do not show proper deference to the sisters. It really is rather a trial to have to live with them. Thank goodness we have none in our coach.

We didn't get a meal until 4 o'clock. We were feeling very starved, as we had had nothing but a piece of bread since the night before. We were entertained by the Moscow Red Cross, who were extremely kind. The British Consul did not come near us.

The Kremlin, which we saw after dinner, is quite the most beautiful and interesting place I have ever seen. The evening was very fine, and we saw a gorgeous sunset over the city and the river. The churches, of which there are a great number, are beautifully coloured in blues and greens. They mostly have one large dome in the middle of the roof and four smaller ones round, or else five crosses in the same arrangement. These are beautifully gilded, and glitter in the sun.

(Lois Turner)

Train Moscow to Odessa

Bowerman *Diary Sunday 17 September*

Rations on train all day, except for lunch, which we had at a wayside station. We walked up and down the platform for exercise, much to the interest of the populace, who gave us a hearty cheer as we went off. The Russian people are always mystified by our uniform – some think we are soldiers – and at Moscow someone asked if we were boy scouts; but on our making a cross on our arm, they always understood.

Tea party with Monfries and Livesay – Dr Inglis was there too. She told us that the day the Transport set out for Liverpool, the War Office had said she was not to take any nurses out of England, but she pointed out that we could not desert our allies in this fashion, and soon the unit was ready to start. She was backed up by the Red Cross people who are sending out a hospital hard on our heels[17] so did not want their own arrangements to fall through. The Serbian army to which we are going is 15,000 strong and has no field hospitals but those coming from England, our two and two Red Cross ones. We hope to be first in the field and so be with the First Division. Dr Inglis said if she had been prevented from taking nurses, she would have come out with doctors and orderlies only, rather than desert the Serbs.

We passed a great many hospital trains full of wounded – one with Turkish, Bulgarian, and German prisoners – some seemed cheerful – others very miserable – the very slightly wounded in horse boxes – the others lying on stretchers slung to the ceilings of the trucks.

Milne *Sunday 17 September*

We had a tea party – it was great fun. Two of the Buffs came – such jolly girls. Birkbeck is the driving teacher of the Transport; she says she will teach me to drive my kitchen – it would be splendid.

Birkbeck *Sunday 17 September*

A lovely day. The train crawled for two hours in the morning. We stopped, and most of the Transport climbed on the trucks at the back of the train and spent the day there. For the first time I really loved the country. Quite flat and lovely colour, patches of dark bluish ploughed land, rye I suppose, and patches of sunflowers. The sky seems more important here than anywhere else in the world, and far bigger. Huge white woolly clouds across a clear rather sharp blue. I lay on my front on the truck and watched them and the horizon changing.

Fitzroy *Letter Tuesday 19 September*

Tea-parties are our great dissipation – and the food we alternately press and have pressed on us is fearful and wonderful indeed! I am even going out to supper tonight with the ultra-exclusive Transport. We have three coaches semi-partitioned off in sets of four. My three friends – Turner, Fawcett, and Bowerman – and I, are, I believe, the only members of the unit who have had sufficient sangfroid to entertain Dr Inglis. She has just left, and of all our chiefs she was the one I most enjoyed entertaining – not excepting the ever-charming Mrs Haverfield. ...She told us a lot about Serbia, and, which was rather a coincidence, particularly about the moment when the other units retreated and Admiral Troubridge tried to persuade her to do so too. As you know, she said she could not leave her men, and they parted somewhat abruptly. Their next meeting took place at Lady Cowdray's, at a party for the SW to meet the Crown Prince of Serbia.[18] Dr I was taken to be presented to him, and his first words were to thank her with real emotion for staying in Serbia. The only other person present happened to be Admiral Troubridge! I must go to my supper party.

Hodges[19]

We all had methylated cooking stoves on which we brewed our various meals. Occasionally we stopped at some bigger place where a real meal was prepared for us. A feature of every tiny station in those days was the *kipyatok*, which was a sort of boiler on the platform with three or four taps on it. It was full of boiling water, and directly a train stopped, everyone leapt out with their kettles and teapots and filled them from it.

Rendel *Letter Thursday 21 September*[20]

We are a very odd party. I don't know what life in the hospital will be like or whether the sisters will ever be able to assert their authority. During the whole journey they have clung together and been sea-sick and train-sick and fainted and quarrelled and flirted and grumbled about the food and been thoroughly unpleasant. ...The part of the train in which they live is called 'Petticoat Lane' because they hang up such an odd collection of clothes. The orderlies who will be under them in the hospital are superior to them in appearance, education, intelligence, and common sense.

Odessa

Grant *Friday 22 September*

Odessa at last. We arrived last night about 6.30 p.m. and got such a reception: the Consul and his wife and Mr Foster, the English Church clergyman and a lot of Serbian officers were there. Mrs Bagge, the Consul's wife, was awfully nice, and asked for me, and came and spoke to me. We then formed up on the platform, and marched out. Outside the station there were *droshkis* and motors; we were put into the former, and driven off at a tearing pace. I pictured us being shot out on the road every moment. We were all taken to a huge sanatorium and given rooms there. It was ripping to see beds, sheets, and pillows once more.

Turner *Friday 22 September*

At 8 a.m. we flocked to the baths. There are two private ones reserved for officers; the rest tubbed in a large room containing five baths, and showers, etc. It was great fun. After breakfast a number of English girls came up to take us round, and Fawcett found a school friend among them, and she and another girl took six of us around. We did much gazing. I bought a fountain pen, a Waterman, which in England costs 12/6, for 12 roubles. Things are on that scale, a rouble going about as far as a shilling. Wherever we go, crowds pursue us.

This afternoon we went down to bathe. It was awfully jolly but rather rough; the bathing place is only about 10 minutes from here, so we are going again before breakfast tomorrow morning.

Gladys Jensen, Ambulance driver *Letter Monday 25 September*

We are really having a great time here, expecting to be off, of course, any day. The first morning was a scream: we were paraded for baths and pushed in like sheep, half a dozen at a time, seized and scrubbed by Russian women clad in no more than a tiny apron and a smile. Today I had my first dip in the Black Sea. It was outrageously cold, but oh! what a glorious 'splogeeka'; one or two had costumes, but the majority were clad in nature's garment only. It is all rocks so you can imagine how torn and bruised we got, especially as it was awfully rough at the time.

Milne *Saturday 23 September*

Moir and I went to the chaplain's house as he suggested at 10.30, and he was waiting for us. He has a perfectly lovely room full of antiques. We started off at once in a wee *droshki* for the Thieves' Market – it was a perfect treat.

Moir *Saturday 23 September*

Mrs Milne and I spent a most interesting morning down at the Market; the English parson, who is a great authority on antiques, escorted us. It's right away down in the native quarters, and such a weird and fascinating spot. We poked about among the old booths, and studied the different people

– Russians, Poles, Greeks and Turks. Mrs Milne procured some treasures, the parson doing the haggling for her...

I arrived at Mrs Bagge's about 4 o'clock, and found that Lilias [Grant] had arrived there before me. We spent such a happy afternoon – Mr and Mrs Bagge are both charming, and were very kind to us. We had a nice English tea, and revelled in comfy armchairs.

Rendel *Letter Sunday 24 September*[21]

Our uniforms are a hopeless failure. Everyone here simply laughs at them. They say that we shall die of cold, etc. They have said this so much that at last Dr Inglis has decided to buy us leather coats tomorrow at vast expense. The absurd thing is that they refused to allow us to bring fur coats of our own with us. I think the committee have tried to do us on the cheap; that is the general feeling, anyway. The blankets we are to use are so thin and miserable that they will be almost useless, and as we are to have no beds but lie on sacks, we shall be pretty cold. However, I suppose we shall rub along somehow.

Jensen *Letter Monday 25 September*

Last night we went to the opera and there was a special gala; the archduchess was present and inspected us. I had a few words with her; she asked if I was a 'shouver' and did I really know how to undo all the screws, etc. It was a magnificent spectacle; all the men were in full military orders, covered with medals. After our inspection, when we returned to our boxes, the orchestra played our national anthem about six times whilst we stood at the salute, and the whole house fixed their glasses on us, and Her Highness bowed several times. Everyone here is delighted with the *angliisky soldatsi* and I believe we shall have a tremendous send-off tonight.

Milne *Sunday 24 September*

Bathe in sea, then church. The tea at the club was a great success, and I ate far too much. The people were very kind and hospitable, and we had a great time. Then opera and inspection by Grand Duchess. She chatted with us here and there – she asked me if I was a nurse, and when I said I was a cook, she wanted to know what I was going to cook. I said, 'Oh, anything I can get.' And she said, 'You won't be able to get anything.' So that is good fun. Everybody was in terrible excitement about the G.D. ... it amused me very much.

Fitzroy *Letter Monday 25 September*

Dr Inglis has just announced that we proceed to the front tonight, and I was going to write my letters peaceably! This therefore is between the courses of dinner, and you must forgive the result...

We got here late Thursday night and have been the guests of the town ever since – having a splendid time – but I think the front will be reposeful by comparison! The opera here is extraordinarily good, and last night was a gala for the Grand Duchess Maria Pavlovna, aunt of the Tsar. We were again treated as guests and given a row of the best boxes. In the first entr'acte the Grand Duchess sent a message that she wanted to see us, so out we popped and were solemnly inspected in the foyer. You would have laughed – I nearly did, but managed to stand firm and say Yes and No Ma'am with propriety. Then when we got back the whole audience, including the Grand Duchess, rose and stood facing our box while they played our national anthem three times and clapped and cheered. It was splendid – and they *do* it so awfully nicely.

I can never say how nice the ordinary people are to us. Again the unequalled four were having luncheon at a restaurant when an old Russian lady came up and put a bunch of roses on the table for us. Of course the Serbs worship Dr Inglis, but Russians will come up to us – both men and women – and tell us how glad they are to see us in their country, and wish us luck and congratulate us, and all so charmingly. The men, I am told, say we are a great relief after their nurses – we look so businesslike – and the papers are funny and most kind.

Train Odessa to Reni

Hodges *Letter Monday 25 September*[22]
The language question is becoming *too* involved. I have now acquired a smattering of Russian and Serbian, I know German and a bit of French, and I converse in those four according to the person I'm addressing; *but now* we go to Roumania, and my mind cannot cope with Roumanian too. I don't know what's to be done.

Birkbeck *Monday 25 September*
After lunch we hurried home to pack; not very easy, as we didn't know whether the journey was to last 24 hours or so many days. My haversack holds enough for days according to our present ideas of cleanliness and the necessities of life. I carry in it one change of clothing, pyjamas, washing things, towel, tin mug and plate, knife, fork and spoon, my little Kodak camera and writing things, and a book. All left at 7 and all our luggage was thrown up on a lorry by our Serbian soldier servants, and off we rumbled in a tram.

Grant *Monday 25 September*

We were all packed into a special tram which took us to the station, and we had a great send-off from the people at the San. ...Mrs Bagge and I had a long talk over things. We had coffee and rolls in the restaurant before leaving, and then at the last we had a scramble for the train, and our friends, who had been so good to us, ran alongside the train shouting us good luck. I can never forget what other people have done for us. It has somehow changed everything to have met such wonderfully kind hearts. We are back in our old train, and into the same compartments. I personally was very sorry to leave all our kind friends, so went soon to bed, and tried to think I was really glad to be off for the front.

Hodges *Letter Wednesday 27 September*[23]

We are now on our way to Roumania – goodness knows when we shall get there. We hear we are to be in the thick of the fighting. I shall be jolly glad when I get over the first day of driving behind the lines – I do hope I shan't funk.

Birkbeck *Thursday 28 September*

Stopped at a little station, where I saw more rats than one can describe; they were all bobbing out under the edge of a barn, to make expeditions to scavenge on the line nearby. The whole edge was crawling with them. [Clare] Murphy, and I armed ourselves with sticks and crept across the line and slashed, but got none. Several dogs watched us rather cynically. I suppose they had also failed. We stood quite close in and let them get well away before we charged. We were so interested in the crusade that we only thought of the train as it began to move. We'd just time to duck under the fence and leap on. We have all learned to treat the whistle with contempt and someone must get left soon.

Grant *Thursday 28 September*

We reached a small village today and had lunch. Moir and I went for a walk through the village before lunch, and were surrounded by natives, two of them insisting on our coming into their house and giving us apples. They said when we wanted to pay that they always gave the troops apples on their way through, so why not us. After lunch we were due to start, as if we did not start in ten minutes we would not get to Reni for two days, so Dr Inglis gave the order for the train to go on, leaving Dr Potter and Dr Corbett behind, they having gone for a walk into the village. We may thank our stars it was none of us who were away when starting time was due, or we would never have been forgiven.

Yesterday evening I went out in one of the trucks and stayed out till after dark. It was a gorgeous night with a most wonderful sunset. I shall never forget that bit of country – mile after mile of land all round one; no trees to be seen, and this part is more hilly, and then the gorgeous colouring of the sky. Perhaps every now and again a cart would be seen coming along, followed by clouds of dust; then gradually it grew dark, and there was nothing but the outlines of the distant hills visible. It was all so large and grand and wonderful.

Hodges *Letter Friday 29 September*[24]

We are now in Bessarabia, expecting to leave the train today – we are now within fifty miles of the fun!

I wonder if you know – I didn't till just the other day – that we are pioneers on this job. There has never been a field hospital run by women before.[25] I hope we'll be successful.

Rendel *Letter Saturday 30 September*

Dr Chesney is an extraordinary woman with a very alarming tongue. Luckily for me she has taken me under her protection. It is just as well to have a powerful ally on such occasions as my position is a little vague and there is a good deal of talk and a certain amount of scrambling for the best berths, etc. The sisters are the chief offenders. They are constantly on the lookout for slights and always think that other people are being better treated.

River steamer *The George* **Reni to Cernavoda**

Fawcett *Diary Saturday 30 September*

Arrived at Reni in the early hours of the morning where we left our train. We were fed at mid-day and 9 p.m. on a Russian admiral's flag ship – quite amusing. We started unloading the hospital stores at 4 and finished at 10. Everything had to be carried about two hundred yards in small coalers. The soldiers, Russians and Serbians, worked splendidly – the cases were fearfully heavy. The majority of the heavy luggage is on this boat, and the remainder with the Transport part of the unit, both cars and people, in a barge.

Ten of us slept on deck last night and watched the sun rise over the Danube. We have passed several barges full of troops going to the front. I saw a corpse floating downstream this morning.

We have just stopped at a little Roumanian town... The agent has just been on board to tell us that they have sixty badly wounded Serbians in the town, and they want to send this boat back when it has landed us to take them to Reni. We are due to land at Cernavoda some time today.

Grant *Saturday 30 September*

We have just arrived at Hirsova – such a pretty spot. On one side of us we have lovely rocks, and of course, the church with its green domes, and on the other very flat green country. We are going to leave the boat today and go by train to as near the firing line as we are allowed, probably ten miles. We left unexpectedly early last night, and in consequence, left a lot of food supplies that had been ordered to be sent on the boat early this morning. Milne was telling us this morning of all the good things we were to have had!

Cernavoda

Moir *Saturday 30 September*

We arrived at Cernavoda at 2 p.m. There is a most wonderful bridge across the Danube here – a railway bridge which carries the line from Bucharest and the west across the river to the Black Sea. It is called the Carol Bridge. It was only built some twenty years ago at a cost of £1,000,000, and it is one of the longest iron bridges in the world. We were allowed ashore for two hours, so had a look round. It is very desolate – houses shattered and bombed, and not a civilian to be seen anywhere; they have all evacuated, thanks to the Bulgarian aeroplanes. They want to get this bridge, of course, as it is the most important thing in these parts. We are now going to start unloading and checking, so I must be off and do my share.

10 p.m. We've got on well with the loading, but oh, dear, it is a big job. We expect to entrain at midnight – a cattle truck, rumour has it, but it's only for one night. I've just been told off to collect the mails, so farewell for the present. Don't worry if you don't hear often – *all's well.*

Mary Henderson,
Administrator
(Mitchell Library)

Evelina Haverfield,
Commandant, Transport
(Myrtle Simpson)

Standing, from left: Turner, Bowerman, Fitzroy; seated, right, Fawcett. Moir and Grant are almost certainly among the unidentified four.

Diarists aboard the *Huntspill (Fawcett Library)*

Camp at Medgidia

Mary Milne
(Edinburgh Central Library)

Sisters Ulph and Edwards
(Edinburgh Central Library)

37

Pitching a Tent at Bulbul Mic
(Mitchell Library)

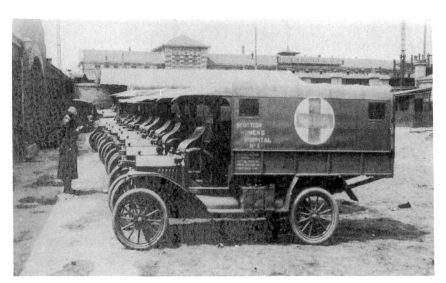

SWH Ambulances
(John Orr)

CHAPTER 2
The First Wounded

(See map 3)

The party of women arriving at Cernavoda on 30 September was a party very tired of travelling, and impatient to get down to real work. They had spent eighteen days travelling from Archangel to Cernavoda, most of them in the train; but the frustrating delays they had experienced were quite normal for those parts of Russia and Roumania in war time, and give some idea of the difficulty of moving troops about. Apart from the single track, which resulted in delays of many hours while trains came from the opposite direction, the difference in rail gauge meant that all goods had to be unloaded at Reni, a Bessarabian river port at the junction of the Pruth and the Danube, and reloaded either on to barges to go up river or to the narrower-gauge Roumanian trains which went from Reni into the interior. The tedious handling of their fifty tons of equipment at Reni and Cernavoda, and the Transport Section's slow journey by barge, reinforced the women's realisation that travel in wartime Russia and Roumania was to be calculated by time rather than distance, and that any journey, whether by rail, road or river, inevitably involved many stationary hours.

The poverty of communications in Bessarabia and the Dobrudga was one of the great handicaps in Russia's alliance with Roumania. Apart from the inadequacy of the Russian railway system for its immense task, most of Roumania's rail links, like her cultural links, were westwards, while those eastwards were few and inefficient. Communications between the Dobrudga Province and the rest of the country were even weaker, for it had been part of Bulgaria until the conclusion of the Second Balkan War in 1913, and in 1916 there were only two railway lines in the province, one from Bucharest to Constanza, and one running south from Medgidia into Bulgaria.

Bounded by the Black Sea on the east and the Danube on the west and north, the Dobrudga is only about 125 miles long from north to south, varying in width from 30 to 100 miles. Cernavoda, where the women transferred from river back to rail, is roughly where the river turns northward, deflected by the Dobrudga Plateau from its easterly course. It then divides into many channels and meanders in a wide marshy valley for a hundred more miles before flowing eastwards again and into the sea. Because of the difficulty of crossing the river, the territory was more easily defended against the interior of Roumania and Bessarabia than against Turkey and Bulgaria: at its narrowest part just south of the railway line the Roman Emperor Trajan had in the second century AD built a line of earthworks to repel the barbarian invaders. In 1916 this was still the most natural line of defence south of the Danube Delta.[1]

By the time the Scottish Women reached Cernavoda, there had been fighting in the Dobrudga for a month. Prompted by Roumania's advances into Transylvania in early September, Germany reinforced the armies of her weaker allies, and put her own generals in command on her south-eastern fronts. General Falkenhyn took control of the augmented Austrian army in Transylvania, while General Mackensen's army, still in Bulgaria after its successful invasion of Serbia the previous year, moved to the southern border of the Dobrudga. When the *Huntspill* was only one day out of Liverpool, a mixed army of Germans, Bulgarians, and Turks under Mackensen crossed into the Dobrudga, taking the defenders by surprise and advancing almost to the railway. Russia countered with reinforcements, and Roumanian troops were transferred from the Transylvanian front, subsequently losing all the territory they had gained. When the Scottish Women arrived, the badly depleted First Serbian Division, along with eight Russian and Roumanian divisions, was holding the line about fifteen miles south of Trajan's Wall. They had already counter-attacked and regained some of the lost ground.

A glance at Map 3 will show why, after the invasion of their southern border, it was important for the Russians and Roumanians to hold the line just there if Roumania was to be held at all: Constanza was the country's largest port, and, apart from the Danube Delta, its only significant outlet to the Black Sea. The railway from Bucharest to Constanza crossed the river and its marshy valley at Cernavoda by an impressive iron bridge and a series of embankments and causeways, together nearly twelve miles long. The Carol Bridge itself was almost half a mile long, and being the only bridge from the rest of Roumania into the Dobrudga, was of great strategic importance. Below Cernavoda the Danube could be crossed only by ferry or pontoon bridge, and then only in a few places, except in a particularly hard winter when the river and marshes froze. In defending the Trans-Dobrudga railway, the Russian commander-in-chief was hoping to protect not only the Northern Dobrudga, but also the port of Constanza, the bridge and rail link to Bucharest and the interior, and the Danube waterway.

The region was hot and dusty in the summer, but wet and muddy in autumn and spring. Roads were few and poor, liable to degenerate into muddy bogs in wet weather, with dangerously steep gradients, particularly in the northern hills. The ambulance drivers who disembarked from the barges at Cernavoda had a comparatively short drive to Medgidia, but because of the bad roads the journey which Captain Bryson, Miss Henderson and Fawcett made in three quarters of an hour on a dry day took the Transport drivers, in rain and mud, eight exhausting hours, and gave them a foretaste of things to come.

The staff had been told that they would divide to form two field hospitals, and the list of equipment brought from Britain confirms that this was Dr Inglis's intention. There were tents and camp furniture sufficient to accommodate staff and patients, and to provide a theatre for operations. The Transport Section had their own camping gear, and it was envisaged that its ambulances, staff car and heavy lorries would serve both hospitals, while each camp would have its own motor kitchen. Behind Inglis's insistence on using her staff and equipment as a field hospitals was a firm belief in the aseptic treatment of wounds as early as possible; many of the deaths and amputations on all fronts in the First World War might have been avoided had the wounds been dressed earlier, and the necessary injections been given; and as the women's diaries and letters make apparent, transport of the wounded was even slower on the eastern front than elsewhere. Although each soldier carried a pack containing lint, two compresses and a fastening pin, so that an initial dressing could be applied on the field,[2] it might be over a week before the wound could be properly cleaned and dressed. If appropriate treatment were provided close to the front, before the dreaded gas gangrene set in, the men would have a much better chance of survival.

Dr Inglis was therefore rather disappointed that the hospitals were not immediately sent to the Serbian Division at the front. After interviewing Colonel Hadjic at the Division Headquarters, and discovering that he concurred with the Russian general's wish that she should remain at Medgidia, she wrote in her third report, 'The ordinary male disbelief in our capacities cannot be argued away. It can only be worked away.'[3] In the light of the volatility of the front line, it is quite probable that the colonel had other reasons for thinking that the hospitals would be more useful a little farther back; nevertheless, when the hospital at Medgidia was in running order, the Scottish Women were asked to set up a field hospital at Bulbul Mic, a village just a few miles behind the front line, where the small Serbian field hospital under Dr Stanojevic was also encamped. All the diarists differ in their estimate of its distance from Medgidia; perhaps the figure depends on whether the writers travelled by rail or road, and how long the journey took. Bulbul Mic was linked by road to Medgidia and Constanza, and by rail to Medgidia, on the line leading south to the occupied territory and Bulgaria.

Hospital B, entirely under canvas, was under the direction of Dr Chesney, a somewhat abrasive personality but a capable and experienced surgeon. Communications being what they were, her field hospital became from this time almost an independent unit. For the first few weeks while the front was quiet, the shuttle-service of the Transport served to link the two groups, but when the retreat began they were as effectively separated as if they had been hundreds of miles apart. Inglis's reports are often vague about Hospital B, and most of the detailed information about Dr Chesney's movements in 1916 comes from the diaries and letters of Rendel, Moir, Grant, Fawcett and Turner.

Hospital A Medgidia

Fawcett *Retrospective Diary Saturday 30 September*
We arrived [at Cernavoda] at about 3 o'clock in the afternoon of the 30th; we were met by an Irishman named Bryson who had been sent by the Russian staff at Medgidia to ask us to go along there at once and start a hospital. As soon as we could get the railway trucks we got about fifty soldiers to work to move the equipment. We finally got off by about 8.30, and arrived at Medgidia at 9.15. Medgidia is the headquarters of the Serbian army, and Dr Inglis immediately went off to get the orders from the Staff. Whilst she had gone, we settled down to sleep in our carriages. Later when we were all comfortably asleep, Dr Inglis came back and said that we were to spend the night in the train, but that we must get out our bed-bundles and make beds for ourselves on the floor.

Mr Bryson told us that the Roumanians had so far not done well; the only thing they could do properly was to run away. (Roumania had only declared war since we left England, so that we knew very little about the Dobrudga – the part of Roumania we were going to.) He also told us that a Russian general had now taken command of the front, and had ordered that every soldier who ran away was to be shot, and every officer to be degraded. The Serbs, he said, had been fighting splendidly, but so far had suffered heavy losses.

Inglis *Report[4] 1 October*
The next morning we went to the Officers' Mess for breakfast, and General Grutskovsky, who is in command here, came in and made a little welcoming speech, and then came and sat down beside me. He told me we had come in the very nick of time, as the offensive was about to begin that very day. He spoke most warmly of the Serbs, and of what they had done in the middle of September... They went into the fight, the Serbian Division, fifteen thousand strong, ...they came out of the fight having lost eleven thousand men. It is almost incredible.[5]

Transport Medgidia

Fawcett *Retrospective Diary Sunday 1 October*

Many things have happened since my last entry, which was made whilst I was sitting on the step of the railway carriage before 8 o'clock in the morning. By 8 o'clock I was going with Miss Henderson (the Administrator) and Mr Bryson in a motor to Cernavoda to meet the Transport with the rest of the equipment. It was a thrilling journey – I was very impressed with the way everything gave place to our car as we had a Russian officer with us. The road was in a frightful condition, being little more than a mere track. The new road then in course of construction was always avoided. We spent one of the most tiring days; it was frightfully hot, and the town, which was bombed regularly at 4 o'clock every afternoon, was practically empty. The barge finally arrived at about 3.30, but as there were two barges full of troops to be unloaded first, our people did not start till about 5 o'clock, and it was long after dark by the time they had finished. We had our evening meal on a Roumanian boat; it was kindly arranged for us by a Russian Red Cross general.

Haverfield *Report*[6]

...the equipment and motor cars [were] unloaded [at Cernavoda] by Russian soldiers, sixteen of whom lifted the two-ton lorries as if they were made of paper. The hospital personnel went on a steamer and we of the Transport into two barges with our cars, the same tug dragging four others also loaded with lorries, troops and impedimenta of all kinds. We were to disembark at Cernavoda, we were told, in a few hours, but found ourselves two nights on board with no food and very cold. We slept in the lorries and ambulances, and just as it was getting dark reached our destination in pouring rain and blowing half a gale. The eight ambulances, three lorries, two kitchen cars and three touring cars were safely got off and I decided to wait till daylight to make a start... We filled up with petrol and after cold and weary hours made a start for Medgidia, where we had received orders to go at once.

We came across an Irishman in the Russian service who volunteered to be our guide, so in streaming rain and seas of mud we made a start. After about ten kilometres the stone road came to an end, and there we saw stuck in the mud in every kind of attitude of helplessness several Russian lorries that had been in the barges next to us on the journey, and that had gone off into the inky darkness the previous evening with much noise and bluster.

The road having come to an end we had to go along a track through fields. Here began many strenuous hours of real labour. There was a specially steep pitch to be surmounted, the soft surface preventing the wheels getting any grip, but with rope around the rear wheels and much pushing and heaving all were got up, including the big lorries. On arriving at Medgidia we discovered we had come all the wrong way in spite of our guide. The distance covered was only about twenty miles, [but] owing to the badness of the tracks, it took more than eight hours to reach Medgidia.

(Ysabel Birkbeck)

Hodges *Letter 1 October*[7]

I've never dreamed of such roads! One was in a cold sweat all the way: mud two foot deep, and enormous holes large enough to hold the car, huge ditches full of water up to your wheel hubs right across the road, and worst of all, the road often on a slant with a big drop off it; with the skiddiness it was a hairsbreadth chance all the time whether you could keep on the road or not. There were hundreds of carts with soldiers, etc., and frightfully restive horses which pranced at you, long lines of them. All very trying and most dangerous. We got to our destination saturated, of course.

Hospital A Medgidia

Fawcett *Retrospective Diary Monday 2 October*

Late in the evening Miss Henderson and I started back for Medgidia – the Transport were to follow in their cars in the morning. We sat on the equipment in the luggage van. The journey which before had taken us three quarters of an hour now took us eight hours – it was the most uncomfortable night I have ever had, and when we got to Medgidia it was simply pouring with rain, and a horrid raw morning. After breakfast – consisting of *chai* (very weak tea without milk), black bread, and many flies, Miss Henderson and I went back to the train to try and get some rest – in the meantime, the rest of the unit saw to the transport of the equipment and to the cleaning of the hospital.

Milne *Monday 2 October*

I had tea ready just as the Transport arrived dead with cold... The supper was a great success. It was much larger than they will ever have again, but just as a housewarming... It is a wonderful life, but I think the confusion here is awful; also, the heads lose their tempers in the most disappointing way.

Fitzroy *Tuesday 3 October*[8]

When you have time to look, or when the rain allows of your seeing anything, this place is distinctly attractive. It's fun being so high up, even though the first Boche shell that comes this way must surely bump into the hospital. The Constanza-Cernavoda railway runs along the valley below, and the ground sweeps up and away on the other side, bare and big and brown. The road to the front runs past the hospital, and vanishes over the rising ground into that world of distant rumbling which is at once so suggestive and so unknown. Only some two hundred yards away the old earthwork that was once Trajan's Wall lies across the steppe from horizon to horizon.

Moir *Friday 6 October*

Medgidia is at present the Staff Headquarters, and very near the war zone. All the civilians have evacuated, and the town is deserted-looking – signs of bombs everywhere. The Russian authorities are most anxious we should keep our hospital going here as long as possible: heavy fighting is going on very near here, wounded pouring in, and no arrangements made for them. They are terribly in need of Red Cross units; there are no hospitals to speak of, and oh, so many wounded. From what we hear things are going very badly indeed, and the Roumanians appear to be allowing the Bulgars a little too much of their own way, and are making a very poor stand. I wonder why the Roumanians came into the thing – I suppose they think the Serbs and Russians will do all the fighting for them...

All Sunday and Monday we spent getting the equipment conveyed from the train to the building which we have got as a hospital. This building is a huge barracks and stands high up on the hill overlooking the town and away from the Cernavoda valley. It is a magnificent situation with a glorious view; but alas! the inside is not so glorious. When we took possession it was *filthy*, so we just set to and cleaned and scrubbed and whitewashed. It is a two-storeyed building; on the ground floor a huge sort of barn with a stone partition down the centre. We have converted it into two long wards, to hold a hundred pallets each side. We have straw mattresses on the floor so close that they are touching – no floor-space regulations here. We brought the ticking out with us, and it was some business securing the straw and filling it. There are two quite nice side rooms, one of which we have converted into a theatre (and a most professional little place it is now), and the other into a theatre dressing room. At the other end are another two apartments, one where we receive the cases, and another which is a sort of office place. We have no water, lighting, or any such luxuries. All water we have to fetch from a pump up on the hill some considerable distance away; then after it has been carted down it has to be boiled, and all we can boast is a small Ludgate boiler. So you see the conveniences are not great; but it is beginning to look and feel like a hospital.

We are billeted in the upper storey, seventy-five of us in the one apartment; it's not a room, just a granary, but not as clean as most granaries. No floor-space regulations here either, methinks!

Turner *Tuesday 3 October*

Such a day! I began by serving breakfast, then scrubbed the store room – an awful business, as the men had been whitewashing and every bit of lime had to be scrubbed off the floor. We seem to live in an atmosphere of preparation or washing up of meals – we had hardly cleaned up from lunch when Dr Inglis came in with instructions to be ready with rice pudding when the wounded were brought in. We haven't got any Serbian orderlies yet, and the great difficulty is water. We have only two samovars going as yet, and one large cauldron on the stove. Every scrap of water has to be fetched either from the Russian hospital next door or from the pump. We staggered backwards and forwards through thick mud fetching this.

Wednesday 4 October

The Transport were called out this morning and went off about 10 a.m., returning about 2 with the first batch of wounded. We had just got the lunch rush over, which was great luck. It was extraordinary how quickly the hospital filled up – the sisters were all in their element. In the evening I went into the ward to take tea to those patients who were allowed it, and was roped in to carry a man out of the theatre and another in. We were on the run hard, and I have not sat down except occasionally for a picnic meal since we came up here. When one is not doing a meal one is fetching water or wood, or running an errand for someone. After almost everyone had gone to bed Fawcett and I did a final stagger with Miss Henderson to fetch water down to the Serbians' kitchen. When we were just getting to bed, Dr Inglis came into the ward and said there were thirty more patients. Apparently the Russian hospital is crowded out and we just had to take them in. They are practically all Russians.

Transport Medgidia

Birkbeck *Wednesday 4 October*

In the morning the cars were ordered out at 10, and we set off for our first attempt to Bulbul Mic. Thus far there was a hard highroad. At a small village where we were told 1,000 wounded were lying, a very nice Russian doctor came out of his tent dressing station and gave us orders. The lorry and five ambulances stayed there to ply all day between the village and our hospital. Mrs Haverfield in Onslow's car and a guide took me and three others on, up to the front. The road became a track of endless mud and mud holes, that would have stopped any other cars except ours. It was very difficult driving. The car boiled and had to be cooled from time to time.

The Road to the Front *(Ysabel Birkbeck)*

In front of me was a line along the horizon with shells bursting. We struggled on over impossible tracks, with an endless procession of carts, horse ambulances, and soldiers returning for rest, groups of less seriously wounded walking back as best they could – all with gleaming white bandages, a strange contrast to their dull drab clothes caked with mud. A dead horse, a dead dog, and then a wrecked village without a house with a roof on it. Here we stopped at the dressing tent, and took on our cases. My car was the first to be loaded – two stretchers as well as one head case, delirious, and another with a fractured thigh. The memory of it will always be there till I die.

...Back to Bulbul Mic, where I took loads more, and then home, where we arrived about midnight. So we spent our first day at our work.

Hospital A Medgidia

Fitzroy *Letter 10 October Medgidia*

Here we are about ten miles from the firing line...I am with Dr Inglis and have got the pick of the sisters in my ward headed by a Bart's nurse – my word what a difference a *big* hospital training makes!

Milne *4 and 5 October*

What a day of work... The wounded arrived last night – and we were up half the night feeding them. As there was no Serbian cook, I had to take it all on. [Today] I began at 6 o'clock to get breakfast for the patients, then for the entire unit – seventy-six of them. I have two baby ovens to cook on, and the most marvellous things are expected of one, and the most impossible things... I have ripping good girls to help in the kitchen, and I don't think any of us sat down all day. We had to see to the Transport girls as they came back with their ambulances, and it went on all day long. The Transport girls were wonderful – they made endless journeys in the dark, bringing in sad shattered men. I was only in the ward for a few minutes, but I could not stand it. We hear the guns in the distance all the time.

Fawcett *Diary Thursday 5 October*

Quite into hospital with the ground floor cram jam with wounded. Already we have had three men die. The house used to be a barrack. There are two twin houses, one of which the Russians have for a hospital, and the other one we have. We are really getting quite straight. It is too awful to go into the wards and hear the men groaning. General Grutskovsky decorated all the men this afternoon.

Turner *Thursday 5 October*

Kitchen orderlies have a thin time when there is a rush and no organisation – there is absolutely none here. One of the joys however is that the powers are too rushed to object to us walking about everywhere quite freely in riding breeks. I take it as a matter of course.

Today my life has been saved by a new job thrust on me, that of getting up the camp. Pleister and I were on it all day and are sleeping out tonight. This is rather a jolly place; I have not had time to drink it in till now.

Friday 6 October

Another day on tent pitching – it is slow work. One has to fish around and collect some Russian soldiers who are supposed to work for us, then one hunts among chaotic masses of stuff for the particular tent one wants, opens the thing out in absolute ignorance of what sort of a tent it is, and with one's half dozen words of Russian finally gets the old thing up. We have got up two latrine tents, eight double ridgepole tents, two small single ridgepole tents, a mess marquee and a big bell tent which is really supposed to be for the kitchen, but was wrongly labelled... Edgington has done the tents in an awfully shoddy way – the second marquee was hopeless. None of the hooks and eyes matched and so the walls hang in graceful folds.

Moir *Friday 6 October*[9]

We had hardly got our wards in order when the first of the wounded began to arrive. That was about 2 p.m. on the Wednesday, and the ambulances continued to pour in till 3 a.m., when all our beds were full. Our Transport girls did splendidly, and went right up the line with their cars to fetch the wounded. We had some appalling cases, nearly all stretcher. Most of our patients are Russian, a few Serbs, but *no* Roumanians. We had a frantically busy afternoon and night getting the patients washed; cleaning them was some job, as they were all simply filthy, caked with mud and crawling. The doctors then had to get the dressings done, and a lot of cases had to be operated on at once. ...Having all the cases on the floor makes it very difficult work – there is so much bending.

The Russians want Dr Inglis to send a few of the staff further up the line to a place called Bulbul Mic, as an advance dressing station. So twelve of the Greys are going, with Dr Chesney in charge, and half the Transport. Mrs Haverfield is of course going with them. Grant and I are among the twelve Greys going, and are awfully pleased, as we shall be more in the middle of things than ever up there. It promises to be most interesting. I am very sorry indeed to leave Dr Inglis and some of my special pals, but one can't have everything one wants. The others here are going under canvas as soon as the tents are pitched, as our granary is required for patients; a good thing too – no one will be sorry to see the last of it as our camping ground.

The poor cooks are having a terrible time trying to get food for us. Supplies are, of course, very short – no meat, no bread, etc. Some of the Tommies' much despised 'apple and plum' or 'plum and apple' would be a god-send to us. How Mrs Milne manages at all, I don't know...

Milne *Diary Sunday 7 October*

B Hospital will be five miles from us, but equidistant from the front. The one thing I regret is that I shall not have the motor kitchen – I have dreamed of that.

Last night we heard bombs dropping not very far off, also the guns from the front – but one never thinks of the danger. Three of the Transport were driving today, and two bombs dropped about ten yards from them – doing no harm. They might have been killed.

Hospital B Bulbul Mic

Inglis[10]

On Friday 6 October we got orders to form the Field Hospital, and on Saturday Dr Chesney went out with one or two others. The equipment was sent out in charge of four of our orderlies, and that was the first time I realised what a first-rate unit I had... They refused to sleep in the passenger carriage provided for fear the equipment waggons should be slipped. So they camped in the waggons. I worried a great deal over their having no food with them when I heard they had not arrived at Bulbul Mic, but they were fed by Serbian officers, and arrived smiling, saying they had 'had the time of their lives'.

Bowerman *Saturday 7 October Bulbul Mic*

Got up at 6.30 to get breakfast. Cleaned lamps all morning. Aeroplane duel just outside the door – glorious day, but shells didn't hit – enemy escaped. In the afternoon went on to Bulbul Mic with Henderson, Chesney, and eight others to help pitch camp for B Hospital which is to be moved on. Passed endless baggage waggons and convoys of wounded on the road. B Hospital to be encamped near the Serbian Hospital and work as a field hospital in connection with them – twenty kilos from firing line – sound of guns all the time. Weather simply divine – encamped on edge of huge plain, with motor lorry and field kitchen – village of Bulbul

Mic on our right. Slept under open sky – camp fires around and soldiers singing – horses and pariah dogs wandering all around. The eight of us dined with Serbian doctors at their little hospital – very clean – good meal of soup and meat.

Sunday 8 October

Woke at sunrise after glorious night – though trifle chilly as all bed clothes fell off – wet with dew but everything soon dry. Cannot pitch camp as tents fail to arrive by train – railway people absolutely vague about them. Spent day measuring out the camp, washing and resting – such a joy after the previous week as we had scarcely had time to wash at all. Fawcett, Turner and Lewis arrived with tents etc. at about 11.30 p.m. having spent about 24 hours to cover eighteen miles. Returned to Camp A – very sad to leave Fawcett and Turner behind.

Fawcett *Retrospective Diary Sunday 8 October*

We spent the night in the luggage van in Medgidia station, waking at 6.30 next morning, still in Medgidia station. However, we left soon after 7 o'clock and by 10 o'clock we had arrived at Merca Voda. We congratulated ourselves, as this was half-way, thinking we should reach our destination by tea-time; but to our horror we were told that we could not possibly leave till after dark. There would be other trains during the day, but all carrying munitions to the front, and as German aeroplanes were circling round all the time trying to drop bombs on them, the authorities would not hear of our travelling by these.

The station master was very kind to us, and gave us bread and tea in his private room, and afterwards introduced us to the OC of the Roumanian Transport Column stationed there. We were given lunch and dinner at the Officers' Mess, and really had quite a good day. The Roumanian officers would not hear of our finishing our journey in the luggage vans, but had a special first-class carriage put on to the train for us.

Turner *Monday 9 October*

Today we went out to breakfast at camp – the motor kitchen was there, and Suche and Hanmer[11] and the rest were encamped gypsy fashion around it. We soon got to unloading, and spent the day at that and at putting up tents. Dr Inglis's beautiful campsite amuses us very much – it has been a ploughed field, and either there has been fighting over the ground, or quite a recent camp. The dogs howl round at night, and dig up the entrails of dead horses.

Transport Bulbul Mic

Birkbeck *Monday 9 October*

Called at 4 a.m. Breakfast was not to be had before we started, so we just took ships' biscuits and set off for another day... As usual we had slept in our clothes and went out without attempting to wash. Royce started up beautifully, and we were away in good time.

At Abequor they were eagerly awaiting us, as the dressing tent was overflowing into the yard. Many lighter cases were left outside. Jensen came up with the touring car and took seven of these straight back to Medgidia station. With the ambulance I took two stretchers and one sitting case. I chose an arm case that could get out if he had to, and we all set off on the track home – with only thirteen. At Bulbul Mic I left only my worst case, dying, I thought, and took the others to our hospital. One of the sanitars was not there, so Hedges was on stretcher duty and we carried the men in together. I hate doing it as they are too heavy for us all, and though one would not drop the stretcher one might fall under it. Back to Bulbul Mic till 10 p.m., when I knocked off, as I had had enough, and went to sleep... The guns stopped yesterday morning, so once we can get this lot cleared, we can sleep. The lorries were out for sitting cases all day.

Tuesday 10 October

Found the Buffs at their transport going into camp, and spent the day there sorting things out. Camp when we arrived looked very attractive but too huge. The Transport had the best of the tents, putting us in threes and twos. Somehow I got one to myself. Lovely weather, and endless flat grassland stretching away to the front, with the station on one side. Slept so happily and hugely for the first time since I left England.

Hospital A Medgidia

Milne *Sunday 8 October*

Another glorious day – what a joy to live in tents in this weather... I still had to cook for everyone, and the ranges smoked in the most awful way – it was misery, and awfully hard work. I never thought it would be so bad, but at least I am told it is the only department that has gone well without muddling from the beginning, and everyone loves the food, so that is a satisfaction.

Fitzroy[12]

We have one Serbian orderly, Chris, who speaks English. 'Chris, Chris, Chris! Where in the world is that man? Fitzroy, go and find that man,' echoes through the ward all day. And Fitzroy does go, and she finds Chris, tall and gaunt and harassed, but intensely important, initiating some sufferer into the mysteries of (forgive me) a British bedpan. And from this occupation he is removed forcibly amidst piteous appeals of 'Seester, but Seester,' to tell another man he must lose an arm or a leg, or that a diet of black bread and sugar is not healthy if you have a bullet in your tummy, or that really the Sister knows best even if she is English and mad, or that his manners are past praying for. I don't envy Chris his job, but he is very worthy...

Bowerman *Tuesday 10 October*

Take up duties as mess orderly – cannot get mess tent in order, as kitchen tent not ready, so cooking must still be done in hospital. Very busy all day with general tidying up.

Thursday 12 October

Another very busy day, trying to teach a Russian soldier to be a mess orderly. Very good man, but impossible to hurry a Russian, and a big handicap not knowing language – have to show him by signs. Large reserves of Russian troops continually going up to the front – big attack expected. Glorious weather continues – not many fresh wounded arriving.

Milne *Wednesday 11 October*

I did my shopping with Bell. I like her very much. She is the first person I spoke to in Liverpool, one of the Buffs, a widow of a few months. She longs, as I do, to get away from the crowd... We did not know the way to Constanza, but she is a *beautiful* driver. We went over hills and moors – no real roads, just tracks. We had taken the wrong road, but we didn't care – we seemed so free, away from everyone. It was glorious, and so was the day – bright mid-summer weather, the first day I have really loved, just being away with a kindred spirit. Bell was in breeches, so of course they thought she was a man, with her short hair.

Hospital B Bulbul Mic

Fawcett *Thursday 12 October*

Have been moved into camp at Bulbul Mic. Our hospital staff consists of twelve: Miss Henderson, Dr Chesney, and Rendel; four sisters, Bangham, Jenkins, Jackson, and Matron Vizard; Ford, our cook, and four orderlies, Moir, Grant, Turner, and myself. My duties are mostly to do with the mess.

Our camp here is awfully jolly. Of course we kitchen people have lots to do, but there are no patients yet; and worse than that, we heard this

morning that the First Serbian Division to which we are attached is going
into reserve for three weeks or so. Having got our tents nicely fixed, we
shall have to shift almost at once. The remainder of the hospital at
Medgidia still have about fifty patients, but they are also very slack.

Saturday 14 October

German aeroplanes passing backwards and forwards, followed by shell
and rifle fire. There are no anti-aircraft guns about here. At one time they
were chased by a Russian aeroplane, and we could distinctly hear their
machine guns.

Moir *Friday 13 October*

Well, here we are, up at Bulbul Mic, all as right as rain. We left Medgidia
on Tuesday, twelve Greys and the bigger half of the Buffs, and came up
here in some of the ambulance cars. We are not worried in the way of
luggage, as all we have with us are our haversacks and bed-rolls – the
latter consist of a ground-sheet, a couple of blankets, and our plaids. The
haversacks hold all our personal belongings – i.e. toilet appliances and
one change; some luggage, what? It took about two hours coming up, and
it was very hot. All along the route it was one continuous stream of troops,
guns, and horses.

We have pitched our tents in an open space just beyond the village,
beside vast stretches of flat land – no country for war – there is simply no
cover anywhere. Everywhere there are guns, camps, trenches, and other
signs of war... Lilias and I have a tent together, and we love it – it's like
Paradise after that awful barrack-room down yonder. Before turning in
the last few nights we've made ourselves a camp fire and sat round it, hour
upon hour, singing and telling ghost stories. In the distance the Serbs and
Russians are playing the same game. I love listening to their singing, it
is so weird and sad... When soldiers on the march sing, there is always a
combination of solo and chorus, and in the chorus there is a kind of part-
singing, which seems to be based on free improvisation, with twists and
twirls and a racing above and below the melody. Some of the Russian
melodies are quaint and stirring, some are simply dull and colourless, and
others are depressing – but all are sad.

Grant *Wednesday 11 October*

Nearly a week since my last entry, and now we are in camp about fifteen
miles further on, and about seven miles from the firing line. We are here
to work as a dressing station and all under canvas. We felt sorry to leave
the others we had been with all through – it felt like leaving home. We
came by road in one of the ambulance cars, our only kit being our

haversacks and bed rolls – no kit-bags allowed. The weather is glorious, and it was a joy getting into a tent for two after having a barrack room for seventy-five. Last night was almost a full moon, and we undressed and went to bed by moonlight. Breakfast at 6 a.m. this morning, and another day of glorious sunshine. We have our kitchen lorry working away, and our camp stove and everything in full swing.

We hear that things are not going well on the front, so I hope we won't have to evacuate before we get to work here. We are really under the Serbian Division now, not as at Medgidia where we had Russians, Roumanians, and only a few Serbs in hospital. We have Serbian orderlies here, and they are such nice willing creatures.

Rendel *Letter Friday 13 October*
...It is great fun here for me. Dr C introduces me to all the officers who come as '*Meine Colleague*, Dr Rendel'. I have also had my salary raised to £100, which is extremely generous of the SWH.

...We all go about in breeches – skirts are put on for tea if officers are expected. Dr Chesney is a great character. She is extremely kind to people she likes and very rude to people she dislikes. Luckily for me she is very friendly to me.

Letter to Ray Strachey Friday 13 October
I am now having the time of my life and enjoying myself more than I have for years. It is really great fun here.

But it's not everyone who is having such a gay time. There are serious dissensions and many difficulties to cope with... Mrs H is the difficulty. She is quite hopelessly incompetent, a thoroughly tiresome woman who goes in for being a charmer. But she is unpractical, unbusinesslike, rather snobbish, and quite foolish. She tries to make up for her incompetence by strafing all the members of her unit until they are all fed up with her. She has brought out a lot of girls many of whom are too young or too delicate for the job, and then she's angry with them for being ill. She has also brought out people who can't really drive a car, or who are not mechanics. The result is that the cars are always going out of order, and no one can deal with them adequately. Apparently she had no test before choosing people, and simply believed them trustfully when they said they could drive. Dr C dislikes her intensely, and doesn't attempt to conceal her feelings; in fact she is consistently rude to her whenever they meet. As our two camps are side by side it is a little awkward.

Dr I is also a difficulty. She flies into blind rages over trifles, and is quickly reducing all her sisters to despair...

I bless my lucky stars every day that I am Dr C's protégée. She is extremely kind to me, and has raised me from the position of boot cleaner and bottle washer that I had at the other place to that of an officer and a gentleman. Dr I wouldn't have hesitated to keep me washing bottles for a year if it happened to be convenient. Dr C has stood by me and given me interesting jobs to do, and taken me with her here without another qualified person... Dr C can be a perfect devil to people she dislikes, so I am really very lucky.

Hospital A Medgidia

Bowerman *Friday 13 October*
Fairly peaceful time, as men orderlies begin to understand their work a little, but still have to tramp backwards and forwards a great deal to explain to them, owing to ignorance of the language. Bulgar aeroplanes over – no damage.

Saturday 14 October
Fierce bombardment of Medgidia by twelve Bulgar and German aeroplanes. Aimed at station – did not do any serious damage, but killed about eight people and wounded several. No bombs near the hospital. Everyone quite unperturbed.

Milne *Saturday 14 October*
This has been a terribly exciting day. I went out with Bell to get meat, and whilst we were on the way the railway was bombed – we had just left it when the first fell. Then they came thick and fast all round us – it was a terrible feeling, watching where the next would come. We drove for our lives along a road which was turned into pandemonium – horses and men flying, hay carts overturned, horses lying dead. We picked up one man and took him with us – he had nine holes in his back. The enemy was just over us all the time – quite awful. Bell was wonderful. She pacified the frightened men, told them to lie down, held terrified horses, and kept us all from feeling upset. I was not really afraid, but I just wanted to get back to William. I felt I didn't want to be killed, and it was just as likely to be me as anyone here. However, we got back to the hospital with the wounded man, and for the moment the enemy has gone off. But at lunch time they came back in double the number, and shelled the town afresh. They hovered over our camp for over an hour; then at tea time they were back again – guns firing and shells flying through the air... For the moment we are all safe, but how long will it last?

Transport Bulbul Mic

Birkbeck *Friday 13 October*

Another hot day and still no sound of guns. An enemy aeroplane over and was fired at pretty wildly, without result, but the town had a pretty rough time: it was bombarded by nine aeroplanes and the streets were littered with dead and dying. The Buffs came back pretty defeated. However, they had secured a real live mechanic to help us out; an immense relief to all of us, particularly myself.

Hodges[13] *13 October*

About this time a stray Roumanian refugee from Constanza, whom we called George, attached himself to us. He was a motor mechanic by trade, and was very useful and helpful. We looked on him as a sort of mascot. He was such a kind creature, and would do anything for any of us, from changing a tyre to filling one's hot water bottle, and later on during the retreat he really saved the unit from being either taken prisoner or shelled to pieces.

Birkbeck *Saturday 14 October*

Had my first real taste of war first hand! Three doctors came for a car and I was sent in Royce. We had not got to the front before we heard bombs. There we found three planes bombing barracks and all the soldiers lying out in the fields on their faces. We took the wounded to Medgidia; there was a bombardment going on there too. As we passed the Red Cross food place, a man was hit and blown to bits... We drove on about six miles to the aerodrome. The planes returned just as we reached it, and we realised that it was the chief object of attack. Bombs were falling in the lower part of the town too, and my passengers screamed, 'Turn and drive as hard as you can.' Quite useless, as the bombs were falling all around, behind and before. I then discovered I had a tyre down, and I got out and started to take the wheel off. Meanwhile my passengers had jumped out of the car and run off to hide in some rubble; I would have too if I had thought anything made any difference.

After what seemed hours the planes moved off and we drove by a different road to avoid the horrors of the station. We stopped at the café, where they left me. After I had been there about half an hour everyone suddenly rushed for their houses, and I realised they were at it again. I far preferred the street, but was shoved into a café; I could not bear the idea of a roof over my head, so went and sat on the steps of my beloved Royce. Some of the officers from over the way came to sit with me... When I got up to crank the car, I found I had stopped her in a pool of blood.

Hodges *Letter Wednesday 18 October*[14]

One of our girls was driving through a town yesterday during an aerial bombardment, and they dropped a hundred and fifteen bombs. She was awarded a Serbian decoration for that drive. She had lots of shrapnel and stuff all over the car, but wasn't hurt. The Russian doctor she was driving was rather scared...

You will probably hear rumours of our being taken prisoner and things, as the Bulgars are doing rather well and are expected to break our defences, but I hope we shan't be. Don't worry whatever you hear; I'll try to get a wire through if anything serious does occur.

The cars are too awful to start in the cold mornings: swing, swing, swing, till your back nearly breaks. One often has to load up one's own ambulance, and it's ticklish work, two girls lifting a stretcher with a huge man lying on it up into the ambulance, especially as they often yell as you move them. They are smashed up too, poor devils: one man we took in the other day had half his face gone, his shoulder broken, a very bad abdominal wound, all one leg in pieces, both arms wounded, and both feet too. He died after two days.

Haverfield *Report continued*[15]

There were a few cases of cholera and we were asked to keep an ambulance separate from the others in order to take cases to isolation hospitals. Ruth Plimsoll had charge of the particular ambulance, and had to take a poor officer all the way to Cernavoda accompanied by the doctor. The poor man suffered much and was most plucky. When they arrived at Cernavoda the doctor had to find the right place to deposit his patient, a long process; meanwhile bombs suddenly began to fall on all sides and Ruth Plimsoll just remained calmly in her seat and when the doctor after a long time returned and the car moved away, a bomb fell in the exact spot where the ambulance had been waiting and made a big hole in the ground. The officer, in spite of his pain, insisted on having Ruth Plimsoll's name written down and told the doctor that if he lived he would see that she got a special decoration for the great courage she had shown. Most of our drivers have been in the midst of falling bombs whilst carrying wounded to the station, and all have shown the highest courage and perfect calmness amidst frantic panic on the part of all in the street at the time.

Hospital A Medgidia

Milne *Sunday 15 October*

Another glorious day... We had three enemy aeroplanes over us, bombing away... I cooked rather a good meal for Sunday – everyone had a slack day but the kitchen, but even Dr Inglis came to the kitchen to say what a good dinner they had had – the first time she has ever said the food was even eatable.

Lots of the girls are off to B Camp, and we are resting; no one thinks of giving my kitchen orderlies an outing – they are a selfish crowd.

Had a very peaceful supper in the firelight of our camp fire. The evenings are wonderful – the sunset across the plains – the sheet of water in the distance looks like blood, and then as it begins to get dark the herds of black sheep come home with their shepherds to the valley below the hospital. We hear the tinkle of their bells till they are far away in their pens; then later droves of cows come home, all by themselves, or herded by tiny boys on ponies. It is all so like a picture – not anything real.

I am burned red – arms, neck, and face – in the sun and strong winds. It is a very healthy life, and in this glorious weather just splendid, but in the rains it will be too awful.

Monday 16 October

Still glorious weather. I got strafed at breakfast today because the girls didn't have any meat – rather absurd – there was no meat to give them. However, they got a top-hole dinner and are to have a jolly supper.

Hospital B Bulbul Mic

Turner *Sunday 15 October*

Yesterday I had a glorious day. Miss Henderson took me down to Constanza with her in the car. Jensen drove us, and two Serbian officers came too. It is about one-and-a-half hours' run from here on a straight road. Along one side of the road there is one of the few woods in this part of Roumania, and the road has trees on each side the greater part of the way. The road was crowded with troops and army transport, both Russian and Roumanian, and also with refugees. The Roumanian peasants are very picturesque, and wear brighter colours than the Russian. There is a large Turkish population in this part of Roumania.

Constanza is an awfully jolly town, like what I imagine Monte Carlo to be – white houses, and the sea and the sky. We did not have much time there, as we had a good deal of serious shopping to do. Everything is ruinously expensive. We wanted a couple of little roasting tins and shelves for our stove, and they asked twenty francs. They are absolutely sold out of cigarettes, so we are getting the Roumanian government to send us large consignments for our canteen.

Today we have been painting our tent with permanganate of potash, as yesterday we had a number of aeroplanes obviously chucking bombs at us. Our camp is very conspicuous, and there are aeroplanes over every day.

Grant *Wednesday 18 October*

Rather an uneventful day after a night of very heavy rain and gales of wind. Moir and I were up several times during the night tightening up our tent ropes. Once or twice we really thought our tent would be blown over. It was a bitterly cold morning, so after breakfast Moir and I went for a sharp walk to Bulbul Mare, a quaint and picturesque village a few miles from here on the way to Medgidia. We got beautifully warmed up, and returned much cheered.

Hospital A Medgidia

Bowerman *Monday 16 October*

Spring-cleaned the mess tent – busy day. Went to tea at Red Cross Hospital next door – found two Russian sisters who had been to Hastings! Just as going out, four Roumanian officers came in for tea – Russian orderly in usual fashion poured away boiling water just as I was going to make the tea. Hectic afternoon – convoy of wounded arrived about 5.30 p.m. – everyone up to the eyes in work.

Tuesday 17 October

Yvonne's birthday. Celebrated by tea on Trajan's Wall at back of camp – scones for tea, thanks to kind Mrs Milne. Mail bag in – three letters. Usual enemy aeroplanes. Inoculated against cholera.

Wednesday 18 October

Busy as usual – no particular excitements except gale in the night – had to get out of bed and peg down tent. Sides of kitchen and mess tents blown up and contents scattered to the four winds – had to collect them together before we could have breakfast. Very cold.

Milne *Wednesday 18 October*

Oh what a mighty wind – there was hardly a tent intact in the morning. It blew and rained and the tent flapped and shook, and every moment we thought would be the end of us; and ice-cold in bed – the wind got into every crack, and we shivered. At 6 a.m. my store was half-way across the plains, so I had to chase it first. Then the mess tent was in pieces, so we had to do a little something there, and the wood was wet and the fires would not burn... but all the same I was expected to have porridge and fried fish ready by 7 o'clock. One is expected to live in a time of miracles... We had a lot of people among the staff down with dysentery, so we had them to cook for also. I was dead tired by 2.30.

Bowerman *Thursday 19 October*

Spent day in bed owing to very slight dysentery – a number of cases in camp, probably due to flies or inoculation. Heavy firing all morning – Russian guns established just near camp – very noisy. Invalids from Camp B and Transport come over to be nursed. Transport and B Camp at Bulbul Mic have to be struck – too great a mark for the enemy – bombs very near to them, and fell between the two camps.

Transport

Birkbeck *Thursday 19 October*

The order came to decamp, just as I was dressed, and we, the sick, and all that were left, fell to packing our goods, and to taking down the tents. The order came from Dr Inglis that all sick, whether they liked it or not, were to go to Medgidia. Mrs Haverfield, of course, expected us to say we weren't sick, but I knew I was and went with eight others. Needless to say, this happens just when drivers are most needed. Onslow drove us in, eight of us. We arrived in utter depression at the camp to find no tent up, and nowhere to go... Meanwhile wounded were pouring into our hospital, and the transport were out all night, I think.

Hospital B Bulbul Mic

Turner *Thursday 19 October*

After days of quiet, the guns began booming away like anything early this morning, sounding awfully near. This was followed by a good old air raid. One fell so near the hospital that Sister Bangham got hit on the rebound by a splinter, but not seriously damaged. There came a sudden order that we were to be ready to evacuate – evidently they did not know which way the battle was going. Down came our personal tents, and before you could look round, the sick Buffs were whiffled off to Medgidia, and Vizard [the Matron] with them, which leaves only three sisters with us.

Grant *Thursday 19 October*

I notice that I wrote that yesterday was an uneventful day. Well, today has been quite the opposite. We were visited by five aeroplanes in the forenoon, and had a very lively time with bombs dropping all round us... By afternoon we had our small tents packed up, but Dr Chesney refused to go, saying it was all nonsense. We had our tents up again before night, but no beds or bed-rolls. The wounded started to pour in about 6.30, and went on all night, over two hundred passing through our hands that night. Those of us who were not on night duty had an awful night of cold and misery. We slept on straw, which was very lively, and it was cold. We took off none of our clothes, except our shoes, and I put my long woollen gloves on my feet, to make bed-socks.

Friday, 20 October

Breakfast we had in the mess tent standing around the tables with everything ready for departure, and only awaiting final orders. About 9 a.m. we were told to pack up and get off as soon as possible. By 10.30 we had all our wounded sent off, and tents down and everything ready for evacuation. News from the front is very bad: the Russians have been withdrawn to go somewhere else where they are more wanted, and as soon as the Serbs are all done for, which from all accounts won't be long, the Roumanians are prepared to give in, or do a bunk. So we started off, and now I am sitting in one of the ambulance cars writing this. We are all dumped down some miles from Medgidia in a kind of yard, with straw, pigs, horses, ambulances, soldiers, and poor refugees scattered about anyhow, and all homeless, waiting just to move on. The mess tent is to be put up, and we are all sleeping in it tonight. No beds again...

No one seems to know what is going to happen except that the war is going badly. The Serbian soldiers are such nice fellows, and a great many of them can speak German, so those of us who can speak that language are able to converse freely with them. Hodges is talking to two Serbian soldiers near me just now, just mere boys with such sad faces, and such utterly worn-out expressions. We hear on all sides how brilliantly and marvellously the Serbs are fighting, but they are worn out, and can't stand it much longer.

Hospital A Medgidia

Milne *Friday 20 October*

An awful morning of bombing – it has been simply diabolical. There had been a Roumanian reverse in the early morning; we heard the big guns – they shook the air. Wounded came pouring into hospital; then at 10 o'clock the enemy aeroplanes were over us, as suddenly, it seemed, as if the end of the world had come. Sixty bombs were dropped on the town just below us at once – the place was in darkness with the earth and debris that shot into the air, and it seemed almost at the same minute the anti-aircraft guns from three quarters were shooting at once: shells were whistling through the air and machine guns were rattling. At that moment

I was cutting up carrots for my boiled mutton, standing over my camp fire – I nearly fell into it with the shock. I had been taking no notice of the enemy overhead, as it puts off so much time watching them, and as to trying to get out of their way, it is useless. When the blackness had cleared away I ran for my camera, and was just in time to get a snap of the clouds of dust cast by another bomb dropped a few hundred yards from us. I do hope I get the film home intact, and that it comes out well. It is a wonderful life, but a very dangerous one. We are awfully busy today – so many are ill with dysentery, so we have had to cook for everyone. I was to have Hanmer of the Buffs sent over to help, but she hasn't come yet...

Bowerman *Saturday 21 October*

Bulgars advancing on east – aerial bombardment today, and cannonade becoming very loud and close. All hospital patients evacuated overnight – orders to pack equipment at once. Worked hard at this all day – struck camp in afternoon – continued in dark and rain – very difficult to find all pegs etc. in the camp field – journeyed up and down to station in baggage carts. Finally everything was packed and entrained by 4 a.m. – the whole thing done within 24 hours. Difficulties increased because of arrival of Russian Fourth Division. Whole station filled with Russian soldiers, baggage, ammunition, and horses. Road to station frequently blocked too – carts nearly overturned often – once two runaway horses charged into the midst of us. No accidents – last waggon closed at 9 a.m. Seven of us to go on to Galatz with equipment – rest of unit to follow later – a few to remain behind as dressing station.

Fitzroy *Saturday 21 October*[16]

I went twice down to the station with the baggage in the evening, a perilous journey in rickety carts, through pitch darkness over roads crammed with troops and refugees, which were lit up periodically by the most amazing green lightning I have ever seen, and the roar and flash of guns was incessant. At the station no lights were allowed because of enemy aircraft, but the place was illuminated here and there by the camp fires of a new Siberian Division which had just arrived. Picked troops these, and magnificent men.[17]

We wrestled with baggage until 2 a.m., and went back to the hospital in one of our own cars. One orderly came in almost in tears. Her cart had twice turned over completely on its way to the station, so on arrival she hastened to Dr I with a tale of woe and a scratched face. Dr I said, 'That's right, dear child, that's right, *stick* to the equipment.' Which may very well be described as the motto of the unit these days!

Milne *Sunday 22 October*

At 3 a.m. we were told an urgent message that all must leave at once, except ten. So we turned out at 4.15, and had to get breakfast of a sort for everyone; and we are waiting still to know what is going to happen. Dr Inglis is asleep, and no one must wake her; so here I sit outside the hospital, writing in my diary and listening to the guns booming nearer and nearer. The great heavy guns are Germans. Last night villages all round us were blazing, and all day long streams of carts crossed the plains with people evacuating the town. Now we are nearly the only people left in it, and there seems no desire to get us away. We shall certainly be caught, but nobody cares what happens to us – it will look well in print, and I dare say that is one of the chief things. Camp B and the Transport are already out of danger, and we feel a little sick at sitting here doing nothing, when we might be well away...

Afternoon. We are still sitting here while the evening closes round us. The guns at this moment are deafening; from a hill near one can see the battle, but I did not go – I had to get food ready. Just a little time ago Dr Inglis came in and said she wanted me to go with the other unit to Galatz, as they were such a helpless crowd; all our little crowd and I were awfully sick. Now I hear we are taken prisoners – what will happen now?

Transport Karakiri ['Black Village']

Hodges *Letter Saturday 21 October*[18]

We went on driving the wounded all day, and at 7 p.m. we were told not to go to bed, but to hold ourselves in readiness to clear out at any minute. As a matter of fact we were out evacuating wounded till 4 a.m., when we lay down on the floor and tried to sleep. At eight o'clock orders came to move at once to a village about ten miles further back, which we did. All our cars were huddled up into a little rick-yard, and we shoved up one tent. We were carrying wounded all day, and at night again were told to prepare to move at any moment. All the time streams of troops were coming *back, back*. It was tiresome driving through them. The guns sounded louder and louder. The next day we again carried wounded, and at 9 p.m. were suddenly told to go at once. From 7 to 9 p.m. I was alone in the rick-yard in charge of the stores there, and I shall never forget it. All the other ambulances had gone up to the front for wounded. It was dark, pouring rain, the guns like incessant thunder all the time, the sky a red flare from horizon to horizon, and in the direction of the village where the cars had gone, flames. They were ages away, and it was awful wondering if they were all right. Well, they were, thank God, though half an hour after they had left the village the enemy had shelled it to pieces.

Hospital B Karakiri

Moir *Friday 20 October*

We said good-bye to Bulbul Mic at mid-day, and came away in cars – I was in No 7 with Carlyon. We left our old camping ground, and were soon hurled into a world of dust and flies, and finally arrived at this little village, where we dumped ourselves down in a farmyard. As we left Bulbul Mic and came through the village, the whole place seemed to be swallowed up by soldiers, horses, carts, and whirling clouds of dust. A wind blew, and through the wind, a hot sun blazed. Everywhere horses were neighing, cows and sheep were driven in thick herds through columns of soldiers; motor cars and ambulances frantically pushed their way from place to place, and always everywhere, covering every inch of ground, from house to house, from corner to corner, was the pathetic, expectant, dreaming, stolid Russian soldier.[19] He was simply part of the intolerable, depressing background.

There can be, I'm sure, few things as bad as our sense of insecurity at present. We have gathered enough from the officers of our division to know that something very disastrous has occurred somewhere, and that things are very serious. It's the vagueness of it all that appals one. We may all of us be prisoners before the night comes – in fact, that seems, at present, no slender possibility. But if it's to be, it's to be, and what's the use of worrying?

Our stable yard is fast filling up: refugees, Tommies, and so forth. The refugees look so homeless and pathetic – like us – only I don't think we've got to the pathetic stage yet. At present we are reposing in straw that is very much alive, and we're very tired and hungry and hot, and ready to grouse at anything. Our tempers are best left alone! The SW have got the starch taken out of them this time.

Fawcett *Friday 20 – Saturday 21 October*

We evacuated on the 20th at about 11 o'clock, and came here and made a camp. The war news seems to be that the Roumanians and Serbs took over the part of the front held by the Russians, as they had to go to the Bukovina district to reinforce their own army. And of course the Roumanians were not so strong, and gave way. We cannot hear yet whether the Bulgars have broken right through or not – there is a rumour that they have got the bridge at Cernavoda, which I believe means that the army here has had its retreat cut off in one direction.

We have heard that Hospital A at Medgidia are evacuating, probably today; we are also probably retreating. The guns are simply blazing away.

We are encamped in a small square enclosure: the Serbian hospital orderlies, drivers, carts, horses, etc. are ranged round the outside, and we have our tents, two marquees and two officers' tents, in the middle with the kitchen car. The horses are tied to their own carts – the men have rigged themselves up little tents with their shaft and ground sheet, and are sleeping on the ground.

Moir *Saturday 21 October*
We spent a wonderfully comfy night buried in straw (which was not of the cleanest, as some can tell), surrounded by Tommies, horses, etc.; the atmosphere was not of the sweetest... The Transport have gone off again for wounded further back the line; they are to get them taken to the railhead and down to Medgidia, and then return for us, so at present we're waiting and wondering. The booming of the guns is louder than ever – they are very playful this morning. I hope those cars will soon come back.

CHAPTER 3
Sticking to the Equipment
(See map 4)

By Friday 20 October the retreat had gathered momentum. Even as Bowerman and Brown tied up the tents and saw the heavy equipment packed and entrained, and the little field hospital sat desolately in the farmyard at Black Village waiting in vain for the cars to return, the Scottish Women were in greater danger than any of them registered, except perhaps Mrs Milne. Though she seems temperamentally always to have expected the worst, her fear that at any moment the Bulgars would come over the hill was in this instance well founded. The Allied lines had already broken, and all around battles were being fought and lost as Mackensen's forces pushed on towards the railway. In a curve which was soon to cut the two hospitals off from both Cernavoda and Constanza, the Germans and Bulgarians advanced on and captured four towns within a fifteen-mile radius of Bulbul Mic: Tuzla, on the coast, fell on 20 October; on the 21st, Cobadinu and Toprasari, where the First Serbian Division was fighting, and, even closer to both hospitals, Murfatlar on the railway between Medgidia and Constanza.[1] By the time the women left on the afternoon of the 22nd, Constanza itself was threatened, and its oil tanks already burning, as all the diarists who travelled by road noted. It was to fall on the 23rd, as was Medgidia, with Cernavoda following on the 25th. All parties were therefore in the gravest danger of having their retreat cut off, and of being captured or caught in the shell fire.

Orders for Hospital A to prepare to fall back came on 20 October, the day Hospital B struck camp and moved to Black Village. Preparing to fall back meant first evacuating the wounded, and next packing the equipment. Since the hospitals had been designed to be independent of billets and buildings, this was no small task. There were the sterilisers, operating tables, X-ray unit and surgical supplies; there were the marquees and tents, camp furniture, stoves, boilers, and pots and pans for the domestic needs of staff and patients; and there were the personal kit-bags, including those of the Bulbul Mic group, who had only light haversacks with them. All this had only a few weeks before been transferred laboriously from the trucks at Medgidia to the little rickety carts which had carried it to the hospital building. Now the process had to be put into reverse, with the added anxiety that the speed of the Bulgarian and German advance (and the haste of the

Roumanian and Russian retreat) made the safety of both the railway and the Danube uncertain. As well as representing the investment of a great deal of public money, the equipment was necessary for the proper running of the hospital, and was not to be abandoned lightly. It is little wonder that shepherding and guarding it became one of the chief tasks of some of the orderlies for the next few weeks.

Working all day Saturday and half the night, the hospital staff completed the packing at 2 a.m. on Sunday 22 October, the day the Bulgars reached the railway at Murfatlar. Supplies for a field dressing station were kept out, the rest being sent off by train in the care of Bowerman and Brown, for Galatz; the staff followed later in the day, some by train and others in cars and on the back of a lorry. The field hospital, thought to be more mobile because it had the bigger half of the Transport Section to ferry it, was nearly left behind when the cars were called back to fetch more wounded; the whole staff of Hospital B made the journey in the tiny springless carts that had been supplied to take their remaining equipment and that of the First Serbian Lazaret out of the danger zone.

In the confusion, the parties split up, lost one another, and made their way in several small groups to safety. For nearly two weeks, each thought that some of the others were missing. As the Bulgarians and Germans moved into Roumania, orders and plans agreed on between Dr Inglis and the Serbian Command quickly became out of date, and those with authority to make decisions could not be reached for consultation. For much of the time each party made its own *ad hoc* plans, while trying as far as possible to conform to the last orders. That every one of the Scottish Women reached safety, and that they seem to have remained in comparatively good health, is one of the many remarkable features of their story; it is certainly a tribute to Inglis's policy of delegation, and to the intelligence and initiative of her subordinates. However, now that they had seen the civil chaos accompanying a military retreat, the absurdity of sending a telegram home 'if anything happened' was clear to all of them; although they do not comment on it, their letters do not again mention that particular measure.

Lorry Party Medgidia to Saragea

Fitzroy *Sunday 22 October*[2]

We were woken at 4.30, and breakfasted on a small bit of bread and butter and *chai*. There were no orders from Headquarters, and the guns were incessant and sounded nearer. We spent a lazy morning, and about luncheon time got orders to evacuate at once. The majority are to go to Galatz by train with Dr Corbett, and the rest, self included, are to go by road with Dr Inglis and work with the army as a clearing station.

The train party got off as quickly as possible, and about 4 p.m. a big lorry came for our equipment. We loaded it, seven of us mounted on top, and the rest went in two of our own cars. The scene was really intensely comic: seven Scottish Women balanced precariously on the pile of luggage, a Serbian doctor, with whom Dr Inglis is to travel, standing alongside in an hysterical condition, imploring us to hurry, telling us the Bulgarians were as good as in the town already, Dr Inglis quite unmoved demanding the whereabouts of the Ludgate boiler, somebody arriving at the last minute with a huge open barrel of treacle, which of course could not possibly be left to a German – oh dear, how we laughed!

At last we started with orders to make for Caramurat. In the town [Medgidia] our driver took us out of our way to pick up an officer, and in so doing we missed the others, who thought we were on ahead. The road to Caramurat proved to be only mud, and quite impossible for a heavy lorry after the rain, so we had to give up the idea of getting there and decided to push on to the military headquarters at Saragea. We heard later that Medgidia fell the afternoon after we left.

Train Party Medgidia to Cernavoda

Birkbeck *Sunday 22 October*
At the station was rather a disconsolate group of Greys, having absorbed every disaster – the most striking of which had been that the Russian Red Cross train we were to have left on, had already gone... Finally, after five or six troop trains came in, we were shoved into a cattle truck. All baggage that had not already been sent off (our rug rolls) was thrown in, and then we heard we might have one second class carriage too. Some had to stay in the horse truck with the luggage, and so one soldier, I, Little, Vizard and Lewis were to have one side for ourselves, and let the wounded have the other. We at once began to clear the place out. However, a terribly wounded man crawled to the door and I hauled him in; others followed, and before we realised it we had fourteen pretty bad cases, and no means of attending to them.

Equipment Party Medgidia to Braila

Bowerman *22-23 October*
Spent the morning on Medgidia station, trying to get our waggons attached to a train for Galatz – hopeless task to get any official to do anything. Suddenly discovered waggons containing our equipment had been attached to a train and disappeared – tore after train hoping it would

stop, but too late. A few minutes later another train left in the same direction. Brown and I jumped on to it, hoping to overtake the first one and our equipment. It was a refugee train, full – mostly horse trucks – got into first class waggon – no seats – sat alternately on step at doorway and on a man's valise in passage. At one end a whole family with several small children, in next carriage a Greek girl and her mother who thought themselves Red Cross nurses – got four wounded soldiers into their carriage. All the girl could do was to hold their hands and give them drinks of water. Terrible to have no bandages so as to do nothing practical for them.

The train crawled about one mile – stopped two or three hours; fierce cannonade going on all the time, especially near Cernavoda, where the bridge was the chief enemy objective. Danube at last crossed – reached Fetesti at midnight – twenty-four hours to do fifty kilometres. Interviewed chef-de-gare at Fetesti re missing waggons. Very busy – most important junction. To our immense joy waggons were eventually found, just leaving the station attached to a train *en route* for Ciulnitza. Greatest kindness from all officials – managed to seize a loaf of bread and a bottle of wine – had not eaten since morning. Wired to Dr Inglis that equipment found – went on train with two Roumanian officers as far as Ciulnitza. They gave us food – chicken, eggs and bread, and – a greater boon than this – some water. They bade us farewell at 2 a.m., and, satisfied that our precious waggons were safe, we sat in the waiting room to wait till morning.

We got our waggons attached to a train going in the right direction, and journeyed as far as Slobosia – next pause for three hours. Waggons again uncoupled and disappeared – false alarm – chased after them and refused to let them out of our sight. In spite of advice and promises of various officials, we sat down beside them near the railway line with a crowd of curious people around who specially admired our strong boots. Left Slobosia at 4 p.m., went to Tanderi, where we got our waggons shunted to the train going to Faurei, the next junction. At Faurei pandemonium reigned – refugees swarming, station crowded with wounded. No adequate provision made for them – those who can walk get on to trains and thus home as best they can – what becomes of stretcher cases, no one knows. Rumours of fall of Constanza, and general panic and depression amongst Roumanians. Russian reserves going up to front constantly passing – seem in excellent spirits.

With great difficulty, at Faurei we got our trucks attached to a luggage train going in the Galatz direction, and spent the night in the luggage waggon on top of a mixture of hospital material, packing cases, stoves, etc. Very cold and hungry. At last started for Braila.

Motor Party Medgidia to Caramurat

Milne *Sunday 22 October*

...what will happen now?

What did happen was that the Serbian officer who was taking charge of us flew into the ward where we were all sitting waiting for the next event and yelled at us – nearly out of his mind – 'You must fly this moment! There is still time.' So in a few seconds we were in the cars. Dr Inglis, Sisters Ulph and Edwards, Onslow at the wheel, and I; in the ambulance car driven by Clibborn were Ellis, Brand, Willcox, Hanmer, and Dr Potter. Then in an enormous motor lorry with all our luggage were Pleister, Wotherspoon, Fitzroy, Johnson, Jenkins, [Agnes] Murphy, Sedgwick. This was the party. The lorry went in front to lead the way we were to fly to a place called Caramurat. We were off with the fear of death upon us – and like the wind, as the hill behind was swarming with Bulgars. The first thing we did was to lose sight of the motor lorry, and of course did not know the way, and had to ask at that awful time. Well, we were told a way and off we went, and instead of being a short cut we went hours and hours out of our way.

The first few hours were over glorious moorland – no roads really – and the flying was an excitement. We saw a sunset the like of which I never dreamed – it was like blood with bold streaks of gold in it. The light faded out of the sky and the scene changed. We turned out on to a road; to begin with there were a few refugees, then more and more, and in a short time there was no room on the road. A thunderstorm came on, and it was inky black, and as long as I live I shall never forget that flight from Medgidia to Caramurat...

At last when we were worn out with the sights and sounds of the road we came to the town, and were told that five miles off the Bulgarians were advancing; it was madness to go there, and we should be off at once or we were sure to be captured. But Dr Inglis said no, we must find the girls who went on the lorry – they would be waiting for us. Then we would sleep there, and if need be start a dressing station there. Fancy our feelings when we heard this.

With awful difficulty we got into the town, crashing into frantic people and retreating troops; then we began to hunt for the girls and the lorry. I, as the young one, had to jump out, and in asking everywhere if the girls had been seen, I was taken from one headquarters to the other: Russian,

Serbian, Roumanian... My German was useful, but all of no use – nothing had been seen of either the girls or the lorry. Of course Dr Inglis was very upset; and one did not dare to think what had happened to them.

We were nearly dropping with sleep and hunger, and at last a room was found for us, and one officer undertook to have supper got for us. There was a lot of straw put down, and some rugs, and in a few minutes we were fast asleep, and only woke up as the meal was brought in. It was awfully good, and we did ample justice to it, and at once lay down on our straw again and were fast asleep, only to be wakened at 9 o'clock again by four of the Transport girls who had arrived – they had been seven hours getting eight miles – had been shelled right up at the front, and had only escaped at the last moment with the troops. They were dead with hunger and fatigue – there was nothing to eat, so they shared our straw.

Lorry Party Saragea

Fitzroy *Sunday 22 October*[3]

The whole country is in retreat, and we had an extraordinarily interesting drive. Behind we could see the shells exploding, and the sky was alight with the glow of burning villages. On our right a bigger glow showed the fate of Constanza, which fell today. The road was indescribably dilapidated, and crammed with refugees, troops, and transport. The retreating troops seem mostly Roumanian; I gather the Russians are protecting our rear.

The peasants are a picturesque lot, not of course purely Roumanian, as the Dobrudga was so lately a Turkish province. Ponies and oxen are harnessed into their little springless carts, all their household goods are packed inside, and they are followed by terrified flocks of sheep, pigs, and cattle. The peasants trudge along, going – one wonders where?

It was showery at first, but turned to a beautiful night, though very dark. Our progress was slow, as the lamp refused to burn, but we cheered our way with frugal rations of biscuits, jam, and cheese. Though lost, we have at least had the intelligence to get lost with the food! We reached Saragea about 10.30, almost too tired to speak; our lorry deposited us in the mud by the roadside, bade us a tender farewell, and left. But the general of the division was very kind, invited us into Headquarters, and refreshed us with black bread and *chai*. We ate amidst a chaos of maps, generals, messengers, and field telephones. The men looked anxious to breaking point, but their kindness to seven lone females is unforgettable. Our kit they stuck under a form of shelter in the charge of a sentry, and we groped our way through deep, deep mud to a house where we were given two rooms. Mud floors, hard but clean.

Motor Party Caramurat

Milne *Monday 23 October*[4]

At dawn our Serbian officer came to say goodbye. 'You understand,' he said, 'the Bulgar makes no prisoners of us; if caught, we are shot.' He left us repeating what everyone had said: 'Get off early in the morning; the enemy is very near.'

About six o'clock [next morning] a motor cyclist arrived with a message for Dr Inglis, telling her the missing sisters were safe: they had been stopped half-way, and were waiting for orders from her how to proceed. It was a great relief to know they were safe... It was arranged that six of us were to leave the cars and travel in small Serbian carts, while Dr Inglis and Dr Kostic, with the staff car, the ambulance, and one of our own motor lorries would join the missing girls and get them and the hospital equipment started for Galatz.

So six of us got into little carts, drawn by three horses. There was just room for the driver, and two on a seat behind him. The back of the cart was piled high with straw; it was a tight fit, and it was impossible to take anything but our haversacks with us. Our guide, a wounded Serbian officer on a beautiful grey horse, led the way, the others all waving us good-bye, and so we started on the most exciting and most terrible day of my life.

Lorry Party Saragea to Hirsova

Fitzroy *Monday 23 October*[5]

We scraped the surface dirt off our hands in filthy water, and then set out in search of news and breakfast. The endless procession of troops and refugees never ceased to tramp past all night, and there was no news of the unit. Meanwhile the general had sent to Hirsova, on the Danube (I think a distance of about 60 kilometres), for two lorries to fetch us and our stuff. A very nice Russian boy gave us boiling water and half a loaf in exchange for treacle and cigarettes. Pleister, I rather fear, looted four eggs, which we hard boiled, and so breakfasted handsomely. The rest of the morning we spent dealing out treacle. The soldiers very soon discovered it, and fell out as they marched past, bringing everything, down to their water-bottles, in which to carry it away. About 11 Dr Inglis and three of our Transport cars drove up. Having invented every awful fate for us, her relief was immense when she found us sitting by the roadside drinking Bovril. Orders to evacuate at once came to the village, and the staff moved off.

It was a pretty heart-breaking sight to watch the people stripping their little houses and packing what they could into some tiny cart, the women sobbing, the men dogged and inert. Here and there on the road, of course, there were moments of panic in which they lost all self-control. Men, at the cry that the Bulgars were coming, dragged women and children out of their carts so as to make good their own escape, and would even in their terror fling babies down on the roadside when these hampered them. I wish that certain people living securely in a certain island could see a country in retreat – not an army only, but a whole country, women and children and beasts – it's not a pretty sight, but it's a very fine lesson.

Motor Party Caramurat to Saragea

Inglis[6]

Mrs Haverfield gave us two more ambulances, and then went off to join Hospital B. We went off to rescue the party at Saragea. We arrived at Saragea about half-past ten, and round the corner we came on the inn and our seven sitting there on the equipment in the verandah, smiling...

The Russian headquarters were there, and we were immediately promised two more lorries. It was quite evident that there was no question of a hospital for the moment.

That was a curious day. Known faces appeared in motors or from houses, greeted us, and disappeared... We waited well into the afternoon for those lorries, and I was nearly asleep in that sunny inn verandah, when somebody suddenly said, 'There is Mr Bryson,' and our Irish friend swam into the centre of the kaleidoscope, unshaved and very tired, with a box of dispatches under his arm. We told him what we were waiting for, and he went and disposed of his dispatches, and came back and stopped the first lorry that passed and turned it round to go to Hirsova. Its driver was very angry, [but] we loaded up with equipment and girls, Mr Bryson gave the man a letter, and off they went.

Motor Party (temporarily on carts) Caramurat to Hirsova

Milne *Monday 23 October*[7]

At first our way led through side roads to the principal part of a town through which we had to pass; from a distance we could see a large building, ...on the roof of which there seemed to be a great collection of soldiers. In a shorter space of time than it takes to write, the roof had emptied itself, and a tumbling, yelling mass of humanity hurled themselves down the steps of the building, all screaming at once, 'The Bulgars are here; they are shelling the town: the town is on fire!' In one instant the place was turned into a perfect inferno. The deafening boom of the cannons seemed just at our backs. As we came alongside the steps, some officers, running down, called to us, '*Aide! Aide!*[8] Hurry, hurry!' and we dashed into the panic-stricken crowd to take our chance with the rest.

Often our little carts were nearly upset, as one wheel would go over a big stone sunk in the mud, but we hung on to each other and hoped for the best. It was late in the afternoon by the time we had outstripped all but an unending stream of ambulance carts winding their way up a long hill; but at last we left even these behind. Then our way led through a narrow pass, which took us down into a little village[9] where, for the moment at least, we were in comparative safety.

The Serbian Hospital, which had left Caramurat earlier in the day, had already arrived, so we joined the little company who were resting on a green knoll with a stream running at the foot, dividing us off from the village. Oh, how glad we were to get out of our carts after being cramped up for so many hours, and it was good to see our plucky little horses unharnessed and fed. We were told that the meal for the officers would be ready in about an hour, and we were bidden to join them. So, till then we had time to rest and employ ourselves as we liked.

The soldiers had been looting and killing everything they could lay their hands on for food; the meal was being prepared, fires made all round, and groups of men intent on their cooking were evidently vying with each other who should have the largest lamb. The lambs were being roasted whole on a long stick, which rested on a stone on either side of the fire. Turning the spit was very interesting, and the odours that came from these cooking groups were extremely appetising, and made us realise that our frugal breakfast in the stable at 5.30 was quite willing to be succeeded by something more substantial. But our time came, punctually at the hour for which we had been bidden, and it was a never-to-be-forgotten meal – basins of hot soup, roast lamb and cabbage, black bread and tea; a very merry party sharing spoons, knives and forks. We had none of our things with us, and the officers only had their own.

One had almost forgotten there was a war on, when a dispatch rider on a motor cycle came up to our guide. When he had read the dispatch he turned to us and said, 'We must be off at once. We must travel all night.' So in a very short time we were back in our little carts, feeling much refreshed after our rest.

About 10.30 we were going along a broad cart-track through a field, when a shout came all along the line, 'Motor cars are behind us.' At once a halt was made, and we waited with breathless anxiety for developments.

We thought it must be Dr Inglis, but could not be sure. How slowly they seemed to come. ...at last word came up that it was Dr Inglis and her party, so we left our carts at once to go to her ...and got into the car and the ambulance.

Lorry Party Saragea to Hirsova

Fitzroy *Monday 23 October*[10]

The Transport were sent off at once, but Dr Inglis insisted on staying with us until the arrival of the lorries. Our orders are to reach Galatz via Hirsova and the Danube, and there report to the Consul. Dr Inglis proceeds with the Serbian Hospital. We waited several hours until the stream of troops had got considerably thinner, and only isolated soldiers straggled by with varying reports as to the nearness of the enemy. One rumour said their cavalry was only three miles away – and this to my mind is quite sufficiently near. The Eighth Army has arrived to strengthen our left flank, and our right at Cernavoda is safe for the present.

At last Captain Bryson passed by in a car, and got out to speak to us. He managed to commandeer a passing lorry, and by 4 o'clock we had packed in ourselves and the equipment, and bidden farewell to Dr Inglis, who was proceeding in one of our own cars by a rather different route.

We found ourselves at the mercy of an insane driver, who dashed along regardless of anybody, wrecked one refugees' cart, terrified all the horses along the road, and stopped for nothing and nobody. As Captain Bryson had had to knock him down twice before the poor little man would consent to take us at all, he no doubt thought here was a chance of getting his own back. At last at dusk he charged a cart, made a belated attempt to avoid it, and drove clean over the edge of the road. Luckily for us the embankment happened to be low at that point. We climbed down, and after much heaving and struggling some soldiers got the car on the road again. A little later we came to the edge of the high ground, and in the distance far below us saw the river glistening. It was pitch dark and our lamp refused to work, though this in no wise affected our headlong career. The next thing we nearly slaughtered was a Roumanian officer in an *droshki*. After that in the interest of the public safety I sat aloft with my electric torch, and we hurtled on by its none too brilliant light. Our driver tipped us off the road once more, but finally landed us at headquarters at Hirsova, shattered but alive. Here again the Russians were very kind. First they took us to supper at a Red Cross canteen, and then two officers turned out of their rooms in our favour. We got hold of a puddle of hot water, and fell to the floor in contented heaps.

Motor Party Caramurat to Hirsova

Milne[11]*Monday 23 October*

As we came to a river with a quite impassable bridge, the drivers both refused to attempt it in the dark. They were also perfectly exhausted, having driven all day through retreating multitudes, and were sadly in need of rest. So it was decided that we should just camp where we were by the roadside. When Dr Kostic, who was with Dr Inglis in the car, heard the decision, he was in a great state of excitement. He begged and implored Dr Inglis to come on with them. He said it was dangerous; it was impossible. If we would not cross the river in the dark we must go back a little way and find a village. We could not sleep out of doors in October. He said, 'I cannot ask any of my men to stay with you. They would not do it. The enemy is too near, and I cannot ask them.' He said, 'Excuse, excuse,' so often, we all laughed, and assured him we would come to no harm, and could very well look after ourselves. We would start at daybreak, and soon overtake them. So, seeing that we were not to be shaken in our resolution to camp for the night where we were, he very unwillingly left us, writing the name of the place for which we were bound, and handing it to Dr Inglis.

After he had left us, a Serbian soldier [Chris] who had worked in the kitchen at Medgidia came up and announced in very American English that he was going to stay with us: he didn't care for 'them Bulgars'. I was especially delighted with this, as it was my job to get a fire and a meal ready. Dr Inglis herself had a most extraordinary way of getting things, and she paid us all the compliment of thinking we had the same power. But when she announced, after we had decided on the patch of ground where we would have our fire, 'And now, cook, let us have a good meal – we are all ravenous,' it rather staggered me for the moment. We had been retreating for two days, and had been unable to get anything. I knew I still had the remains of a roast of pork from which we had lunched before leaving Medgidia – if it had not been taken out of the ambulance in the meantime. So with trembling I looked into the basket where I had put it; and not only was it there, but a loaf of bread had been added to it, which was to have formed the lunch for Dr Inglis and the drivers, but they never had an opportunity to stop... So with triumph I produced these... and soon we were all sitting round the fire waiting for the water to boil for our tea, and a more delightful, merry meal could not be imagined. We all told our experiences of the day, and Dr Inglis said, 'But this is best of all: it is just like a fairy tale.' And so it was; for when we looked up, there were groups of soldiers holding their horses, standing motionless, staring at us; we saw them only through wood-smoke. The fire had attracted them, and they had come to see what it could mean. Seeing nine women laughing and chatting, alone and within earshot of the guns, was more than they could understand. They did not speak, but went quietly away as they had come.

Train Party Cernavoda to Braila

Birkbeck *Monday 23 October*

Cernavoda – at about 9.30 a.m., having taken fifteen hours to cover as many miles. Here Little and I got out to buy bread, or steal it. The town was deserted, and glass from every window was smashed. We did not go far, but, by the bridge, marched into what appeared to be the headquarters of the military. Two officers were quite interested, and gave us two loaves of bread, black *sukharki*.[12] We were too grateful – it was more than we had got for a week; but then, when we heard the everlasting bombs, the train got away at once, and we had to run for it. I landed in a horse truck on my face; Little fell, and I grabbed her in. As we made for the bridge, they were trying for it, and I was more afraid than ever in my life. They hit it, but behind us... Once over the Danube we all felt as safe as houses; then, when we got bombed twice further on, we took it quite nicely.

At Fetesti a huge great official in uniform signalled me to follow, took me to a frightfully nice doctor on a Red Cross train who took me inside, gave me chocolate, introduced me to some lovely *krestovya sestry*,[13] and finally sent me off with an orderly with a sack of sterile dressings. ...A boy led me to a cattle truck on my own and introduced me to what was afterwards known as my ward. Here, lying on the floor on a heap of dry manure, were seven stretcher cases. There was no question of dressing their wounds thoroughly in such filthy surroundings. It would have been folly to uncover anything, so we just packed those that had been dressed, fixed up slings, and rough washed all that we could who had not been washed. None were fit to move, and we had nowhere to put them. We decided it was better not to disturb the floor, and so left it. I got them hot tea and bread.

Awake all night, so I made a kettle full of tea for my ward by holding it over the primus flames, then ...prowled along the train in the dark and up into the horse truck bringing the hot tea. They were all awake and terribly cold, but some went to sleep before I left them – I think the hot tea made them sleep.

One man in the truck was evidently suffering from shell-shock. He moved restlessly around the crowded truck in delirium. Every now and then he screamed, and then shouted all the time. I got Little to come in. He got worse, and we soon saw he was quite raving mad. The difficulty was to keep him from stumbling over the bodies of the other men on the floor. One man with a fractured thigh suffered terribly, and at any jolt he screamed. A man shot through the face cried quietly all night...

The candle burned lower and lower – Little and I began to talk rather feverishly about other things, when the shell-shocked man jumped up, and as the candle gave its last flicker, he crumpled up, dead.

Equipment Party Braila to Galatz

Bowerman *Tuesday 24 October*

After wretched night in waggon found ourselves at Braila in morning – less confusion reigning here – chef-de-gare promised we should be attached to next train to Galatz. Restaurant actually available – tea and coffee never more welcome. While drinking I suddenly saw Little and Birkbeck and others of the SWH who had come on behind us from Medgidia – similar experiences to ours – just escaped bomb on bridge at Cernavoda. Invalids with them – Matron and one or two others who have had really bad dysentery. Overjoyed to know the equipment safe. Dr Inglis with a few sisters and orderlies (including Fitzroy) staying behind in fighting area to establish dressing stations.

At moment of writing still sitting on cattle truck waiting to be shunted on to next Galatz train. Hooray! Huge bump hurls us against the packing cases – the engine is on, and we hope soon to be in Galatz. Alas, our hopes rise too soon; station master a beast, continually promising to attach our waggons to next train – we saw train after train departing and we were left behind. Went round to chef-de-gare's office for last desperate effort – happily a Roumanian general was there, and said to chef-de-gare that we must be attended to. At last attached to train and started at 4 p.m., getting only as far as Barbosi, a few miles from Galatz. Horribly impudent station master told us no train till six next morning. We knew he was lying, but felt very helpless till Brown had the brilliant inspiration of wiring to the British Consul at Galatz. Went into the telegraph office, and in front of all other clerks, etc., dictated wire: 'Chef-de-gare says we cannot proceed from Barbosi. Kindly arrange by telegraph.' At mention of his own name, Chef was alarmed – immediately went and telephoned to someone – returned and said there was a train at 8 p.m., and treated us with marked respect after this. We had one or two other amusing bluffs on this journey – we made great use of the name of General Popovic, with marked effect. We imagined this was the name of the general commanding Medgidia, but discovered afterwards that there was no such general in the district. However, this name served its purpose.[14] Trucks were fastened on, and we got into a first class carriage – mostly officers.

At last arrived at our goal at about 9 p.m. Went to chef-de-gare, got the famous trucks sealed up for the night, and telephoned through to British Red Cross Hospital, where we found that those who had already arrived were installed. Motor came to fetch us – we had had visions all the way of a bath and a bed in a hotel when we arrived in Galatz, but found the Red Cross had erected a tent for us in the garden where we all slept. Moreover we had missed the hot supper which the others had, so our hankerings after the fleshpots were doomed to disappointment. The Red Cross people were awfully good, though – gave us all they could, and we turned in on our ground sheets in the tent.

A little later Fitzroy and six others arrived, having had the most thrilling adventures... Dr Inglis and several others still missing – also B Camp, the Transport, and Miss Henderson.

Lorry Party Hirsova to Galatz

Fitzroy *Tuesday 24 October*[15]

The general called us at 4.30 a.m. in person, to enable us to catch a boat for Galatz. In the end we had a long wait, and the opportunity of watching a delicious sunrise over the Danube. A party of Roumanian officers, still very 'well dressed', refreshed us with *chai*. As we sat at our little iron tables outside the restaurant, with our lovely glasses of deep amber *chai* and heaps and heaps of sugar, down the road came the weary, muddy figure of a soldier. With a cry of 'David', we all simultaneously leaped to our feet. It was our laundry orderly from Medgidia. The poor fellow had lost the others, had walked all the way, and had quite, quite given up hope of seeing us again. He was too touchingly happy for words at finding us.

After considerable difficulty we all got put on a barge with our equipment in immediate succession to a regiment of cavalry. The condition of the deck was awful. They crowded on a whole army of wounded, Roumanian and Serb, the worst cases on wooden shelves below deck with not a soul to look after them, and the rest strewn about on the filthy deck with soaking bandages and not even a bench to sit on. We did what we could, but it was not much, and found a fairly clean spot where we camped, and where Sedgwick improvised the most wonderful meals. Mercifully it did not rain, and the afternoon was clear and beautiful. We left about 10 a.m. and they landed us on a Russian hospital ship at about 9 this evening.

The little sisters looked far too beautiful to be really hard worked, but for the moment to look beautiful seemed the more essential, and the officers, who all spoke French, were charming. While the sailors landed that something equipment, they took us in, gave us water to wash in, and a delicious meal. They were optimistic as to eventual success, but spoke very bitterly of the slaughter and suffering the retreat had entailed. But of course, one must not forget that the Roumanians had a very stiff time of it for any army, let alone an untried one, and no artillery to speak of.

Ambulances from the British Red Cross Hospital here were sent to fetch us, and we went off to the hospital, where we found Dr Corbett and all the train party, including Bowerman, who had saved the equipment and generally covered herself with glory. We spent the night in a tent on the hard damp ground – a most bitter disappointment!

Motor Party Hirsova to Galatz

Milne *Wednesday 25 October*
It was a terrible feeling still being in Hirsova in the daylight. We had hoped to get off in the dark, but not so; but at last we were off – a double barge crammed with cars, soldiers and horses, all the soldiers with bayonets on which I several times spiked myself trying to get from our car to the others. We buttered a little bread for breakfast – we had no drink – hadn't had since yesterday at 2 o'clock. When we had been away about an hour we stopped and turned round, and we shook in our shoes, thinking we were going back – but it was because we had come to the pontoon bridge and the cavalry was crossing, and we must wait till the bridge was open again – so we got through when the time came, and have had a very pleasant journey. For the moment the idea of being taken prisoner is behind one.

Thursday 26 October
10 o'clock. We have only now left Macin for Galatz. We have had rather a trying night – we spent all night in the cars. The smells in the small port were too awful. All night long wounded soldiers came on board, and the second barge was laden with heavy things, so the noise all the time was incessant. I didn't get much sleep, and it rained, but at least I kept warm, and we had our breakfast at 6.30 – the captain of the tug gave us two new loaves and some sugar, and we made cocoa, so we were quite well fed. Since then we have been tying up wounded, and now we are off – where?

We arrived in Galatz towards evening, and glad we were to get there, though I'm afraid it may not be for long, as they expect this to be taken.

Train Party Galatz

Birkbeck *Saturday 28 October*

The inhabitants regard us with utter bewilderment. We have none of us a thing other than what we stand up in, and find the manicured nails of the Roumanian officers very irritating – but it's difficult to look one's best after a retreat. The Russians cannot contain themselves on the subject of the Roumanians. Their wish is now that the Roumanians had joined in the fight against them; that surely would have stopped them hampering them, and us. The Russians have little but contempt for them, and indeed, after the panic along the roads during the retreat one could hate them. The Transport brought stories that hardly bear repetition, of the wholesale loot and plunder of the retreating army, and of individual cases of brutality as they took their cars through the fleeing crowds. They were besieged by people who hung on to the already overloaded ambulances and implored to be taken up. One man seeing a car threw away a little baby and jumped on. They took the baby and its mother. Another worse case was of an officer who pulled a woman and her child off a peasant cart and kicked the man till he was forced to drive on. Another of their stories was of an old, old woman whom they found with a bundle and her dog, a refugee from Constanza, crying by the roadside, having given up all hope. Her horse had broken down. She offered her dog, a black demon, when Edwards landed her safely at Braila...

When we all met later one saw on every face what we have since called 'the mark of the Exodus'. We have all agreed not to talk about it. It's no use soaking one's mind in horror, especially if it's real, and we have all seen things we are trying to forget. No, we never, never shall.

CHAPTER 4

The Field Hospitals and the Transport Retreat

(See map 4)

With few exits even in peacetime, the Dobrudga was a complete cul-de-sac by the time Hospital B and the Transport got away. The Carol Bridge was damaged on 23 October as the train party crossed, and although it was subsequently repaired for a few more trains to cross, the Russians blew it up when Cernavoda fell a few days later. The remaining outlets for the retreating civilians and the army were the river ports of Hirsova and Tulcea, and the pontoon bridges at Macin and Isaccea, leading to Braila and Russian Bessarabia respectively. Not only were the available routes quite inadequate for the strain imposed upon them, but road and river travel were to some degree in competition, for the long pontoon bridges at Macin and Isaccea blocked the waterway and held up steamers and barges for days at a time, while the bridge traffic had to be interrupted at intervals to allow vessels to pass through. As the whole army retreated northwards and westwards via these meagre and uncertain ways, its progress was further impeded by the fresh Russian reserves hastily entering the Dobrudga by the same routes. Once having broken through the line of defence, the Bulgars made rapid progress, and were not checked until just north of Hirsova, which they reached on 25 October, only hours after Dr Chesney's party and Mrs Milne's group had left it. There was good cause to be alarmed; although the pursuers halted at Hirsova, those fleeing did not know this at the time. Tension was particularly high in the remnant of the First Serbian Division, because of the prisoner-of-war status of most of the men. While the notion that 'the Bulgar takes no prisoners' may have been something of an exaggeration, the Yugoslavs of the Serbian Division were technically deserters and traitors, and had every reason to believe that they would be shot if captured. According to Rendel's entry of 24 October, this was understood to be the fate of the wounded who had been left behind; hence the anxiety to get away, and the pressure on the Transport to keep returning to the firing line to pick up casualties.

Even on their first drive from Cernavoda to Medgidia, the Transport drivers had very soon found that motors were at a disadvantage on the steep and muddy tracks, which were never intended for cars. Now there were other hindrances as well. They could go no faster than the carts, pedestrians, flocks and herds that crowded the roads, yet they were presumed to have the advantage of speed, and were always left to the last. Petrol was in short supply, and several drivers made hazardous but necessary trips back to Medgidia to refill the cans. Even before dysentery struck the camp there had been a shortage of drivers, for nobody had foreseen the need for so many reserve drivers to cope with the long hours and difficult road conditions. All groups found the retreat an arduous and exhausting experience, but perhaps for the Buffs it was even worse than for the rest.

The supposition that ambulances could double as transport for the hospitals had been naive and ill-considered. They might have been able to move staff and equipment in an advance, but in a retreat they were urgently required for ferrying wounded. In the last days before the lines broke even the heavy lorries had worked as ambulances, making many trips loaded with light cases, and this conflict of duties combined with the condition of the roads to prevent the Transport from fulfilling their promise to convey the staff of Hospital B to safety; they simply could not get back to them in time.

An extra anxiety was the nervous breakdown of Angela Bell, who was in no state of health to be left wandering alone in an occupied country. Refusing to remain with the unit, she had to be conducted to safety, and Miss Henderson and her driver were exposed to additional danger by returning to Constanza at the last minute to deliver her, with an attendant nurse, into the care of the British Consul.

For Hospital B, only a few miles from Medgidia but most of the time out of touch with Dr Inglis, the retreat was a different experience from that of the Buffs or the base hospital staff. Able to keep together as a group, they moved back with Dr Stanojevic's field hospital, sharing the adventures and anxieties of their Serbian allies, but also sharing their comradeship and protection. None of the women mentions possessing or even seeing any map at the time; their Dobrudga experience is recorded in terms of actuality rather than symbolic representation, and they knew the direction of their progress, not from any plotted routes or compass readings but from the lovely dawns and brilliant sunsets, and from the burning towns and villages behind them. Their analysis of where they had been seems to have been reconstructed afterwards. They went eastward towards Constanza, north-west to Caramurat, and then westward to Hirsova, where they expected to get a barge down-river to Galatz. By this time the Bulgars were very close, and the congestion of people waiting for places on the barges caused Dr Stanojevic to push on along the river valley to Macin, where there was a pontoon bridge leading to Braila. The Transport crossed this on 24 or 25 October, but by the time the field hospitals reached it, it was being reserved for Roumanian soldiers and refugees; so without stopping more than a few hours, the two field hospitals moved on again, continuing to follow the Danube valley to Isaccea, where they were at last able to cross into Russian territory. Because of the uncertainty about where they would be able to cross, their route was much longer than necessary. Even Dr Stanojevic was in unfamiliar country, had lost touch with the commanding officer of the division, and could only, in his own words, 'follow the crowd.'[1]

In Rendel's brief account of 22 October, she records that when they had clambered up on to the carts, they started off in the direction of Constanza. This is puzzling, because Constanza was then being heavily bombarded; but if one looks at the military positions which had by then been lost – Cobadinu, Toprasari, Tuzla and, on the railway line to the coast, Murfatlar, it is evident that the hospitals were almost surrounded, and the flight towards Constanza was a race for the gap that was closing fast as the German and Bulgarian army moved northward from Tuzla on the seaboard towards Constanza and eastward from Murfatlar. No wonder the convoy of carts travelled most of the night, stopping for a few hours rest only in the early hours of the morning, and going on at daybreak.

Progress was very slow, not only because the fragile carts were heavily laden but because the traffic was at times all but stationary. At first it seemed largely a civilian retreat, and all the diarists, like those of Hospital A, wrote detailed and sympathetic descriptions of the peasant families and the assortment of possessions they had chosen to load on to their carts. Soon, however, soldiers and gun-carriages began to preponderate, and often the peasants were pushed aside for ambulances or for the army. Hodges, as an ambulance driver, does not seem to have done much pushing, and most of the diarists give rather the impression of having themselves been pushed; but it is interesting that Miss Henderson was offered, and accepted, an armed soldier to sit in front of her car and clear the road. This, with the loud swearing mentioned by Turner and Fawcett, seems to have been the normal method of claiming priority.

In the weeks that followed, many of the Scottish Women had conversations with Russian and French officers, and gradually they pieced together what had happened. The Russians, including the Serbian Division, had been holding the centre of the line, with Roumanians on either side. The Roumanians on the right abandoned their positions without informing the Russians and Serbs, who went on fighting. Meanwhile, the Roumanians on the left also retreated, and, according to a modern historian, 'fled along the Black Sea coast, pursued by Bulgarian cavalry over the sands'.[2] By the time the Russians realised what was happening, they were in danger of being cut off, and had nowhere to go but back. The retreat does not seem to have gone according to any plan, except that the Serbian First Division went on fighting for another twenty-four hours, thus covering at least the evacuation and retreat of their hospitals, but at the price of further depletion of their already diminished force.

The women's understanding of events was necessarily filtered through the anti-Roumanian prejudices of the Serbian and Russian doctors and officers they encountered, and no doubt also through the constraints of a third language. There seems to have been a general consensus that the Serbs had fought magnificently, as they had done in the earlier Dobrudga attack, and that the Roumanians were badly officered. The Serbs and Russians felt that the Roumanians had let them down, while the Roumanians complained that the Russians had been niggardly in sending reinforcements. The women were not competent to assess the relative merits of the armies, and some of them were careful to report what they heard as opinion, not as fact. Almost without exception, however, they commented on the impeccable grooming of the Roumanian officers, on their powdered and painted faces, and on the indifference of the officers and civilians behind the lines to the disasters at the front. Earlier they had observed the toll in civilian suffering which the scorched-earth policy of both sides levied, and they now noted the extremes of behaviour which the stress of danger evoked. Warmed by the comradeship and generosity of many whom they met, and horrified by the erosion of normal human decency in others, they felt that their education in human relationships had progressed far beyond the limits of their respectable homes and colleges.

With more to write about than before, and with the inevitable disruption of their sense of place and time, they had more reason than ever to keep a record, if only for the ordering of their own memories. There is a gap in most of the correspondence, because for a while there was no prospect of sending letters, and because a consignment of outgoing mail was jettisoned from an overloaded car. But the efforts of the regular diarists, in spite of the long hours of travelling and the makeshift bivouacking, ensured that the retreat became the best documented chapter of their time at the front.

While the local Russian and Roumanian newspapers praised the women's calm behaviour, all their diaries and letters home – which arrived uncensored if they arrived at all – refer to the disorderly panic of the armies around them. Perhaps one stereotype had been exchanged for another: foreigners panic, but British do not. At least they had put to rest the myth that men are brave and women are weak. Contemporary British newspapers and journals such as *The Spectator* and *The Illustrated London News,* which they saw some months later, described the Dobrudga retreat as a disciplined strategic withdrawal;[3] the women, when later they read these accounts, poured scorn on them. What they had seen was an unseemly rout.

Transport Karakiri to Caramurat

Hodges *Letter Saturday 21 October*[4]

We all started off [last night] at ten o'clock in pitch darkness along dreadful roads, went about ten miles, and then the road was so hopeless – enormous cavities, river to ford, etc., that we all struck and said, 'Blast the enemy; we'll camp the night on the road in the cars', which we did. At 4 a.m. we started off again across country, making for a place where we were to meet the Serbian First Division and get further orders. All the time we heard the guns nearer and nearer, as we were going to another part of the front near Constanza. We eventually found the general in a field in a valley with crowds of soldiers and guns, etc. We waited there an hour, and all the time just over the hill the shells were bursting and flames from the burning town and oil wells could be seen. Two or three shells burst over us while we waited. Then the order was given to get on, *retreat*, and all the soldiers had to go first.

We were the very last of all, and when we'd got about a quarter of a mile our blasted car stopped and wouldn't budge. So with great calmness, with shells coming nearer and nearer, we cleaned the plugs, oiled various bits, and eventually after half an hour's playing about, she started, and we raced after the others. We then went about ten miles on, all this, mind you, across fields, no road at all. Then we halted again while the military authorities burbled to each other. It was getting towards sunset; there was a scarlet sky, a vast undulating plain ahead, and behind us the crash of ever nearing guns and the long lines of soldiers coming wearily back. Again orders to move, and again we were kept to the last, and it began to pour. Off we went, and I shall always see that sinister plain, and the grey ghost-like figures of the soldiers and guns retreating. We had gone on for about two hours when we discovered that one of our big lorries had stuck. We waited and waited while they tried to get it going and the shells got closer and closer. At last we had to abandon it, after smashing the engine with a hammer, and removing the magneto. Then we went on till about 10 p.m., when we came to a village, and we slept in the cars there, as we were all done and couldn't see an inch; and besides, no one knew where to go, as the charming army had jolly well cleared off without waiting for us, after keeping us to the last. That village was pandemonium all night, with guns, guns, guns crashing, and Roumanian, Russian, and Serbian troops all mixed up in hopeless confusion in the retreat, not knowing where to go or what to do.

Haverfield *Report*[5]

After about a mile the last ambulance in front of me (I always bring up the rear) stopped, so I sent on all the others and watched the driver and her assistant pull it all to pieces with the same patience and interest she always displayed just as if no shells were falling on the hills behind us. After about twenty minutes we started all right and got on well to a large farm called Caratai, where we again awaited events. The surfaces of the field tracks were better, but the rain as usual came down and made the going for the cars a perfect nightmare. From this point Jensen and the mechanic made a dash back to Medgidia with all the empty petrol tins, as I feared running short, and joined us at the next stop, Caramurat. They reported the place deserted and shells falling on the hills behind the town.

We could not start the Seldon lorry, so with much difficulty I got eight oxen to pull her, but the guns got nearer and my second-in-command got into a stew and I was forced to abandon her with her load of Ford tyres and alas no means of replacing them. Streams of troops, refugees, waggons, guns and animals of all sorts were trailing along all day, and as darkness fell all converged on Caramurat; the streets or rather muddy lanes between houses soon became one mass of terrified humanity screaming, crying and cursing, cars and scared animals adding to the noise: scenes of terror and despair never to be forgotten. We remained in the mud in our cars till about 2 a.m. when a start was made, and at the corner of four crossroads I found our two lorries and Dr Inglis and her two cars, so we all had a yarn about our various adventures.

Hospital B Karakiri to Caramurat

Turner *21 October*

Miss Henderson, the Administrator, has gone off to Constanza to take Bell, who is one of the Transport girls and seems to have gone off her head; anyhow, she has been making trouble at Medgidia. The Transport personnel is diminishing – except for Mackenzie, who drives the kitchen car, we are to be quite independent of them.

Rendel *Diary*[6] *Sunday 22 October*

We sent off all unnecessary luggage including beds, pillows, stores and all our tents except four. We kept the mess tent, two small tents and a hospital tent, a box of emergency rations, a few cases of provisions, and a small quantity of hospital stores. At 2 p.m. an orderly galloped up with bad news and at 4 p.m. we were ordered to retreat. We started at 5 p.m., i.e. Dr Chesney, three sisters, four orderlies, a cook and myself. We were under the orders of Dr Stanojevic, the head of the First Serbian Lazaret. He had 120 men under his command and about 40 waggons. We each climbed on a waggon – already piled high with equipment – and started off, destination unknown. It was then almost dark, and there were no lights. The guns were going hard the whole time. We went in the direction of Constanza.

Grant *Sunday 22 October*

The Transport that we had been counting on to take us to safety had all been sent off, we suppose to take in wounded, so we were obliged to mount on top of our carts. Moir and I got on top of the personal luggage one, and off we started on our trek. As it got dark, everything became more wonderful. The sky was lit up with the glare from the guns, and at one point we were within three miles of the fighting line, and could see shells bursting all round. Through it all we had no fear – at least, I believe some had, but Moir and I agreed we were absolutely confident that we were being cared for by a greater power than any earthly one. We bumped and jogged along, and every moment one wondered how the whole thing didn't come to bits. A nice Russian officer who spoke German rode alongside of us most of the time, and gave us lots of information. We saw poor Bulbul Mic, that we had left only twenty-four hours ago, in flames, and all around us places were burning. We did not know what had become of Miss Henderson, who had gone to Constanza with Bell, or of Ford with the kitchen car. Finally we arrived at a village, where we are now, got our tent pitched, and all slept here, first eating our emergency rations of ships' biscuit and bully beef. We all lay down on straw, and slept the sleep of the overtired. But we were all as cheery as possible, and Dr Chesney said she was awfully pleased with the way we had gone through everything so cheerfully.

Turner *22 October*

Mackenzie, driver of the motor kitchen, had been sent off, apparently by Mrs Haverfield, on an ambulance. Our things were packed and we set off, nine of us on our five little carts, Ford being left behind on the kitchen [at Karakiri], presumably to be taken to Medgidia later. We trekked on until about 10.30 p.m. It was a most wonderful experience; as we wound in our long train across the plain we saw columns coming down from all directions. Our flock of sheep and two or three bulls were driven across the plain too. Just as we started a great fire burst out on the horizon, and we were told it was Bulbul Mic, the village we had left the day before.

When we arrived at our sleeping place we just pitched the mess marquee and all turned in. Though we had done no real work, but merely hung around all day, we were jolly tired. We thought we had lost the Transport for ever, likewise poor little Ford sitting alone with the motor kitchen in that village which is called Black.

Fawcett *Diary Sunday 22 October*

We got here about 9.30 last night after a somewhat exciting ride. There was quite a nasty thunderstorm on the way along, but luckily Turner had her mackintosh and ground sheet with her, so that we didn't get wet. We are supposed to have gone within three miles of the firing line, which I can quite believe. We seemed to see the flashes of bursting shells on three sides of us, and the roar of the guns was far more distinct than we had heard it before.

The tent went up very badly. The Serbian Sergeant, who speaks English and had to see to the tent, is a most objectionable person in a fur hat. He thinks he knows more about tents than we do, and will insist on having the pegs hammered in before he sees where the guy lines come – with the natural result.

Transport Karakiri to Caramurat

Hodges *Letter*[7] *22 October*

At 4 a.m. we started off again, and from then on it was Hell. Imagine to yourself an enormous stretch of country like the back of the Downs, only gigantic, and through the centre of it one not very wide or good main road running to the River Danube and the frontier, and from every direction on this plain, as far as you could see, behind and before and all around, streams and streams of carts and horses and women, men, and children, herds of cattle and sheep, soldiers, guns, bullock waggons, and every conceivable thing, all converging on this road. A nation in retreat, and only one road... We had awful difficulty in moving at all, and every yard we were beseeched to take people. We couldn't, because we had wounded with us in most cars, and the others were full up with stores and petrol...

At about 10 a.m. a rumour spread that Bulgarian Cavalry were coming over the hills at our back, and then panic seized the poor wretches. The soldiers and the waggon-drivers whipped up the horses and drove furiously on over everything and everyone. All the people began to scream and scream and run for their lives. They tried to jump on the cars, and one man with a little baby in his arms ran in front of one of the cars, threw the baby on the ground, and jumped on to the step. We jolly well chucked him off, and gave the baby to a woman. Never can I forget the terror on the faces of those people.

Henderson[8]

The last few days the sound of the guns got nearer and nearer, and the order to evacuate came on 19 October. We went back to a village near Medgidia, where we stayed one night. The next day I had occasion to go on business to Constanza, one of the Transport drivers, Miss Mackenzie-Edwards, driving me in the staff car. I found the city practically deserted, and the enemy took it next day. On the return from Constanza we got into the midst of the retreating Roumanian army. The enemy must have been very near, for the soldiers were crouching low as they went along, taking what cover they could. When we got back late in the afternoon to where we had left the field hospital, we found that Dr Chesney and the staff had gone on in horse carts, leaving the Transport, with which I followed that night; but the weather was bad and the roads in a shocking state, and we got stuck in the mud a little way out of Medgidia. On the following day we were able to get on again, and eventually found Dr Chesney and her staff encamped in a small village. We stayed there a couple of hours, and were then told to proceed at once.

Hodges[9]

Two Roumanian businessmen plagued us for lifts, and we let them hang on to the steps of the car. During one of the halts they went to Mrs Haverfield, and said that of course we must all be *demi-mondaines*, and some of us were quite pretty; how much did she want for the pretty ones? We were told later, with how much truth I do not know, that in both Russia and Roumania a great percentage of the nursing staffs were recruited from the *demi-mondaine* class. We certainly had instructions in Petrograd to remove our Red Cross armlets, as otherwise we should be taken for ladies of the street. All honour to them for the fine work they did.

Hospital B Karakiri to Caramurat

Grant *Sunday 22 October*

About 9 o'clock a shout went up as the Transport was sighted coming along; we *were* glad to see them, and they us, as they couldn't think how we had got here, and imagined us walking all the way. We heard their adventures, and they ours. Miss Henderson and Mackenzie-Edwards only escaped out of Constanza by the skin of their teeth, and poor Bell has been sent to Bucharest. We are now sitting outside our tent awaiting orders to move on, or rather, back. The poor Serb and Russian doctors who are with us are dreadfully worried over us, and our nice captain who was with us last night said he was very cheered at seeing us so bright. He asked Moir and me where we came from, and he said we were the most cheerful of the lot. We told him we were Scottish, and he said that when the war was over he would come to Scotland, as we seemed more warm-hearted than the English.

Turner *Sunday 22 October*

This morning we woke, and of course there was no grub, as we had devoured our emergency rations. Great was our joy when it was discovered that I had a box of coffee tablets, and that, with a ration of bread that the Serbs gave us, did us very well. The Serbians have a delightful boiler thing, better than our Ludgate boiler, quicker to get going and to put out at night, and in the morning there is generally boiling water to be got. It was a lovely morning, and we were very happy sitting outside waiting for orders. We watched the streams of soldiers passing – guns this time seemed to be in retreat. At about 9 o'clock the Transport arrived and the motor kitchen, and don't forget the cold stew. The latter we soon heated up and devoured, for Dr Chesney says always eat a meal when you can get one on a retreat. We certainly were jolly glad, for just as we had finished we had to go off again, leaving Ford and the motor kitchen with the sucking pig hanging on behind.

Fawcett *Monday 23 October*

We stopped twice yesterday, when the motor transport caught us up. As it has rained most of yesterday and the mud is already fearful, I feel sure they will have to burn their cars and come along on carts if they don't want to be taken prisoners. We are rather anxious about Miss Henderson – she went off yesterday in the touring car to find Dr Inglis, and as it has rained pretty hard since, the car may get stuck. It is very serious to go back towards the firing line, which is not so very far away. Already Bulbul Mic where we were encamped is in the firing line. As we came along the other day, we saw fires all along the horizon from where we had come the day before. The worst part of the war is the lot of the women and children. All the villages we are passing through have had orders to evacuate within 25 hours.

Transport Caramurat to Macin

Henderson[10]

Being in the 'run-about' (my own staff car) I went on with the Transport and lost sight of Dr Chesney and the hospital again. That afternoon we had to abandon one of the lorries and the kitchen car, as the Bulgars were so close that the shells from their guns got the range of the retreating army, and we could see them bursting quite a short distance off.

That night we reached a village called Caramurat, which Dr Inglis dubbed the 'Alice in Wonderland Village' because of the way people kept turning up there. Arriving in the dark, we found that Dr Chesney and her staff had passed through it before us, while Dr Inglis and her contingent were putting up there for the night. Dr Inglis greeted me next morning quite as if nothing out of the way had happened, and after passing the night in the automobile, I went on next morning with instructions to try to find Dr Chesney and then go on to Galatz.

I struck across the country with Miss Ford and two of the Transport drivers, Miss Mackenzie-Edwards and Miss Glubb, and all that afternoon we scoured the country, and eventually came upon a detachment of the Serbian army. They were very good to us, and the officers found us a little peasants' cottage in which we passed the night, being, as a matter of fact, left behind by the army, which went on, having orders to proceed, as there was a rumour that Bulgar cavalry was in the neighbourhood. That night was one of the most anxious I have ever spent in my life, as I felt considerable trepidation and responsibility for the three girls who were with me – the prospect of their being caught by the Bulgars was not a pleasant one.

Hospital B Caramurat to Hirsova

Turner *Monday 23 October*

It was quite late this morning, about 9.30, when we started on our trek again. The road ran just in front of our camping ground, and an endless stream of traffic passed along it last night. The carts were constantly in trouble, and the women implored the men to help them out. I must say they were awfully good about it. These men are awfully decent to each other, too; they share things out charmingly. Our driver this morning pressed us so much that we positively had to drink a little wine out of his cup.

We have been passing through more interesting country today. Dr Chesney calls it slightly undulating, but it is really quite hilly. Our road early this afternoon wound down through a sort of pass with cliffs on either side and a stream running down the centre. We got out and walked for a long time this afternoon. After the pass we went through quite a sizeable village, where all the inhabitants were leaving.

Fawcett and I had made up our minds to procure even at a fabulous price one of those jolly little Roumanian pots something like a gypsy pot without legs which they use for drawing water. As we passed a cottage we saw two of the very things through the doorway, but on entering we found confusion and *personne*. A Russian soldier followed us in and explained that they had all gone, and when I told him what I wanted, he said 'Take it,' so I took it. Here we see the transformation of more or less respectable Englishwomen into looters; the men loot ad lib. It doesn't seem to matter much. The people have gone, and if we don't take things, the Bulgars who are behind us will have them. Our driver looted a goat, which we carried alive in our cart for some time. She is now dead, and I think, hanging up behind. The Serbian boy perched on the barrel behind rather adds to our picturesqueness. We now have a live goose in front.

Moir *23 October*

We 'looted' a goose *en route* the other day, and it afforded us no end of amusement preparing it 'for table', and no end of joy in consuming it. It lasted us for three days! We got the goose, but had no pot, so that had to be our next loot, and all was complete. The soldiers assisted us with the plucking.

Grant *Monday 23 October*

Moir and I got out and walked for a long time this morning. It has been lovely and sunny, and such a treat after the rain of yesterday. We all have to be out of Roumania within twenty-five hours, we are told, as the Bulgars are hot on our heels, but I don't somehow think we will get into Russia in that time. We go at a walking pace all the time, so don't get along very fast. Moir and I have struck up a friendship with such a dear Russian officer who is with us. He is a doctor, and he always comes and asks us how we are getting on, and rides alongside of us, giving us all the news. In fact we have both fallen in love with him. I share my rations with him; he so often has nothing but a chunk of black bread to eat.

Tuesday 24 October

We are a little farther on our way, and sitting round a camp fire making a stew of goose, pork, and potatoes. We are just waiting to go on. We came across Dr Inglis last night, but only spoke for a few moments, as she was with two of the touring cars; she was going to remain where they were for the night, as the road was too bad for the cars in the dark. She told us that one of our lorries had gone into a ditch of muddy water. We were thankful it was not the lorry with the kit-bags.

The Roumanians are retreating as fast as they can, and making no attempt to stand. The poor Serbs have had all the worst of the battle, and one can see there is no love lost between the two. The Serbs seem to have been dragged into this just to bear the worst of it. They tell us they are not prepared for a winter campaign at all, and have no overcoats, and a great many of them no boots, while on the other hand the Roumanians are loaded up with garments of all kinds. The soldiers we are with do a great deal of looting on the way, and it is rather pathetic to see the poor people standing at the doors of their little mud huts watching the soldiers catch their pigs, hens and geese. The men are all awfully good to us, and give us their meat and bits of bread. They say they are all so sorry for us.

We pitched our tent in a rather dirty spot last night, but were only too thankful to turn in anywhere. I had mice occasionally dropping on my head, and Dr Chesney found a dead mouse in her bed bundle in the morning. We have one camp bed with us, which was brought by mistake, so we put it up last night for Dr Chesney, who is quite lame from a nasty kick from a horse a few days ago. We were afraid her ankle was broken, but though very painful, it is only badly bruised. The men have just brought us up a large hunk of cheese, and have gone to fill our water bottles with wine, so we really will do well in the food line today.

Transport Caramurat to Macin

Hodges[11]

Once out of the gloom a car pulled up, going in the opposite direction to us, and someone hailed us. We went forward, and in it was a Russian general and some of his staff. He first of all warned us on no account to try and take that particular road, as he had found it quite impassable, and had had to return. Then he said suddenly, 'What are you women doing here?' 'Driving Red Cross ambulances,' we replied. Whereupon he bowed to us, and said, 'Mesdemoiselles, I salute you. You have great courage, and I thank you for your services.' With which he saluted, and departed, leaving us all 'took aback'!

Some time during that confusion of days we drove down a long hill, at the bottom of which there was an empty farm. We were all terribly tired and hungry. Mrs Haverfield gave the order to halt, and suggested that the cook should take a very battered goose that we had been given and make some sort of meal for us. Everybody trooped into the farmyard and began collecting sticks to make a fire, when down over the hill came a Russian staff car. It pulled up beside me, and a very brusque general barked at me, 'What are you doing here?' I explained that we were just halting for half an hour, whereupon he went off the deep end and said, 'Are you mad? Do you wish to be taken prisoner? The enemy are just over the hill. There is no time to be lost; you must proceed immediately.' I fetched Mrs Haverfield, and after a brief interchange of words he departed, and orders were given to abandon the goose and start off at once. I was standing by the farm gate with Mrs Haverfield, who was considerably older than most of us, and as one of the cars slowly backed out, she said to me, 'You know, Hodgie, I don't very much mind if we are taken prisoner. I've had my day.' I remember staring at her, roaring with laughter, and saying, 'Well, you may have, but we haven't.'

Henderson[12]

We started at daybreak and passed through Babadag, where we were informed that the Transport was in the neighbourhood. We eventually got to Tulcea, where we were most kindly treated. The Roumanian general in command of the district to whom I went provided us, next day, with a soldier, who sat with fixed bayonet in the car, and helped us to clear the road before us when we went to Isaccea, as it was so thronged with refugees and soldiers as to be almost impassable.

We went across the Danube on the pontoon bridge, and after a further drive of about thirty miles reached Reni, and were most kindly received by the Russian authorities, who provided us with baths and food and sent us on to Galatz by boat. There our troubles, for a time, were ended.

Hospital B Hirsova

Rendel *Diary Tuesday 24 October Hirsova*

Left at 10 a.m. and got to Hirsova, a town on the Danube, at 5.30 p.m. We heard that Medgidia and Cernavoda had fallen, that the disorganisation was complete, and that no defence could be made. The Roumanians had started to run away at once, and had been running hard ever since. The Serbians fought most wonderfully, and have been, owing to those miserable Roumanians, almost destroyed. Four thousand or so are all that are left of the First Division. There are no wounded for us to attend to, because they had to be left behind for the Bulgars, and the Bulgars are not taking prisoners. Dr Stanojevic came to see Dr Chesney that evening. He told her that he had been ordered to consult with her if he was in a tight place. He said he was in a very tight place; that the position was very serious. It was impossible to communicate with the staff, as no one knew where they were. It was impossible to cross the river at Hirsova, as the barges were all too crowded already. He didn't know the country or the roads, and his only plan was to follow the crowd and hope to find a pontoon bridge at a place called Isaccea. As far as he knew there was no reason why the Bulgars shouldn't swoop down on us at any moment, as there were no troops between us and them.

Fawcett *Diary Tuesday 24 October*

Started at about 11.30 and stopped at Hirsova for the night. Wild rumours of Bulgars swooping down and taking us prisoner; also rumours of Dr Inglis being in the town. The kitchen car is said to have been abandoned, also one of the lorries.

The Transport are all supposed to be safe at Staravargan, and the rest of Dr Inglis' unit are I believe at Galatz. Captain Petrovic, one of the Serbian doctors, met us here – he had been 'told off' to direct the Transport safely out of the danger zone.

Transport Macin to Braila

Hodges *25 October*[13]

We were incredibly hungry, having had nothing but a little black bread and some Brand's beef lozenges for some considerable time, and tired doesn't describe it, to say nothing of the dirt. At last we got to the Danube, where the congestion was again frightful. Eventually we got over the river and into Braila. The first little restaurant we saw on the outskirts of the town, we fell upon, and ate a huge meal.

Then, still exhausted beyond description, and simply filthy from head to foot, we proceeded into the heart of the town. Out of all that terror and anguish and chaos, we suddenly emerged into an open flower-bedded garden in the centre of the city, with gay restaurants and brilliantly lit shops all around. We parked our cars beside the gardens. Suddenly crowds of people arrived and began to cheer us and throw flowers at us, and before we knew where we were, someone had taken us into an enormous brightly-lit restaurant filled with smartly-dressed people. We were installed at a long table in the centre of the room, and people stood on their chairs to see us. A magnificent meal was brought to us, which, needless to say, after the one we had just eaten, we could hardly swallow. We were so tired we could hardly hold up our heads. Crowds surrounded us, and people gave us more flowers, cigarettes, and chocolates, literally mobbing us as we struggled through pushing, cheering masses to the place in which we were to sleep. We were taken into a huge hospital ward nearly filled with soldiers, and were given beds at one end of the room, quite unscreened. However, we were past caring in what company we undressed and slept, as long as we could, after a week of being in our clothes, get rid of them and get into bed.

The next day our first effort was to find somewhere to bath. The only place we could discover was a Turkish Bath, and I shall not easily forget my embarrassment at having to go into the room, according to the custom of the country, quite nude, with about forty perfectly strange women, equally stark. I felt so dirty, and was, too, for when the bath attendant had scrubbed one side of me it was a totally different colour to the other. D was with me, and she always laughs at the remembrance and says I held a sort of court, sitting on a bench in the hot room, mother naked, with all the other equally naked ladies round me besieging me with questions about conditions at the front.

That night the British Consul very kindly took pity on us and had some of us in his house and found accommodation for the rest. He and his wife were most awfully good to us.

Hospital B Hirsova to Bolgrad

Turner *Wednesday 25 October*

Still on trek. Last night we landed near Hirsova, a most picturesque town on a hill commanding the Danube and capped by its cathedral. I wish we could have seen the city. All day we had hurried through quite beautifully hilly country. We did not start till midday. I had got up very early and found wood and water and made tea over a real camp fire – how we enjoyed it. We then had time to cook the goose in the cream which had been looted for us, but we kept it and hung it on the back of our cart and heated it up over a camp fire in the evening. Last night we had quite a beano – wine and the Turkish delight which I had kept. Early in the morning I was up again with another camp fire heating up the remains of the stew for breakfast.

This morning we started off in rather a hurry. It seems that the Bulgars are in hot pursuit. They have got Medgidia and Constanza and our only outlet remains into Roumania proper across the Danube. There is a stretch of flat marshy country between the mountain cliffs and the river itself. It winds tremendously, and round every corner we expect to find the pontoon bridge by which we are to cross. The Roumanian artillery, which is very smart, is in full retreat, and the Russians also. As we pass through each village we find the inhabitants just preparing to go off.

Moir Thursday 26 October

The news is bad. Cernavoda has been occupied by Mackensen's troops, Constanza has fallen, and the Russo-Roumanian forces are falling back rapidly behind the line of the northern Dobrudga. The capture of

Cernavoda – at the Danube end of the trans-Dobrudga railway to Constanza – seals the fate alike of the railway and of the famous 'Carol Bridge', and is the object which the enemy have been making for for some days.

We passed through some beautiful country yesterday, very hilly and rugged, with deep gullies and high rocks, and far away in the distance the wide-sweeping Danube. The sunset was most gorgeous, all the sky golden, and the blue rugged hills standing out clearly against the crimson and gold. Why are we in the midst of war? The sheep and cattle – big silvery grey beasties – and the tinkle of their bells add to the irony of it all.

All through this voyage there really seems to be some special Providence taking care of us and watching over us. We are all so wonderfully fit too. Of course we're a bit fagged out, and always hungry, but that's hardly to be wondered at. You should see us – we're all so weather-beaten and brown – or is it black?

Turner *Thursday 26 October*

And still we trek towards the Danube and Roumania proper. Last night we did not stop till after midnight. It was a most extraordinary night ride. The Roumanians seem to be in a state of panic; dashing along the road they were always trying to push in front of us or the Russians, all swaying and shouting and cursing at each other. The road was bumpy and not very wide, and all the drivers were drunk. Finally, in trying to pass some Roumanians, our cart gave a dreadful lurch, and the whole cerbooch turned turtle. Captain Petrovic, who, since his return from the Transport, has attached himself to us, came off worst with a bruised hip and a cut face. Fawcett merely banged her nose. Mine was the most interesting position. I could not move, being entirely eclipsed by the waggon and its load, which had to be removed before I could get up. It was fearfully late before we got our tent up, as that cart got left behind *en route*. Things were so congested that it was only by loud swearing that we made any headway at all.

I never knew a retreat was like this. Expecting something very depressed, it was a great surprise to find that all the men are most merry, looting and getting drunk as lords. The refugees are the worst part of it. They, poor things, have very little chance of getting far with their heavy waggons and slow oxen. They are always breaking down, and always get pushed aside for military or Red Cross columns.

Fawcett *Diary Thursday 26 October*

We got to our resting place last night at about 12.30 after various vicissitudes, including being turned out of the cart and being left behind. We had Captain Petrovic on board, and he came off the worst with a hole in his nose and a knock on his back. He is fearfully sorry for himself to-day. It is quite an original experience to feel yourself being thrown head first into a Roumanian ditch. As a matter of fact the driver had been drunk all the day before, and was still suffering from the effects. We got left behind simply through his stupidity: he did not notice when the cart in front started off, so that we got mixed up with a train of Roumanians. The result was that we simply followed the stream of carts for the next hour or two till we finally met one of our own sanitars, who was looking for us with a light.

The Roumanian officers are extremely smart in their powder blue uniforms with black or white pipings and brass buttons, but they are frightfully hot tempered. We have just passed two having a scrap, and last night when we got mixed up with them they swore like anything.

All the houses in the villages we have passed through are made of mud, beautifully whitewashed and decorated with blue, and thatched with reeds. They nearly all have verandahs in which are suspended long strings of bright red peppers.

The Serbian staff have just passed us, travelling in carts just like ourselves. I was very amused at one of our own Russian officers, who said when he saw them, 'Oh – the staff – always careful to be first.'

Moir *Friday 27 October*

We started at 5 a.m. yesterday and went on all day and all night, and are still moving on, ever on. We didn't even stop for a couple of hours during the night as usual. Things seem worse, and the main thing now is to reach the pontoon bridge. We went through some magnificent scenery yesterday – gorgeous high mountains towering above us, big, blue, glorious hills that made me think of the Abriachans, and made me wish they were the Abriachans, too. Just before dark, we went through the little town of Macin, a beautiful little village nestling amongst the hills. The view from the top of the hill, before we descended into the valley, was too lovely: peak upon peak rising against the evening sky of orange and flame, at our feet Macin with its thatched houses, and stretching far, far below, the beautiful valley of the Danube and the broad beautiful river flowing peacefully on, undisturbed by war and rumours of war.

We trekked on, and spent anything but a restful night; we were all so tired, and we could get very little sleep huddled in those joggly, bumping carts, cramped and cold and cross, and so hungry. We do feel grubby and fuggy; we've not had a wash or our clothes off now for ten days.

Fawcett *Diary Friday 27 October Isaccea*

We arrived at Macin at about 5.30. It was the most perfect place for camping, and we were quite disappointed when we heard that after three hours we were starting again and travelling all night till we reached a place opposite Reni, where we could get across the river by pontoon bridge. We had quite a peaceful night. Turner and I took it in turns to sleep on the back of the cart on some straw that the Serbs had put there for us. We reached Isaccea in the morning, and took our places in the long queue of soldiers and carts waiting to cross the bridge. Whilst we were waiting we saw part of the remnant of the poor Serbian army. Poor fellows – they looked half starved and had evidently walked miles that day – they could hardly crawl along. When they were greeted by our Serbs, who looked fat and well fed beside them, they hardly had spirit enough to respond. We also saw a hospital for horses pass – some of them had most terrible wounds, and others looked pitifully sick.

The bridge is made of fifty-six pontoons, and looks very pretty in the sunlight with all the carts and things passing over in an orderly manner. This is the only part of the journey where there has been anyone to organise the traffic. At all the other places it was the party with the officer that could talk the fastest that got through first. I'm afraid that Englishmen would be out of the running with the Roumanians and Russians – I have never heard anyone talk so fast or look so furious. On one side of the bridge there is a Roumanian flag, and on the other side a Russian, but the whole thing here is run by Russians. There are only two bridges, this one which leads into Russia, and one at Braila, a place we passed yesterday, which leads into Roumania, and is being reserved for the refugees.

Coming along last night and this morning we have passed some mountains on our right. The Bulgars are supposed to be on the further side of these. The doctor looks very anxious, and is scurrying us along as quickly as possible.

Moir *Friday 27 October*

We reached Isaccea and the pontoon bridge today – farewell to Roumania and long live Russia! We've done it, and I don't think the Bulgars will get us now. They very nearly nabbed us, all the same; from what Stanojevic, our CO, tells me, it's been touch and go on several occasions. He himself never for a moment thought we would get away. Stanojevic is a splendid little man, so brave and cool, and it's thanks to him that we are where we are. He and all his officers, and in fact the whole crowd, officers and men alike, have been more than good to us all the time, and we've come to look on them all as very real friends indeed. On the whole, they think we're not a bad lot; and we afford them some amusement, most certainly our clothes do, anyhow. They think our attire 'unusual'! Perhaps it is, but it's sensible. A shower of rain, for instance, will produce oilskins and sou'westers which no fisherman on the wettest day in the West of Scotland could beat. The size of our boots is designed for a flood, and we affect hats of uncompromising sternness. No mountain-climber, no huntress of wild beasts, ever wore clothing so abnormally practical! It even soars, in some cases, to masculinity! In consequence, we guileless maidens always nervously explain to Serbian and Russian officers, that the Scottish Women do not as a general rule (at home) dress in breeches and puttees!

Fawcett *Diary Saturday 28 October Karagaci*
We travelled about 20 kilometres after we passed the bridge yesterday, and arrived here at about 6.30. The Serbs brought us lots of dry straw, and in spite of the pouring rain we managed to have an excellent night under our mackintoshes.

It is pouring with rain, and the tent leaks horribly, which is a nuisance. Poor Turner is cooking a goose on the camp fire. Rather a wet job for such a beastly day. At present we are all sitting round the tent on our bed bundles writing our diaries.

Grant *Sunday 29 October*
We left our camping ground yesterday afternoon as the rain was soaking everything and everybody. We came into the village and are in two rooms in a dear wee cottage. We were all very glad to get under cover from the torrents of rain. One room is smaller than the other, and in it is a long divan, so Rendel and Bangham are sleeping on it, and we put up our one camp bed for Dr Chesney. The other room has a mud floor. We just put our ground sheets down for our bedding; it was cold and hard, and we all slept very badly, but we were glad to get out of the wet. We have put up our baths and are enjoying plenty of hot water; we had much needed baths, and actually went to bed with our clothes off.

Dr Chesney has just come in and told us that our hospital is to help in the hospital tent run by the Serbian doctor – I expect Moir will have to go there, as she speaks German. The patients will be mostly maladies, we hear, but it will be good to start some work. Dr Chesney and Rendel were over at the Serbian hospital this afternoon, and heard that the Roumanians have blown up that lovely bridge at Cernavoda to prevent the Bulgars making use of it. It seems dreadful to think of all the places that we have been in now being in the hands of the enemy: Bulbul Mic, Cernavoda, Constanza, Medgidia.

Fawcett *Diary Sunday 29 October*

War news according to the doctor: the Russians already on this front have not retreated across the river as we supposed. The Bulgars have been pushed back from Hirsova – they probably got there in the evening of the day we left. The bridge at Cernavoda has definitely been destroyed. The Russians are sending a whole army corps down to this district, which is more hopeful. The Hungarian Prime Minister has been assassinated by a Socialist.

Grant *Monday 30 October*

Sisters Bangham and Jackson and I went over to the Serbian tent and helped there. We have got our tent up now, with a few patients in it. This evening we were told that we are moving again tomorrow, fifteen kilometres back towards the pontoon bridge. The wounded are all going over it, and this is too far for them to come.

Moir *Tuesday 31 October*

We got sudden orders to move this morning, so bade adieu to Karagaci at 9 a.m. Back to the old game of trekking. We stopped before dark at a little village, and another mud floor was found for us. We are now sitting round our camp fire telling ghost stories, 'writing up', and singing ragtimes to celebrate Hallowe'en.

Fawcett *Diary Tuesday 31 October*

Yesterday we were told that we should be here for at least three or four days, and now this morning we hear that we are to go off at an hour's notice. At present we are waiting for the horses to be put in – we are usually ready ages before the men are. We have a new Serbian orderly – frightfully smart in a Roumanian officer's coat, etc. – who takes great care of us, bringing us hot water in the mornings and such luxuries. He speaks German quite fluently, which makes him very valuable. He says he is a Serb, but I strongly suspect him of being a deserter from the other side.[14]

Wednesday 1 November

We are to travel 40 km today to Bolgrad, and tomorrow we go on to Ismail. The ride yesterday was frightfully cold; the wind today seems to have fallen, so I hope it will be warmer.

This is a pretty little village; the inhabitants are mostly Roumanian or Russian, and are quite friendly. In the last village they were chiefly Bulgarians, and were not at all pleased to see us. Four of us went for a walk last night and saw the most beautiful sunset – mountains in the background and a lake in the foreground. Up till the present we have seen heaps of wild geese flying overhead; now as the weather gets colder, we see very few.

Thursday 2 November Bolgrad

Yesterday we had a perfectly beastly trek – the worst we have had. The wind was bitter and there was no sun at all. We finished up at about 11.30 p.m. in quite a nice house at Bolgrad. We started off again at about 2 o'clock, having explored the market. It was quite the most exciting market we have come across yet. Turner invested in a ripping sheepskin with coloured illuminations and a charming full skirt which swishes as she walks.

Moir *Thursday 2 November*

We had such a day of it yesterday – it was so cold – a biting wind all day. We got to Bolgrad about 1.30 a.m., all very cold and weary, once more found a cottage, and just dropped. We have been here all morning, so have just been out exploring. Bolgrad is quite an important town in Bessarabia; a railway junction between Odessa and Reni. It's an interesting old place, with some fine old churches and a fascinating market. We went up to the top of the fire-station tower, and had a topping view of the surrounding country. We move on again in half an hour.

There is talk of a dispatch-rider going through to Headquarters from here, so we may have a chance of sending letters. I'll finish this off and send it in the hopes of your receiving it. I've been worrying dreadfully about not being able to let you know anything – all I hope is that Dr Inglis has cabled home to the HQ and that they have informed you that we are all right. Only the unfortunate thing is that Dr Inglis can't have the remotest idea where we are; we seem to be 'lost' and cut off from the Unit, just the nine of us on our ownie-oh.

This is some life, but I wouldn't have missed it for anything. It's such an interesting experience, and in time we'll forget all the nasty parts! I wonder where my next letter will be written – some unheard-of spot in the depths of Bessarabia, I've no doubt.

CHAPTER 5
The Hospitals Reassemble
(See map 4)

Dr Inglis had named Galatz as a gathering point for the various parties which had left Medgidia and Bulbul Mic on 21 and 22 October. With a population of about 59,000[1], it was a railway junction and river-port on the Danube between the Sereth and the Pruth Rivers, and boasted a British Consulate. Among the hospitals recently established to deal with the emergency were the two units of the British Red Cross under Dr James Berry who, with his wife Dr Frances May Dickinson Berry, had worked in Serbia in 1915, and Dr Clemow, who had been in charge of a Red Cross unit in Montenegro.[2] Like the Scottish Women's Hospitals, they had come specifically to provide medical care for the newly-formed Serbian divisions, but since the Second Division was not yet ready to go into action,[3] they had been sent to Galatz, where they and a Roumanian hospital shared the premises of a large school. In the grounds they put up a couple of tents to receive the refugees of the Scottish Women's Hospitals as they arrived.

First came Dr Corbett and the train party, with Birkbeck and other invalids, from Medgidia; next, Bowerman and Brown, with the precious equipment, after their circuitous journey in its pursuit and care; then Fitzroy with the lorry party; Mrs Haverfield, with some of the Transport; and, a little later, Miss Henderson in the touring car, with Glubb and Mackenzie-Edwards as drivers, and Ford, forever parted from her motor kitchen. Mrs Milne with her party of seven followed by barge, and a few days later they were joined by the rest of the Transport. All were hungry, dirty, and exhausted, but once they had established contact with Dr Inglis, who had stayed behind at Braila with Dr Potter, Sister Edwards, and Hedges, all of Hospital A were accounted for. Hospital B and the First Serbian Field Hospital were still making their way to the pontoon bridge at Isaccea.

The retreat did not mean that the work of the hospital staff stopped; on the contrary, all the diaries mention the plight of the wounded, and the attempts of the VADs to dress their wounds and make them comfortable. It did mean, however, that for a while the organisation broke down, and what help could be given took on an improvised and temporary character. The train party organised the cattle trucks as hospital wards, and were given dressings by the Russian Red Cross; those with Mrs Milne did what they could in tying up the wounded who accompanied them on the barge; and the ambulance drivers continued to ply between clearing stations and the overcrowded hospitals in Braila and Galatz. Dr Inglis, an experienced surgeon with specialised skills to offer, had no problem in finding work for herself and a number of VADs and ambulance drivers at Braila, where they borrowed supplies from the British Red Cross; but it is clear that in the general disorganisation of the retreat, the coincidence of helpers, wounded, and the necessary supplies depended for a few days on chance and on the capacity of individuals to seize the initiative.

By 28 October, all the groups of Scottish Women were safely across the Danube, and by 3 November both hospitals were working again. Dr Inglis may perhaps have had some wry thoughts about a comment she had made in a letter to the Edinburgh Committee three months earlier when she was discussing her needs for the Russian expedition: 'The CMO, the administrator, matron and sanitary inspector will be in charge of both hospitals. As we are working with a definite division of the army we cannot be very far from one another...'[4] Now the division was a diminished entity, and the two hospitals were indeed separated, travelling time between them being out of all proportion to the actual distances involved. Mrs Milne, nominally 'only the cook', was put in charge of the Galatz party; and all the nursing staff of Hospital A were moved to Braila, where there was a concentration of work. Hospital B was necessarily left to Dr Chesney.

The remnant of the Serbian Division was for the moment quartered at Ismail, the capital of Bessarabia. This was on the northern shore of the Danube, though not on the railway, its nearest railhead being Traianoval, near Bolgrad. Here Dr Chesney's group set up their small hospital, and having sent couriers to Galatz for more medical and surgical stores, continued to nurse sick and wounded Serbs. At first they were busy, as Moir's letter of 6 November indicates; but as the patients recovered, or were sent on to base hospitals at Odessa, the doctors and nurses found themselves with less and less to do. It is the common lot of military hospitals to be either overcrowded with a rush of wounded or to wait in the wings with little to do; but having begun with such frenetic activity and excitement, Dr Chesney's party found it very difficult to accept that its present role might be simply to be ready and waiting. Like the Transport, who were bored unless they were doing their 'proper work', and like the few at Galatz who began to get restless within five days of their momentous retreat, the women of Hospital B had a low boredom threshold. Winter was setting in, their clothing was inadequate, particularly until they were reunited with their kit-bags, and their quarters were crowded, unhygienic and uncomfortable. There was nothing to read, for a while no mail, and nothing much to do. The Serbian officers came to the rescue by lending them horses to ride every afternoon, and the orderlies indulged their fondness for exploring, but Ismail was a dull place in a wartime winter, and all the diaries reveal an eagerness to get down to really hard work again.

In spite of the general panic which the women had witnessed, all was not yet lost in the Dobrudga; the Russian reinforcements had made a stand in the northern hills, thus protecting the northern river ports and the pontoon bridges, and keeping the vital waterway open between Braila and Tulcea. For the next seven weeks there was uncertainty about whether the new line of defence could be held: at the end of October it extended across the northern end of the Dobrudga, from Ostrov on the Danube to the mountain village of Babadag, now the headquarters of the Russians under the new commander-in-chief, General Sakharov. For the moment, the river ports of Galatz, Reni, Ismail and Tulcea, and the crossings at Macin and Isaccea were safe; more reinforcements poured across the pontoon bridges, and the Transport crossed and recrossed many times with their sad loads of wounded.

(Ysabel Birkbeck)

Hospital A Galatz

Bowerman *Diary Thursday 26 October*
Arrival of Miss Henderson, also of more people who have been with Dr Inglis. Terrible experiences behind the firing line. Dr Inglis, Dr Potter, Hedges, and Sister Edwards still left behind. Roumanians arriving, still in full flight, no attempt at a stand having been made. Transport all safe at Braila.

Fitzroy *26 October*[5]

Mrs Haverfield arrived. The Transport, except for the five reported to be with Dr Inglis, are all safe at Braila, and Miss Henderson, with three others, turned up here later. Rumour says that Hospital B is safe with the Serbian Hospital, and that Dr Inglis is still at Hirsova, working at a dressing station at the request of the Roumanians.[6] The town has been evacuated. I went into the wards after tea – work very heavy.

A charming black terrier, with a white shirt front, has adopted us.[7]

Letter to father, 26 October

I sent you a cable to the office yesterday as I did not know what sort of account the papers at home would be giving of the retreat in the Dobrudga, and in case you might be wondering if we were in the middle of it. I, with six others, got through safely, though the squeak was not very wide, and reached here the day before yesterday. The advance guard we found already established. The Transport, including Babs[8] have all got through except one. Altogether there are seventeen of the unit still missing, including Dr Inglis. But knowing they are with her and Dr Chesney we feel sure they'll turn up any time now. The irritating part is that we are fed on rumours only – real news is as rare as lies are plentiful.

Equipment Party Jassi

Bowerman *Diary Friday 27 October*

Started off at evening with Miss Henderson and six others to take equipment to place of safety; Ungheni chosen, just over the Russian border off the main line. Arrived at Jassi, found we could not take equipment on to Ungheni without transferring it all to new trucks, as the Russian railway gauge is different. Decided to stay in Jassi for the night to await developments. Had a splendid dinner at café.

Saturday 28 October

No news as yet from Galatz. At present we are all sitting by our respective beds in the ward lent us by the Russian Red Cross sisters, and Miss Henderson and Little (our interpreter) have gone to make enquiries and arrangements. Jassi seems a charming place, full of picturesque peasants, as well as good shops and cafés. Whole atmosphere feels like a musical comedy: officers in bright coloured uniforms going about, gay crowds, etc., just like *The Chocolate Soldier*! People don't seem to realise the state of affairs in other parts of Roumania. This total lack of preparedness and foresight perhaps accounts for the disasters in the Dobrudga. There was no attempt at entrenching the Roumanian army – they simply sent the men out into the open country where they were mown down by German artillery. Constanza, Medgidia, and Cernavoda fell with scarcely any resistance – it looks as if there had been some understanding between the German and Roumanian governments, and from the appearance of many of the upper class and officers, one could imagine they would have no scruples about accepting bribes, etc. It is to be hoped the Russians will now take over the whole front, but of course they have been very slow to arrive owing to the deficient railway system; and we have not seen much artillery going up. But only seeing small bits of the campaign as one does, it is difficult to judge what is happening to the whole country. We know the bridge at Cernavoda was blown up by the Russians on Tuesday 24 October; we crossed on Sunday night, and we did not see any extraordinary preparations to defend it, though more than six weeks ago we had read in the English papers that this would be the main point of attack. It is amazing that no greater effort should have been made to defend it. It seems now as if the way to Bucharest and Galatz were quite open to the enemy, but we hope this is not really so. Our chief anxiety at present is for Dr Inglis and the three with her. The last heard of them was at Hirsova on the Danube with the Roumanian army, the place already bombarded by the Bulgars. The Russian general had washed his hands of them, as she refused to leave when he wished earlier in the day. She desired to stay on and dress the wounded.

Hospital A Braila and Galatz

Inglis *Thursday 26 October*[9]

Late in the evening the Roumanian doctor came down and said we must go. The Russians left next morning, and Hirsova was shelled half-an-hour afterwards.

At Braila we found the river closed by the bridge of boats, and the doctor, who was stopping there, said we must go to Galatz by train. We dragged ourselves reluctantly from the boat. At the pier head we met the Russian sisters from Medgidia. They told us our Transport were here. We went to find them, and while we were at a restaurant with them a Roumanian official came in, and begged us to come and help in a hospital near at hand. We went and found that in Braila there were eleven thousand wounded and seven doctors, and here we have been since...

Milne *Saturday 28 October Galatz*

Had rather a rotten night – cold and wet. At breakfast time Dr Inglis arrived – she is at Braila with the Transport. We are to be told presently what is to happen. All the nurses went through to Braila, and fourteen of

109

us stayed behind to start a canteen for the soldiers passing through. I do wish we were doing some real work and not pottering about in places where we are not wanted.

Sunday 29 October

Onslow and I went to interview all sorts of officials about the canteen. She and I were left in charge of it. All seemed to go well at first, but in the afternoon we found that the authorities expected us to provide all the meat etc. for the soup, and as we can supply nothing but the people to man the show, they were not having any of us. We went to see the Consul, Colonel Baldwin, about sending a wire to Dr Inglis to say it was impossible. He is awfully nice, and what is more, he has asked us to come to a big room in his house – all of us – and here we are, fourteen of us in a room, all watered and fed... We are all having baths, but fourteen rowdy girls in one room is rather the limit. I never was very fond of girls, but I like them less now. It is rather fun being a CO, and they obey very well. They call me 'the duchess', because I have been wearing a fur coat belonging to someone else. We all hope so much that Dr Inglis won't turn up tomorrow and take us out of our happy home – it is such a joy to think we are in the same house with an Englishman.

Fitzroy *Saturday 28 October*[10]

Nearly all our nursing staff are to go forward to Braila. I hurled a few things into a rug, and just caught the boat. Braila is about an hour's journey up the river, and Dr Corbett is in charge, as Dr Inglis has gone to Reni for a day or two to see Hospital B.

...Six of us went off after supper and worked at a dressing station. Wounded were lying about on the floors of five or six rooms in their uniforms without so much as a mattress. We carried in one or two who were helpless, but only the cases that really needed attention. The rest just slept, and slept, and slept, as if they could never be deep enough asleep. We are told they have 11,000 wounded here, and only seven doctors. Got back to the Consulate about done. We had no baggage, so we lay down on the floor as we were.

Transport Braila

Hodges[11]

When I look back on those days in Braila, it seems incredible that any place so near the fighting zone, in which such a terrible and utter collapse was taking place, should appear so ignorant, and to the outward eye, indifferent to the state of things then existent. Their hospital preparations were ridiculously inadequate, and there was only one surgical and one medical hospital in the town. There were practically no medical supplies. We ourselves had got separated from most of our hospital unit and stores during the retreat, and had only two doctors, Dr Inglis being one of them, and a few nurses with us. Our doctors and nurses offered their services to the military hospital at once, and as wounded were beginning to pour in in thousands, they were most thankfully accepted.

I have never seen anything so awful as that hospital, because in a day or two the beds were all full, and patients were lying on the floor, all along the corridors, down the stairs, and anywhere that there was enough room to lie them down.

We used to drive to the station, which had a huge open space in front of it, and as cattle truck after cattle truck of wounded arrived, they were taken from the train and laid on the ground in rows. We used to get our stretchers out, load up the ambulances, then drive around the town until we could find access to an empty house, get the wounded out and into the house, where we unloaded them on to the floors, go back to the station and fetch more till the house was full, and then go off to the main hospital to see who could be sent to take charge. As a rule a nurse or a VAD would be dispatched to do the best she could until such time as a doctor could get along.

Equipment Party Jassi to Galatz

Bowerman *Diary Sunday 29 October*
Went to Mass at Metropole Church, Jassi; Greek Orthodox, wonderful singing – a large number of soldiers there brought various possessions to be blessed by priest.

Miss Henderson learns by telephone in the evening that Dr Inglis is now in Braila, working in hospital there. Things seem a little more settled, so she decides to return at once to Galatz with all the equipment.[12] We return once more to our third class carriage, get trucks hitched on; we are to start at 7 p.m. – spend whole evening waiting to go. Miss Henderson pays frequent visits to chef-de-gare. At 1 a.m. an official comes along to our carriage to ask us what is our destination! We eventually start at 4.a.m. – freezing cold – wooden seats to lie on – no heating – expect to be hours *en route* – not very cheerful. Serbian orderly Chris gives us 'hot water' – cherry brandy.

Monday 30 October
All dozing in our railway carriage when Brown suddenly awakes and discovers we have arrived at Galatz at about 2 p.m. – we have come

quickly. Bundle out of train with our various belongings. Find Dr Inglis, sisters, and nursing orderlies away at Braila, working very hard in a hospital; dressings, etc, lent them by British Red Cross. Remaining people installed in a large room under the British Consulate awaiting re-arrangement of the hospital. Miss Henderson, through the Consul, finds a delightful little house for us to sleep in – had belonged to some Austrians now interned – so we are very comfortable. Beds and fires!

Hospital A Galatz

Milne *Monday 30 October*

A perfectly glorious night in a cosy bed. I slept like a top. We had breakfast late, and had a real good time – then a long talk with the Consul – he is *so* nice. I have been out all the morning seeing the old part of town – it is very smelly, but interesting. I also bought a hat, in which I look less awful than in the old beast. We fed in town, then came back to the Consul's house, and were just beginning to enjoy the warm life when Mrs Haverfield came in... We feel our happy time is at an end.

Tuesday 31 October Galatz

Eight more of the Transport have come on from Braila – and now we are no more the happy family we were... It is Hallow Eve tonight so I got lots of apples for the girls to duck, and cakes for them to eat afterwards. We are making ourselves as happy as we can.

Transport Galatz

Birkbeck *Thursday 2 November*

We spent five nights in the tent, during which the ground and our blankets got wetter every hour, as it rained so. We had no chance to dry them as our only fire was the camp kitchen outside. The last day there I was driven out into the rain to sit by the fire – the doctor rescued us, or rather the British Consul. He offered us a room in his house. I went straight to bed as near the fire as I could, with a temperature, and thawed my bones out after four luxurious days in bed. The doctor was in often, I think, as I could not eat the food provided by the unit, and the tinned milk that usually comes to my rescue was not to be had, so I just lay and ached. The third day someone found some real milk, and I got on then. Varying rumours reached us all the week – some said the advance had been checked, but the retreating army never ceased to pour into the town when some of the inhabitants left it. Some of our people left too – on 2 November Clibborn, Monfries, and Grey Mackenzie[13] went home with an Englishman in the diplomatic service.

Hodges *Tuesday 31 October*[14]

[Soon] we received orders to move from Braila to Galatz, some miles down the Danube. We had to go on barges, and it was a terrible job getting the cars on and off them. Two planks were put from the riverside on to the barges and you had to drive up them; as the barges were very narrow, it was great fun when you had successfully negotiated the perilous planks and got aboard the barge, having to back and turn the car in the very tiny space available. It was bad enough with the Fords, but it was awful for the driver of the big lorry. To start with, as the lorry got on to the end of the planks the weight of it caused the other ends to tip right up in the air; then as the lorry proceeded on to them, down they went again with a bang, and it was always a toss-up whether they would bang on to the barge or not. On one occasion they began to bend in the most ominous fashion. We all shrieked, 'Hurry, hurry!' and the poor driver tore over them. It was a very nasty moment, for we all thought those planks were going to snap and dump driver and lorry in the Danube.

We were told that we should be only a short while on the barges, which were quite open. It was extremely cold, and pouring with rain. At last we started, and went a few miles down the river, which was immensely broad. Suddenly we stopped, and the tug which was towing us departed, leaving us planted midstream, and there we stayed.

The bargee and his wife were very kind and let us go into their little warm room downstairs sometimes, and gave us a little coffee and one loaf of bread. We had no other food with us, and we got colder and wetter, and hungrier and hungrier... After about forty-eight hours a tug appeared, to our intense relief, and very soon we were in Galatz, where we were billeted in villas around the town.

Hospital A Galatz and Braila

Bowerman *Diary Tuesday 31 October*

Arrival of eight more of the Transport who had been working at Braila – sent down river by barge which for some unknown reason anchored in the middle of the river for about 24 hours. They had had nothing to eat, so were feeling very sorry for themselves. No definite plans arranged yet re new hospital – awaiting further developments at the front. Lull in fighting owing to bad weather – hope this will give the Russians time to establish themselves and bring up artillery in Dobrudga. Everyone becoming very bored at inaction – we hope Dr Inglis will soon make some definite and practical plans for the winter – unit beginning to get rather dissatisfied.

The house we live in is still very comfy. We find it belonged to a single Austrian man – old housekeeper left behind. She is washing our clothes for us – such a boon, as the washing at Medgidia was distinctly half-baked. Our other attendant is our Serbian orderly Chris, who has been with us ever since we left Medgidia. He washes up, fetches hot water, etc. – very funny – talks English quite well – he had been in America and made lots of money, settled in Austria, and lost everything. At the outbreak of war he was forced to fight in the Austrian army, but together with a large number of Serbs, ran over[15] to the Russians. These men formed the nucleus of the First Serbian Division to which our hospital is attached, but which is now practically annihilated. Twelve hundred ran over at one time, but four hundred were shot by the Austrians *en route*. Chris says nothing would ever induce him to go back to Austria. He has lost track of his entire family – wife and four children – says he has no one now but the sisters, as he calls us. Odd the way he marches in and out of our bedroom and waits on us, regardless of the state of dress or undress we may be in.

Supper and Hallowe'en party with the people living under the British Consulate – ducking for apples, etc. No news of Dr Chesney and B Hospital. Rather disturbing, as we had hoped they were safe with the First Serbian Division.

Inglis[16]*Braila*

That first night we all turned to in that hospital. Then a message came from another hospital, and Dr Potter took two of the girls and went there. The people here had been working thirty-six hours without stopping. The women of the place had turned out splendidly, but of course they are not trained. Of the seven doctors only one was a surgeon. The man at the hospital Dr Potter went to was so worn out that she simply sent him to bed and took the hospital over. It was just a case of going on dressing blindly, and the wounded coming in and in and in.

Now more doctors have arrived, but they have given me an operating theatre in one of their temporary hospitals, and we are working there and in our original hospital all day. There is a woman doctor in charge of the hospital where our theatre is.

Bowerman *Diary Thursday 2 November*

Orders for everyone (except Lewis, Brown, me, Mrs Milne, and one or two invalids) to go to Braila to help with the work there. I have to collect the kit-bags of all the people who are going and make arrangements for them to go on the boat – also for the unpacking of the equipment into the store which Miss Henderson has taken for the purpose – busy day doing this.

Milne *Friday 3 November*

Miss Henderson and the rest of the girls went off to Braila, and I was left in charge of three of the Greys who were not well – and we are very happy – but how long will it last?

Bowerman *Diary Friday 3 November*

Saw off party to Braila by morning boat – all luggage safely on board – spent whole day unpacking equipment from train to store. Red Cross kindly lent us lorries for this purpose – our own not available. It is now certain that the Transport are quite inadequate to transport the hospital. They are merely an ambulance column, though of course they do excellent work in this capacity. They have orders to rejoin the Serbian Division at Ismail, so are getting their cars in order.

News of Dr Chesney and B Hospital, who are safe and well – they have had a great task with their division, and many adventures – great relief to know they are all right. It remains now to get the equipment in order and definite work for A Hospital. We do hope Dr Inglis will decide to go straight back to Odessa for the winter and have a base there. We do not seem really to get in touch with Serbians here, and we know there are large numbers in Odessa and great need of a hospital. As we have no transport we are useless as a field hospital, and much too unwieldy – perhaps small parties could be sent up for dressing stations, but it seems to many of us obvious that the bulk of us should be in a place where we can find plenty of work for a considerable time, and where there would be no danger of losing the equipment. Dr Inglis clings to her idea of a field hospital, and we feel she will only give it up at the last possible moment. None of the other officers are really strong enough to put the case before her. Dr Corbett is very nice – a gentle, lovable woman and a good physician, but very afraid of Dr Inglis, will do nothing on her own responsibility, and we are sure would shrink from expressing her views strongly. Dr Potter is good-natured, but tactless and short-sighted. Miss Henderson, our administrator, is a perfect dear – a fat, comfortable, lovable soul, kindness itself – calls us all 'dear', and, as she herself says, only wants to get us to Odessa and have us all 'safe and comfortable' – a dreamer and sentimental to boot. This character naturally does not make her a good organiser or business woman, or able to cope with the present situation.

It is rather lamentable that plans cannot be made and the hospital re-organised at once, as every day of delay means waste, as of course we all have to be kept and looked after. Those at Braila are being fed and housed by the Roumanians in whose hospital they are working, those at Galatz by the Russians – but we feel we want to justify our existence more than we have done up to the present.

Henderson

The following poem by Miss Henderson is dedicated to the rank and file of the SWH, Dr Inglis' Unit.[17]

'Like that'

'No wonder Britain is so great if her women are like that.'

Prefect of Constanza

'Like that' – Like what? Why, British to the core!
You went beyond our sheltering British shore,
Out to the peril of an Arctic Sea,
Bearing the flag of British Liberty.
You laughed above the lurking submarine,
Clothing Death's terrors in a happy sheen
Of debonair lightheartedness – I've seen
How very gallant women's hearts may be
Though torn the while with deepest sympathy,
British and women – women to the core.

I've seen you kneeling on the wooden floor,
Tending your wounded on their straw-strewn bed,
Heedless the while, that right above your head
The Bird of Menace scattered death around.
I've seen you guiding over shell-marked ground
The cars of succour for the wounded men,
Dauntless, clear-eyed, strong-handed, even when
The bullets flung the dust up from the road
By which you bore your anguished, helpless load.

I've seen you, oh my nurses, 'under fire',
While in your hearts there burned but one desire –
What British men and women hold so dear –
To do your duty without any fear.

November 1916

Bowerman *Diary Saturday 4 November Braila*
Brown and I go by boat to Braila. Dr Inglis wanted me to go into wards – explained I had no experience and didn't want to, so I am to be mess orderly. The great rush is over now – we seem to be merely marking time here till new plans can be made.

Sunday 5 November

Mess orderly work. We are living in a house next door to the Roumanian Hospital where our people work, and five of us up at the British Consulate (Consul away), three of us in beds on the drawing room floor, the other two in the Consul's bedroom. Service by Dr Inglis in the afternoon – read the piece out of Hebrews[18] about martyrs wandering about in sheepskins and goatskins. I thought of my peasant's *cojoc* hanging in the Consul's front hall to get the smell of sheep out of it! We all had sheepskin rugs served out to us at Odessa.

Tuesday 7 November

Returned to Galatz to help with the equipment – cold reception from friend Little, who says there is nothing to do! Forsooth! Living in room under Consulate with Mrs Milne and others very cosy – delightful suppers always round the fire, cooked for us by Consul's nice old cook – an Austrian Pole.

Fitzroy *Friday 3 November Braila*[19]

Our kit-bags arrived – oh, such good, clean, clean clothes.

Letter to mother Sunday 5 November

Your letter of 5th October has just arrived, but judging from all reports at least three of our mail bags have gone astray, and equally, some of our letters home. It *is* sickening. I wrote you several letters from Archangel and a long one from Odessa, besides several since. I wonder if all or any have turned up? You ought to have had more than one by 5th October.

We are still working for the Roumanians, but return to our Serbs very soon, I believe and hope. They are resting and there was a big rush here. The Transport and B Hospital are with the Serbs, except Babs [Clare Murphy], who is at present driving Dr Inglis, but is by way of joining the others in a day or two. Meanwhile she and I are sharing the Consul's bed at the Consulate, he having tactfully fallen ill and been detained elsewhere! And it's very nice too, not to mention his hot water and arm chairs. Three of the others are luxuriously spread over the drawing room, and the rest are packed into a little house next door to the hospital.

I did two days' rather interesting work at a Roumanian dressing station before our bit of the hospital was handed over to us – just dressing the whole while, and it was good to be on one's own and to chivy instead of being chivied! I am becoming no small linguist and it really is a pleasure to feel one's French getting a bit less sticky once more, and to even succeed in strafing a photograph shop in German. Which reminds me they have promised to have my films ready by tomorrow, so I shall keep this open and send some prints on if they are decent. Three of the unit have gone home, but unluckily from the other camp, or you should have had your ikon as a Christmas present. It sits among my combinations and has retreated whole.

Hospital B Ismail

Rendel *Diary Friday 3 November*[20]

Arrived at Ismail at 3 p.m. and were given our present quarters. I wish we were going back to the front, but it's not very likely that we shall do so just yet, as the poor Serbs need a rest badly. Everyone says they fought magnificently. The news is now much better. The Russians have sent a large army to the Dobrudga... I gave an anaesthetic the other day, and to my great joy the man was not sick afterwards.

Moir *Monday 6 November*

We nine are still under the wing of the army, having arrived here three days ago. We have such a nice little hospital here – three fine wards in a very good building about ten minutes' walk from where we are billeted. It's so funny having a stationary hospital again, after tending the men in tents, in ambulance carts, on stretchers, on the field, anywhere imaginable! We are billeted in a small three-roomed house in the back part of the town, and surrounded by a stable. Damp, horrid, smelly quarters – and the ordinary, everyday conveniences are nil, the sanitary conditions being *too* appalling for words. The town is choke-full of wounded and troops, and it was with the very greatest difficulty that we found a corner at all. We secured the building for the hospital first, and then just had to dump ourselves down in the nearest available vacant corner.

The first few days we were busy getting the hospital in order, and very soon we were filled up. Our patients are chiefly Serbians – a few Russians, but they are in the minority. The more I see of the Serbs, the more I like them; they are such dears.

Ismail is a very old Russian frontier town on the Danube; it is beautifully situated, and in spring and summer must be just perfect. At present it is a wee bit cold and bleak, but wonderful considering the time of the year. The town is very picturesquely laid out, with rows of trees along all the streets and beautiful gardens situated in different parts of the town. It's a great summer resort, with lots of bathing and boating, and it seems to be a great place for schools and colleges.

To our great surprise and joy on Sunday night, a lot of the Transport appeared – all our lot, who had been with us at Bulbul Mic. We were so glad to see them again, and all safe and well too. They all thought we had been taken prisoners, and were in a great state till they got the news that we were safe and sound here. They are to work in conjunction with us – to bring in the wounded to our hospital, and to evacuate the men when they are fit to move on. We got all the news of the unit from them. Dr Inglis is at Braila – they have a big hospital for the Roumanians there – glad I'm not with them. A few of the girls are at Galatz looking after the stores; we hear our kit-bags are all intact, and safe at Galatz. How I long for a rummage in mine, and, first and foremost, a change of undies!

The Buffs are charmed with our hospital; it really is a nice little place, so sunny and bright, and the men are all so happy and so grateful.

Transport Galatz and Ismail

Birkbeck *Saturday 4 November Galatz*
Moved to the Watsons' house, a real proper bedroom with chintz curtains, only two others in the same room, and no cooking smells or smoke.

Hodges *Sunday 5 November*[21]
We had received orders to go to Ismail for a quiet time after the strenuous period we had been through, as it was necessary for us to recondition the cars, and incidentally ourselves, as we were all a bit the worse for wear. We got on to barges again and proceeded, this time without being stranded mid-river, to Ismail, which was a funny primitive little Russian town. Here we parked in various small cottages with a central mess room in another house. The cottages were quite comfortable, but the sanitation was unspeakable, practically non-existent. The system of heating was extraordinary in some of the houses. The end of a wall had a small door in it; this was opened, and bundles of reeds, about twelve feet long, were pushed in, right along the whole length of the wall. These were ignited, and the fire burned in the centre of the wall, thus warming both sides of it. It was really a primitive method of central heating, but I never quite understood why the houses didn't catch fire.

Hospital B Ismail and Galatz

Moir *Tuesday 7 November*
On hearing that Dr Inglis was near Galatz and that our stores were there, Dr Chesney thought it advisable to get in touch with the unit and also to get hold of some medical stores for our hospital here, so Grant, Rendel and I were sent on that little jaunt...

119

We got to Reni at 7.30, but found we could get no boat on to Galatz that night, so as Reni is merely a small frontier town and boasts no hotel or inn, we were stranded. But not for long.

Grant *Tuesday 7 November*

Rendel and Moir agreed to go to the flagship where we had dined and lunched on our way to Cernavoda some weeks past, and ask for the admiral... They soon came back full of bounce, having been received on the flagship by a Roumanian prince serving in the Russian army. Almost as though they expected us we were given a beautiful dinner... Our prince then took us to another ship where he said we could get beds for the night, as there was no boat on to Galatz till the next morning. He took us along to what turned out to be our old friend *The George* that we had gone to Cernavoda on.

Moir *Wednesday 8 November*

We had an early start, and arrived at our destination at 10 a.m. We drove direct to the Consul's house, and found three of the unit there, the ones who are arranging, checking, and looking after the stores. The Consul has given them a nice, big, airy basement room below his house, and there they are encamped, and there we were given floor room. We were so glad to see the others, and how we all talked! The first day and all next morning we spent seeing about the stores and getting them packed and ready to take back with us. We also had a good rummage in our kit-bags, and are each taking a bundle back with us – also bundles for the rest of us nine. In the afternoon we had a look around the place, and enjoyed ourselves hugely. Galatz is quite a large place, beautifully situated, but very dirty and smelly! We spent such a jolly evening, and we talked and talked, all relating our different experiences, and revelling in a glorious fire and real chairs. I feel as if I were living in a dream, everything is so luxurious after what we've been accustomed to.

Hospital A Galatz

Milne *Wednesday 8 November*

Rendel, Moir, and Grant arrived this morning from Ismail – we are so glad to see them, and have spent today together. We are having a jolly supper all together. Dr Chesney wants me to come to her as cook for a bit. I will go if Sedgwick can come with me.

Thursday 9 November

Bell turned up while we were at lunch – poor girl, she certainly isn't accountable for her actions. I wonder what will be done for her...

Bowerman *Diary Thursday 9 November*

Rendel, Moir, and Grant arrived from Camp B to fetch stores. They have been trekking with the Serb Division ever since the retreat – now arrived at Ismail where they have set up a small hospital. Have had great adventures – made me long to have been with them – been on the move in carts for three weeks. All looking very fit, if weather-beaten.

Friday 10 November

Visitors from Camp B still with us – unable to obtain boat to return. Great fun – most hilarious party at the Consulate. Rendel mercilessly ragged because of her adoption of the Chesney manner.

Hospital B Galatz and Ismail

Moir *Saturday 11 November Admiral's launch*

We are travelling in state this time, no barges or cargo boats, thank you. On making enquiries yesterday, we found we could not get a return boat for some days, so as it was medical stores mainly, we went to consult Admiral Spirapol, who is in command at Galatz. He was most kind and charming, and said at once that he would send us back in his own launch today. So here we are, installed in his lordship's own cabin, with a nice warm stove, and surrounded by every comfort, instead of shivering with cold on board a dirty old cargo boat for 48 hours.

Fawcett *Letter Friday 10 November*

We are still at Ismail, having quite a peaceful time. Dr Chesney's temper is still troubling her and us a good deal.

There is no railway to Ismail, although it is the capital of Bessarabia. All communication with the world is by road or by the Danube. In peace time the Danube is the chief highway for this part of the world, but now this is impossible, as the Bulgars have Tulcea, a town just down the river on the opposite side.[22]

The house we are in belongs to Bulgars, who now live in one of the rooms and an outside shed. Like most Russian houses, the rooms are all on one floor and have double windows. We have three bedrooms, a mess room, and a verandah and a tiny kitchen with a grate that smokes. This is a great nuisance, as firewood is very scarce; we use blocks of fuel which is made largely of cow dung, and the smoke stings our eyes horribly. Luckily Turner's eyes are stronger than mine, or I'm afraid the unit would fare badly, but she is often reduced to tears.

Diary Sunday 12 November

Dr Inglis has been along from Braila today to settle things. It has been arranged that the Transport will now be attached to her unit. There was rather a row the other day between our doctor, Dr Stanojevic and Mrs Haverfield about a car or something.

We are probably all moving to the same place about six hours journey from Odessa where we shall still keep with our own hospital but still be under Dr Inglis.

Transport Galatz

Birkbeck *Tuesday 14 November*

Recovering from jaundice, thanks to Mrs Berry.[23] She made them get a nurse to look after me. I rather think I should have died else.

Rather worried to hear several people have wired to the Consul asking what has become of the unit, so I suppose this retreat has been in the papers and that the wires never got through. I sent one the day I got here three weeks ago.

Wednesday 15 November

Mrs Berry had a long talk about going home. I am quite prepared to if I really cannot eat the food, but think I can, now I have got really well, and she is willing for me to have another try at keeping the Transport going. Meanwhile we are not a cheerful party here. Suche cried for three quarters of the day and night, and Livesay scraps with Hedges next door, day and night. Why can't we get some regular work again?

Hospital A Galatz and Ismail

Milne *Tuesday 14 November*

We got to Dr Chesney's house, to be told that I was not coming to them after all, but going to Mrs Haverfield. Dr Inglis had arranged it. I was awfully angry, and told Mrs Haverfield so when I met her later on. She wanted me to come to her and teach her cooks – such perfect nonsense. She just thought I cooked well and wanted me to be with her, but I wouldn't do it, and went to Dr Chesney and told her so... So it is fixed up that Sedgwick and I should stay with Dr C while the two cooks went off for a week's holiday.

Thursday 16 November

The supper was a success. Everyone is very nice – quite a jolly little party – much nicer to cook for than eighty.

Hospital B Ismail and Galatz

Fawcett *Diary Friday 17 November*

Had a most exciting night. Arrived at Reni at 7 and found there was no boat on, so had dinner on the admiral's boat and were sent on to Galatz in a jolly little tug. When we arrived everything was pitch dark, so we shouldered our baggage and sallied forth. A Roumanian gendarme person took us under his wing and said he would take us to the Hotel Metropole for the night. We were handed on from one gendarme to another until we finally reached the Hotel Metropole. We asked for a room, but were told that they had not a single one left as the place was full of officers. However, two officers said they would get us a cab and send us to the British Consulate. After wandering over half the town one of them finally succeeded in getting us a conveyance. He kindly paid the man and sent us on to the Consulate, where we arrived to find that the others had moved out that very day into a house, and there was consequently no one there except a maid. However, she said we might spend the night there, which we did, and found the others in the morning.

Turner *Saturday 18 November*

Miss Henderson is going back to England almost immediately. We are sleeping with the Watsons in her room while she is away. In the a.m. we went up to see the Serbian Hospital.[24] Some of our sisters are working up there, as they are very shorthanded.

Tuesday 21 November

Went over to Braila for the day. It was jolly to see Fitzroy and Johnson again. We came back on a train, more crowded than any I have seen before. The corridors were chock-a-block, and likewise the roof. We expected Dr Inglis by the same train, but the crowd was so enormous that it was impossible to see whether she was there or not. It was full of refugees and wounded from Transylvania, going, most of them, to Galatz. We travelled, Bowerman and I, in a carriage with several Roumanian officers. They are most amusing, these people, with their endless questions. They are most curious about English women, our age, whether we are married or single, likewise the cost of our clothes.

Hospital A Braila

Fitzroy *Letter to mother, Tuesday November 21*

I *am* sorry you have had such a worrying time... I feel I ought to have suffered far worse perils. I wonder if my cable from Galatz ever got through? Anyway, long ago now you will have heard that the SW have turned up smiling, a little habit they have, so don't worry! Besides, we are going to be positively indecently safe all the winter, I am told. Rumour also says that the *Daily News* told of our prowess in carrying wounded on our backs! All I can say is – *has* the correspondent of that paper ever, by any chance, beheld a Russian soldier? We know, of course, that we are hefty, but it would take several correspondents, even *Daily News* ones, to shift the average member of the Tsar's armies, bless them, let alone one unfortunate SW. But even that cannot beat the tales about us in Odessa. The richest story tells of us jumping into the Black Sea at Constanza to escape the Bulgars! We are very busy again in hospital now, and no sign of moving.

You would hardly believe it credible, but *I* am the one who rises first at the Consulate and calls the rest. The more I think of it, the more oddly assorted a company do we appear. Of the four [who made friends on the *Huntspill*], besides Bowerman and me, there was Fawcett, a National School teacher at the East End, and Turner, who worked at the Board of Trade and possesses every virtue save an overpowering affection for a certain conscientious objector, now happily residing at Wormwood Scrubs! Of the company at the Consulate besides myself, there is a nice child called Johnson whose father stood for Hastings in 1910 as a Liberal, but was beat; Brown, once governess to Roger Fry's children and then one of the assistants at the Omega workshops in Fitzroy Square; and Mackenzie, a member of the Transport... At the moment we have another Transport visitor – one Mackenzie-Edwards, a merry soul who was working with a mechanic at Derby, and used to see us all frequently coming in the cars from Eggington with the men. Babs [Clare Murphy] has gone back to the Transport Headquarters, where they are all kicking their heels with fury and have nothing to do. The other camp too are slack, and we give ourselves horrid airs.

Hospital B Ismail

Rendel *Letter Tuesday 21 November*
We are learning Russian industriously from one of the Russian doctors attached to our lazaret. He is very kind and takes a lot of trouble, but unfortunately he has no idea of teaching. His only notion is to make us read aloud from a Russian reading book meant for small children. The words are mostly quite useless to us. There are little sentences such as 'Scythe, mow the grass while there is dew.' In return we teach him English. The lessons are rather difficult because he knows very little English, and he always speaks and teaches us in German with occasionally

a French word thrown in. It is most confusing. Another difficulty is that all our patients are Serbs, and we have to learn and use a good many Serbian words. The result is that our brains are whirling and the confusion is great.

Turner *Wednesday 22 November*
Returned home from Galatz. We brought Sammy, a little black dog we found, who had attached himself to the Greys at Galatz. He was quite black with some white about him, and we thought Dr Chesney would be delighted – but he was not greeted with the joy we expected, chiefly owing to the mud in the yard. After a brief evening spent in trying to train him to stay outside, he went for a walk, from which alas, he never returned. Our journey back was more or less uneventful; we just caught a boat to Tulcea, so did not as usual get hung up at Reni. At Tulcea we just had time to scramble off our boat with about half a dozen little boys staggering under the weight of the petroleum and other things we were bringing back, and dash along a muddy quay to a boat for Ismail, I with Sammy mixing himself up with my legs the whole time.

Fawcett *Letter Thursday 23 November*
We hope that we are not going to stay here for the winter, as already the roads are thick with mud, and the yard at the back of the house is one large pool of mud. This of course is not surprising, as we have already had a great deal of rain, and there is no drainage at all. Besides this, there are about thirty horses tethered there, there is also a Serbian kitchen, and all the hospital laundry is washed there.

Yesterday we had quite an amusing experience – we were asked to a ceremony connected with Dr Stanojevic's Saint's Day. When we got there, there were lighted candles on a sort of altar they had rigged up in their mess room, and a fat old priest prayed loudly. Then they cut up a very rich cake into three pieces to represent Father, Son, and Holy Ghost. The priest took one of these, and two of the officers the other two, and they twiddled them round and round on the tips of their fingers. This they continued to do whilst the doctor prayed for each of his family in turn. When we came away, they made us drink a glass of neat brandy.

In the evening we went to a soirée, where we danced the Kola, the Serbian National Dance.

Grant *Wednesday 22 November*
We went to an entertainment this evening, at about 9.30. There were about thirty to forty Serbian and Russian officers, all more or less drunk.

There were two long tables down the room, spread with cakes, wine, and the cake of the day before. We were given the most delicious cake to eat, and great huge glasses of wine which none of us except Turner could manage at all. It was beastly stuff. At intervals the men got up and danced the Kola, just in and out amongst the tables; as the evening wore on they got more and more uproarious, and we were all wishing Dr Chesney would come away. The tables were covered with spilt wine, it was on the floor, and on the men's uniforms, and altogether the whole scene was disgusting. Stanojevic himself was the only one who remained unruffled, and the little Russian doctor. They were as neat and calm as ever, though they managed to put away a good deal of drink. There was a string orchestra, mandolin and a cello, all playing pizzicato, and one of the orchestra sang very well. One of the officers (a former opera singer) sang very beautifully too. At last Dr Chesney suggested our going, and we were all given flowers from the tables by the men, but I'm afraid we were all so disgusted that most of us threw them on the road when we got outside.

Turner *Thursday 23 November*

We just came back from our jaunt to Galatz at the right moment. Even on our way up from the quay, when I was staggering along with two large parcels of instruments and drugs, and with Sammy on a lead, tying himself up round my legs, and fairly wading through the worst mud I have seen since Archangel, I met Petrovic in the most awful state about a *slava* they were going to hold and to which we were invited. Such a do I have never seen before, and I wouldn't have missed it for worlds. At about 9 o'clock Petrovic came to fetch us. The Canzelaria is only just around the corner from us, which was fortunate, considering the mud. They had apparently fed, and were sitting over coffee and wine and cakes. The Headquarters staff from the village had come in and the room had been marvellously decorated for the occasion. A little Russian doctor who is evidently an artist had done a gorgeous poster effect representing Russia rescuing Serbia from an uncomfortable-looking rock in the middle of an angry sea. He had also done a number of awfully good caricatures, notably one of Petrovic, which he gave me to keep.

As soon as we arrived some started dancing the Kola, and presently, after we had been introduced to people – those who could speak anything but Serbian – we were invited to join in. A few of us did so; it is a jolly dance. Generally, I believe, it is done very slowly and majestically, but on occasions, like last night, it is danced very quickly, and at the end they curl up into the middle, and I believe thereafter occurs a sort of kiss-in-the-ring game for the innermost couple. I unwittingly was the innermost girl, but mercifully Stanojevic ordered the unwinding process when he thought the situation looked dangerous. After the Kola – or I should say the first Kola – we sat and ate a queer cake which had been blessed two days ago, and drank pints of wine – mercifully a light *vin du pays* from the Caucasus which does not easily go to one's head. On the whole it was a lurid evening. As they each got thoroughly squiffy, they started a fresh and wilder Kola which we did not join in. Four Serbian NCOs and men formed the band – a cello and three little scratch things they call guitars, but weren't. One quaint little man came out and sang – he really sang very well indeed – and one or two of the officers also sang. At about midnight more coffee was served, after which Dr Chesney, in mortal fear lest any of us should drink too much, came away. As a matter of fact I was the only dangerous one, as the sisters sat lumped together as is the wont of such people, while Dr Chesney and I sat with the officers, so that we had to drink healths all round.

They kept it up till 4 a.m., and the little Russian who comes to tea with us every day told me that by 2 a.m. even he was squiffy. Last night he told me in an awed voice that certain of the others were 'how do you call it – *ivre en français.*' So I told him 'squiffy' and he knows that word now. One day he will come out with it in polite society.

Petrovic, by a Russian doctor
(Felicity Blake)

CHAPTER 6
The Work Continues

(See map 4)

Because of its position at one of the two pontoon bridges on the lower Danube,[1] Braila continued to be an important hospital centre for the reception of wounded, and for the rest of 1916 Hospital A was still hard at work. Ismail, a long day's trek from the railway at Bolgrad, was a different matter. The First Serbian Division was now in reserve, and as the few sick and wounded recovered – and only the lightly wounded had been able to undertake the arduous journey with the division – the hospital was less busy, and in this state of comparative inactivity, the personal tensions noticed in earlier and busier times began to be more serious. Dr Chesney had already quarrelled with Mrs Haverfield at Bulbul Mic, and now that they were together again at Ismail for a short while, the two got on no better. There was also a quarrel between Mrs Haverfield and Dr Stanojevic, of the Serbian Hospital, 'about a car or something.' Probably this quarrel was related to the 'taxi work' which the Serbian officers seem to have expected the Transport to undertake when they were not otherwise busy. It resulted in the transfer of the Transport to the Russian Headquarters at Babadag, where they were restored to feverish activity and more urgent anxieties.

Within the groups, too, there was discord. Many of the Transport were unhappy under Mrs Haverfield, and although Dr Inglis made several tactful arrangements, keeping the unhappiest drivers with her to drive the staff car, this was not a permanent solution. The rest continued to do admirable work throughout November and December, but trouble was brewing between them and their commandant. In Hospital B the dissension was mostly related to Dr Chesney's rudeness, not only to her staff but to many visitors, including some of the Serbian and Russian officers. All the orderlies' records reflect great anxiety about the effects of her tongue, not so much on themselves as on the various visiting dignitaries with whom it was necessary to maintain friendly relations. Surprisingly, none of the diarists complains about her obvious favouring of Rendel, although this must have caused some ill-feeling. Rendel's frequently expressed thankfulness for Dr Chesney's patronage seems to contain a substantial measure of alarm at the vision of what it would be like not to be so blessed. Fawcett and Turner, whose work in the kitchen did not slacken, in spite of the slackening of the hospital work, felt Chesney's displeasure keenly, and when they got the opportunity, asked to be moved, Turner to the Transport and Fawcett to Hospital A.

Working relations were much happier in Hospital A. While Dr Inglis was impatient with inefficiency, and sometimes lost her temper, she valued good work, and appreciated the capacity for responsibility which she had seen in the sisters and orderlies. Her praises are generous, and in all her comments one can discern tact, a capacity to see the other side of the question, and a desire to be fair. Though not prepared to delegate her final authority in matters of policy – and at the time the normal style of discipline in all British hospitals was hierarchical and militaristic – she was obviously willing to give responsibility where she believed it would be worthily borne. At Galatz, Fitzroy was given a ward of her own; and later, at Reni, she, Murphy and Fawcett, by then thoroughly trained in ward work, were often to be in sole charge of the ward during the night. Rendel's criticism that Dr Inglis was shy, and did not seem to take any personal interest in people, must be measured against the evident respect and affection which Fitzroy, Bowerman, Fawcett and Turner felt for her, and against the evidence in her letters and reports of thoughtfulness and concern for her patients and staff.

Personal difficulties were not helped by the serious money problems of foreigners in Roumania and Russia. In Russia prices had risen by January 1917 to almost four times their 1914 level.[2] The funds the women had brought out with them, including their private pocket money deposited with Miss Henderson, had at the beginning of October been changed into Roumanian currency, which by mid-November was worth a fraction of its original value, even against the rouble. A few of the Buffs, always more independent than the Greys of the general rules of the organisation, and perhaps on the advice of the veterans of the Serbian campaign, had managed to hold on to some private funds in gold sovereigns and half-sovereigns,[3] but most had handed in their £10 or £20 as instructed, and did not understand why Miss Henderson could not give it back to them when they needed it. Rendel seems to have blamed Miss Henderson's incompetence, but although she was a poor book-keeper, and indeed had failed to keep proper records in the momentous days before and during the retreat,[4] it is not to be supposed that she was at fault in failing to overcome a collapsing exchange rate. There seems to have been little understanding of this at the time, and Miss Henderson came in for more blame than she deserved. For a while Hospital B was very short of money, and even when things had settled down and banks were operating normally again, the funds of the SWH were so depleted that they had to ask for advances from the Foreign Office, which the London Committee subsequently repaid.[5] No doubt the parlous state of the unit's finances contributed to Miss Henderson's decision at the end of November to go home for a month or two to raise more money by lecturing on the London Unit's Roumanian adventures.[6]

Fighting continued in the Dobrudga for another two months after the October retreat, but Roumania's allies now took more positive action. General Sakharov was appointed commander-in-chief of Allied Forces in the Dobrudga, and his augmented army gradually pushed Mackensen's force back until Hirsova had been regained. Earlier, in mid-October, a French Military Mission under General Berthelot had arrived – too late to prevent the Dobrudga disaster, but in time to take over the retraining of the Roumanian army, which had now been withdrawn from the front. The French airmen whom Hospital A met at Ciulnitza on 8 December were evidence of this increased French interest in the fortunes of the eastern front. There was also an oil-destroying mission headed by Colonel Norton Griffiths, whose hotel room Fitzroy and Bowerman borrowed while they waited at Braila. The Scottish Women may have felt at first that they were seeing only little bits of the war, but in their subsequent travels they came across many of the key commanders and units on the Roumanian and south-western fronts, and heard from them what was going on in their theatre of the war. By the end of 1916 they had learned a great deal, and were conscious of their lives having touched the lives of many of those directly involved in the battles around them.

With the reinforcements Russia poured in on her southern front, and with the help of the division of British Armoured Cars which arrived at Hirsova on 27 November,[7] the front line was pushed forward again almost to Cernavoda and the crucial bridge and railway. This exercise was very costly in human terms, and it was the wounded from this front whom the Transport were ferrying to safety during their stay at Babadag in November and December. The Serbian Division, which had sustained very heavy losses, was put into reserve, and took no further part in the Dobrudga campaign.

Meanwhile there was a new development, which led to another upheaval in the work of the hospitals. On the night of 22 November, some of Mackensen's forces crossed the Danube south-west of Bucharest, having hidden their boats in the mass of islands and meandering channels into which the lower Danube divides as it enters the Dobrudga plain. Once across in sufficient numbers, they built a pontoon bridge, by which more troops crossed and then marched towards Bucharest, which was already in the path of Falkenhyn's army as it advanced through the mountain passes between Transylvania and Roumania. Caught thus between Mackensen in the south-west and Falkenhyn in the north-west, Bucharest fell on 6 December, and Braila and Galatz were also endangered. It was this envelopment of the Allied positions that led to the decision on 14 December[8] to withdraw from the Dobrudga, to abandon all of Roumania except the small eastern province of Moldavia, and to make use of the natural barriers of the Sereth and of the Danube below Galatz as a front line. When this decision was taken, Dr Inglis was working at Braila, Dr Chesney at Ismail, and the Transport between Babadag and the outlying field hospitals and dressing stations. All these places were threatened, and the Scottish Women prepared to retreat once more.

Hospital B Ismail

Moir *Thursday 23 November*
This afternoon when Grant and I were off duty, we went for a lovely walk along the Danube. We came home by the trenches and Danube fortifications. We made love to some Russian soldiers, and quite got round them, and they took us all over the trenches, on the condition that we would keep it dark where we had been. They took us all round, showed us their 'funk-holes', and explained everything to us. It was most interesting – the whole thing was so complete – even to their little gardens and gravel paths; very different from the hastily-made attempts right up the line that we saw at very close quarters during our sojourn in the Dobrudga.[9]

There are such a lot of troops here – soldiers everywhere. It is a fine sight to see a body of these troops come swinging down the road, with the slow, steady, side-to-side gait peculiar to them. They nearly always sing, too; one leads off, another and yet another joins in, until all are taking part; and then the men and their song seem to merge into one moving, vibrating whole. They say the origin of this singing dates very far back, when they sang to keep off the evil spirits lurking in the darkness of the endless, lonely plains.

Grant *Friday 24 November*
The Duchess and Alice [Mrs Milne and Sedgwick] left this morning. All sorry to see the last of them. I went back to the surgical ward this morning, and didn't get in till lunch time.

Monday 27 November
This morning we hear the news is very bad. The Bulgars have crossed the Danube and are now on their way to Bucharest. The court have fled to Jassi. Our people at Galatz and Braila will have to make another hurried

departure, and all the equipment will have to be removed from Galatz. Our officers were in a great state of excitement this morning over the news.

On Saturday last, Moir, Fawcett, Turner and I all went a lovely walk. We visited the trenches on the shores of the Danube. They have several guns, and trenches with beautiful funk holes. The men took us down and showed us everything, and then showed us a communication trench. We had to go along all crouching down because it was all covered in over the top with branches. We were taken to where they had a place for storing their ammunition. It was all very interesting, and the men were so nice, and seemed to take such an interest in us. Their last words were that they hoped to meet us in Berlin. The Danube was really blue that day, and looked prettier than I have ever seen it.

Tuesday 28 November
Dr Chesney performed two small operations this afternoon: amputation of a thumb, and two fingers as well. The poor sister got into trouble over something foolish she had done, and accordingly was given nothing to do. Moir assisted Dr Chesney, and I took Moir's place. By the end Dr Chesney was calling Moir her assistant doctor, and me theatre sister! Everything went all right, with one or two rather funny episodes. It turned out it was only the second time Rendel had given an anaesthetic, and she always seemed uncertain whether the patient was over or not. Dr C asked, 'Is he over now?' Rendel replied, 'Yes, I think so.' Then Dr C started jabbing her knife in, and the patient kicked. This went on several times before the operation proper was begun. I think after today I never want to nurse under women doctors.

Turner *Wednesday 29 November*
Rumour that we are moving tomorrow, also that the Transport are off to Babadag. Mrs Haverfield is going to ask for Fawcett and me to come with them.

Thursday 30 November
Dr Inglis is here. She will not let us go to the Transport till our six months are up.

Hospital A Braila and Galatz

Fitzroy *Friday 24 November*[10]
Meat rations failed. A busy day. Franz Joseph is dead.

Letter to father Monday 27 November

Thank you so much for your letter of 22nd October. I was *very* sorry to hear you had all been so disturbed about us. Is the death of the old Emperor of Austria at all likely to affect the position? Do tell me anything you can; it is so interesting and out here one gets occasional facts but more usually nothing but a complicated elaboration.

Our news is not good, is it? And one feels desperately sorry for these people with the lesson of Serbia and Belgium before them. Since the junction at Ploesti fell they seem to have lost heart with a rush and I think it has been a terrible blow to have to abandon Bucharest. On their new line, as you see, little more than Moldavia and the north of the Dobrudga remains to them. The Dobrudga front has been handed over to the Russians entirely... Owing to the fact that for the last two years the army has been concentrated at short intervals, labour has been short and the harvests have been largely stored untouched. The country is therefore hugely rich in grain, which has been allowed apparently to fall into the enemies' hands and not destroyed. These and the petrol mines must mean a vast haul.

Bowerman *Diary Wednesday 29 November Galatz*

Dr Inglis came over with news that Hospital A is to go to Isaccea to nurse Russians until Serbs require us again. B to remain with Serbs; Transport to go to Babadag – this place and Isaccea not far from firing line, so hope for plenty of work.

Thursday November 30

Rumoured fall of Bucharest – panic from there – trains arrive crowded with people, some on roof even. Government has been moved to Jassi. Oil fields at Ploesti destroyed to prevent them falling into the hands of the enemy; as much petrol as possible being sent here.

Hectic lunch with Bell at the Metropole – saw her safely off to Braila in the afternoon. She is to be sent home, and Sisters Ulph and Edwards are to go back as far as Petrograd with her. Fitzroy and I would have liked the job.

Transport Ismail and Babadag

Hodges[11]

We were all terribly bored at Ismail. We didn't do much ambulance work as we were supposed to be resting, and we really became taxis for the various officers and doctors. Although when we first knew we were going to have a rest we were delighted, after a very short time of this taxi work we were aching to be back in the midst of things and getting on with our proper job. At last orders were received for us to return to business, and once more we got on to barges and returned to Tulcea. From there we drove over part of the road of the first retreat – and how different it seemed this time – to a village called Babadag. It was set in the midst of beautiful country, with wooded hills and lakes with masses of snipe and wild duck, and lovely sunsets over the smooth still waters. ...I think it was during our stay in Babadag that we heard we had all been awarded the medal of St George, and later on the order of St Stanislav.

Birkbeck *Sunday 26 November Galatz*
Orders at last. They are, in brief, 'Back to the Bulgars'. News from the front is very bad. The enemy are across the Danube, and advancing on Bucharest. All wounded from there are being evacuated here; hundreds are expected. All the churches and synagogues are being prepared to receive them. We leave now, to be attached to the Russian cavalry near Constanza. We might have guessed it, for Constanza is the headquarters of the Bulgarian cavalry – I did hope we would be given to the Bulgars *after* Xmas, not before! Heaven knows what we can do on those roads though, and here we could work all winter in town.

Tuesday 28 November Ismail
Edwards and I left for Ismail by the only boat, leaving at 7.30. Ismail is indeed 'the abomination of desolation', street after street of houses bordered by acacia trees before low one-storeyed houses all made to the same pattern. Only the high road and main street are made roads, the rest just beaten tracks, knee deep in dust and sand in summer, and knee deep in mud in winter.

The mess room was my joy when we arrived at tea time. A great ornate gramophone was trumpeting ragtime at a room full of Buffs eating a huge tea. All have lost 'the mark of the Exodus', and most have put on a stone in weight, I should think. After supper Hedges gave us our first lesson in ballet dancing. As we pounded into the figures of 'the Buffet Ballet' we must have looked pretty funny. Most had field boots on, and Suche came in, in her pyjamas, and joined in.

Wednesday 29 November
The cars are all in a farmyard and Royce looked a new automobile. Jensen had cleaned her inside and out. The whole engine was bright and free from rust, and the body had been oiled and the red cross repainted. She started up the first turn. Really rather wonderful in this weather, considering they have slept out for months and months. Lots of others had to crank theirs

up. I am accused of talking about her in my sleep. I certainly think a lot about her, love her dearly, at present.

Thursday 30 November

Dr Inglis harangued the Transport after breakfast. The first part was against the nasty habits of the Transport; somebody's been swearing, it seems, as if there's not plenty to swear about. The last – a bouquet: we were told our work had been very good, and the result – the Russians had asked for us for the winter. We were warned that the next venture would be harder than anything we had had before. It will certainly be colder. After the harangue we all trooped to the yard and collected our luggage and drove down to the quay.

Friday 1 December Babadag

We got off the barge at 11.20 over the usual horrible little planks. Faithfull's Burford refused, as usual, and stood kicking up the planks that were laid down for her. Faithfull just backed her till they were rearranged and drove off without turning a hair. I hate it even with my little Ford; they leave such a yawning chasm between the planks...

The kitchen car kept us amused. She refused, as usual, to budge, and then had to be towed. Once off, her driver could not engage the brakes, and she buzzed three times round Tulcea to the delight of the town, and the disgust of her driver.

At 1.30 we streamed off to Babadag; the road was fairly crowded, but good. Some lorries passed us and cheered tremendously. I recognised them as some of the people who had camped near us at Cernavoda, before we started work at Medgidia. We have all been through it since, and recovered too. We came to an arm of the Black Sea before we arrived. As Edwards says, we have most of us given up admiring the scenery, but it was really lovely. It looked like a lake among the mountains. As we arrived it was getting dark, and there were rich reddish reeds in the foreground among which a flock of geese was feeding.

Sunday 3 December

Spent the day pottering around the cars again – bitterly cold. All cars out at 2. We streamed up to the hospital and cleared thirty-five. Marx had arrived from England the night before, full of ideas, and wrote many lists of directions. I was to be last; however, with Mrs Haverfield on board, I had to get off first. We waited over an hour for the other cars to fill up.

The road to Tulcea is one of the few 'stone roads' of Roumania. It happened to be a good one; usually they are distinguished from the other roads – mud tracks – by a few boulders chucked down anyhow with rifts and gaps between, to wrench a tyre off. Onslow stopped for me to catch her up, and I did myself down by biffing her wing – just touched it, but it all counts. At 8 we got back; we did sixty miles.

Hospital B Ismail

Fawcett *Sunday 3 December*

Dr Inglis was here on the 1st... Our plans are still fermenting – the most exciting scheme is for us to form a base hospital at Odessa where we should collect up all the wounded Serbs from the Russian hospitals and have them all together – the other is that we should go to Voznesensk and form a typhus hospital.

I had a chat with Dr Inglis and asked to be transferred either to her hospital or to the Transport, but it could not be managed – we are to stay where we are for the present. Later she may put us into the wards.

Turner *Sunday 3 December*

It looks as if it is going to snow. This morning Sammy came back to us. We met him in the town, and he was awfully glad to see us – I am delighted to have him again.

Moir *Wednesday 6 December*

The hospital is still full, and always there is plenty to do. The weather is intensely cold, and as we have no heating or fire in this hut of ours, and our barrack-room is very cold, we are not relishing this climate!

The news seems very bad, and Bucharest may fall any moment now. 'Our gallant little ally Roumania' is making a brave show! Why did she ever interfere in this war? The whole country is pro-German. The men mightn't be so bad if they were properly officered – but their officers are *impossible*, conceited, dressed-up fops, powdered and painted and dressed up to the nines. All they think about is their personal appearance.[12] When fighting is the order of the day, they run away – they are experts at that game. Oh, yes, we've got a brave and noble ally, we have!

Rendel *Wednesday 6 December*

Dr Chesney has gone off to find Dr Inglis and consult with her as to what is to be done, and I have been left in charge here. Heaven knows when she will return. Travelling in this country is so uncertain you can never be sure of getting a steamer or a boat, and you can't send a postcard as you would in England. People just walk in. We are also expecting two of the unit from Galatz. One is bringing money and the other is to go on to Odessa in advance with Dr C. We hope that they will also bring us letters.

The wind is howling dismally and I would willingly pay five pounds for a good English fire and an arm chair. If only I had a pair of Jaeger bedroom slippers or fur-lined shoes. But I have nothing. The others are out riding. Two of them have never been on a horse before. I hope they won't come back with broken limbs which I shall have to deal with.

Hospital A Galatz to Ciulnitza to Braila

Fitzroy *Letter to mother Monday 4 December*
The news is better, and rumour has it that the oil fields have been destroyed, which I hope is true... The real Roumanians have been charming to us – the ladies are very pretty and delightful, but alas, so are the men, worthy only of a musical comedy chorus at the Gaiety. One – a minute one – was talking to one of the Transport at Cernavoda. Apparently he was being more professionally charming than ever when down the street swung three magnificent Cossacks. He twirled his moustache – *'Nos Alliés,'* he said, *'nos Alliés sont bien barbares'*!

Bowerman *Tuesday 5 December*
Dr Inglis returns with orders for the two hospitals to be ready to start – A to Ciulnitza, B near Odessa – busy all day packing and preparing to go. Broadbent and I to go with equipment as far as Braila, there to await further orders, as it is again rumoured that Bucharest has fallen, and Ciulnitza may be evacuated. B and I took our places in the baggage waggon at Galatz goods station – slept in Wolseley valise on floor of waggon. Train started about 6.30 a.m. – had great luck, arriving at Braila 8 o'clock – distance about fifteen miles.

Wednesday 6 December
Saw baggage from Braila on to train and with great difficulty the Russian commandant obtained one coach for us to travel in, and one more horse truck for our twenty-five Russian orderlies. Sisters, doctors, etc. in coach – Brown, [Agnes] Murphy, Wotherspoon, Fitzroy and I in baggage waggon manage to make ourselves very comfortable.

Friday 8 December Ciulnitza
Breakfast at station restaurant – afterwards walked about till lunch time. Met French aviators quartered in chef-de-gare's house – four English ones living at a farm a few kilos away. Saw machines – five small biplanes belonging to French – three large ones, English, had flown over from Imros. Such a joy to have a talk with French and Englishmen – Naval Air Service. They tell us they have orders to evacuate by lunch time, so are very busy preparing to go. They confirm our opinion of the Roumanians

– unpreparedness, inefficiency, and funk. They say communication is very bad – they have great difficulty in getting orders or information – are told to fly over Germans and they will find out where they are when they begin to be fired on.

At lunch Dr Inglis tells us we have orders to return at once, as the whole place is to be evacuated. Cannot understand why Russian Red Cross sent us down here when they knew, or ought to have known, that the district was evacuated.

Ciulnitza to Braila

Saw airmen off about 1 p.m. – Englishman leaned out of his machine and waved to us. Waited in station till about 5 o'clock, when suddenly there was a great flare by our engine – an oil tank set on fire. The train moved out at once, past the fire. A young Roumanian officer told us that they wanted to get the train out of the station as we had several trucks of ammunition attached. It was most thrilling rushing through the blaze. Almost simultaneously several other huge fires broke out on the horizon. This was the Roumanians firing their stores, etc., to prevent them falling into the hands of the enemy. We learned that the station and railway at Ciulnitza were to be blown up almost immediately after we left – ours about the last train to go.

Journeyed by slow stages to Slobosia, accompanied by a young Roumanian lieutenant, M. Radu Codreanu – gave him supper and had quite an amusing time. Codreanu a better type than we had met previously, but not strong, or any use as a soldier – in usual way blamed Russians for everything. Admitted lack of organisation and preparation in Roumania – said several 'Boscophiles' in power – his own family remaining at Bucharest, best from an 'economic' point of view – said three Boscophile ministers in Bucharest would prevent any serious harm occurring to that city. Roumanian generals admitted no use, except Averescu, and one who had already committed suicide. Lack of transport – single railway lines – one of chief causes of failure. Arsenal and stores, mainly at Bucharest, will fall into the hands of the enemy.

Amusing supper of soup, bread and cheese, bread and sardines, bread and chocolate. Bade farewell to M. Codreanu at Slobosia and settled down to bed – Fitzroy and Wotherspoon on bales of blankets, Murphy in the laundry trough, Brown on a bed which she had unearthed with great energy, I on the floor in my Wolseley. Funny sight to see us lying in sort of tiers, one above the other. Man tried to get in at one period during night, but desisted when Brown and I shouted at him *'Nyet'*, *'Inglesi'*, 'Hospital

Aide', and various other interjections which we had learned for use on such occasions.

The Wolseley valise *(Army and Navy Stores' Catalogue 1914)*

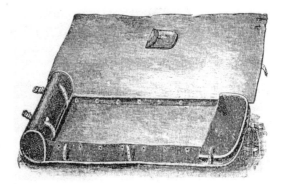

Fig. 1 Open

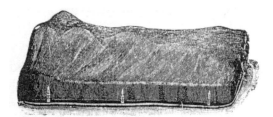

Fig. 2 Occupied

Tuesday 12 December Braila

Arrived Braila in the very early morning after a good warm night. Fitzroy and I sent up to town for news and to arrange for baths. We found water supply broken down – not a drop to be had – spent morning wandering around and sitting in hotel. All officers of English Mission who have been burning oil fields[13] are quartered here – hall half full of them when enter Broadbent and Jenkins carrying large linen bag – we all covered in mud and dirt and grime of the journey must have looked a wonderful sight! Colonel Griffiths very kindly gave us the use of his room for the rest of the day. Had most interesting afternoon gleaning the news from the various officers who came in and out of it, French and English. They tell us that there is a big battle being fought at Buzei – if the Russians cannot manage to hold this it means that Braila must go. There are tremendous stores there – all of which would have to be destroyed. The oil fields have all been successfully scrapped but the Germans have captured very large quantities of wheat. If the English had only been able to get here a month sooner, this might also have been prevented. The whole situation looks extremely black at present – probably the Roumanians will only be able to hold Moldavia. We are told that they have betrayed the Russians right and left, and they don't seem to make any attempt to withstand the enemy. We also hear that before coming into the war they gave the Allies false figures with regard to their supplies, troops, etc. The extreme difficulty of transport has also been a great handicap to the Allies.

Transport Babadag and Cogealac

Birkbeck *Wednesday 6 December*

Up at 6.30 to lay the table for early breakfast. We were wired for to go to Saragea about 30 miles off, to fetch thirty sick. We went off in the usual kind of way all following on each other's tracks, the staff car leading, and Donisthorpe with her weak steering brought up the rear. We went south, round behind the mountains that are the background to the inlets of the Black Sea, as we see it from Tulcea. Again we came upon the troops moving up. They wanted to get on our cars, and we took all we could. Again the road was lovely, and better, the horizon all round, which was wave on wave of blue hills. We crossed the range behind the inlet, through a wood of birches, past endless little hill tops; these were all entrenched. We ran to look at some of the trenches – they were very shallow, and the dugouts about the size of a badger's earth. They had been used, and the place had a decidedly Medgidia feel about it; one felt nearer the front. Perhaps it was the bodies and skeletons of dead horses lying about.

The entire staff at Saragea met us as we arrived, and took us into their mess. Here after an hour they gave us a delicious meal – all fifteen of us. Talked to the soldiers as hard as we could for two hours. At 11.30 we left to take the wounded.

Friday 8 December

Marx was furious as no cars were out except the Burford to go to Tulcea. No ambulances are to use the road till the stones have settled down a bit. They [the driver of the Burford and her companion] were not in to dinner, and I as mess orderly, had to wait up; at 12 they arrived. Faithfull had ditched her lorry with four bidons of petrol inside. A car came along on the wrong side and instead of holding the road as she should, she flew into the ditch. Her cargo was deposited and they got her on to her feet again. Bucharest has fallen, we fear – so soon.

141

Saturday 9 December

We prepared for the 'party'. Edwards and I felt awfully smart in the shirts we had washed the day before. We cleaned our thinnest shoes and set out in our cars for Cogealac at 2.30. Most of the Transport went, and the sanitars. We were to bring back wounded the next day...

We arrived fearfully conscious of our comic appearance, and I came in feeling just as one does at one's first dance. In the hall was a band, and as we changed, kicking off our gummies in a corner, we really felt on the razzle-dazzle again. In the ballroom, which was beautifully decorated with flags, were a crowd of officers in a bewildering number of uniforms, standing round the walls in rows. The old general was rather daunting; thankfully he was very nice to us, and held our hands rather tight for the first half hour.

Endless hors d'oeuvre courses, then fish, chicken, and some jelly stuff – the food was excellent. It was amusing to look round and see the Buffs all smugly gassing away in foreign tongues... For *vis-à-vis* I had a Caucasian who claimed to have taken me out riding at Bulbul Mic, and I remembered him well. His store of English conversation began and ended with 'Kiss me quick', and my Russian was even more limited to *'khorosho'* and *'nevazhno'* – 'All right' and 'It's of no consequence', which I answered in turn. He sat and glared at me all through dinner, and insisted on drinking my health every five minutes....

Russian sisters came in after dinner and then the dance began. One's partners came up and clicked their heels, whirled one round into the wildest of dances, and then dropped one like a hot brick and wandered off. The polonaise and the mazurka were really an effort, but we were undefeated and capered into everything. As time went on they all got pretty drunk in a harmless way. It struck me as odd that they were not removed, but none of their friends seemed to mind....

Hodges *Saturday 9 December*[14]

Some of the unit were sent from Babadag fifteen miles further on just behind the lines. We were quite busy again now. The general commanding in that area had his headquarters at the village where the rest of our unit had been sent. On St George's Day[15] he gave a party to which he invited all of us. It was a *mad* party, just behind the lines in the village schoolhouse, with a marvellous supper sent from Moscow, and lashings of wine; after the meal Cossacks came in and sang and danced too wonderfully for us. There was a terrific offensive going on – in fact our lines broke two days after, and it was a strange, crazy feeling – this amazing party, and the wild songs of the Cossacks combining with the angry thunder of the heavy artillery. A photograph was taken at the end of the evening, and I think I am right when I say that the Russian general, who had obviously looked well on the wine that was red, sat on the floor with his head resting heavily on Mrs Haverfield's lap – much to her horror! He was fast asleep when, after much manoeuvring of the group, the picture was finally taken.

Hospital B Ismail

Grant *Sunday 10 December*
We have had some fun riding while Dr C was away hunting the country for Miss Inglis. We got horses every afternoon, and it was sport. None of us can really ride, so we had rather fun comparing notes as to our methods of sticking on. The most trying part to me is that these dreadful dogs that live in these parts come out in batches and bark and snap at your heels. The horses don't relish this at all, and as one wishes to stick on, and at the same time preserve the dignity of the SWH, it becomes very trying, especially as there is usually a crowd of villagers all standing round watching. However, no accidents occurred. We are all feeling very sore and stiff, and have developed a cavalry-man's walk, not from any desire to appear like a cavalry man, but from sheer necessity...

Dr C and Rendel came today during the cooking. Neither of them knows anything about cooking, so the results are anxiously awaited, especially by us orderlies. Dr C seems to have spent most of her time beating the meat. Our meat is killed in the most inhumane manner here. It is driven into the yard, and if one cared to look, one would see it being killed...

Petrovic came into tea this afternoon, and brought a budget of bad news. Headquarters have had a wire to say that one automobile and five English ladies have been taken prisoners by the Bulgars near Babadag. Of course it is some of our Transport girls, and we are all feeling horribly down about them. And we can't hear which of them it is, either. It was folly on Mrs Haverfield's part taking them down there in cars when everyone knew their big cars could do nothing on roads like these at this time of the year.

Fawcett *Sunday 10 December*
Petrovic came to tea and brought thrilling but not pleasant news. Five of our Transport people and one motor car are supposed to have been taken prisoners by the Bulgars; Bucharest fell two days ago; Odessa is evacuating

all its refugees; the Bulgars are advancing against the Serbs at Monastir; and Greece has at last joined in, but against us.[16] The evacuation of the refugees from Odessa may mean that they are expecting a rush of wounded or it may mean that they are preparing to evacuate the town.

I feel awfully sorry about the Transport people – we do not know any details. We guess that as there were five people and one car, it must have been a run-about car. Several of them had a bet on before they left Ismail that if it was possible their chiefs could muddle things so that they would be taken prisoners, they would.

Dr Chesney and Rendel have been cooking all day – Rendel gave in at lunch time with a sick headache. The meat was of the toughest, in spite of having been beaten for half an hour with a wooden spoon.

Rendel *Monday 11 December*

Dr C never found Dr Inglis. She, Dr I, left Isaccea and has gone off with the unit into space, leaving us without nearly enough money. Dr I is really rather mad. She promised to send us someone with our letters and money, and then forgot all about it apparently. We have had no letters now for more than a fortnight, and shan't get any now for another fortnight.

Fawcett *Tuesday 12 December*

Dr Corbett and Johnson have come along from Galatz... They have brought a mail and are taking letters back. The news about our Transport people being taken prisoner turns out to be untrue; it is some of the British Armoured Car men who have been captured.

Turner *Wednesday 13 December*

Dr Corbett and Johnson returned to Galatz this morning, taking Sammy with them. I was awfully sorry to part with him, but Dr Chesney does not smile on him, so he will be happier there. Brand will be pleased to see him back.

Rendel *Letter to Ray Strachey Wednesday 13 December*

I am writing this letter to you by the request of Dr Chesney and all the members of the unit who are here. We wish to protest very strongly:

1. Against orders which, we hear by letters received by some members of the unit, have been issued to the effect that no parcels are to be sent out here via the office. Miss Marx, apparently with the approval of the committee, refused to take anything, and we hear that Lady Ashmore has said that no one coming out here from England is to be allowed to take things. We all feel that considering the inadequacy of our original

outfit, the discomfort of our surroundings, the scarcity and enormous cost of everything in Russia, this order is simply outrageous...

2. Our second protest is against the arrangements made about money. Orders were sent out before the expedition started that all money taken by individuals was to be banked with the SWH. The result of this arrangement has been that no one has been able to get her money. The arrangement broke down at Archangel, and has remained broken down ever since. There has apparently never been enough cash in hand to pay the running expenses of the unit, with the result that Miss Henderson simply refused to give people their private money. On the retreat we were left very unpleasantly short of money. Since the retreat we have been left for six weeks still without our money. I made one effort to get money from Miss H shortly before she left, and all she would do was to offer us Roumanian money, which is perfectly useless in Russia. To exchange it into Russian money meant a serious loss, as Roumanian paper money is not at all in demand. Everyone in the unit has been treated in the same way. As the committee insisted on our banking with them, they should see to it that things are better organised.

I don't wish this letter to be shown to the committee, but I do wish you to look into the matter and to make a good old row about it. It is quite a delusion to think that we don't want money out here. The more Lady Ashmore prevents things being sent out, the more money do we want.

P.S. Whatever you do, don't make use of this letter so as to give me away.

Hospital A Galatz

Bowerman *Wednesday 13 December*

I am sent to Galatz by boat to take various messages to our people there. Arrive at the quay at 10 a.m. – thick fog over river – sit on board all day – finally start at 4 p.m. – boat very crowded and stuffy – nothing to eat all day. Arrive at 5 p.m.

Friday 15 December

In the afternoon Dr Potter turns up from Braila, having walked most of the way and left the rest of the party stuck in the train halfway between Braila and Galatz. Tells us a hospital is to be formed at Galatz. Food and wood becoming very scarce, however, and we wonder if this will be really feasible – unit somewhat unsettled in consequence. Majority anxious to go through to Odessa and form a base there.

Fitzroy *Saturday 16 December*[17]

Reached Galatz about 5 a.m., fifteen miles in thirty-six hours! ...I am billeted in a dear little house with five of the others. Sambo, our terrier, is here. He was with the Transport for a time, then returned to Galatz with a Hospital B orderly. He is the most perfect gentleman I have ever met.

Transport Cogealac

Birkbeck *Tuesday 12 December*

The guns most perceptibly nearer. Talk here is all of retreat again. This time it may go ill with us, for we have no petrol for the motors and my own is hung up till Marx gets back from Babadag with my new cylinder joint and a pipe for the radiator. We stop in our work and listen to the ever-louder guns, and wonder why we bother to work on our cars.... Slept in my clothes as we'll have to retreat in a day or two if not sooner.

Hospital B Ismail

Fawcett *Friday 15 December*

Peter [Petrovic] came to tea this afternoon. The news was thrilling but very bad. Mr Asquith is no longer Prime Minister in England, but Lloyd George is in his place with a Unionist Government. The alteration seems to have taken place over some disagreement about help to Roumania – Lloyd George wanted to send more help to 'our gallant little ally'.[18] The Russian Minister is also changed – he wanted to make peace.[19] They have had two ministers in two months. The Russians are retiring in this part of the world. Braila is evacuating, and we suppose Galatz will soon do the same. What will happen to our equipment?

CHAPTER 7
Retreating Again

(See map 4)

The second Russian withdrawal from the Dobrudga, though foreseen, began a little earlier than expected, when on 17 December the Bulgarians suddenly broke through the lines south of Babadag, and plans had to be hurriedly adjusted.[1] At this time Hospital B was on the way to its new quarters in Odessa; Hospital A was still hard at work in Galatz, having decided to stay in spite of the inability of the Russian general to guarantee its safety; and the Transport drivers, some of them based as far south as Cogealac, were busy evacuating wounded to Isaccea and Tulcea. Owing to the shortage of Russian ambulances, the SWH Transport unit took over the evacuation of all the field hospitals in the northern Dobrudga,[2] and as before, the drivers were almost the last to leave. Again the women got away, all safely, but only just in time. On this occasion, although the roads were just as crowded, a rear-guard action had been planned. For the drivers, the dangers and difficulties were much the same as before, but for all parties, a new element was present which made a difference to the safety and efficiency of their withdrawal.

This new element was a division of British Armoured Cars, a pleasant surprise in a foreign land, for although the Scottish Women knew there were British naval officers at far-off Petrograd and Archangel, and some of Hospital A had met Colonel Norton Griffiths and his oil-destroying mission, no one had expected a British fighting force on the eastern front. The sudden sight of a number of Englishmen in khaki, to all intents and purposes a collection of real 'Tommies', was a reminder that Britain was not as far away as it had seemed over the past four months, and a reassurance that the Scottish Women were not alone. Throughout December, small groups of women came across Armoured Car men in unexpected places, and they were able to exchange news and views, to the delight of both parties. In addition, the retreat of the Transport and later of Hospital A was eased, not only because their fellow-countrymen voluntarily assumed responsibility for their safety, but because the BAC leaders were good organisers, and had the power to commandeer barges and arrange transport by river and road. Previously the Transport and hospital staff had been left till last, and sometimes they thought they had been forgotten; but this time their presence was taken into account, and their evacuation planned, by senior officers so important to the Russian army that the promised lorries and barges materialised, with men to help load them, and they left on time. Not since the *Huntspill* days of cabin inspection and military drill had life been so well organised; and seldom before had the practical and diplomatic value of a group of women been given such immediate recognition by a group of British men.

The British Armoured Car Division, (known in Britain as the Russian Armoured Car Division), had begun as a division of the Royal Naval Air Service, and most of its officers were from the Royal Naval Volunteer Reserve. Its several names point to its amphibious origin, the first British armoured cars having been commissioned by the RNAS to supplement their reconnaissance missions and to rescue pilots shot down in Belgium behind the enemy lines.[3] The division which came to Russia in 1915 was in fact quite small, its strength being forty-four officers and four hundred and fifty-five men.[4] Like the Scottish Women's Hospitals, it was privately sponsored, at least in respect of its cars and equipment, and was under the command of the British MP Oliver Locker Lampson. Armoured cars were at the time very new, and most of them, including Locker Lampson's own Rolls Royce, were converted private cars, looking in photographs like vehicles papered over for a float parade. Most of the personnel who manned them were volunteers, encouraged to join this particularly daring and dangerous unit by being offered the starting rank and pay of a naval petty officer, a considerable improvement on the rank and pay of a private in the army.[5] The BAC rank and file were therefore not strictly speaking 'Tommies' at all; but for their ordinary military duties they wore khaki, and the women would have distinguished the petty officers by their speech as 'not officers'. Locker Lampson's unit had come to the Dobrudga front after a year in the Caucasus, and had reached the recaptured Hirsova on 27 November 1916, in time to join General Sirelius's 4th Siberian Corps, which was defending it. Though a small force, the Armoured Cars were very valuable to the Russians, and played an important part in the rear-guard action after Hirsova was evacuated on 8 December.[6]

Acting Commander Gregory's report gives a good idea of the intelligent and effective responsibility which he took for the evacuation of the SWH Transport, and of his detailed planning and execution. The action of the Armoured Car men in pulling Faithfull's heavy lorry out of the mud[7] became the forerunner of a number of other rescues, and of many cheering if brief encounters between the Scottish Women and their countrymen. The Armoured Car men seemed to be ubiquitous, turning up at all the places where the women were working, smoothing their way by arranging their last-minute evacuation, helping them to pack and move heavy equipment, sending them emergency rations, and, in the case of Surgeon Scott and his orderlies, rolling up their sleeves and working with women doctors. The method hitherto employed on their various travels by Bowerman, Brown, Turner, Rendel, Moir and Fawcett, and described by Turner as 'getting the interest of a bigwig', was not necessary on this retreat. The women were recognised as important in their own right. Moreover, they were appreciated, not as foreign curiosities whose gender was questionable, but as the brave, enterprising, and capable young women they were. No doubt the admiration was mutual, and the recognition of their courage by their fellow-countrymen and women must have given a welcome boost to the morale of both groups.

Armoured Cars Tulcea

George Martin, Petty Officer. *Diary Saturday 9 December*
All the Russians leaving this place, as the Bulgars are advancing. We started to load up our stuff on barges. Roumanians running back – cannot hold them.

Wednesday 13 December
The barges were unable to be taken away the last three or four days as no tugs about, but they left this morning with the spare men, and the rest of us were told we were to fight a rear-guard action as the enemy were coming on. We were left alone in the place except one or two cavalrymen.

Hospital B Ismail

Fawcett *Friday 15 December*
We are leaving Ismail on Sunday. It will take us two days to trek to Bolgrad. There we have a train which leaves on Tuesday. Dr Chesney and Grant have gone to Odessa to arrange what we are to do – we are all longing for a hospital in Odessa. It would be so jolly to be near Natasha Harris – besides, we should probably all go raving mad if we landed at a place as dull as Ismail.

Hospital B Ismail to Odessa

Grant *Thursday 14 December Reni*
It was no easy task getting the baggage off the boat, as the boat was chock-a-block with refugees and soldiers. However, I managed to get hold of a soldier who was fairly intelligent, and got him to understand what I wanted done. Dr Chesney returned with the joyful news that she had

found an English officer on board the flagship, so we toddled back there. I could have hugged him, he looked so nice and clean and English. He was a Captain Edwards, who is acting as interpreter to the British Armoured Cars that are fighting on the Roumanian front. He arranged everything for us, got dinner for us, and told us all the latest news. He told us that the Roumanians put off and put off setting fire to the oil fields, till finally our troops took the law into their own hands, and fired every blessed oil field in the place; meanwhile, the Roumanians fired on our troops – brutes! That is what our English papers are calling 'our gallant little allies'! We turned into our bunks early, as we were all sleepy and tired.

Friday 15 December

Slept very badly, owing to three Russian sisters who shared our cabin; they came to bed late, and talked most of the night. Captain Edwards took us to see some of their armoured cars. They were awfully interesting, and we crawled inside one. These were new ones that had just come out from England. Captain Edwards arranged about our tickets and the journey. We had to go to some offices to get a free military permit. We all had a jolly tea together on board, about ten of the officers, and Dr C and I. We heard news of the new Cabinet, and were greatly surprised. We then went off to the station, to find it packed with refugees, all waiting for a train. We were very lucky in getting into the only first-class carriage on board, along with a fat old Russian general, and a fat female companion.

Sunday 17 December

We are still crawling along in this miserable train. Really, the way one travels in Russia one would think it was the dark ages. You go for one hour, and stop for eight. Dr C and I nearly got left behind today at one of our many stops, and well away up the line we heard the train whistling and the guard blowing on his little penny trumpet, so we had to run for it. Had it been one of our trains, we would have been left behind, but it is not difficult to catch up with a Russian train.

We have got two young Russian officers with us, whom Dr Chesney has been very rude to. She has just remarked, apropos of one of these men sitting opposite me, 'A very ugly little man, but he would have made rather a decent-looking pig.' Fortunately they don't understand English, although if they did, it wouldn't trouble her in the least.

Hospital A Galatz

Bowerman *Diary Sunday 17 December*

Dr Inglis tells us the Russians have given us a building for a hospital which will be ready in a few days – also a house for ourselves. At the same time we hear that people are evacuating this place – also that the British Red Cross Hospital is thinking of leaving owing to the impossibility of obtaining adequate wood and supplies. Situation at front very grave – Bulgars reported a few miles from Braila; also it is said that Hirsova has been retaken by the enemy. All Roumanian troops have been withdrawn from Braila, which is being held by the Russians. Jassi now closed to refugees, as it cannot hold any more people. Even Dr Inglis admits that things are very complicated.

About 9 p.m. orders come that the equipment is to be sent away by steamer to Odessa – must load up at once – Fitzroy and I sent down to store and spent rest of day helping to get the stuff on board. Many difficulties – at one stage lorry disappeared – we had to spend ages in the Russian agency trying to get another – eventually borrowed two from the British Red Cross hospital. Finished loading about midnight – party started for Odessa by the light of the moon.

Fitzroy *Monday 18 December*[8]

The Russians are evacuating all their own hospitals, and we have got to go too. The enemy are already this side of Faurei, and are threatening Braila. We could hear the guns today, and the station was a seething mass of refugees all fighting to get on the platform – everything guarded by sentries.

Tuesday 19 December

We are to stay here. The Russians say they will not take the responsibility of getting us away, but nevertheless would like us to stay. Am glad.

Transport Cogealac to Tulcea

Birkbeck *Wednesday 13 December*

Got orders after breakfast to evacuate. This, it seems, is not a retreat, but *the* retreat: Roumania is to be abandoned. All turned rather wearily to our packing.

Away at two with all the wounded left in our hospital, to Babadag... We stopped at Babadag to have some hot tea and get a little warmer before driving the wounded to Tulcea. My car was not fit to go and I went with Hedges as her second driver. Two of the other cars came on too. A thick fog stopped us on the way – it was bitterly cold, and there was some difficulty about taking our men when we did get to Tulcea. We hung about for half an hour. We drank hot coffee before returning, and would all have preferred something more bracing. It's no joke driving wounded with practically no lights along these roads packed with the retreating army, then a fog. We got back at midnight. Robinson's car with the baggage had broken down, so we had no blankets or bed bundles, and our coats were wet. Lay on a stretcher till 5.30 a.m. when Onslow came and called us. All night carts had rattled by as in an ordinary methodical retreat.

Thursday 14 December

We packed the cars and lorries, and then things began to happen... Hedges and I got away first, and waited for the others by the road. It was too lovely: bright blue sky and mountains partly hidden by heavy clouds – it's a lovely country, the Dobrudga. Hedges and I waited hours in the car until the others began to turn up. Barges were being packed with soldiers and lorries, but all very quietly. The chances of our getting off seemed pretty thin. They offered to get us off without our cars. Mrs Haverfield preferred to chance it... Some time after dark, they got a deserted club for us, and we left the cars and squelched into what must have been rather a smart place once.

Hodges *14-18 December*[9]

We moved back from Babadag to Tulcea, where we were billeted in a large public building with a gigantic ballroom, on the parquet floor of which we slept. We met Commander Locker Lampson's unit here. How glad we were to hear English voices again.

We were two or three nights in Tulcea, I believe, and then we were ordered to proceed further up the Danube to Isaccea, and then to a hospital over the river. We went at night and had to wait countless hours to get over the pontoon bridge – a very swaying affair – as by this time troops and guns were pouring back. Eventually we landed up at a field hospital by a monastery... We stayed there a night or two, sleeping in a big hospital tent.

Transport Tulcea to Aregori

Birkbeck *Saturday 16 December*

Finished off Royce's toilet – she's rather smart now – then pottered about the town and loafed a bit. No prospect of work until 6 p.m. Then we had orders: four ambulances were to go up to Aregori to join a hospital train.[10] Edwards, Hedges, Onslow and I went. We found that the hospital we were looking for had either departed or had changed its plans. We were taken into the Russian canteen and given the offer to sleep there for the night. We lay on the floor like sardines, tightly packed in.

Armoured Cars Tulcea area

George Martin. *Thursday 14 December*

Up early in the morning and away, I riding a cycle. The road was awful, impossible to run a cycle on. We cyclists were riding on the banks and fields. Later on I was getting along pretty quick in front of all the cars, when I suddenly saw an old trench two or three yards in front of me. Because of the slope impossible to see the trench a few yards away from it, so before I could stop the bicycle fell into it, and I was picked up later lying in the mud unconscious, with my nose broken and my face badly cut – was picked up by an ambulance, and camped at Alibakshee.[11]

Monday 18 December

Had orders after breakfast to be on the road in half an hour. I rode on a car, reached Tulcea about dinner time, waited on quay for barges – enemy advancing. The Scottish Women here with their cars. Barges came in very late and we started to load up – the Scottish Women and some of our light lorries left to go by road. The Scottish Women attended my nose.

C.J. Smith, Chief Petty Officer.[12]

We had many varied jobs to do. One section moved right up on the right flank to fight a desperate rearguard action in an attempt to hold up the enemy long enough to allow the Roumanians to retire in a more or less orderly fashion... Another ticklish job was that of extricating a motor detachment of the Scottish Women's Hospital marooned far behind the fleeing populace and in peril of capture at any moment. It was a ghastly job for us to press through the solidly-packed advancing throng and avoid running down demented individuals. At times we came to a dead stop with a sea of vacant faces stretching for miles around us. We reached the beleaguered nurses and we got them out, but with only a matter of minutes to spare.

Transport Tulcea

Birkbeck *Monday 18 December*

At 12.30 we arrived just as the others were rushing off to a hurried lunch before evacuating the hospitals. All our cars went out to the *otryad* hospital and also to the Russian lazaret. We worked to and from the quay till we had cleared them. Then we went on to the next, and the next. Then the rest gave up as there were only four more in another hospital. The four of us worked hard clearing thirty typhus cases; some of the Armoured Car people helped at the quay with the unloading of stretchers and carrying them on to the barge. Some of the sitting cases were very weak indeed and could hardly walk across the planking without help. One of the BAC men asked us to supper with him in his car. We refused hungrily. There would have been a stink about it. The SW work you like ten men, then round on you and tell you, 'You are a girl, and must behave like a lady.'

Armoured Cars

Reginald Gregory, Acting Commander. *Report 18 December*[13]

At 9 a.m the whole force left Alebei Chioi and proceeded to Tulcea, arriving at 11.30 a.m. on 17 December. The cars were parked on the quay, and the men were billeted pending the arrival of the barges. Great confusion existed at Tulcea, orders having just been received that the town was to be evacuated within 48 hours.

At 10 p.m. I was informed that at 2 a.m. I would be given one barge for the British and Russian armoured cars to take them to Reni, and also that I would be given half another barge to take some of the transport cars to Ismail. The matter being urgent and barge accommodation very limited, and having the additional responsibility of saving the Scottish Women's Hospital cars and nurses suddenly thrown on my hands at the last minute, I divided the force as follows:

1. All the light transport and touring cars (including the SWH cars) under Lieutenant-Commander Belt I despatched at midnight by road to Isaccea to cross the pontoon bridge at that place and proceed to Bolgrad to await further orders from me.

2. All the heavy transport, including two transport waggons belonging to the Scottish Women's Hospital, with the attendant nurses,[14] I placed on the barge proceeding to Ismail under Sub-Lieutenant Turner, with orders to proceed from Ismail to Bolgrad to join Lieutenant-Commander Belt, and await further orders from me.

3. All the fighting cars, ammunition, etc., I took under my command on board the barge with the Russian armoured cars and proceeded to Reni.

We were delayed 24 hours on the way up owing to the non-opening of the pontoon bridge at Isaccea, over which refugees and troops were continually passing in an unending stream.

Transport Tulcea to Isaccea

Birkbeck *Monday 18 December*

It is too nice to have them [the Armoured Car men] here, and hear English at street corners. They look so clean, so friendly, and we are fearfully interested in each other. They congregate round our cars to hear our adventures and tell of their own.

At 10 someone came for our cars for the typhus hospital to be cleared. Out came all our baggage again, and off we went. I drove until 11, and when I returned I found we were moving off at once. It was not till 12 however that we got off. The armoured cars came too. Two of our cars were to go by barge with the rest of the Armoured Car unit. My lights gave out at the moment of starting, so I had to do it in the dark again. A pitch dark night. The road was an absolute jigsaw puzzle, zig-zagging up and down the mountain, with black in front and precipices on each side for a mile. The road was fairly clear. We passed several camps with many fires round which soldiers were grouped, asleep or standing round the fires. We arrived at Isaccea at 4.

The last bit of road was negotiated with one of the Armoured Car officers in our leading car, and we slowly bored our way through to the bridge. Oxen, sheep, carts with refugees lying across the road and camp fires in the middle of it made the last mile very trying without lights. Once at the pontoon bridge we drove straight across into Russia once again.

The place where the others were camped was one huge camp, dotted with fires. Plimsoll, Hedges and I made a lovely fire. We bribed a Russian soldier to get wood for us, and kept it going from 4.30 till 6.20 when it got light. We ate some bread and one of the Tommies produced some bully beef for us. The ambulance crew were frozen out of their ambulances, and joined us till all the Transport were round the fire and many Russians and others too. Below us lay the Danube, purple and black, and the gently shifting long bridge over which refugees never ceased to pass. With the light we were off at 6.30. We stopped almost at once at a Red Cross hospital to look for friends and found both the Isaccea and the Cogealac lots.

Beyond the mountains came the boom of guns – must be the battle of Babadag going on. We hear that Cogealac has fallen, also Isaccea and Babadag. There are rumours about Galatz and Braila.

The sanitars set up an absolute triumph of a tent. One side was divided into two; one half was ours with our own door, wooden beds, and straw mattresses, and a stove in the middle made it the most luxurious quarters we have had for months. The walls were double, and proved as wall-like as they looked. The other half was divided into four rooms. In one of the rooms we all fed and in the others the doctors slept, and one was a kitchen. Never was such a tent! We had supper with the sanitars at about 7, and went to bed as soon as we had finished.

Hospital B Ismail to Bolgrad

Rendel *Monday 18 December*

We left Ismail at 8 a.m. on Sunday 17 December. It was dark and very cold and disgustingly muddy. We each sat on an ammunition cart beside the driver and we drove along about two miles an hour. Once we were clear of the town the roads were better and we walked most of the way. At 3.30 we got to the village where we spent the night.

The news is very bad and I should think it is quite a question who gets to Benderi first, ourselves or the Germans. Braila has fallen and Galatz is evacuated. The Roumanians appear to be the worst soldiers in the world and neither the Serbs nor the Russians have a good word to say for them. I see from *The Spectator* of October 28th that people in England are still chattering about 'our brave little ally Roumania', etc. I wonder how long that fiction will be kept up. *The Spectator* says that the retreat was done in good order. As a matter of fact it was the most hopeless confusion. Everybody was lost, and the Roumanians ran like hares in absolute panic. They say the present retreat is as bad.

Moir *Monday 18 December*

We started, each perched up sky-high on the top of a rickety cart containing hospital stores; hard packing cases which seemed all corners, and it really was so terribly uncomfortable and sore that one by one we climbed down and footed it most of the way. It was such a desperately cold day, too, that we were thankful to walk, to help to keep warm. It was very heavy walking, thanks to the mud, and by the time we reached Cismea Varuita and had secured a hut, we all felt about at the end of our tether. We made ourselves some tea, retired to the floor, and did not budge till 5 a.m. next day. This morning we were off again at 6 a.m., and we got to Bolgrad about 2 o'clock.

Fawcett *Diary Monday 18 December*

The roads today have been far less heavy, and Turner, Rendel, and I had the good luck to meet three nice Serbian officers who gave up their horses, so that we rode practically all the way to Bolgrad.

We have arrived in Bolgrad and have quite settled into a nice house. Our settling in consists of putting up our camp beds and undoing our bed bundles. We have just heard that the day we left Ismail the town was bombarded by enemy aircraft.

Afternoon. Moir and I have just seen some English Tommies and officers. It was so nice to see Englishmen again. They had just come from

Tulcea, which is evacuating. They travelled by road with their transport and sent their armoured cars by barge. They have seen our Transport, who have been doing splendid work the last few days carrying wounded all day and all night. They were then about 5 km inland from Isaccea awaiting orders. The Armoured Cars people have lost three cars and six men taken prisoner.[15] The car the men were in was not taken by the Bulgars. Before leaving it they put it out of action, as it was stuck in the mud and they could not drive it away – then the Bulgars advanced and took them prisoner. The same day the Russians advanced again and pulled the car out of the mud. Moir and I met Acting Commander Belt and Surgeon Scott. Really the commander is Oliver Locker Lampson, who comes out for a fortnight at a time, according to one of the Tommies.[16]

Turner *Monday 18 December*

We arrived in Bolgrad about 12 noon, and having had coffee with Petrovic and Brasio at the principal café, we got our quarters straight and most people went to sleep on their beds. I strolled out about 2.30, and suddenly seeing a lot of cars somewhat un-Russian in shape, turned down the street where they were and came face to face with three RNVR officers. We fell on each other's necks, metaphorically speaking. It was awfully jolly to see them. This Armoured Car Division has been out here for a year, first to the Caucasus, then to the Dobrudga front. They only arrived there after the retreat, and they went forward to Hirsova when the Bulgars evacuated it. Now they are *en route* for Odessa. They caught up with our Transport yesterday, and found the Burford lorry sticking in the mud, and helped to heave her out. Imagine the joy of the Transport in this unholy country where on retreat every man rushed off and would never dream of helping the Scottish Women unless some bigwig was interested in the matter. Just imagine suddenly meeting English armoured cars and Tommies to pull you out of a hole.

Hospital B Odessa

Grant *Monday 18 December Hotel de Paris*

We arrived most unexpectedly about 11.30 p.m. We took a *droshki* and drove to this place. It sounds very fine and large, but is rather like a pigsty. However, we are lucky in having a room to ourselves – no other inhabitants! We both slept like tops last night, getting to bed about 1 a.m. and not getting up until 10 this morning. We went to the Consulate to see Mr Bagge, and incidentally to get our mails. We then trotted round to the Serbian Headquarters, and also the Russian ones; and after much pow-wowing got them to understand that we were anxious to start a hospital for the Serbs in Odessa. It is just fine going round seeing all these bigwigs, who bow over you and kiss your hand – mine being encased in a very grubby glove. It always made me want to laugh. The difficulties are great, but I hope we are going to have what we want.

We lunched at a restaurant, went to see some more officials, and then took a *droshki* and went out to tea with Mrs Bagge. It was ripping to see her again, and her pretty drawing room with pretty English chintz was most grateful and comforting.

Tuesday 19 December

After visiting the Serbian Headquarters to see old General Zhivkovic, we went to the British Consulate to meet Mrs Bagge, who was going to take us to the cathedral, where there was a great function, this being the Emperor's name day. Mr Bagge looked very nice in his consular uniform, and we also had one of the Armoured Car officers with us. The function was a gorgeous display of uniforms, medals and orders, and I have never seen such a wonderful collection of armaments hanging on people before. The Grand Duke Cyril was a very commanding figure amongst them all, with his breast covered with medals, and a very pretty pale blue order tied across him. The priests were very gorgeous, two of them with what Dr Chesney described as golden halos on their heads. We lunched at the Bagges' along with some other people, and then Mr Bagge came with us to the Russian Croix Rouge place to interview the chief there.

While we were having our dinner this evening, a great surprise came in the form of a telephone message from Mr Bagge to say that some of our people from Galatz had arrived by boat with all the stores, as they are evacuating Galatz now.[17] Matron and Johnson have just arrived here, and Dr Chesney received them very coldly. Of course they had to come, as Dr Inglis had sent them; at the same time, it is rather a difficulty to find them accommodation at such short notice, and also a place to put the hospital stores. They are sleeping on the boat tonight, and tomorrow we ought to have it decided whether to stay here or not. I am just afraid now that Dr Chesney will, out of sheer devilment, go careering off to Voznesensk.

I heard of a poor English girl who has been teaching in Bucharest, and in her spare time doing Red Cross work. She left the town all by herself while on night duty, as she was told the Germans were entering the town from the other end. She walked about 17 *versts* along the railway line till she got a train, and then took days to get here. She had nothing but the uniform she stood up in. Her hair has turned quite grey in consequence of what she has been through. One hears endless pitiful tales. One of the

Armoured Car officers was shot in the leg in an action with the Bulgarians. They took some of his men prisoner, and as his leg was broken, said they would come back for him. In the meantime he, poor fellow, managed to crawl back, on his back, to where our troops found him. He is now in hospital here, after having an awful time with the Russian doctors on his journey here. Every dressing station he came to they said, 'Ah, English officer,' took down the dressing on his leg, examined it, and did it up again. This occurred more than once, the consequence being that his leg will take some time to be right, and even then will be wrongly set, I expect.[18]

Hospital B Bolgrad to Odessa

Rendel *Tuesday 19 December*

We were told that Sakharov and his staff were expected, but finally only the staff came. General S has left the Roumanian front in a rage because the Roumanians refused to obey orders. One of the officers we saw told us that the Russian, French, and English officers refused now to speak to the Roumanians. He also told us of a terrible scene in the Duma in which the British and French ambassadors took part, and which ended in the fall of the Russian premier. I don't dare tell you all the details... This man heard them from a friend of his who was a member of the Duma and had been present. He was very mysterious about telling us and insisted on walking up and down out of doors so that he could be sure no one was listening. If what he says is true, and I think it is, the situation is very serious.

Moir *Wednesday 20 December*

We kicked our heels at a little wayside station all afternoon yesterday, waiting for General Sakharov and his staff to pass. We were sitting in the 'feeding room' when they came in, so had a good view of them – they were attired in very gorgeous uniforms and were very much bemedalled. Their curiosity proved too much for them, for very soon one of their officers came across and spoke to us and asked a few questions, but we found he already knew as much about the SWH as we did ourselves. From what one of the officers said, things are *not* as they should be in the Russian Duma. The Tsarina is decidedly pro-German and *not for us*. Her party – a man of the name of Rasputin and Stürmer being the chief instruments – are all for peace. Their idea is to make a separate peace and then declare war against us. This may read as an exaggeration to you people at home, but it's not; the army and the people are up in arms against the Tsarina and the court party, who are playing into Germany's hands.

The poor weak Tsar seems to have no say in the matter, but they have one very strong man, the Grand Duke Nicholas, and fortunately he is in command at the front. He's very popular, and a fine character.

There has been a terrible row in the Duma on the head of this 'peace talk' – the Prime Minister Stürmer has been deposed and the Duma suspended. Our ambassador in Petrograd, Sir George Buchanan, made a very strong and impressive speech, in which he told the Duma that they had proofs of the secret meeting which was held with the German War Minister, arranging for a separate peace between Russia and Germany. Altogether it looks as if there would be internal trouble in Russia ere long. One hears rumours of a revolution in Petrograd. The army and the people are all against a separate peace, and *all* against the Tsarina and her party – Rasputin is evidently the worst offender, and is said to have extraordinary power over the Tsarina. There'll be some fun in Russia soon! Enough of politics, or this letter will never get through.

Fawcett *Diary Thursday 21 December*
We have passed Benderi and Tiraspol. At Benderi, Moir and I took Peter [Petrovic] into the market, where the poor dear got his boots very dirty. He tells us that Germany is talking of peace. There is a kid in the officers' coach with chicken-pox. We tease Peter and say that he will have chicken-pox when we get to Voznesensk and we shall take Dr Chesney to see him every morning. He simply hates her.

We probably arrive at Odessa tonight, where we must try and find Natasha Harris.

Grant *Wednesday 20 December Hotel de Paris*
A most successful and satisfactory day. We went along to the British Consulate and found Matron and Little there. We discussed things, and then Dr Chesney and I went to the Serbian HQ and parler-voused there. Later we met two Serbian officers, who took us in their car to the Greek school where we are to have our hospital building – we are to have one floor of it. It all looked so nice and clean, and I think is going to pan out most successfully. Our people from Ismail will be glad we are going to stay in Odessa.

Saturday 23 December
The rest of our unit arrived from Ismail yesterday morning. Petrovic arrived at our bedroom door at 7.30, and Dr Chesney received him in her pyjamas, I in my bed. He was as usual very excited, and said that they were all at the goods station, a long way out. We found them all there,

looking very fit, and very glad to get here – I'm afraid they had not had a very nice journey. Moir and I were left in charge of the equipment while the others went back to Odessa.

Transport Isaccea to Front

Hodges[19]

Suddenly we got fresh orders that we were to go back again, and we set off over the river once more, along the main road for a bit, and then turned off into a little lane leading up to the mountains. As we turned from the main road we saw a wonderful picture: a large field full of troops camping for the night. Every little group of men had a wood fire burning; the dark background of trees threw the leaping flames into bright relief, and the figures of soldiers moving in front of the flames became sharply defined dramatic silhouettes.

We climbed up and up, getting nearer all the time to the sound of guns, until we came to a little valley in the top of the hills; here we found a quiet white convent. The nuns, their serenity apparently untouched, came out, gave us their schoolroom to sleep in, and some hot coffee. We were told that we should do nothing till morning, and that as it was bitterly cold, we should empty all the radiators, which we did. Then we all went to the schoolroom to rest. I was just going in when George called me back and said, 'Don't say I've told you, but pass the word round to fill up your radiators again, and each of you take it in turns to slip out quietly to go and turn your cars.' The ambulances were parked in single file facing *towards* the front, and the road was very narrow, so turning the cars took quite a little time. 'Why?' I asked George. 'Well,' he said, 'I've heard that this place is none too secure, and we're liable to have to get out very quickly, so we'd better have the cars turned now.' I duly passed on the information, and we acted on it, and very glad we were that we had done so.

It was a strange night. When the big guns stopped at intervals, you could hear the rifle fire. The enemy were, we were told, just on the crest of the hills above us...

Early next day orders suddenly arrived that our lines had broken, and the enemy might be on us at any moment. We left very hurriedly, and retreated back to the main road, which was by this time terribly congested. After a few miles we had to turn up a very narrow lane into a little village to fetch wounded, and there we sat for hours. At last the cars were loaded up, and went off one by one as soon as they were ready. I had two bad stretcher cases, one man with a shocking head wound, the other an abdominal one, and a boy sitting by my side with his arm blown off that morning.

These poor fellows had been taken to the hospital in the village to have dressings, and their clothes had been taken away, as they, presumably, were to have stayed in the hospital, for no one was expecting to have to evacuate so quickly. So all they had on were coarse cotton hospital pyjamas, and it was December, and very cold. I had one rug which I put over the two inside the ambulance, and I put my leather coat on the boy next to me, but I fear it didn't help them too much. I plied the boy with cigarettes, which helped to keep him going, poor lad.

At last I started off. The lane was very narrow, and by now congested to a degree that is almost indescribable. I don't think it was more than three quarters of a mile from the village to the main road, but it took me from midday to nearly five o'clock to cover that distance. I moved about a foot and then waited half an hour, and so it went on. It was hardly better when we reached the main road: we were making for the pontoon bridge again, but so was the bulk of the Russian and Roumanian armies. The confusion was awful.

There was a turning to the right which led to the river and the bridge, and at last we reached this turning, and sat and waited and waited and waited. The road was not very wide, and on the left hand side there was a drop of three to four feet into marshy ground. Suddenly there was a terrific commotion behind, and beside me a fearful crash, and I was thrown forward on to my steering wheel. The next thing I knew was a huge horse crashing over my bonnet, another by my head, and then a grinding, rending noise: my car was being dragged along rapidly, locked into a gun-carriage. Fortunately I had enough sense left to hang on to the steering wheel. The leading horse started off to the left, plunged down the steep bank, and we were over the edge of the road and had dropped on to the marshy ground. Mercifully the leading horse was pulling madly to the right as we went over, which was the only thing that saved my car from landing on its side with the gun-carriage on top of it. As soon as I realised the drop was over and saw the horses pulling to the right, I rammed my steering wheel hard over to the left, and with a grinding rip and a tear, the gun-carriage tore past me, leaving me stuck in the marsh, but thank God with no harm done other than shock to my wounded. Poor things, they were in a terrible state, and I myself was very shaken. The mudguards and a huge strip of canvas had been ripped off one side of the car, but mercifully the wounded weren't touched. Crowds of soldiers ran down, Donisthorpe appeared, and between them they got me debogged and back on the road again, where after another long wait we at last got down to the river and to a camp on the other side. There my wounded were transferred to another car, and taken to another hospital about three miles on.

We slept on the ground that night, and I slept between two big Russian soldiers who kept me warm, as it was freezingly cold. I cannot say enough of the wonderful kindness and simple charming way in which the soldiers treated us. They took us for granted as comrades, there was never a difficult moment or feeling of embarrassment, and they were always ready to give us some of their food and tea, or to lend a helping hand if we needed it.

Transport Front to Isaccea

Birkbeck *Thursday 21 December*
Up at 7. The Bulgars are admittedly where we supposed them last night, on the other side of the hill at the back of the village. The guns formed an almost unbroken line all over the hills. Machine guns sounded in a staccato accompaniment to the convoy – very near.

I, Carlyon, and Gartlan had orders to take the wounded into Isaccea. We lunched at the hospital first, and ate like wolves; ships' biscuits and *sukharki* soon pall. They gave us goose – it's far the most common dish here, and one does not wonder, seeing the flocks of geese about. While we were at lunch the doctor came with orders for us all to clear out at once. He himself was to return with his hospital to Ferra Ponta. We loaded and were soon off, at 2. We got wounded from Nicolactso, where they were pouring in. When we got a little way on the high road we found the usual pack of retreating infantry walking in masses, carts in a single line, plodding back, wounded walking as best they could. The carts had picked up all we had come for, others hung on behind. We each picked up all we could. I took three extra, and kept changing the less serious cases for weaker ones I passed later. All looked absolutely expressionless and marched in silence, bone weary. The pack thickened till we could only edge through a little at a time. In the middle of Isaccea the street was blocked with a mass of wounded outside a hospital waiting to get dressed. We then left our sitting cases there and took the others to hospital after hospital, but all had either evacuated or were evacuating. We heard it was out of the question to leave the wounded anywhere this side of the river. As we were all consulting Mrs Haverfield turned up with the touring car and lots of news. The Burford had stuck miles back with our luggage on it. The driver had come in on foot. We went across the bridge to Ferra Ponta. By now it was dark, as dark as it always is when we cross that marsh. My wounded screamed the whole way...

When we got back to the head of the bridge the others had all turned up, with wounded. I had to take on Onslow's as her car was wrong. I found more lights and did it all over again – after trying to make myself drunk with brandy, but there was not enough. We arranged once again to form three sides of a square, and I lit a fire and got the kettle out for tea. Russian lorry drivers, infantry and cavalry dribbled up. We lay on sheepskins round the fire; others sat behind; the outer ring stood. The back row were all shivering; passers-by came and warmed themselves, and passed on. It was interesting watching the faces in the firelight. It was bitterly cold beyond the ring of warmth of our fire. After a bit we sang 'The Long Trail' and all the songs that keep us going, and then we started the Russians off. One would begin and sing a little, and then all would join in with a chorus. We sang too the songs we have learned. They sang the song they never ever miss, 'The Song of the Volga', of the man who loved the Volga so much he wished to give it his most precious gift: he threw in his lady love as an offering.

Hodges[20]

During this retreat from the mountains, Faithfull, the poor lorry driver, had a frightful time. The gradients were really far too steep for the heavily-laden lorry, which contained all our petrol and kit-bags; and the difficulties encountered in getting it up and down the shocking mountain roads were appalling. Eventually the gear lever snapped in half, and the first and second gears were out of action.

Faithfull had only a young Russian nurse with her, and Mrs Haverfield told them to stay with the lorry, saying that she would try to send a car back for them after the wounded had been evacuated. They waited, alone in their glory, while troops and guns surged past them in ever-increasing haste and confusion. At last, when it was quite dark, someone told them that they really must not wait any longer, as the Bulgarians were only about two miles behind, and advancing with the utmost rapidity. They decided that they would have to abandon the lorry, but just as they started to walk, a Ford approached, and with joy they recognised it as one of their own. If this car had not been able to get back for them they would certainly have been taken prisoner or killed by the firing of the advancing enemy. The lorry was left at the side of the road.

At the time there was such a rush that we did not think much about it, but the next day when we had got over the river and landed all our wounded in hospital, we realised that we were not only minus our kit-bags, but minus petrol, bar the small amount left in our tanks. After some discussion Donisthorpe volunteered to go back and see if she could reach the lorry. Mrs Haverfield was very much opposed to this, as it was a very risky proceeding. However, eventually Donisthorpe, with George, set off with all our spare petrol cans, and found the lorry, which was in the process of being looted by passing troops. The road was being shelled, but they filled the cans, and piled them and as many kit-bags as they could into Donisthorpe's Ford. While she started off, George, who on examination found that the gear lever of the lorry had snapped off about two inches above the gate change, got a soldier to steer the car while he sat on the step and changed gear by gripping the broken lever with a large pair of pliers. Thus, complete with petrol, luggage, and lorry, they returned triumphantly to us.

The next day we were ordered to retreat to Bolgrad, about fifty miles back. We spent Christmas Day in Bolgrad; the only things that stand out in my mind are the excellent mince pies produced, heaven knows how, by our cook.

Hospital B Odessa

Rendel *Letter to Ray Strachey Sunday 24 December*

Since I last wrote prospects are looking better. Dr Chesney has succeeded in getting hold of a hospital for a hundred beds, and now that there has been all this fighting in Roumania again, I expect we shall be quite busy. We are hard at work getting things ready.

Dr Chesney continues to befriend me, so I am very prosperous still. The position is a little difficult at times, because some of the orderlies are inclined to be annoyed. Dr C will say to me, 'Don't do that, Miss Rendel. Get an orderly to do it for you.' Also the matron is rather huffed occasionally because I eat and sleep with the doctors, and she has to preside over the sisters. However, she is a nice creature, and is very kind to me really. But you can imagine that there are difficulties of this kind from time to time. Dr C can be a perfect devil when she chooses; but her good points largely outweigh her bad, and she is exceedingly amusing.

Fawcett *Diary Christmas Day*

Thank goodness we have landed here after all. At first it seemed too good to be true. We have the top floor of the Greek School as a hospital. There is one large ward which will hold about sixty beds, and four medium-sized rooms leading out of it. At present we are only getting straight, and we sleep in the rooms leading off from the main ward. The beds are all ready for the wounded, but we have to wait for a Prince something or other to come and see it before it is properly started. I only hope that Dr Chesney will be civil.

Turner *Monday 25 December*

The English Colony here keeps the Russian Christmas, so we did not take any notice of it. As a matter of fact we were working very hard getting the hospital in order. In the evening when the doctors had gone to bed we got up and danced the Kola in the ward in our pyjamas. There is a most gorgeous parquet floor, and we want to give a dance before the patients come.

Hospital A Galatz

Bowerman *Christmas Day*

Got up at 6 a.m. to get breakfast for Dr Corbett who has to catch early boat for Reni. Breakfast for unit at 8 a.m. Cleared away and tidied up – went to Catholic Church 10.30 – services all over. Lunch at restaurant with Fitzroy, Brown and Murphy. After lunch went to do shopping for Christmas tea, with Brown. Wandered down by the river – found new pontoon bridge had been made across the Danube. Went across it to the Dobrudga – large number of refugees coming towards Galatz – nearly got caught on the wrong side of the river as preparations being made to open the bridge when we were halfway back. However, hurried across, and just got over in time. Can now hear guns in Dobrudga very distinctly – news very black.

Unit had jolly Christmas tea together in the hospital building – played games, charades, etc. afterwards. Dr Inglis as knight-errant in breeches, with bowl on her head.

Fitzroy *Christmas Day*[21]

They have flung a pontoon bridge across the Danube here, and the Dobrudga guns sound nearer...

A most wonderful spread awaited us at tea, and we played games and chanted carols far into the night. I'm sure the Russkies think we worship strange gods indeed!

Transport Bolgrad

Birkbeck *Sunday 24 December*

There was a very good Sunday market. There was street after street of stalls, grouped according to their wares: fruit, vegetables, bread, boots, leather, sheepskin coats and caps, poultry and meat, live fowls, pigs, and stalls where trash and items from boot polish to pencils and beads were jumbled together. Among the stalls the most picturesque of purchasers crowded: men in white sheepskins and women in gay coloured velvet coats lined with fur. We had great fun buying our Christmas presents.

Everyone lost their heads before Christmas Day. Hedges, Gartlan, Onslow and I were sad, sleeping round the fire when the Armoured Car people all came in after supper. We rolled up our beds, and really the packed earth floor made quite a good floor to dance on. They came, ten of them, and formed a very cheery crew indeed. It was too funny to see khaki dancing with khaki. It all reminded one of a charming musical comedy chorus. It was everything to find English people at Christmas, and it was as it should be, that the only English units there should be together.

Christmas Day Bolgrad

Worked on cars and got them ready for the next exodus. It was a Christmas dinner, goose and a turkey bought in the market – rather a disturbed meal. Mrs Haverfield had not come in; she arrived after lunch, and arranged for all there who were going, to go at once to Odessa. The rest of the day was spent in packing the others off, and rather sadly giving them a hundred messages for England. At 6 they all left – Donisthorpe, Hodges, Carlyon, Suche, [Clare] Murphy, Gartlan, Reaney, Cunningham, McDougall, Maguire, Faithfull and Plimsoll. The Armoured Cars sent a lorry down. Edwards and I went with them to the station; we did not stay, knowing Russian trains. They got off at 2 a.m.

Hospital B Odessa

Fawcett *Diary 25 December*

Tomorrow – Boxing Day – we are going to a show given by the English Colony to the British Armoured Car people stationed here – the orderlies are going at 5.30 to help with the dinner, and the doctors and sisters are to follow at 8 for the sing-song. We mean to enjoy ourselves.

Turner and I spent the first two nights at the Harrises'. We thoroughly enjoyed hot baths and sheets – not to mention fires and food that we had not had to prepare ourselves.

Today I have told Dr Chesney that I am going home at the end of my six months. Really I hope to transfer either to the Transport or A Hospital, but it was useless making a row.

Wednesday 27 December

We enjoyed the party at the English Club last night very much indeed. There were about sixty or seventy Tommies there and about five officers. They were all quite fun.

We hear that Ismail has fallen exactly ten days after we left it. This puts a stop to the retreat by river and sea, which was the way the equipment came.

Hospital A Galatz

Fitzroy *Tuesday 26 December*[22]

We were woken at 2 a.m. by a terrific explosion, followed by two less violent. It proved to be a Zeppelin – our first night raid – and the bombs were very near. News is bad, and plans uncertain. Tulcea fell last Thursday or Friday, and our Transport are believed to be at Ismail.

Wednesday 27 December

Ilyachenko, the chief of the Russian Red Cross in these parts, visited the hospital. He said that in four or five days they will know whether or not it is possible to hold the line from a point between Isaccea and Macin in the Dobrudga, up to Buzei, where a battle is now raging. If Macin falls, Galatz must follow in three or four days' time, in which case we are to move north to Foltesti, which lies at the head of a pontoon bridge on the Pruth, and set to work there. The Transport have done *very* good work in the Dobrudga.

Commander Locker Lampson's Armoured Cars have all turned up here. They say Galatz will be bombarded from two sides, and blown to little, little bits. Today the guns were incessant.

Thursday 28 December

I am to have a ward to myself, and am absolutely *thrilled*.

Hospital B Retreating
(Mitchell Library)

Trouble with the Heavy Lorry
(Mitchell Library)

Camp Cooking
(Edinburgh Central Library)

Motor Kitchen
(Edinburgh Central Library)

Serbian Slava *(Imperial War Museum)*

171

Staff House, Reni
(Roger and Patrick Cahill)

The Kitchen at Reni
(Roger and Patrick Cahill)

CHAPTER 8
New Quarters
(See maps 4 & 5)

The withdrawal from the northern Dobrudga left Russia's south-western front dangerously vulnerable, so that for several weeks the immediate future of the hospitals was again in the balance. The effective defence of the southern frontier now depended on holding the few river ports on the lower Danube; these were Galatz, Reni, Isaccea, and Tulcea. Tulcea fell on 24 December, a week after the bulk of the equipment had been sent off from Galatz via the Danube and the Black Sea to Odessa. As Fawcett points out, this route would not have been possible once the Bulgarians had control of any of the river ports downstream. Fitzroy, in her diary entry for 27 December, mentions Ilyachenko's hope that the Russians might hold on to the north-west corner of the Dobrudga, where the river takes a bend that includes Macin, Braila, Galatz, Reni, and Isaccea. But Macin fell on 4 January and Braila on the 6th, exposing Galatz to attack from two sides, and causing Hospital A to retreat from there to Reni. For the first few weeks of 1917 Reni was likewise in jeopardy; but having cleared the Dobrudga, the Germans stopped short of entering Galatz, and transferred most of their troops to the western front, leaving the weaker Bulgarians and Turks to hold the south bank of the Danube and the west bank of the Sereth.

In winter it was possible to penetrate the frozen marshes on foot, and on 22 January the Bulgars succeeded in crossing one arm of the Danube Delta near Tulcea; but without the German stiffening they were unable to sustain their attack, and were beaten back the next day.[1] For the rest of the winter the line stabilised, and the pressure eased, although both Reni and Galatz were subjected to sporadic air raids and shelling from across the river. The British Armoured Cars, having set up their headquarters at Tiraspol, maintained one squadron at Galatz, and when the severe winter precluded the use of cars, they helped the Russians by manning machine guns in that area.[2] The front line now followed the Sereth River along the Moldavian border to its confluence with the Danube just above Galatz, and eastwards along the north shore of the Danube to the Black Sea.

With the First Serbian Division still in reserve, and likely to be so for the rest of the winter, Dr Inglis arranged that the Scottish Women should continue to work for the Russians until required by the Serbs. The building she was given at Reni, another barracks, was in No Man's Land, dangerously between the first line of Russian trenches (with its artillery batteries) and the river. Some of the requests for transfer were now granted: Sister Jenkins and Fawcett were moved to Hospital A, and Turner to the Transport, while the London Committee was asked to send a new batch of nurses and orderlies to replace those whose six-month contracts were about to expire.

A substantial group of Transport members quarrelled with Mrs Haverfield, and left Bolgrad either on Christmas Day or on the day following. Both Hodges and Birkbeck draw a discreet veil over the reasons for the large-scale rebellion, but Rendel, whose opinion must be taken warily as sometimes reflecting Dr Chesney's prejudices, complained about Mrs Haverfield's unpracticality, snobbishness and foolishness (for which there is not much objective evidence); adding, more tellingly, 'She tries to make up for her incompetence by strafing all the members of her unit until they are all fed up with her.'[3] Casual comments by other diarists support the impression that it was her manner of asserting authority that was the main cause of discontent. All the Transport had been under severe strain throughout their work in the Dobrudga, and were much of the time physically exhausted. Mrs Haverfield must have been so too, and no doubt responded to her unit's tendency to question her orders by more adamant insistence on obedience.[4] Whatever the reasons, her relations with her drivers and orderlies deteriorated so much that by the end of January, seventeen of them had either gone home or joined another hospital or ambulance column.[5] Later, leaving the Transport in the care of Margaret Marx, who had arrived in early December, Mrs Haverfield and Onslow returned to Britain to recruit more drivers, and, at Dr Inglis's request, to see the London Committee about these difficulties. Minutes of the committee reveal a great measure of doubt in all minds about whether the rebels had resigned or been dismissed: there appears not to have been any clarity on the matter. Five of those who returned home were interviewed about their resignation (or dismissal), or asked to give their reasons in writing. Of these five, all complained about the bad cooking; three mentioned the state of the cars and the lack of work in the winter months; two were reluctant to impute any blame to Mrs Haverfield, but three gave her unwillingness to delegate authority as a serious cause of dissatisfaction.[6] This last explanation is unwittingly corroborated by Mrs Haverfield's own statement to the committee that all she required from members of her unit was that they should drive a car and do as they were told. To the modern reader it seems almost inevitable that young women who had the personal and financial independence to drive and in many cases to own their own cars, and who had shown great courage and initiative in dangerous situations, should rebel when required to obey arbitrary orders.

Another serious problem was revealed in a report from Marx, probably written in early February, and read to the London Committee on April 28. Marx was asking to be allowed to employ men as drivers, at least for the heavy lorries, which had a stiff clutch pedal, the resistance of which, she said, was too great for a woman's strength. She then added:

> Also the original Transport unit had too few drivers for the heavy cars – each lorry requires at least two drivers. The Russians have three men to each lorry, and they of course know the conditions and strain well. Drivers should be required to do nothing else but drive and do such roadside repairs as may be necessary. It is impossible for tired drivers to attend properly to the oiling and daily care required for a car in use. Unless this care is given daily and not just when there is slackness of work, the cars suffer.[7]

The justice of this complaint is borne out by the many references in the diaries to the long hours worked by the drivers, to the lack of sleep and to the missed meals, as well as by Birkbeck's evidence about the unreliable state of the cars in November and December. Mrs Haverfield's expectations of what drivers and cars could do seem to have been based on her experience of peacetime driving on a macadamised road, with the support of regular servicing and a supply of spares, none of which was available in the backward and rural Dobrudga. The punishment the cars had sustained was something not envisaged by their original designers, and the repairs needed went far beyond the scope of the elementary motor mechanics in which some of the women had been instructed. In recognition of this, the SWH had in early November recruited two professional mechanics, George Day and Percy Cowland. They had travelled out with Marx, bringing with them spare parts for the small workshop which they set up in Odessa, where the few remaining drivers and orderlies worked under their direction.[8]

Even if the cars had been in good order, however, they would not have been of any use until the spring. It was the hardest winter for seventy years, and for several months wheeled traffic was out of commission. Carts were put on runners, sledges became the normal form of passenger conveyance, and there was a significant lull in the fighting. With both motor transport and the army in a state of hibernation, there seems to have been some anxiety about how to keep the handful of remaining Transport personnel busy until the spring. Although the Dobrudga experience had seemed like a lifetime, the six months' contracts had not yet expired, and some women had committed themselves for a year. With the exception of one or two drivers to be attached to each hospital, it was not certain when or where the team would be required. As early as February it was rumoured that the Serbian Division might be transferred to Salonica, and it was probably this possibility, combined with the slackening of work and the shortage of food and fuel, that persuaded Dr Inglis to send the remaining six-monthers home a little early and to allow others, including Birkbeck, a few weeks leave. Birkbeck, Hedges, Onslow, and possibly others, intended returning in the spring, but as it turned out, not all were able to: from early January onwards, travel to, from, and within Russia became increasingly difficult.

Transport Bolgrad

Hodges[9] *Tuesday 26 December*

For reasons too controversial to give here several of us were going to leave the unit, and the day after Christmas we were told that we were to go from Bolgrad to Odessa to see the British Consul there and obtain information from him regarding the continuation of our journey back to England... That train – I can see it now. We were in it for a solid month; in fact when we finally left it we felt quite sad, for it had become a sort of home from home. A very dirty, very surly gentleman called by us 'Joseph' was in charge of the coach. He lived in a horrid little fuggy cubby-hole at the end of the coach, with a stove in it, which he plied with wood all day, and this somehow heated it. He used to get this stove red-hot, and the heat was positively tropical. We used to fling open the windows to get some air, and Joseph would rush at us shouting with rage. The most tempestuous arguments took place, till finally he screwed the windows shut with much muttering to himself the while. Imagine his horror when he found these dreadful Englishwomen had unscrewed them and thrown the screws away. He never gave up trying, though, and the battle continued daily throughout the entire journey.

Birkbeck *Tuesday 26 December*

Bad news – Tulcea is flat, Isaccea and Reni both No Man's Land. The place is evacuating ahead. Meanwhile the Armoured Cars have gone off again to Galatz and a few Red Cross people remain here, waiting like us, for a train to get to Odessa.

Hospital B Odessa

Turner *Friday 29 December*

Last night some of the Transport arrived on their way home – apparently they have had a pretty thin time with Mrs Haverfield. Dr Chesney, as usual, behaved in her odious manner, and the poor dears, who are penniless, were obliged to sleep in the train. They, like us, are frightfully fed up with the SWH.

Moir *Friday 29 December*

We have been busy all week getting our hospital in order and getting in patients. It all looks so nice now, and quite professional. I'm in the theatre – I'm most awfully pleased I've got that job, and am quite in my element. The theatre is perfectly ripping; it might have been specially designed for an operating theatre. I hope we get plenty of ops.

The rest of B Unit arrived at the beginning of the week – at least, not quite all, but the larger half: Matron, four sisters, Fordie (the cook), and Clack, the laundry superintendent. They came from Reni, where Dr Inglis is at present. So now we are fully staffed – over-staffed, we feel, compared to what we've had since the days of our base hospital at Medgidia. Our patients are all Russian, except for one Serb, one English Tommy, and an English officer – both Armoured Car men. At present our beds are full, but there are no very bad cases. We are not rushed at all with such a big staff.

Monday 1 January 1917 Odessa

Last night I was down at the station seeing twelve of the Buffs off home – back to Blighty. The Transport has been practically dissolved, the roads are impossible for cars and will be for some months to come, and the cars are badly in want of repair, so they are all in Odessa at present being overhauled, and most of the Transport are going home. Some of them are coming out again in the spring. The first contingent went off today – I was *very* sorry to see them go, as all my special friends were in this lot.

Transport Bolgrad to Odessa

Birkbeck *Saturday 30 December*

Left Bolgrad. After waiting a week for a train, we decided to take the vehicles to the station and pack into a waggon for ourselves. We drove down after lunch, or began to drive down – it was one of our best departures. Marx from the first light was driven distracted by us. The station habit having entered our bones, it took us several hours to get the first under way and the things packed. I spent the whole afternoon with George tinkering away at the ambulance in the yard. We got Royce to go in the end with a good deal of pook-pooking. The *sestritsa* [a Russian Red Cross sister] thought she would be unlikely to be able to drive Rolls. She had never driven a car alone before, and hung her up on a post in town. It was really awfully funny. When we got her off, she went one mile and stalled her engine, and refused to drive her, saying she had 'broken the engine'. I got in Rolls, and she [the *sestritsa*] simply shot down the hill in Royce as I had forgotten to tell her the brakes weren't working. At the bottom she got out and returned to Rolls. She tried again – no good – so gave up as useless. We then got going again. The comedy was continued by Hedges, who ran her car across two train tracks and off the next, where it hung by its heels over a ledge. Between us we got it righted, and then sat on our luggage on the platform or in the restaurant. They promised to make up a train, and it was made up at midnight with a few extra coaches. We shall make ourselves comfortable with two layers of bunks. It looks just like a Wild West shack with the wooden ceiling and a stove in the middle; after the cattle truck of the retreat, it is a palace indeed.

Wednesday 3 January Odessa

Thanks to the thieves at Bolgrad we had very little petrol, but decided we had better get off. However, the cars coughed and gave up all along the water front, and a car had to go along and fill them up with borrowed petrol. Rolls had a nasty adventure. The car in front of her stuck in the gate turning into the garage, so the driver left her car across the train line and ran to shove. I sat in mine and watched with breathless interest a train charge it at 40 and sweep it seventy yards along the line. It was a very spectacular smash. She was ticking over quite gaily after, even with the side smashed in and her four wheels spread apart like a gutted fish.

Arrived in the Greek School, a huge building of innumerable classrooms, most of which have been seized by various parties of refugees. We took one. Camp beds again, and a good night.

Hospital A Galatz

Bowerman *Saturday 30 December*

Just as we were sitting down to lunch, convoy of eighty wounded arrived – hard at work for the rest of the day – theatre and dressing orderlies did not get to bed till 5 a.m. Fresh convoy in at about 11 p.m. so hospital completely full – a hundred and nine cases. Lack of fuel still great difficulty, so I looted a large pine trunk lying by the railway – commandeered six Russkies to carry it and we brought it back in triumph. Wounded men so delighted to get wash, bed, and food – very tired and fell asleep almost at once. Mostly from the Dobrudga front – several slight cases. Such nice cheery fellows – such a delight after Roumanians, and so plucky – never utter a sound. One man died in the night from gangrene owing to a neglected arm.

Sunday 31 December

Foraging expedition in the morning – got hold of two of the Armoured Cars to bring the bread home. Three Tommies to lunch – Surgeon Scott helped in the hospital all afternoon. Cars ordered to front, so most of them leaving today. We hear the Germans are afraid of them, so they are most useful – whole Russian village was able to get up to a certain place in safety because the Boches knew our cars were there and so would not come near.

Inglis *Report 1-3 January 1917*[10]

The wounded were pouring through Galatz at the rate of about one thousand a day, and we got nothing but bad cases at our hospital. Dr Potter has a story that she gave orders for any cases that could walk to come down to the dressing room, and a few minutes afterwards the door was burst open and a man crawled in on all fours. That was the nearest we could get to a walking case!

The night we opened we got 109 cases. We bathed and dressed them all, and began operating the next afternoon at one o'clock, and then went on without a break until five o'clock the next morning. We owe a debt of gratitude to Mr Scott, Surgeon to the British Armoured Car Corps, who met one of the girls and asked whether he could be of any use. I sent back a message at once that we should be most grateful, and he worked with us without a break until we evacuated. He is a first-class surgeon, and it was a great thing to have him there. The cases stayed in a very short time, and we evacuated again down to the barges going to Reni, the hospital filling up, and more than filling up each time.

Bowerman *Monday 1 January 1917*

147 more wounded arrived – hospital only equipped for 100. Terrible sights and sounds – a lot of very bad cases of gangrene – smell at times almost unbearable. Operations continuously all day and all night till 5 a.m. Nurses up nearly all night. Mr Scott came up to help, also three orderlies from the Armoured Car Corps – most awfully helpful in the theatre and carrying stretchers all the time.

Tuesday 2 January

Much the same as yesterday – terrible suffering of the men, and some deaths. One man Wotherspoon and I particularly attracted to in one ward – better type than the others, and most awfully plucky – turned out to be a German!

Armoured Cars

G.B. Scott, Staff Surgeon. *Report* [11]

On 29 December I recalled Surgeon M. B. Scott[12] from Braila. I made arrangements for him to work at the Scottish Women's Hospital at Galatz. Owing to the loss of the Dobrudga, Galatz became too dangerous a place for the hospitals, and they had left or were in the process of leaving.

Between the 30th December and 5th Jan, a large number of wounded passed through Galatz, coming from the Dobrudga. At the Scottish Women's Hospital Surgeon Scott did, or assisted to do, 20 amputations of the leg, 5 of the arm, 5 abdominal operations, 4 excisions of the eyeball, 2 trephinings, and a large number of smaller operations for drainage of wounds and setting of fractures. Surgeon Scott with three sick berth staff worked for the first 33 hours without a rest, and after three hours again returned to duty.

On my return to Galatz on the 6th I was able to make arrangements for Dr Elsie Inglis and three others of her staff, with some Russian orderlies and a few remaining stores to travel to Reni on our barge, which was taking part of our force back. With the help of one of our lorries Dr Inglis's hospital was entirely evacuated by 8 p.m.

Hospital A Galatz to Reni

Inglis *Report 4 January*[13]

On Thursday, 4 January, the evacuation officer ordered us to evacuate the hospital. I told him our orders were to stay until the 'last moment', and he said that the 'last moment' had come. He arranged to send ambulances for the patients at eight o'clock the next morning, and we went up to the station to arrange for waggons to take us to Foltesti. We found, however, that the line to Foltesti was absolutely blocked, and we could neither get there direct nor by going round by Jassi, for the line was blocked northwards. While I was there debating what to do, Commander Gregory sent down a message to say that he would take us all over to Reni in a barge which had been given him for his corps. We therefore cleared out all the equipment on Thursday afternoon, and the personnel went that night, except four who stayed to evacuate the hospital the following morning. The committee will not be surprised to hear that at least half the staff came and asked for leave to stay; in fact one said she thought the whole twenty-two ought to stay. Late that evening, when I went down to the barge to see how the loading was getting on, Mr Scott came up with a fresh message from Commander Gregory that he did not wish any of us to stay. However, it was obviously impossible to leave the hospital, which at that moment contained sixty-six cases – every one of them bad cases – and I assured Mr Scott that we would find our way out. As a matter of fact, this was not necessary, for another barge belonging to the Armoured Car Corps went next day, and we came off in it.

Bowerman *Thursday 4 January*
Packed up the hospital things and our own with all speed. Armoured Car men loaded up our goods on to lorries and took them down to their barge – finally took us all down in a lorry. Brilliant moonlight, splendid night – such a relief to get away from the atmosphere of the hospital, and to be with jovial Englishmen whom we can depend on, after coping with foreigners and not able to speak their language. As we reached the barge we heard several explosions and saw brilliant flares in the sky – this was the destruction parties at work destroying stores, etc., to prevent them falling into the hands of the enemy. Our quarters are in the hold of the barge, so we were able to get out our beds and lie down – really comfortable. Tommies had lighted a lamp and stove for us – brought us porridge for breakfast and were most awfully good to us.

Saturday 6 January Reni
Dr Inglis arrives in the morning, having successfully evacuated the rest of the patients – five very bad had to be left in Galatz – the rest were sent by motor ambulance to Foltesti. Braila fell yesterday at 10 a.m. No orders or plans decided upon today.

Fitzroy *Letter Sunday 7 January Reni*
This goes to Odessa tomorrow by those immensely fortunate people the six-monthers. They may not take letters home but Johnson will come and see you and tell you personally of our adventures. And in another month Elsie Bowerman has got to go home. It is very sad for me – but she will be yet another visitor for you. Murphy, the medical student, is the only other orderly besides myself staying the full time, but she is a dear, so I feel comforted even in the midst of hating all these home-goers.

By the heading on this letter you will see that we are once more retreating, but this time we did it in state with the Armoured Cars and myriads of English Tommies to do everything for us. It was wonderful. We got here the day before yesterday after a week's work in our hospital in Galatz, and it was a week which none of us are likely to forget in a hurry. My ward was eventually turned into a straw ward, and the men were laid side by side as they came in, as close as possible. There was an enormous

181

percentage of the worst possible cases, and it was pretty terrible. Mercifully though we were always all too nearly finished to be capable of much thinking. We were always on all day without a stop, up till anything between two and six the following morning. The Armoured Cars Surgeon, Mr Scott, came to help, and brought with him four English orderlies, who proved the most unutterable blessing.

My CO has just discovered I possess a pack of cards, and she bade me a most affectionate good-night with 'One day we will show each other our patiences, dear child'; the rest of the unit had the impudence to giggle. I wonder why!

Bowerman *Monday 8 January*

Walk with Pleister up to the village of Reni to try and do some shopping – the *most* appalling mud I have ever seen. Fortunately got a lift part of the way there in an armoured car and back in a Russian car. Nothing to be found in the village, as it is a fête day – apples the only thing to be bought. Armoured Cars kindly sent us two days' rations – delicious English corned beef, jam, etc. – otherwise we should have been rather up a gum tree. They have two years' supplies with them – everything of the best.

Got a chimney fixed up to our portable kitchen stove, so we are now able to cook our meals and get heaps of hot water. The water supply very bad here – very dirty Danube water. Russian bath just opposite our billet, though, is a great boon. It consists of a very hot room with several huge boilers of water and a large supply of small buckets. You pour the water over yourself with these, and it runs away through a hole in the floor – heat tremendous.

Tuesday 9 January

Mrs Milne, who is going back to Odessa, Sedgwick and the other three six-monthers, set out for home on the train belonging to the Armoured Car Corps. We all feel very envious of them.

Armoured Cars Reni to Tiraspol

Milne[14]

When Dr Inglis told me that I was to accompany the four orderlies to Odessa, I was very delighted. The six months of the 'half-timers', as we called them, were nearly up. I was a 'yearling', and not on my way home, but Dr Inglis wished me to try baths and electricity for my neuritis, which had not improved during our strenuous ten days in hospital. The Armoured Cars train was leaving on the 10th for Tiraspol, and they had offered to take any of us so far with them. My two orderlies were of the party, and I think we three enjoyed the rest on the train more than anyone can imagine. To sit still and be waited upon, instead of being torn in all directions at once, and to have meals brought to us of which we had known nothing beforehand, was a rest which perhaps only cooks can appreciate. The journey took four days, but we would have been quite pleased had it taken double the time, it was so peaceful. And our hosts did everything that could possibly add to our comfort.

G.B. Scott, Staff Surgeon. *Report 7-11 January*

On the 7th the force left Galatz, with the exception of some cars and thirty officers and men. Surgeon King was left with this detachment. As we left Galatz the first shells fell near the arsenal, five bursting in quick succession.

At Reni the cars and men were embarked on two trains, and on the 11th January the first arrived at Tiraspol, followed two days later by the second. At this town which is to be our base for some time, I have formed a hospital of forty beds, for our own and the Russian sick and wounded.

Hospital B Odessa

Moir *Sunday 7 January*

Today is the Russian Christmas, thirteen days after ours. We gave the patients a Christmas tea, and had a tree for them. We lighted it up about 4 o'clock, and distributed little presents – crackers, sweets, fruit, cigarettes, etc. to each of them. I think they've all enjoyed their day immensely – they were all very happy and jolly anyway. The ward looked so nice, and quite Christmassy – we spent yesterday evening decorating.

We all enjoy being here. Think of it, we've got our camp beds and kit-bags once again. Our kit-bags! We were like children exploring a Christmas stocking when we first got them to ourselves. They seemed to be full of all sorts of unknown treasures.

Transport Odessa

Birkbeck *Monday 8 January*

Our room seemed large after the cattle truck, but the walls have contracted since, as walls will. Round the edge of the room are our nine camp beds, in the middle one long table, and here we eat, sleep and work. The chief difficulty is having nowhere to put things except under one's bed.

Work began at the garage. Day, and Percy, his boy, turned up long after us, and we were late enough. All the cars are packed into this very small space, leaving just enough clear for one car to be taken down at a time. A very inadequate little stove pretends to warm the place, and the doors have to be left open for light. Holme, Walker, Edwards and I did not work on the cars; the cars had to be unpacked, and it was an unpleasant filthy job, sorting nondescript débris, the collection of weeks.

Tuesday 9 January

Back to work, valve grinding, painting, valves that would not be ground, scraping paint that refused to come off, and painting with paint that would only go on in waves. Bitterly cold. Had tea at Franconi's. It was well peppered with khaki. Transport were there in force and all the Armoured Car people, mostly a new lot, but not quite as new as they used to be.

Hospital B Odessa

Turner *Saturday 13 January*

This morning Mrs Milne, Sedgwick, Kent, Brand and Ellis arrived from Reni, where they have left Dr Inglis and the rest of A Hospital. They brought orders for Fawcett and me to go to A, taking hospital materials. While Mrs Milne is in Odessa I am to take her place as cook. However, I am due to go to the Transport, and if I don't start that soon, there will not be time to learn before the cars are in working order again. Of course I have got to go, and shall enjoy roaming the country in search of Dr Inglis, but it will be awfully difficult not to get roped in to stay with A altogether.

Grant *15 January*

Poor Moir got very bad news from home. Her mother died on the 31st December, so we hurriedly decided on coming home.

Moir *Monday 15 January*

Since writing last, everything is changed, and after the cable I talked things over with Dr Chesney, and am going home as soon as Mr Bagge can secure a place on the train. Crowds of refugees are going up to Petrograd just now, so travelling is rather difficult. However, Mr Bagge thinks we may get off tomorrow or next day. Some of the others from A Unit – those returning at the end of their six months – have arrived here *en route* for home, and are likewise waiting for places on the train, so there will be several of us all going together.

Later. Mr Bagge has arranged for three of us to go tomorrow, so we leave here at 6 a.m. and get a train at 7. We should be at Petrograd in three or four days. I will be *very* sorry indeed to say goodbye to my old unit; we've been very happy together... Will write from Petrograd – should be home in twelve or fourteen days.

Fawcett *Letter Monday 15 January*

Turner and I are just off with thirteen packages of equipment to join Dr
Inglis at the front. Our orders are to report to the Russian Red Cross
Headquarters at Bolgrad, where we shall be told where to go. We are so
thankful to get away from Dr C.

Hospital B Odessa to Reni

Turner *Tuesday 16 January*

Here we are on the move again. Owing to the crush which prevented
Natasha getting into the station till 9 p.m., we nearly got left behind. At
the last moment they insisted on weighing our luggage. By a great stroke
of luck we met a big bug who went and turned two officers out of the only
through coach and got us a top berth between us. The other top berth is
occupied by an officer who knows how to make himself comfortable even
in the most trying circumstances. Below, there are four a side, and they
kicked up the most unholy row all night. There were men standing in the
corridor all night, and some are still there, although a few have got off at
this station.

At Tiraspol we heard that there were *Anglichane*, so we hastily bundled
out to find a whole crowd of Armoured Car men. They seem to be living
in trucks, and all look rather grubby. We had met most of the officers
before, so we sprinted up and asked for news of Dr Inglis. At Tiraspol also
our train picked up a whole crowd of French Armoured Car men just
arrived in Russia. As we got out of the train we were greeted with shouts
of 'English girls', and '*Vive l'Angleterre*', to which we replied, '*Vive la
France, Vive l'Entente*'. They look awfully jolly – their uniforms are
ripping. They are only distinguishable from the Roumanians by their Sam
Brownes, and their faces, which are *not* powdered. They have just gone
off to Jassi.

Thursday 18 January

Still perched like two hens on a roost... Last night our friend the toff on
the top bunk gave us his opinion of 'that dog, Rasputin', who was
murdered the other day to the great joy of Russia. A most romantic event,
quite like the Middle Ages. A set of young men drew lots as to who should
murder him, and the one who did escaped to the Caucasus. He [the toff]
laughed like anything when I referred to him [Rasputin] as '*cet homme
religieux*', and recounted some scandal at court.

Arrived at Traianoval at 4 p.m. and drove into Bolgrad by *droshki* –
awful mud there, infinitely worse than last time. And the dear people are

185

still trying to make a futile road between Bolgrad and Traianoval. At the Red Cross Headquarters we were received by General Krupensky, who is charming, and speaks English perfectly. He seems to have a great admiration for Dr Inglis. It is very refreshing to meet someone who understands and appreciates us and who has nice manners, after the piggish man on the train.

Friday 19 January

After breakfast we were sent into Traianoval by the general's equipage. While we were waiting in the buffet for lunch a naval man came in who we thought was French; I therefore cast the glad eye at him, and he came and sat by me. Then to my horror I discovered it was a washout – he was a Roumanian. However, it appeared that he was with an admiral who had commandeered a special train to Reni, and who later invited us to travel with them, which simplifies things for us. So here we are installed in a first class compartment to ourselves. The admiral and his three officers came to supper with us.

There is a quaint youth, very young, and educated in Austria. He has quite fallen in love with Fawcett's classic profile and has been making love to her hard. I have to translate for them as F can't speak French, and he can't speak enough English. It's great sport. Of course it loses all the cream in translation.

Hospital A Reni

Fitzroy *Letter to mother Saturday 13 January*

I am waiting for the cart to come and fetch the kitchen luggage. (*Later.* The cart came, so I must try again. I am now waiting for the cart to come back!) We are just moving up to our newest hospital – part of the barracks here – with a very nice little house for us, so I am told. Our new chief came and called upon us yesterday – the original head of the Russian Red Cross has been superseded. He [General Krupensky, the new chief] speaks English, knows England well, and inspired us all with much confidence. Instead of our having to fight for things as hitherto, everything is beautifully and expeditiously arranged, and we ought to be in working order in a day or two. They seem to have confidence Reni will not fall, but if it does, do not worry, as we have orders to evacuate and go to Benderi long before that event...

Our house is delicious – rather a tight fit, but on high ground with a really fine view over the Danube.

Saturday 13 January[15]

Murphy has found a deserted black kitten, and so is of course perfectly happy.

Bowerman *Saturday 13 January*

Moved into our new quarters – very busy day getting our new house straight. Delightful kitchen with boiler and range, but water scarce, also wood. In evening went on foraging expedition in a cart with General Krupensky's secretary and the Russian sister – not very successful – usual Russian promises but not much actual gain. We hear the position of Reni *very* precarious – may only be here a few days – rather disheartening to unpack under these conditions.

Monday 15 January

In the evening some of us were invited to a concert by some of the officers quartered in Reni. They came to fetch us about 8 p.m. in three *droshkis*; they had told us to be ready at 7 p.m., so for Slavs we really thought they were quite punctual. Lovely drive under the stars – passed a regiment of soldiers who were singing their evening hymn – sounded beautiful coming across to us through the darkness. Concert strange entertainment – started with good pianist and violinist – items by the Regimental Band of Cossacks quartered here. Then weird Cossack songs and dances accompanied by triangle, concertina and tambourine... afterwards there were round dances in which everyone joined. The 'English Sisters' also came in, though most of us were wearing gum boots, which did not add to our agility. The Russians, we gather, kept it up all night, but we left about 1 a.m. after partaking of supper of cold goose and cabbage, lemonade and claret, provided for us by the officers. Returned home and found wounded just arriving at the hospital – about forty of them – so Dr Corbett and eight of the sisters had to set to work at once.

Tuesday 16 January

Everyone very busy in hospital all day. About eighty patients admitted altogether, most of them pretty bad. Fifteen Austrian prisoners attached as orderlies – perfect godsend, so clean, *quick*, and intelligent. I have two to assist me in the kitchen – after my one old Russki it seems too blissful for anything. They are quite pleased to be with us – a real case of loving our enemies. Heavy bombardment in Galatz direction.

Fitzroy *Wednesday 17 January*[16]

Sambo has received official recognition. It became necessary. Dogs and puppies abound, and the unit is developing a weakness for the adoption of any and every waif they meet. So now we have 'The Official Dog'. Dr I loves him, as we all do, and even poor unofficial Pushkin (the black kitten) has almost won her heart.

Wards all day up to 12 midnight. No news, and the firing less violent.

Bowerman *Wednesday 17 January*

No orderlies arrive before breakfast, as they are not allowed out without guard. Have to cope with lighting fire and getting breakfast – porridge which has to be stirred all the time – tear my hair – lose my temper with offending Russian who comes in for stores when I am at the most preoccupied stage of my manoeuvres on the stove. However, manage somehow. Rest of the day goes smoothly – kitchen uncommonly clean owing to the efforts of Bender and Luschke, our two 'enemies', at present my best friends.

Saturday 20 January Reni

Fawcett and Turner arrived from Odessa, bringing some equipment and mails. Delightful mail, including two parcels – book and sleeping socks and gloves, also lots of newspapers. F and T have taken nearly a week to come from Odessa. Weather intensely cold – snowed nearly all day.

Fitzroy *Letter to father Friday 26 January*

I expect the HQ of the Hospitals in London had only heard of Camp B when they referred to the unit as being in Odessa. They returned there with a Serbian hospital at the beginning of December, and have been leading a more or less peaceful and blameless existence ever since. So peaceful, in fact, that Dr Inglis has got suspicious and has flown off to Odessa to enquire into the matter. What are left of the Transport are also there – in fact both they and Camp B have been indulging in the absurd luxury of rows – so I am thankful to have been so far removed from them. We are usually too breathless and always too sleepy to do more than grumble – a very British safety valve, isn't it? Besides, Dr Inglis is a remarkable leader.

Elsie [Bowerman] is making the pudding for supper, and chanting in a doleful voice:

> The jam has given out;
> The marmalade has given out;
> The butter has given out;
> The margarine has given out.

Sad voice of an invalid: And what are we going to eat?

Elsie (sternly): Bread and *rice.*

The country is just a white glare, and floweth not with milk and honey. To cheer us we hear there is better news – what a thrill it would be were our next move an advance.

Transport Petrograd

Hodges *End of January*[17]

Petrograd was as crowded as Odessa, and we were shunted into a side platform and allowed to remain in our carriage home for the time being. One evening Donisthorpe returned to the train in high fettle. She had found an English woman doctor who was running an epidemic and surgical hospital on the Galician front, under a Russian society called the Union of Zemstva. This unit had been promised ambulances, and the doctor was on her way to England to collect funds and drivers. D had told her that some of us might be available, and after a good deal of weighing of pros and cons, four of us decided to join this unit with D instead of going on to England.[18]

Transport Odessa

Birkbeck *Sunday 21 January*

Went to church. The snow is beaten hard as hard, and the sledges swing from side to side recklessly. The air is ajingle with the tinkle of a hundred bells. Edwards and I went to lunch at Franconi's and then in a sledge to Arcadia. We went along at a good pace, till we got to the cliffs overlooking the Black Sea. Here we left the *droshki* and ran down the cliffs to the rocks. This year the sea is not frozen, but the rocks were covered in ice and the most wonderful icicles of frozen spray. It was too cold to play about, and we returned the same way.

(Ysabel Birkbeck)

Monday 22 January

I have to take hospital stores to Reni, and spent the morning getting a pass from the Russian Red Cross. My French was utterly exhausted after three hours of grimly insisting that tomorrow would *not* do. Finally I found the right administrator in one of the rooms I strayed into. He was just going off to lunch, he said, but I absolutely refused to let him feed till I had my pass. The pass came in two minutes and we left together. He was very amused at my insistence, and said he had waited four days for his. As he spoke English perfectly, I was able to tell him what I felt about it all. Like so many of his countrymen, Ilyachenko has spent a year or so in America. It must be rather a shock to such as he, for they are as far apart as the poles in temperament.

At 6 Edwards and I set off with one enormous bale of pyjamas, my bulging valise, a canvas bag of food, and our two haversacks. At 9 the inevitable kind official came and rushed us into a train which we only discovered later was not for Reni...

Hospital A Reni

Turner *Sunday 21 January*

Dr Inglis was pleased to see us but rather unfortunately put us on to get breakfast this morning. We were just dumped down in the kitchen knowing nothing about times of the meals or the whereabouts of the stores. Dr Inglis is quite a dear, but knows nothing about cooking. In speaking of the various meals to be provided, she said, apropos of the night sisters' breakfast, 'It's so easy to toss a pancake, isn't it?' We saw ourselves solemnly tossing pancakes with first and second breakfasts still in the kitchen, and the lunch just going on.

Monday 22 January

Last night we went to a dance given by a Cossack regiment quartered here. It was sad having nothing but nailed boots. I couldn't dance, so had to content myself with being a spectator. They dance ripping Russian mazurkas, and of course they are just tiptop when the man has spurs to clank. They had collected quite a number of Red Cross sisters. A dance at the front is rather amusing – no mufti present except one girl in green. I don't know who she was, as Reni is evacuated.

My own best-beloved dog, Sammy, here at A. He has been adopted by Murphy, but he recognised me at once, and lives on my bed. Murphy has also got a kitten called Pushkin, a great dear. Sammy and Pushkin play together in a most attractive way. This afternoon Sammy and I went out chasing crows, our old game of Ismail days.

Fawcett *Letter Tuesday 23 January*[19]

Today has been a good day in the kitchen. Yesterday everyone was late for everything – breakfast started at 7 a.m. and the last supper was at 9 p.m. Today the fire went properly, the lunch was good, and people were more punctual, so we all feel more cheerful.

The guns have been very silent the last few days, and it is possible to go to Galatz, which Dr Inglis left about three weeks ago as they thought the town was going to be bombarded. From our house we can see right across the Danube, across miles of marsh to a gorgeous range of hills. The Bulgars are supposed to be amongst them. The actual Russian first line trenches are at the top of the hill behind the hospital – so that we are really in 'No Man's Land'.

Turner *Tuesday 23 January*

This afternoon Fawcett, Brown, Jenkins and I went to the baths – gorgeous. One small room where we dressed, and the bathroom, also quite small, and so full of steam that one can't see across the room. At one end there is a bench and some attempt at a couch effect, and at the other four large boilers and a cold water tank. One gets little wooden tubs of water for washing purposes – there is no real bath about it. One stays there until reduced to an almost fainting condition, then staggers out into the cooler atmosphere of the next room, and thence out to the gorgeous snow. Matron suggested it was very dangerous, but Dr Inglis insists on us all having baths once a week at the unit's expense. Not much compulsion needed.

Reni I suppose is always something of a naval and military headquarters. There is a swanky building on the quay with six balls in front of it under a painted slatted green and yellow roof. Behind this are little houses, evidently for the housing of odd officers, etc., who pass through; a smithy and a bath, and then there are gardens with terraces overlooking the Danube, and fountains and a band stand and a sort of toy building with painted wood, where evidently refreshments are sold in peacetime – now, of course, there is nothing doing. The Dobrudga mountains look simply ripping with snow, and from time to time we can hear firing out beyond Galatz. The admiral's yacht and the *George* and other boats have all disappeared, and only one or two barges remain hastily loading with stuff for the Front.

Inglis *Report 24 January* [20]

Fortunately we have solved the question of the wood supply, thanks to the kindness of the commandant of the 'Expedition'[21] at Reni. It took about three days to solve this question of meat, wood, and water. Reni itself is quite a small place, and it is only its geographical position that gives it importance now. The Expedition has made practically a new village for itself on the docks. There was no Intendance, where one usually gets supplies, and if it had not been for Captain Yermakov, who is head of the Expedition and an old and tried friend of ours, I don't know what we should have done.

However, the doctor in charge of the Evacuation Hospital (a kind of clearing station) at the railway, was bent on our staying, and things gradually cleared up. We were very amused, however – the day we *promised* to have the hospital ready, when everybody was hard at it putting things into shape, and the wood and water problem was only being temporarily solved by the kindness of individual officers who lent us water-carts and gave us wood, two officers of the 30th Cossacks arrived on the scene with an invitation to a *concert*! And the 'premier line' seven versts off, and the guns booming all the time! I accepted conditionally on there being no wounded, and at 7 that evening, the majority of the unit off duty, with Dr Corbett in charge, went off to the concert, which ended in a dance, and they got back at 1 a.m. just as the first batch of wounded arrived. They [the 30th Cossacks] invited us to another one the next week too.

Those first days we did not know how long the hospital would remain at Reni. Our own guns were firing from the hill above us and we saw Galatz on fire. Our orders were to stay until ordered to go by the doctor in charge of the Evacuation and then to go to Benderi.

The hospital at Reni is being run with Russian Red Cross money, and a clerk has been attached to us – Captain Bergmann, who is very useful in many ways, besides accounts. The Russian sister has left. She was a nice little thing but not very strong, and knew nothing about keeping accounts. She helped us a great deal, however, as she knew personally such numbers of Russian officers. All her brothers are in the army. She met a colonel she knew in Galatz and got us enough wood for a week, and at Reni she got us a sheep a day out of another acquaintance, until the meat problem was solved.

Turner *Thursday 25 January*
This morning Holme, Pleister, Bangham, Hedges and Walker-Brown turned up with a bit of a mail, and orders for me to go back by the train that brought them along.

Friday 26 January

After lunch Hedges, Fawcett and I went to find the sanitary train I am to go back on. It had moved five *versts* down the line. The Russians generally have lunch at about 2, so we hoped to arrive just after the meal. However, we found they were lunching at 3 p.m., and were made to stay for four courses and *chai*, not to mention two glasses of lovely lavender-coloured vodka. The only place where one can get drunk in Russia, except on methylated spirits, is on a sanitary train; they get vodka as a medicine. It is very nice warming stuff on a snowy day like this – and very like brandy, except for the colour.

Tonight I am sleeping down at the cottage by the baths with Hedges and Fawcett. It is awfully jolly. I love the ten-minute walk through the snow to bed.

Saturday 27 January

Slept very happily at the cottage. Breakfast very late down there this morning at 8.30. Matron came along and I asked if I could have a job. She jumped at me, and I spent a gorgeous morning at the Privia Lista. First I held two compound fractures while they were being dressed. In the middle of the second I had to be shot out and stood on my head in the corridor, but after ten minutes I went back and behaved properly.

Sister Wilcox is ripping. She let me do two dressings and quite a lot of bandaging myself. Russians scream all the time, too, except a few awfully plucky ones who realise how unnecessary it is.

After lunch Edwards and Birkbeck arrived with a mail, and we all went straight off to the baths, I getting back at 2.30 to help in the Privia Lista again. After tea the head of the sanitary train and a sister turned up to say the train was probably leaving tonight. Hastily we packed our bed bundles, and at about 6 p.m. trundled off amid many goodbyes, with Theodore and two Russian orderlies carrying our luggage. Sammy also followed us, and though we had to tramp about nine *versts* along the line in the dark, ploughing through the snow, he came on with his little sore foot to the train, and I bribed a soldier to carry him back to the hospital. Dogs are not permitted in the Transport, and I'm under military discipline now.

The hospital train is most wonderful, half a *verst* long, with mess room, operation theatre, Privia Lista, wards, and first-class carriages for the personnel. The mess is more like a pleasure yacht than anything I have struck yet; the chef is first-rate. The train is endowed, like most hospital trains, by a big bug, in this case Prince Konstantin Konstantinovich. His monogram is painted on the carriage, and the sisters have brooches with the same device.

Fitzroy *Saturday 27 January Reni*[22]

Busy day; a rumour about that Braila has been retaken, and fried eggs on toast for supper! The line between here and Galatz is under fire, which explains why our convoys always arrive at night.[23]

Monday 29 January Reni

Mrs Haverfield turned up late. She has been at Galatz all this time visiting the front. The Braila rumour is quite untrue, but nevertheless the situation is quite encouraging. The line is held on the Sereth, and they say that all the German troops have been withdrawn from this front.

Some of our men were evacuated today. They go in the same open carts even in this awful weather. It's an appalling thought. They would hardly be given so much as straw and blankets if we did not send our own. On one occasion during the worst of this terrible weather one of the aforementioned carts arrived, and when we went to carry in the wounded we found only two bodies frozen stiff under coverings that were just a sheet of ice. They had only about a quarter of a mile to travel to reach us. This may serve as an example of the conditions under which the men fight over here, with no hope of a commission of enquiry.

Fawcett *Monday 29 January*[24]

On Monday Holme and Hedges, two of the Transport, arrived, Holme to help in the kitchen and so relieve me for the hospital, and Hedges also to help in the wards; and Turner has been allowed to go back to Odessa to begin her work with the Transport – poor kid, she was sick of the kitchen and was thankful to get away. I miss her most awfully.

We have quite a nice hospital here – there are three wards, one large and two small. There are about fifty patients. I have been in hospital now for three days and like it immensely. Hedges and I are in the big ward with Sisters Cliver and Hopkin.

Dr Inglis left about two days after we arrived, for Odessa; she wants to find out if the Serbs really want us. She does not mean to stay here and pander to the Russians.

Transport Reni to Odessa

Birkbeck *Tuesday 30 January*

Spent the day either jolting reluctantly along slowly towards Odessa, or playing in the snow. It has hardly stopped snowing since it first began ten days ago; now the snow is knee-deep and the peasants' carts are all on runners.

(Ysabel Birkbeck)

During the night we only travelled five *versts*. They are clearing the line by hand before us – but came with a second engine. We hardly progress at all. Further north the snow is far deeper, but they are prepared for it there. Here so far it is a poor show – they have no snow plough.

Thursday 1 February Odessa

Back to the garage. No 1 touring car is up, body and all, and she looks very smart. Studdy is being taken down, and high time too. The garage was almost impossibly cold: everything we touched stung our fingers till they were too numb to feel... The Black Sea is freezing far out from the shore, and the wind that blows off it is agony.

Sunday 4 February

Colder still: 37 degrees of frost. Spent a long day under Studdy with Turner, scratch, scratching mud into our eyes, and we warbled our songs to the accompaniment of our grammy and to the distraction of the others.

In the evening wounded were coming in sledge after sledge, packed in straw, the very bad cases in huge wooden boxes. They say fighting has pretty well ceased all along the line. In this weather stores cannot be brought up, and food is unavailable.

Mrs Haverfield and Onslow returned from Galatz at 1 a.m. They want us to sign on for a further six months. Turner and Edwards are not being advised to; I am. Mrs H has to be here to receive eighteen drivers. Had a hell of a time, but decided to stick it out.

Monday 5 February

Best news of the stunt. I am to be given a few weeks' leave to go home with the others, and sign on again to come over with the new draft. Carriage paid both ways. The office has lost its reason...

CHAPTER 9
An Eventful Spring

The danger to Reni having been considerably reduced by the transfer of the German troops from the Dobrudga, Hospital A was able to settle down to work as a base hospital for the next seven months. Although the severe winter caused a lull in hostilities,[1] there was sporadic shelling from the troops across the river, particularly in the Galatz area, where a small detachment of British Armoured Cars had been left to support the Fourth Siberian Corps. These skirmishes and the periodical bombing raids on Reni caused enough casualties to keep the hospital busy, and there were also maladies and long-term patients recovering from surgery. Hospital B in Odessa, where there were other base hospitals, did not get much work, and Dr Inglis agitated for it to be sent nearer the front where it might be put to better use. Even when it had been agreed in principle that this would be done, there were inexplicable delays which caused their orders to be altered and their departure to be postponed. It seemed either that the Russian Red Cross general was uncertain of the immediate future, or that he had other things on his mind.

It is not clear from their records how much the Scottish Women knew initially of the political life of Russia. Although some had made great strides with the basic practical language of the hospital, few had acquired sufficient linguistic sophistication to conduct political conversations, and until their Russian was more fluent their information necessarily came through conversation with German- or French-speaking officers and from their own observation. They probably knew very little in their first few months: in 1916 topics of conversation on the south-western front had been the retreat, the behaviour of the Roumanians, and the conduct of the war. But in the new year, as they began to meet Russian officers socially, to travel in small groups, and to mix with the English colony in Odessa, many of them heard rumours of revolution – whether fear of a popular revolution or plans for a palace revolution,[2] they do not say. Certainly they heard talk which some regarded as too dangerous to record in their diaries or letters.

As it turned out, at least three separate revolutionary movements were gathering momentum, and as the women learned more of Russia's social and political life, they foresaw trouble. A number of forces tending towards revolution were deeply embedded in Russia's complex history, but the three most clearly discernible were an aristocratic concern about Rasputin's influence over the Tsar; a long-standing political agitation for a more democratic form of government; and the pressures of the socio-economic conditions of the peasantry and proletariat. All three thrusts were accelerated by the conditions of the war, and were soon to be visibly expressed.

The cumulative desperation of a group of troubled aristocrats culminated in the melodramatic assassination of Rasputin on 29 December 1917.[3] This was the first revolutionary event to come to the women's attention, as distinct from the talk which they had heard, and was a direct response to criticism and insinuations in the Duma about the influence of 'dark forces' close to the Tsar, of which Hospital B had been told on their journey from Ismail.[4] Although the aims of the conservative Prince Yusupov and his accomplices were very different from those of either the Constitutional Democrats or any of the Socialist parties, the murder of an influential adviser so close to the imperial household appeared to the Scottish Women and to many of their Russian friends to be a startlingly revolutionary act. Yusupov claimed that it was meant to be a blow for autocracy, aimed at restoring the authority of the Tsar, which had been dissipated by Rasputin's influence over the Tsaritsa, and by her attempts to promote the appointment of government ministers friendly towards Rasputin, and allegedly pro-German.[5] Certainly the assassination seems to have met with the approval of the officers with whom the women discussed it, and with the sympathy of the women themselves.

A less personal force which had for many decades threatened the stability of the old order was the growing pressure for a more liberal form of government. In spite of a number of concessions won since the emancipation of the peasantry in 1861, the political system was in 1916 still highly undemocratic. The Council of Ministers was appointed by the Tsar, to whom each minister was directly responsible, so that it did not operate as a council, but as a collection of individuals whose term of office depended entirely on imperial favour. From its inception in 1905 the Duma, the elected parliament, had possessed very few real powers. It had no independent authority to pass laws, and was dominated by the landed gentry;[6] it could be, and had been, prorogued by the Tsar's decree, and was always under threat of dissolution. In 1916 however, within the Duma, the several reform-minded parties formed an alliance known as the Progressive Bloc, which continued to oppose the autocratic government, and also to operate outside the Duma through the *zemstva*, the local bodies of rural self-government.[7]

In addition to the political dissatisfaction, and partly underlying it, were serious socio-economic problems which had existed in Russia for centuries, and which were compounded by the war. For the Scottish Women, impressions were initially dominated by the manifest patriotism of the Russian soldiers, by the enthusiastic welcome they gave to their foreign allies, and by their unquestioning obedience to higher authorities. At first this had seemed right and proper for a country at war, and in October 1916 Fawcett had been impressed with the way the traffic had given way to their car because a Russian officer, Captain Bryson, was with them. During the first retreat, Fitzroy expressed no distress at Bryson's rough treatment of the driver who refused to take the lorry party to Hirsova: officers were permitted to strike soldiers, who were expected to stand at attention while the punishment was inflicted. In the diaries the first criticism of such blind obedience appears in Fawcett's entry of 17 February, when she describes the plight of the soldier who obeyed his unreasonable orders to travel over the thawing marshes. Gradually the Scottish Women were becoming more critical.

As they grew more used to their Russian patients, and better able to communicate with them, they also realised the widespread poverty and backwardness in the country. They noted with some dismay that the pension of a rouble a month which went with their St George's Medal was regarded as a lifelong sufficiency by the patients, and they were horrified when they learned that the compensation due to a mutilated soldier was a government licence to beg.[8] Several diarists comment on the common soldiers' lack of boots, the most basic item of equipment for infantry. It was also apparent that many of the patients had not heard from their families since their conscription two years before – could not hear, because neither they nor their families could read or write – and that they had very little social or financial security. There had recently been industrial disputes: in 1912 there had been 2,032 strikes,[9] and although industrial action had been suspended in the early wave of patriotism at the outbreak of war, the grievances remained, and many were plain even to foreigners. By 1917 two-and-a-half years of war had taken their toll on the economy, and the government had resorted to raising more foreign loans and printing more rouble notes. In an age when inflation was little understood, even the recently-arrived Scottish Women could see that money was buying progressively less, that food was short in the cities and at the front, and that the railways were not capable of moving passengers, munitions, food and fodder where they were needed. They may not have known that the Social Revolutionaries, the Social Democrats, and especially the Bolsheviks, were working systematically to harness the natural discontent over these problems, but they were certainly aware of many of the problems. If the hospital staff at Reni were at first surprised by the news of the revolution, they were quick to welcome it as necessary and justified. Those in Petrograd and Odessa were not even surprised – they had heard it talked of, and seen it coming.

Hospital A Reni and Odessa

Fawcett *Diary Sunday 4 February*

Quite a quiet week. Mrs Haverfield and Onslow turned up for a day and night, and left Thursday for Odessa. Dr Inglis is expected back soon; we are longing for letters...

We have one patient who squawls all the time. He is a bad fractured femur case. My pet case – 'Baby', a poor boy with an amputated leg and dysentery – is just at his last gasp. I hope that he won't last the night.

Monday 5 February

We were so sad this morning – poor Baby died. Last night at about 8.30 forty-five new patients arrived – the poor night sisters had 'some night'. Dr Corbett was up till 5 or 6, also Lewis, Wotherspoon, and Captain Bergmann, our little interpreter-secretary person.

It has been thawing hard all day – the snow which blew into the loft of this house is now melting and coming through the ceiling of the mess room.

Fitzroy *Monday 5 February*[10]

Forty-four admissions last night, but light cases for the most part. The Bulgars are only six kilometres from the farther bank of the Danube, and here we are between the first and second lines of defence. What fun for us when they start bombarding! A hostile aeroplane was over today.

Fawcett *Diary Tuesday 6 February*

Quite a peaceful day. Writing on duty in the ward. A sharp frost last night, and no more thaw today. The official cat was lost, and found shut in the attic. Broadbent has made some holes in the roof of the house to let the air in to air the clothes – the result, heaps of snow which are now thawing and coming through the mess room ceiling.

Thursday 8 February

Hospital in the morning – fifty patients were evacuated yesterday, as food is running short and there is no wood. Went foraging with Sister Hopkin and bought a ham and 6 lbs of dripping – most useful stuff in this god-forsaken hole where there is neither butter nor jam. As we came back, the Germans started to shell the station at Reni – we heard the discharge and the shell whistling through the air, and then the explosion. One shell fell about two hundred yards beyond the station. We are about a mile away the other side.

Bowerman *Diary Wednesday 7 February*
At last Dr Laird arrives from Odessa bringing mails and messages from Dr I. Very disappointed that the latter has not come, as she would be sure to let us start for home now. Fitzroy is to be allowed to go to Odessa to have her teeth attended to, and we do so want to go with her. To add insult to injury Fitzroy is to be sent to B Hospital, which is now going to Bukovina – Dr Corbett is also going. We are all fed up. Murphy and I went to see the two travellers off by sanitary train in the evening – very very cold – drove down to the station in cart over the snow, and thought as we did it that for once we were living up to the reputation for enduring hardships, etc., which our various families have imagined for us. Very sad at saying goodbye to Fitzroy, but hope her teeth will take a long time so that we can meet in Odessa next week.

Fitzroy *Letter to mother Thursday 8 February Train to Odessa*
Of course Mr Broderick was shown *les latrines* – wait till you visit Russia. They almost take precedence of the wounded as a subject of conversation of absorbing interest. In fact our much-tried sanitary inspector (she's a pioneer, by the way) says she should be far more suitably named lavatory attendant.

Dr Corbett and I are having a peaceful and comfy journey, and it's rather fun getting a doctor to myself and making her talk shop – which she does very kindly even to humble me. If it wasn't for leaving all my friends and the abominable prospect of having to go to B for a while, I should be quite bobbish. As it is I'm horribly blue... Anyway if it has to be, I expect the Bukovina will be interesting. The sisters at A said they would have got up a protest had they thought it would be the slightest use; the orderlies, I regret to say, counselled rank insubordination and mutiny. However, here's poor me, and there's no one I like in B save one small sister, and I shall be the only orderly. A bitter world! Still, I'm to have my choice of changing when the new lot come.

Bowerman *Diary Tuesday 13 February*
Dr Inglis suddenly arrives from Odessa with news that we cannot go home as the way across the North Sea is blocked owing to violent submarine activity after the severance of diplomatic relations [between Germany and America.][11] We determine to go to Odessa and see for ourselves if we cannot get through. Brown and I win consent to do this –

if unable to go we are to have a fortnight's holiday and return to Reni! Dr P in great haste to be off too.

Wednesday 14 February

No sanitary train available. Dr Potter decides to go at once by passenger train – we wait one more day for sanitary train, also that Hedges may travel with us. She is returning to Odessa, and probably to England as well, as there will be no more work for the Transport for the next few months. Mrs Haverfield and Onslow have started for England to collect new people to come out and drive the cars.

Fitzroy *Letter 14 February Odessa*

It's too wonderful living in this land of daily posts. Your letter of 14 January has just come...

I am having an excellent time here, and feel rather ashamed of myself, as you are probably picturing me being a noble woman under the worst possible conditions. The dentist is doing his lurid worst, but at least he's a really good man, and a painless, if toothless, future awaits me. As a matter of fact he has only pulled out one, and I feel thankful I came when I did. And best of all, I am to go back to A Camp at Reni, and shall be travelling with Mrs Milne, so all is as it should be.

No women are allowed to go home at present, by order of Sir George Buchanan and by reason of submarines, so there is much weeping and gnashing of teeth amongst the few remaining Transport. As a unit they have completely broken up, and they are all for home. Miss Marx too, I believe, though I am told one or two new drivers are coming out to take charge of the cars which will be attached to each hospital and under the direct command of Dr Inglis and Chesney. This is only a rumour; another rumour which has been afloat for some time speaks of the entire unit being moved to Salonica – via London! – if the remains of the Serb Divisions are sent there. I hope this does not happen – it would seem a terrible waste of time.

From you two letters today, and also some soup, a lovely hanky, chocolate – of which the censor was kind enough to leave me three bits – boot laces and Oxo. Thank you ever so much. I am so glad you got the photographs in the end. From Father's description I should gather the photograph in the *Sunday Pictorial*[12] was one I took on the retreat – which encourages me to hope my films and the parcel got home safely.

Fawcett *Diary Wednesday 14 February Reni*

Holme and I went for a ride yesterday afternoon, but my horse bolted with me as soon as we got outside, so it was rather spoilt. After galloping about a mile we rolled over in the snow. Luckily it was quite soft, so we neither of us got hurt, but I ricked my knee mounting again.

Friday 16 February

Dr Potter started on Thursday – Bowerman and Co. on Saturday. My left knee has been getting more painful ever since Thursday, and today I am staying in bed. Dr Inglis orders rest and fomentation – very dull indeed, but I have a bed by the window, where I can bask in the sun all the afternoon, and I have several nice books to read and many letters to write and stockings to darn. So I should not be dull.

We have had enemy aeroplanes over for the last three or four days, but they only seem to come for scouting purposes. The Russian guns blaze away at them, but so far have not brought one down. We also have searchlights on us every night. The Russians have put barbed wire entanglements on the Danube, which is now frozen, and have two battalions of Cossacks on the further side of the river.

Saturday 17 February

We had a heated discussion this morning as to what day it was – it rested between Friday, Saturday, and Sunday. Had a rotten night, but my knee is distinctly better today, so hope to get up soon. Captain Bergmann is going – we are all awfully sorry, as he has been a brick. He fell out with Dr Inglis. Goodness knows what will happen to us when he has gone. We have a little Russian sister with us now who speaks English, French and Russian.

Letter 17 February

The Danube is frozen across, and it is possible to walk to the other side if you go on planks where the ice is thin. It is frightfully uneven – I think I told you about the icebergs that have been floating downstream for three weeks or so, and now we imagine they must have got jammed somewhere, and so the whole lot have come to a standstill and been frozen together.

There have been a good many casualties amongst the soldiers marching over the frozen marshes. One of our sanitars nearly came to grief the other day. He had orders to take a horse and cart by the marsh road to Galatz, and there await Captain Bergmann, our Russian administrator. When he got along the road he found it to be practically impassable, and awfully dangerous – but being a Russian soldier and accustomed to blind obedience, he still went on instead of taking the longer and safer road along the hills, and very nearly got drowned. As it happened, Captain

Bergmann only got as far as the Pruth, which is about a quarter of the way, got a ducking, and came home again.

The mountains the other side of the Danube are looking their best – they are covered with snow, except just at the top where it has melted.

Diary Monday 19 February

Knee much better; have been for a hop. Lieut. Hunter of the Armoured Cars was here this morning. He called on me in my bedroom. Little snow.

Bowerman *Sunday 18 February Odessa*

Disembarked from train about 9 a.m. – felt just like soldiers back from the front – the first time Brown and I had been back since we left Odessa in October. Delicious coffee and rolls at the restaurant – drove in sleighs to the hospital. Found B Hospital have not left yet – somewhat chilly reception from Dr Chesney – acrid remarks apropos of sheepskin hats. No one has succeeded in getting through to England since Dr I left. Brown and I resolve to try our luck with the Consul tomorrow. Tea with the Harrises – it feels odd to be back in real civilisation.

Fitzroy *Letter Sunday 19 February Odessa*

Bowerman and Brown arrived yesterday *en route* for England, and are even now wrestling with the Consul, who declares he can let no women through. But I think in the end they will go – it is important for both of them that they should. Dr Potter left early and suddenly one morning before I had time to see her, so will be carrying no films of mine; I am glad my others have got home safely and are being useful.

Miss Marx has been very kind, and we had a great evening at the opera. There is a niece of old Lady Birkbeck amongst the remaining Transport. The political gossip is lurid – how glad I am we are not working here and victim to all these rumours...

I am *frightfully* smart in my new uniform.

Tuesday 20 February Odessa to Reni[13]

We left Odessa about 6 p.m. and have sixteen packages and cases of hospital stuff to steer safely to Reni. About 12 midnight we got ourselves and our baggage into a sanitary train at the goods station, where a little Jewish man, with wavy golden hair and tight mauve mufti, made himself most agreeable in French.

Wednesday 21 February

We saw a wolf quite close to the railway line, and so feel we have beheld true Russia at last! It is pathetic; they only give us one meal a day, and we brought no provisions. Also, I did think I was looking my very, very best, in all the glories of a new uniform and Odessa-waved hair. But to no purpose. The mauve Jew became very confidential this morning, and gazing at my new, new tunic, said mournfully that it was sad indeed that we wore such clothes, for was it not the duty of every woman at least to *try* and look her best!

Milne *Saturday 24 February Reni*

Arrived at Reni at 6 this morning – Fitzroy is now away to the hospital to tell them we have arrived, and to send the carts to fetch the luggage, so I am waiting for Fitz to come back. She was in a vile temper over her bed bundle – she is very easily upset.

Monday 26 February

Very busy and dead tired – I am alone in the kitchen, but for two adorable Austrian orderlies – perfect dears – so I am very happy speaking German and loving my enemies.

Fawcett *Diary Saturday 24 February Night duty*

Waited an hour for a bath this morning, and did not get to bed till nearly one o'clock. Have been expecting an attack this evening. Captain Bergmann has been on duty with his revolver ready – I don't know what he thought he could do. It is quite thrilling waiting. There are Turks and Bulgars on this part of the front, and there is a German Army Corps between Galatz and Fundeni. This is the hardest winter that has been known for seventy years, and the marshes, which are really impassable, are now frozen hard, and promise to stay frozen – hence the expected attack. We now have a Russian searchlight near us – there have been two enemy ones opposite us for a long time.

Fitzroy and Mrs Milne arrived with letters this morning.

Hospital B Odessa

Rendel *Letter to Ray 23 February*

Here we are still stuck fast in Odessa and in a state bordering on homicidal mania. Every day we expect to get our orders but they never come. Our only hope is that Miss Henderson will arrive with parcels and news from England. There is nothing to do all day except smoke and play patience. We can't even go home as the Consul has orders not to allow people to go as the crossing is too dangerous.

Dr C has gone this morning to interview a certain Prince Somebody about our journey. With any luck she may succeed in stirring him up. We can't go until they have got us horses and waggons and that they won't or can't do. Until we go I have nothing to write about except my own temper which is in a threadbare condition. I am simply longing for an armchair and a fire and some books. Considering all things, outwardly we keep our tempers in very good control but it is a great and increasing effort.

We have for a long time now had no marmalade or coffee. But I suppose Miss H will bring out such things with her.

Hospital A Reni

Fawcett *Diary Sunday 25 February Night duty*
No attack last night. Unit went to another party – this one given by the Black Sea Dragoons. Slept until 2.30 today, and went for a good walk this evening. Have just had a most interesting talk with Dr Inglis about the starting of the Scottish Women and the difficulties they had to contend with. Just read quite a good article about us by Miss Henderson in *The Common Cause* of 5 January.[14]

Inglis *Letter 5 March*[15]
Should Hospital B be considered a separate unit? Personally I think not, because though in many ways Dr Chesney is a splendid head, – conscientious, and a thoroughly good doctor, – she is so uncertain in her temper, and takes such strong dislikes, that she is apt to be unfair to certain people in her unit. This matters less when I can transfer them to my own, – but might make great difficulties if she was entirely responsible. The unit now is thoroughly happy and working well, but I have had to remove Miss Fawcett and Turner and Sister Jenkins, because they were all miserable, – 3 people out of the 12 she had with her in the field hospital! I am writing quite frankly for the information of the London Committee. As I brought Dr Chesney out, for my own sake I must make it clear that I should never have recommended her as head of a unit. As assistant to anybody she likes she could go anywhere...

This brings us face to face with another difficulty. Dr Chesney and Mrs Haverfield cannot bear one another! And they are neither of them people who can hide their dislikes, though they have tried heroically. Both Mrs Haverfield and Dr Chesney are such bricks, and it seems absurd not to be able to make it work. But on the other hand there are enough difficulties without having personal antipathies to cope with!

Here we have had all sorts of gaieties – every regiment which comes entertains us in some way – till, I confess, I got very tired of it! But the girls enjoyed it. Personally I am thankful it is Lent at last! The entertainments were most varied, from a regimental concert in a dug-out to a very smart concert and dance which the Black Sea Horse gave. (Isn't the Black Sea Horse a delightful name?) The concert in the dug-out was most interesting. One company was entertaining the rest of the regiment. I had no idea the Russian soldier had so much fun in him. So the slackness of the work hasn't bored us; we have got to like our patients immensely.

Fawcett *Diary Monday 26 February*
Broke a tooth at breakfast this morning, so got Dr Laird to pull it out for me. She funked horribly – I began to wonder who was going to have the tooth out.

Sunday 4 March
We had an inspection yesterday by the head sanitary inspector of the army or the front or something. He came round the wards and hunted for lice on the men. The patients were quite clean, except for one man who had one louse in poor Fitzroy's ward. However, the sanitars were quite dirty enough to make up for the cleanliness of the patients.

Inglis *Report 4 March*[16]
...it was indeed a thorough inspection. The men's pyjama suits were taken off and searched for lice; the sheets were turned up, and the mattresses beaten to see if they were dusty; the food was tasted and the orderlies' rooms raided. The report eventually ran that the patients were very clean, well cared for medically, and well nursed; but that the condition of the orderlies was disgraceful. This report is absolutely true. But the condition of the orderlies shall no longer remain 'disgraceful'. I am afraid I rather thought they were not my business, as Captain Bergmann always said he was in charge of the orderlies. But during his inspection the Chief of the Medical Staff suddenly turned to me and asked, 'Do you hold yourself responsible for the condition of the orderlies?' I answered, 'Yes, and next time you come you will not find a single louse,' at which he was very delighted and amused.

Fawcett *Diary 4 March*
There was to have been another inspection today by the GOC of this front, but like many other things in this country, it never came off. Captain Bergmann says, 'These visitations – I do not like them; they are not agreeable.' Captain Bergmann starts for Bolgrad tomorrow. Sisters Cliver and Hopkin are due to arrive from Odessa.

Tuesday 6 March

The sisters arrived from Odessa, bringing a mail, sweets, and cigarettes. Alas! I only had one letter from England. Natasha Harris has just received a letter from me – posted from near Medgidia, presumably Bulbul Mic – which travelled all the way to England and back to Odessa again. Turner seems to have enjoyed life at Odessa. They were leaving for Petrograd the day after she wrote.

Fitzroy *Letter 4 March*

I wonder if you have any suggestion of spring at home yet? Here the snow gets deeper every day, and the ice harder. Outside our gates there is a drift well over twelve feet high – and we *dream* of spring. Not that we'd mind if the sun shone every day as it is doing now – but it doesn't, and the blizzards are terrific. As soon as the spring comes Mrs Milne and I are going flower-hunting with zest, and I hope to get you some seeds or plants. She is a frightfully keen gardener.

Marx was most exceedingly kind to me at Odessa, and I liked her so much. I feel had she been out from the beginning it might have made the whole difference to the Transport. She said she was going to write and tell you I was alive and no shadow. Birkbeck was contemplating going home when I left and coming out with the new drivers. She promised to visit you, and (should she come out again at once, which I doubt) to bring out a parcel.

Hospital B Odessa

Rendel *Letter to Ray 5 March*

We are still here – doing nothing. Apparently there is no fighting going on and there are also all kinds of black rumours going about. We heard some very interesting gossip yesterday about people in high places, but I don't dare to repeat it. We have had no letters dated later than 31 January but they say that boats are running again. No Miss Henderson!

They say now that there is an epidemic of typhus and that they are bringing in 600 cases a day so we may get a chance to do some work after all.

Hospital A Reni

Inglis *Report 6 March*[17]

One case of typhus appeared in the wards ten days after admission. It had evidently been contracted outside. It speaks well for the care and cleanliness of the sisters that not another single case has occurred, even though the patient was in the wards for ten days after his temperature began to rise. This was owing to the fact that the rash did not appear until the tenth day, and we could not diagnose the case.

There have been great difficulties here owing to the shortage of wood and the difficulty of obtaining pure water. Captain Bergmann, the representative of the Red Cross here, secured wood for us in various ways, and eventually made an arrangement with a Cossack regiment to cut wood for us on the other side of the Danube. We send our carts over the river to bring the wood back, but it is green and difficult to burn.

The weather has been bitterly cold. One snow storm nearly cut the house off from the hospital owing to the great drifts between. I wish we could have got for you a photograph of the staff struggling over to roll call in the morning in their top boots, short skirts, and peaked *bashlyks* over their heads. The Danube has been frozen over, and the carts for wood crossed over on the ice. That is another photograph I wished I could have got: streams of men carrying wood across the river. They say that it has not been frozen for seventy years.

Captain Bergmann has been with us now about a month. He is very keen and interested in the hospital, and anxious to help us. But the question of his duties will have to be settled by General Krupensky when he comes in a few days. The Sister Marie who came to us in Braila left us when Captain Bergmann came. Since then Sister Vera Kolesnikov has been attached to us. She is an able and pleasant little woman, and I very much hope she will be allowed to stay. She speaks English beautifully.

Fawcett *Diary Saturday 10 March*
It has been thawing hard, and the night sisters are very sorry for themselves, having to walk up from the Expedition in the dark. We don't waste any sympathy on them. The Captain has returned from Bolgrad, and General Krupensky is expected in a day of two. We have the two small wards at the hospital full. There are two Armoured Car men at the Expedition; they are waiting for the ice to break up so that they can get their yacht[18] along to Galatz.

Our hospital is between the Russian first line trenches and the enemy, who are on the other side of the river. We occasionally hear firing, now that the weather is finer.

Tuesday 13 March
The thaw continues. Three new patients in today. General Krupensky was here yesterday afternoon; he arranged that the Captain should leave us. Guns have been blazing away all day.

209

Wednesday 14 March

Great excitement: we have just heard that Baghdad has been taken by the British Army. One of the Russian doctors sent up to tell us.

More firing today. We are expecting a huge bombardment some day soon. The hillside is simply riddled with dug-outs. It is only a week since I went along the railway towards Galatz till tonight, when I went to the Pruth. There are dozens of new trenches all the way along, and several new gun positions. It is so interesting to pass from Russia into Roumania, although I did not actually go on to Roumanian territory. The railway from Reni onwards belongs to the Roumanians. The Roumanian railway gauge is smaller than the Russian, so that hospital trains from Galatz have to leave their wounded here to be taken on again to Odessa in Russian trains.

Milne *Diary Tuesday 13 March*

We have had a great day of guns – the enemy has been shelling poor old Galatz – and we saw clouds of smoke, so I suppose the town was in flames. I wonder when our time will come – soon, certainly; a shell whirred past today, but did not burst, and a general was killed this morning on his way to Galatz with his men. We live in stirring times – I wonder if we shall be taken prisoner?

Fitzroy *Letter Wednesday 14 March*

At dinner we were sent a message by some friendly doctor on a train: 'Baghdad is by the English army taken.' *Oh* how splendid.

Fawcett *Diary Saturday 17 March*

Pushkin was away all day yesterday, but came back in the evening with two friends and howled outside all night.

Murphy, Fitzroy, Lewis, Broadbent and I went for a long walk along the Galatz road, or rather the railway line, as the road was under water most of the way. We watched the water break through the sandbags at one place, and almost immediately, there was a torrent right across the line. We watched some exciting firing at a Bulgarian aeroplane on our walk, but it was very wide. The mud is horrible, and the river is rising rapidly.

Sunday 18 March

Thrilling news: the Captain has just arrived with news of the Russian revolution. Sister Vera is frightfully pleased, and so is the Captain.

Milne *Sunday 18 March*

Tremendous excitement – we hear today of a revolution in Petrograd – it is grand living in the midst of history like this. The brother of the Tsar, Michael Aleksandrovich, says if he is properly elected he will be Tsar, and Nicholas Nikolaievich is to be head of the army; so we are expecting a great push on all the fronts. The Tsarina has been shot at by a prince from the country – he is to be hanged. The Tsar ordered out the military and they refused to fight – so it must be very exciting in Petrograd. The Tsar is said to be taken prisoner and shut up in Tsarskoe Seloe. What will happen now? Shall we have an advance? I do hope so – perhaps it will bring the war nearer an end. I shan't want to go home if we are really in the midst of interesting times.

Hospital B Odessa to Jassi

Rendel *Diary Monday 19 March*

Orders to pack up everything and start Monday. Rumours of all kinds going about. The Grand Duke Nicholas is said to have appeared at the Duma at the head of the Guards and put himself at the service of the Duma. The Grand Duke Michael has refused the crown.

At 3 p.m. no train in sight. All the stores packed and sent down to the port.

7.30 No train; 12 midnight no train.

Tuesday 20 March

Great military demonstration in Odessa. Soldiers marched through streets waving red flags and wearing red ribbons; Marseillaise played. Crowd orderly but excited. The mayor and two other officials arrested. Got on board train at 8.30. Third class carriage – no room.

Wednesday 21 March

Tiraspol in middle of day. Benderi in evening. Excitement in Benderi. Soldiers seized policeman and pulled him about. Turned machine gun on Cossacks, who fled without damage being done.

Friday 23 March Ungheni

Very cold day. Station master insolent; ordered Mr Rothe to unload at once. Refused to let us go on to Jassi. He says he has orders not to let any more trains through. Very impertinent. Red flag waving. Mr R appears to be rather nervous. He is afraid of a Terror. Very deprecating towards the officials.

Miss Little and Sister Edwards sent on in a sanitary train with letters to Red Cross in Jassi and to Sir George Barclay.

Saturday 24 March

Miss Little telephones from Jassi. We have permission to go by train but horses and men to trek. Unloaded carts and horses and fodder at 4 p.m. Mr R and men set out. Cold wet day. Roads almost impassable. Started for Jassi at 9 p.m.

Letter to Ray Monday 26 March Jassi

We have been in this filthy hole for four days now waiting for a train to take us on to Barlad. From there we are to go on by carts nearer the front. We are living in the train which brought us here from Odessa. Our food is running short and there is nothing to eat in Jassi. The first day we came we tried to get a meal in a restaurant. In the best one in town they had nothing at all. In the second best we got cold beans, black bread, and a little vinegar they call wine. Our food which we brought with us consists of hardboiled eggs now eight days old, bread of the same date and so stale that you have to cut it up with a knife and fork, a little cheese and tea. We also have a little sugar. Our candles are almost finished and we have to sit in darkness most of the time. Milk can't be bought, nor can anything else. More than half the shops are shut. There is no tobacco in the town. Before we came we heard reports that there was a bad outbreak of typhus and also plague. This we find was much exaggerated. There are only 1000 cases of typhus and no plague. But the town is in a wretched state, overcrowded with very dirty soldiers. There are swamps of dirty water everywhere, the mud is chronic, and the smells horrible. Dead horses and dogs lie about, and heaps of dirty dressings and other refuse are thrown all over the station, which is crowded with hospital trains.

When we arrived it was bitterly cold and snowing. The last two days have been very warm. This is a strange existence and very chastening. Dr C is a very amusing companion and she can be extremely pleasant. But she has the gift of losing her temper badly, more suddenly, more unexpectedly and on a smaller provocation than any person I have ever met. The result is that I am always kept on the jump. One minute she is laughing and joking, the next second she will say, 'Confound you, you idiot,' in a towering rage. It is really very difficult to adapt oneself to such lightning changes. I am left gasping and quite unable to retort in kind. Her motto is 'An eye tooth for an eye tooth' [sic] so I don't suppose she'd mind if I cursed her back, but I'm never quick enough. Perhaps it's just as well because it would be fatal to quarrel with her and I'm really extremely fond of her.

As for Miss Henderson, she is a traitor. We want our stores very badly and also our medicine cases which we fear very much now will go to Dr Inglis by mistake. I suppose Miss H was too frightened of submarines or revolutions to set sail.

Hospital A Reni

Fawcett *Diary Tuesday 20 March*

We were all decorated this morning by Prince Dolgorukov, the GOC of this front. He first of all decorated the wounded in the ward, and then the staff in the Privia Lista. Dr Laird had not been under fire, so had a different sort of medal with a red and orange ribbon – others have black and orange – she says it is a consolation prize. It is so nice that they give us the same medal that they give the soldiers.

Milne *Diary Tuesday 20 March*

A great day this has been. Prince Dolgorukov, General Krupensky, and several other generals visited the hospital. We were just at breakfast when word was brought to us that all the staff must come at once to be presented to the prince. So we all darted off with our cameras in case we could get a group of the big folk. When they arrived in the hospital the prince at once presented us with medals – St George, 4th Class – for bravery under fire. As he presented the medal he shook hands with each one and thanked us for what we had done. Of course we were terribly excited, much to the amusement of the prince and suite. We pinned the medals on at once, then we took photographs of all the guests alone and with the hospital staff; and later in the day we took snaps of each other with our medals. I got a half-day off, and Dr Laird and I went for a very long walk by the Danube and home by the fortresses. It was perfectly lovely, especially the sun setting over the river. The snow-clad hills across the river in Roumania were beautiful. As we went on our walk a German aeroplane was being fired at from three sides, and the noise was awful – it all reverberated across the river. I did enjoy the walk with my medal on – awfully proud of it. Some soldiers drove us home the last mile in their carts.

Fitzroy *Letter Tuesday 20 March*

We've had the most breathless day, and I must catch the mail bag. It began early this morning with the arrival (quite unexpected) of our chief, General Krupensky – the CO of the troops here – and Prince Dolgorukov – the commander-in-chief of the Russian forces on this front, with all his gilded staff. After they had inspected the hospital, we were lined up – and decorated! It was a word and a blow indeed, as the telegram announcing their arrival only reached us long after they had taken their departure. Our medals are the same as the soldiers get, which adds to their value – the 4th Order of St George. It has attached to it a pension of a rouble a month for life! Silver metal with an orange and black ribbon; on one side the Tsar's head (rather an irony!), on the other an inscription which reads 'For valour'. It only means we've been under fire, so don't imagine we have achieved the Russian VC. The men were charming, and when we returned to the wards we created a far greater sensation than the revolution ever did. I was very touched by the dear old NCO of the Austrian prisoners, who came up to me in the ward, saluted and said (in German, of course), 'Congratulations, Sister.'

Letter Wednesday 21 March

Work is very slack, which Dr Inglis says is bad for us. Therein I don't the least agree, and it is only terribly dull people who would not find endless resources for any amount of spare time in the sunshine and the country. But the dear lady forgot how to play *many* years ago.

Milne *Diary Thursday 22 March*

This morning the priest came to bless the hospital and four new icons that Dr Inglis has presented to the hospital. It was terrible mummery, I thought – and then he blessed us all, sprinkling us with the whisk broom that was used to brush lice off the beds – *sehr gut!* – everything is really very funny, but a perfectly wonderful fascination about everything – and I don't think I shall be able to tear myself away when July comes, especially as the war must be over by the winter. I shall have to see it out.

Friday 23 March

Galatz was bombarded in the night by Bulgar 12-inch guns – during the day an aeroplane dropped a letter to say all the civil population had to leave as the town was to be bombarded – and so it was. We were wakened by the awful row: it seemed as if they were just in the garden. I wonder how much of the town is left?...

Fawcett *Diary Thursday 22 March*

Sisters Wilcox and MacElhone came back from Odessa last night – we all fumed. They had lost the one case they had to take care of – the atmosphere was really rather electric. Dr Inglis was really cross. Of course, our letters were in the case – however, Dr Chesney wrote that there had hardly been any letters for a month, just one or two coming through at a time. We also heard that all letters are kept for three weeks before delivery.

Yesterday's paper said that Russia had been granted freedom of speech, freedom of religion, and freedom of the press.

Of course we have started the sleeping difficulties – they wanted Fitzroy and me to go down to the Expedition, and Dr Inglis was coming to act as chaperone. However, we objected, and Broadbent offered to have the two of us up in the turret, and Murphy, like the sport she is, is going up into the loft above, so that we shall really have rather a nice colony.

Saturday 24 March

Dr Inglis promised me a salary one day last week if I stayed on, so I said I would.

These are two stories of the SWH.

> An Armoured Car man and a British Red Cross orderly were discussing the merits of the SWH and the BRC sisters respectively. 'Oh,' said the orderly, 'you should see our theatre sister. She is ever so quick – why, she has the man on the table within five minutes of hearing of him.' 'That is nothing,' said the Armoured Car man. 'Why, in the SWH the theatre sister has the next man on the table before the last one is off.'

This is one of Mrs Milne's, and is supposed to come from one of the Armoured Cars' officers: one of his men said to him one night, 'But you don't expect us to sit on the quay all night, sir; you know we aren't Scottish Women.'

Fitzroy[19]

We have a very mixed lot in just now, and through our being in quarantine they have had to stay in some time, so that we have got to know them rather well. We have one smart young man who can read and write, is a smith by trade, and in times of peace earns an astonishing number of roubles a month. If there is one thing he abhors, it is the uneducated! And then there is Nikolai. Nikolai has been desperately ill, and with us a long time. He will say you are the most perfect of all created beings if he is feeling in the mood, and will bite you if he isn't. And so it goes on. The young ones are for the most part delightful. Our youngest patient is a Cossack sergeant of fifteen. He was adopted by the regiment when he was a child, and has won all the four medals of St George, and all the four crosses. He is quite frightfully naughty, and a great darling.

Letter Monday 26 March

The revolution has reached us at last, and yesterday we attended a republican meeting in the market square. The speeches as later conveyed to us by the Russian sister seemed distinctly to the point, in as much as the *first* duty of the Russian peasant was insisted upon; and this was not to please himself and flout authority, but to fight for Russian soil. The Tsar of course – along with other tsars – was attacked; and I hope it isn't true that he is taking refuge in England? I only wish we had been able to understand all they said.

The crowd was very good-tempered and appreciative, composed almost entirely of soldiers, and the most effective moment of the meeting came with the short chant and prayer for those killed in the revolution. So far, so good. It is a big task for those responsible – the men are just beginning to realise the change, but to our eyes it seems ever so slow in reaching their understanding.

Fawcett *Letter 26 March*

Yesterday we went to a revolutionary meeting in Reni Market Square. It was really most impressive – there were about three hundred soldiers and just a few civilians, all crowded together outside the church. It was all most orderly, but we were rather disappointed that the two chief speakers were Jews. There was a lot of talk about *Angliya* and *Frantsiya*, and we found out afterwards that they said that England and France knew that Russia had been betraying things to the enemy, but that since the revolution it was up to the soldiers to make them once again trust them. The general opinion seems to be divided between the desire for a constitutional monarchy or a republic. Most of the officers we have spoken to are in favour of the former; they say that Russia is not yet ready for a republic.

The local war news is good. The Bulgars are being pushed back the other side of the Danube between here and Braila, and are burning the villages as they go – we can distinctly see the fires from here. We also heard that for the first time two women have been elected for the Duma. We hear that the Tsar and his family are being sent to England. I wonder if it is true.

Since the revolution we wear our medals 'inside out', with the inscription part outwards. If we don't do this, the soldiers turn them round.

CHAPTER 10
Upheaval in Petrograd

By January, with the retreat of rich Roumanians to a safer city and the understandable wish of many foreigners to leave Russia altogether, Petrograd was overcrowded with refugees and other travellers; and Germany's ultimatum that from 1 February her submarines would sink even neutral ships on sight[1] meant that foreign consulates forbade sea travel for their nationals in all but the most urgent cases. As Moir's entry of 19 January indicates, the capital had become a bottle-neck; in addition, it was short of food, and alive with rumours of coming troubles. The eighteen Scottish Women[2] held up here felt themselves to be at the very hub of modern history.

The discontented Buffs had been the first to arrive, and although those who wished had managed to get a passage home before the submarine blockade began, several had remained to work with other hospitals in Russia, at least one in Petrograd itself.[3] The six-monthers followed, then those of the Transport who were not needed until the cars were again functional; and one or two who, like Moir, had personal reasons for returning before they had meant to. Miss Henderson, on her way back from Britain with hospital supplies, reached the capital on 18 or 19 March, just after the news of the Tsar's abdication had been broadcast to the world; she too was delayed.

Moir and Grant, who had arrived on 19 January, had plenty of time to see the city while they waited for a passage. They were able to visit the British Embassy and the Anglo-Russian Hospital, and to make friends with the English colony in Petrograd. They heard all the rumours then circulating among the English residents, shared the general expectation of trouble on the day the Duma was due to open, and understood the seriousness of the bread riots and the unofficial strike on International Women's Day, 8 March.[4] Starting with women in the textile factories, the strike soon spread to the Putilov arms works and other industries, involving about 90,000 workers.[5] Two days later this became a general strike. Called to control the crowds, many regiments mutinied, joined the strikers, and turned against the police who were firing machine guns previously concealed on the rooftops. Although the Tsar dissolved the Duma, its members refused to leave the building, and waited in an adjoining room to take control.

By 12 March political prisoners had been freed by the crowd, the Red Flag was flying from the fortress of St Peter and St Paul, and the released leaders and other public figures had formed a Provisional Committee of the Soviet of Workers' and Soldiers' Deputies, which took over the provision of arms and the issuing of orders to the crowd.[6]

Having waited so long, and having seen the trouble escalating, Moir, Grant, and two others left Russia secretly on 8 March, presumably with the necessary papers from the British Red Cross, and made their own travel arrangements. Ironically, their choice of vessel was an unfortunate one, and having left well ahead of the others, they took nearly four weeks to get home. Those who were present during the disturbances appear to have enjoyed the excitement, and to have sympathised with the aims of the revolution; like the staff at Reni, they were infected with revolutionary enthusiasm and were able to share in the general euphoria. Despotic autocracy had been displaced by democracy, and this was something that British constitutional monarchists could rejoice in. Among the Scottish Women, eye-witnesses of the events of 8-12 March were unanimous in their support for the revolution, and in their praise of the restraint of the crowds, the orderliness of the first few days, and the early return to normality.

Petrograd

Moir *Friday 19 January*

We arrived here at 9.30 this morning, very thankful indeed to get off the train... This is a general holiday in Petrograd, 'The Blessing of the Neva' festival. The people come from far and near, and bring receptacles to be filled with blessed water from the Neva. The festival is held once a year.

We had a most terrible business finding a corner to go to when we arrived. The place is chock-a-block with refugees. We finally secured floor-space in this hotel, but just for one night – we will be homeless again tomorrow. We expect to be here for a week or ten days, as the permit question is the difficulty here, and takes time. We interviewed numerous officials this morning, and both the Embassy and Consulate people are to do all they can to help us.

Grant *Saturday 20 January*

We arrived in Petrograd yesterday about 10 a.m. We were dumped out of the train into the snow and there was a great steep bank of snow, at the bottom of which was a road with *droshkis* on it. So we hailed to the drivers and sent our kit-bags rolling down the hill, much to the amusement of the people who were standing by. We drove each in our own *droshki* with our possessions, and landed at the Regina for the night.

Moir *Sunday 21 January*

We couldn't get into any of the hotels yesterday; in the end we went to the English padré, Mr Lombard, and he has got us a room in the British Nursing Home here. This home is run by Mr Lombard and the English Church, and is for the benefit of the English colony in Petrograd. It is such a beautiful little place, and just the essence of comfort. Mr Lombard was just too kind for anything yesterday. We spent the afternoon and evening with him – revelled in a real English fire, comfy armchairs, hot buttered toast, and such unheard-of luxuries. And last night we slept in real beds and between sheets, the first time since we were in Odessa, over four months ago... There are two very nice sisters here, and they are so good to us. We sleep in in the mornings, and are waited on hand and foot – changed times, I can tell you! We're feeling loads better already.

We went to the English Church this morning, and in the afternoon we went to the Anglo-Russian Hospital. We had tea there, and were shown all round. It is a fine building; the walls and ceilings are all beautifully carved. It was given by some prince or other for a hospital, and is a sort of diplomatic hospital.[7] They can take two hundred patients, all Russian of course. We were highly amused to see those thick-set, bearded Russians in our hospital blues. We are to go to the Embassy to tea tomorrow – Lady Georgina Buchanan and her daughter called to see us today after church, and they were so kind and nice.

Grant *Wednesday 24 January*

Went to the Hermitage and felt we could spend months there looking at all the treasures in the art world. Murillos, Rembrandts, Gainsboroughs, French, Spanish, Italian, German and Dutch schools there, but alas we had only two short hours so could only look at a few... We then went and shopped and had tea in a café, and so back home – to find, to our horror, that four more of the SWH had arrived! Fortunately they, after much difficulty, found rooms in the Regina, though goodness knows what they may have to pay.

Moir *Sunday 28 January*

Still here, but we hope in another few days to get our permits. We've spent a lot of time this past week running between the Consulate and the Red Cross commissioner's, worrying them about our permits. It's easier to get into Russia than to get out of it! And from what we hear, it will become yet more difficult – there are rumours of a *revolution* on all sides – one hears it everywhere. Things are becoming very serious, thanks to the Tsarina and her party. They seem to be trying to starve the people and the troops into making peace. The people in Petrograd are dying of starvation; no flour is coming into the town, they can't get bread, and the prices are simply impossible. It can't go on. Of course Rasputin's death is still *the* talk. It's a blessing they've got rid of him, and that he's safely down the Neva. The Tsarina seems to have been quite bereft about him; it's extraordinary how a dirty common peasant priest could have had such an influence over her. He is said to have 'cured' the little Tsarevich on various occasions, and in that way played on the feelings of the Empress. The Tsarina appears to be cordially disliked and hated here. The people say she is a German, that all her sympathies just now are with Germany, and that her party is working for Germany – and pretty successfully, if all one hears is true.[8]

We have been seeing as much of Petrograd as possible this last week. It is a most attractive town. The streets are broad and straight; the first-class ones are called 'prospects', and most of them are paved with wood. The longest and most important is the Nevsky Prospect, which is four miles long... The swiftly-running carriages in which the élite drive – with runners instead of wheels – with their fine horses, are very striking. They fly along with no sound but the sound of the bells, the crack of the whip, and the subdued crunching of the snow. The coachmen pad up their robes of blue to an enormous extent, so that they seem to bulge out over the seat.

Odessa

Birkbeck *Friday 9 February*

Beginning to think I have spent all my life, a very, very long one, under the Studdy. The chisel has been exchanged for a long lean paint brush. Grey paint wanders slowly down the handle and into my sleeve. Some of the complicated corners were worth picking out, but it's not an enlivening occupation. Studdy is very smart; I can't help hoping that when she dies, she'll die on her back, that her under painting will show. Not before long – I fear her frame is cracked right across. Onslow thinks this happened when she stuck at Antwerp, before Studdy retreated her first retreat.

At Franconi's we heard some people discussing the end of the war; they all say from 2-6 months, till one has excited oneself into thinking one feels in one's bones big changes coming. We talk of it always, everyone does. Meanwhile, in the nearer future, people are betting on the length of the blockade. I am betting on these people being held up three months.

Petrograd

Moir *Monday, 12 February*

Further delay and fresh complications. There's no saying when we may get away now, since Germany's ultimatum saying she will sink all neutral ships after the 5th. No one is allowed out of Petrograd. All passenger boats are off, and even cargo boats are not running from Norway. The Ambassador says there's nothing for it; we must just stay here. The SW are very furious and rebellious, I assure you! There are hundreds of people waiting here to get away, and hundreds more in Sweden and Norway. The congestion in Norway is terrible, we hear, so after all we're better off here, in comfortable quarters and among friends. The English colony here are more than kind, from Lady Buchanan downwards, and we feel we have made some very true friends.

We are getting to know Petrograd very well, and go sight-seeing somewhere nearly every day, despite the awful cold.

Odessa

Birkbeck *Saturday 17 February*
We are all standing on our heads again, not knowing whether to go or stay. Hedges turned up from Reni, the last of the Buffs at war. The next will be Marx. I must go too. It's best, only very, very hard to make up my mind...

Monday 19 February
Put in a plea at the Consulate, and were sent home to give written reasons for returning – the real reason being a wish to see everyone at home. It was awfully hard to think of any reason that could not be used to prevent one rejoining and thus ending my career for ever as a Scottish Woman. Ill health and so on were barred, so I merely said I wished to go as I wasn't wanted for the next two months at least. Marx certified to the truth of the statement, and we waited breathlessly till Walker returned to say we were 'considered' for it.

Monday 26 February
We were all marshalled at the Consulate, those who were for home – Brown, Bowerman, Hedges, and 'the Firm',[9] and all were asked what we were going to do when we got home; and having been already primed, we said with one voice, 'War work.' The chorus made Mr Bagge laugh.

Petrograd

Moir *Tuesday 27 February*
Nothing doing, but still hoping! Petrograd is becoming more and more unsettled, and the strikes are spreading. There will be a big bust-up one day soon. The Duma opens today, and warnings have been sent to

civilians on no account to go out in the street. Some fun is expected, evidently. There has been quite a lot of shooting in the streets, and guns are concealed all over Petrograd. The Cossacks are in possession – a regiment has been sent up from the Caucasus...

There seems to be a spirit of excited anticipation abroad among the public. In certain distant quarters of the city, the attitude of the mob has been so dangerously defiant of late that recourse by the soldiery (or rather the police) to firearms has been necessitated. Who can blame the people? They are starving here in Petrograd. There is no bread for them; there is no shortage of grain in the country, but it's being held up. The cold is terrific, and the people are suffering terribly. If the Tsarina and her party think they'll starve them into making peace, they're mistaken. They'll rebel. Already there have been bread riots all over the town; a little more, and there will be a general upheaval – and a big one too!

'Butter Week' is just past – it is the week before Lent starts, and during this week no meat is eaten, just butter and eggs and such diet. A feature of Butter Week are 'blinnies', a sort of pancake eaten with sour cream, melted butter and caviare. They are very thin, and twenty is an average to eat at one sitting!

The chances of this letter getting through are microscopic! *Our* chances are too, I'm beginning to think, especially now that things are so very unsettled in Petrograd itself, and all the riots, etc.

Odessa to Petrograd

Bowerman *Diary Friday 2 March*
Left Odessa 8 a.m. by express for Petrograd – very comfortable train – two first-class compartments reserved for the seven of us and one sister from the Red Cross Hospital who is returning to England with us. Walker, Hedges, Brown and I in one compartment – Birkbeck, Edwards, Turner and the Red Cross sister in the other. Very clean train – wide berths, electric light, and an electric bell which when rung brings a most useful conductor who makes us *chai*, washes up for us, and makes us feel back in civilisation again.

Turner *Saturday 3 March*
The country is looking lovely – white snow, white sky, silver birch and rushes, and an occasional village or sledge. It's like a perfect etching. It looks like the Russia one reads about in fairy tales.

Monday 5 March
At about 4 p.m. we arrived in Petrograd, and while we were still

struggling with our luggage, a Red Cross man turned up and guided us and our luggage in eight *sankies* to this hotel. The Select Hotel is extraordinarily comfortable. The Firm nearly fainted with joy when it discovered itself in a luxurious bed-sitting room – quite large, so we can easily ask our friends to tea. There is a large restaurant upstairs, and the food is excellent. Moir, Grant, Sedgwick and Brand are still in Petrograd; they are quartered in some nursing home, not having had the Firm's luck.

Birkbeck *Tuesday 6 March*

Petrograd indeed. The Firm breakfasted on its own, and then set out in a smart sledge to explore the city. Really one never gets used to sledges being taken seriously; always at the back of my mind I expect someone to say, 'There isn't enough snow really,' then I see the *droshki* harnessed to the pony ready to go. But to see people like one's father skidding about there is still a little odd. We saw a funeral and a fire engine, all in harness, the latter drawn by four beautiful blacks. All along the Nevsky Prospect we trudged, gasping at the length and breadth of the street. At tea we met Moir, Grant, Sedgwick and [Clare] Murphy who have been here seven weeks, but who leave for England tomorrow. They had all been shoved into nursing homes, charity institutions, and we consider ourselves most lucky in our quarters. The peace of our sitting room cannot be described.

Friday 9 March

We went to the Red Cross commissioner for our passports. He held out hopes of getting us off to Christiania soon *en route* for England. Coming home we heard a new tune and saw some magnificent Cossacks, and made a friend, as one does abroad.

Petrograd to Stockholm

Moir *Saturday 10 March*

I'm writing this in the train *en route* for Stockholm and I hope home! We have actually got out of Russia and shaken the 'snow' of Russia from off our feet! We left Petrograd at daybreak on the 8th; the day before, we decided to take the law into our own hands and risk it, and anyhow, we've got so far, it now remains to be seen when we will actually get back to Blighty. We thought the sooner we got out of Petrograd, the better, as things were beginning to get 'some' warm there. In a very short time there will be news from there, if I'm not mistaken. The outside world may be surprised at the news to come, but those who have been in Russia and more especially in Petrograd for the last few months will not be surprised at anything that happens there. There's trouble ahead, methinks.

We reached Torneo, right up in the very north, between Finland and Lapland, about 12 o'clock on the 9th. From there we sledded across the Gulf of Bothnia to Haparanda. There was such a fuss there about luggage, passports, etc., and some of the poor things had a terrible time. We four 'Scittish Widows' (our Petrograd title!)[10] escaped scot-free; we found everyone most kind, and they seemed to know as much about us as we did ourselves! We appear to be rather a notorious band, I fear!

We entrained at 8 o'clock and started our journey through Sweden. What a difference there is between these Swedish trains and those of Russia; we have every luxury here – restaurant car, etc., and a refreshing change is realised in the smoothness and speed of running!

Sunday 12 March Stockholm

We arrived at Stockholm yesterday morning and have spent two very enjoyable days sight-seeing.

Everyone in Stockholm looks so happy; everywhere are sunny faces and high spirits and sprightly chatter – what it is, *not* to be at war! Of course the Swedes are decidedly pro-German – undoubtedly their sympathies are with the Boche – that one sees most plainly. This is a most comfy hotel, and we are revelling in the numerous comforts – hot baths, comfy beds, and no lack of food! We leave for Christiania at 9 o'clock tonight and should arrive there at mid-day tomorrow.

Petrograd

Birkbeck *Sunday 11 March*

Turner and I went out after lunch to see what was happening – immense crowds, surging up and down the Neva. A general strike is on. Opposite the Nicholas Theatre the police were backing up into a crowd with a machine gun. Bands of Cossacks rode up and down pretending to do the same, but charged along firing into the air. People got hit. Someone inside a house opened fire at the crowd, who hurried into areas and courtyards. At one point the crowd were pressing towards the Neva, and Turner and I got on to a food sledge just as someone shot, and we found ourselves taken to a detention house in the Ligovskaya – captives in earnest. After that drama we thought the Select might be the best place after all. Messrs Blake and Bennet[11] joined us after dinner.

Monday 12 March

All shops shut. All day we prowled about. We have just realised the importance of the big bread riots: the army was nowhere, and are putting through the rebellion, and so it is all right. Today the soldiers have gone over entirely and are only seen scattered through the crowd. All officers have had their swords taken from them, and soldiers and civilians alike are armed with rifle, revolver, or dagger. Any *droshkis* still about are held up, the passengers turned out, and the man sent home. All cars are commandeered by the revolutionists who crowd aboard them. All wear red favours...

During the day there was much shooting. Blake took the Firm out after dinner, but we had not got far before we were in the middle of a fight. Two army lorries full of soldiers and armed civilians were fired upon from a house held by the police in the Ligovskaya. The lorries replied with volley after volley, and a fierce fight raged for some time. We, meanwhile, had fled like the rest of the crowd into a courtyard opposite, where we got an excellent view in comparative safety. The strikers in the cars and lorries scattered copies of the manifesto of the new liberal government to the crowd, and were met with cheer after cheer. Some kind of mass meeting was taking place in the square.

Wild rumour has it that the soldiers of the Litovsky Regimental Barracks mutinied and murdered their officers.[12] The cry of the crowd was 'Down with the *nemka*, the German.' Returned to our room for tea, saying as usual, what wonderful people the Russians are.

Bowerman *Diary Tuesday 13 March*
Up early for Mr Kimens,[13] who did not turn up. Great excitement in streets – armoured cars rushing up and down, soldiers and armed civilians marching up and down – attention suddenly focussed on our hotel and house next door – round of shots directed on to both buildings as police supposed to be shooting from top storeys – most exciting. Several shots went through windows. Presently our hotel searched by rebels – came into each room searching for police spy. Very nice to us – most polite – several civilians as well as soldiers. One 'revolutionary' came into our room to dress – didn't know how to wear his sword – we had to assist with the strapping up.

All hotel servants, also the manager, disappeared – nothing to eat – picnicked in our rooms. Shooting and shouting continuously all day in the street – several search parties through the hotel at intervals. Sat at hotel window in afternoon and watched crowds in the streets, and lorries crowded with armed men. Youths left in charge of the hotel kitchen, armed with ferocious carving knives and muskets. Managed to loot some glasses of milk – all other food locked up.

Fresh alarm in hotel in evening – rifle shot suddenly heard in building – merely one of the revolutionary sentries banged rifle on the floor in his excitement and shot went through the ceiling. One of own officers immediately appeared and remonstrated. Heard from nice Russian man everything most satisfactory. Trains coming in punctually, and soon banks will reopen, also factories. Wire has been sent to Tsar asking him to accept the new government.

At 5.30 p.m. three police spies with machine guns said to have been found on third floor of our hotel – no more search parties after this. Revolutionary officer left in charge. Rumours that hotel will be fired during the night, so we packed our haversacks carefully in case we had to make a hurried departure in the night. Retired to bed – great luck to have such comfortable quarters – Astoria[14] has been sacked and guests turned out, and some hotels have had no food over the weekend. Brown and Hedges went to the Embassy in case there were any orders for British people. They 'wished us luck' – no other suggestions to offer.

At intervals during the day motors rushed by, scattering news sheets and declarations to the people. Brown and Hedges ran into a street affray.

Birkbeck *Tuesday 13 March*

Woke to a great deal of noise outside our hotel when an absolute fusillade at the corner made us wonder what was coming next. We leapt up and dressed in record time. Then the revolutionaries poured into the hotel. Every room was searched. Someone had fired from one of the windows, and they meant business. Such a mob as poured into our room: soldiers, factory hands, old men and young all carrying firearms or knives. We cordially welcomed our visitors (never anger a man with a gun) and gave them cigarettes. After a brief glance round the room, they saluted and clattered off.

The servants all cleared off, and no food was to be had. Bennet and Blake saved the lives of the Firm by getting several yards of sausages and some brown bread. We continued with our repast during the several times the room was searched by similar parties. It was not till the evening, when the fatal second shot was fired that the police officer was discovered on the third floor. He shot himself, and spent a good deal of time in the hall. Many people left the hotel, thinking it a particularly unhealthy spot. Only Russians remained, and hated it. They huddled together in frightened groups and made each other miserable by repeating rumours. The favourite was that the hotel would be blown up in the night. The revolutionaries took over the top floor and sentries were placed on each landing. Rather dangerous people: three times one let off his rifle by mistake outside our door, in the afternoon, and another upstairs during the night. When we were washing up the tea things some of the waiters came back, one wearing a sword.

Turner *Wednesday 14 March*

Everything much quieter today. Manifesto has been issued asking everyone to go back to their job – giving 24 hours grace. Tomorrow things will get going again. The train service is still going splendidly. New police have been appointed; they are in civilian kit, sort of 'specials' wearing a white brassard with red on it.

We went down the Nevsky with Blake – who has been adopted as a new member [of the Firm] – and saw signs of yesterday's fray – bullet holes galore, and a bomb hole. We strolled up to see how the Astoria had fared, and found all the ground floor windows knocked out, piles of broken bottles and burnt papers outside. We learn from an English staff man we met that they were given half an hour to clear out and they lost some of their kit, but I gather not much. While we were out we still heard a certain amount of firing, and returning along the Nevsky saw bits of someone on the wall of a house – not very pleasant. We then went to a café which seemed to show signs of life, and a girl was serving tea to soldiers and temporary soldiers. As we had the red cross we also were given *chai*, but the girl would not let us pay. It was significant to see an officer and a private sitting at the same table. We came on a whole regiment of infantry marching with a band – carrying red on their bayonets – and officers marching with their men, and some as officers in front – it was really awfully impressive.

The hotel provided two meals today, all served at two long tables. The hotel staff has come back now, except a few. Tomorrow all will be working again.

Birkbeck *Wednesday 14 March*

All the first floor windows of the Astoria are smashed, the curtains making a torn and draggled track in the snow, outside. By the door was a huge heap of broken bottles. We heard the revolutionaries had drunk the contents of the cellar, and we saw the remains of a bonfire of papers. It [the Astoria] is now the headquarters of the sailors, who peer out through windows barricaded by chairs and tables. It was too odd to see civilian soldiers on guard in the hall among the palm trees, where so recently gayer blades had strutted last time we were there.

On returning we were hailed with much enthusiasm, and told that England and France were in accord with the new government – as English we are hugely popular. Who could fail to be in accord with a government that stands for freedom of speech, freedom of religion, liberty of conscience, universal suffrage, and the responsibility of ministers? Rumours about the abdication of the Tsar circulate.

Bowerman *Letter to her mother 15 March*

If there has been much in the English papers about Russian affairs, and more especially Petrograd affairs during the last few days, you must have been rather anxious. I am sorry if that is so, as there has been no cause for worry. We are in a very nice hotel and have been most comfortable all the time. For one day there were no meals to be had here, but fortunately we had some supplies of our own so were not inconvenienced. The servants have now returned and everything is in running order again.

Of course it has been a most *thrilling* time – I shall have loads to tell you when I get home. Our great regret is that we cannot read the Russian newspapers so as to be able to understand the political events which are so intensely interesting. We are so glad to have been here while all this has been happening. If we had been a week later we should probably have had to stick in Odessa for ages. I tried to wire you yesterday, but the telegraph system is not yet in working order again. Everything is much quieter today, though. It has helped matters tremendously that the army has been with the people, as they have helped to maintain order. We have met with the utmost politeness from everyone – even in street crowds they are awfully nice and ready to let you through when they see the Red Cross brassard on your arm. Such a wonderfully organised revolution deserves success.

Letter to a friend Tuesday 20 March[15]

We arrived here just in time for the revolution. It has been a perfectly wonderful experience, and we are so glad we did not miss it. I only hope nothing will happen to spoil things now...

My friend Joy Brown and I were out on Wednesday and had an exciting escape. We came in for a street affray when the soldiers were trying to dislodge a policeman from a house – or so we thought – so we took refuge in a church, when to our surprise just at the moment when we were crossing the courtyard a hail of bullets came in our direction. The people were being fired on from the *church* and not the house. So we had chosen rather a warm corner for shelter. Needless to say we soon vacated it. It is surprising how one can get used to things, though. They always give warning when they are going to fire down a street – people took cover in doorways and houses, then came out when it was over just as if it had merely been a shower of rain. The street firing only lasted for about two days, though – just until the people had cleared out all the police agents and pro-German and pro-Government officials. This week everything is practically normal again. Even the trams are running, which is a great achievement, as of course all the rails were frozen over at once directly they stopped using them, so it has been a great work to get them free of ice again.

Turner *Thursday 15 March*

We were able to ring for a *café complète* this morning, and even got a bath as usual. Last night we went out with Bennet and Blake after supper – quite a long tramp – the streets are quite calm now. We came upon a bonfire of police documents. People have great joy in burning up their dossiers.

We got up late and only got a little way down the Nevsky to get cigarettes before lunch. After noon, Blake, Birkbeck and I went out street-gazing. The pamphlet-casting game is still going on, and very few shops are open. The Tsar, they say, has arrived in Petrograd, and has abdicated in favour of the Tsarevich; and the new cabinet comes into power today. Milyukov is Minister of Foreign Affairs.

As we were going down the Nevsky we suddenly saw two lorries full of English bluejackets – we were awfully bucked, and rushed after them shaking them by the hand – they were tremendously cheered all along. Everyone thinks they have come to help the revolution – lucky moment for them to arrive. We acquired reflected glory and collected quite a crowd. Had tea at a café, which is now running as usual.

(Lois Turner)

Bowerman *Diary Friday 16 March*

Hedges saw Mr Kimens in morning. We are to go home with special military pass – hope to be through in about three weeks. Mr K says the way affairs have been conducted amazing – inner history of revolution as wonderful as external results.

In afternoon went down Nevsky – huge crowds in every direction. Presently motor came along, drew up opposite arcade. People flocked around – officer and also man in civilian dress made two short announcements from the car, namely that the Tsar had abdicated in favour of his brother Michael, and Michael had placed the power in the hands of the people. Therefore to all intents and purposes, *Russia is now a Republic.* People cheered and cheered in wildest excitement – rushed off and fetched ladders to take down the eagles off various public buildings.

Monday 19 March

Miss Henderson turned up – much diplomacy on all sides. Brown and I bought Russian boots – very cold and snowy. Hedges went to see Miss Henderson in the evening.

Thursday 22 March

Lunch with Miss H in new restaurant. Birkbeck and Mackenzie-Edwards also there. Heard from Miss H reports re revelations since revolution. Marconi on Winter Palace in communication with Berlin; pro-Germans had wished to provoke civil war – police agent cut down woman in street to start revolution. Fortunately the party now forming Provisional Government got hold of the movement in time and turned it in the right direction, thus preventing civil war and consequent chaos.

Lerwick, Shetland

Moir *Thursday 22 March* **SS Smolensk**

'Scotland for ever!' – so near and yet so far! We've got so far, but can't get no further! We're 'interned' here. After a few days wait in Bergen we got aboard a cargo boat and set sail on the morning of the 17th – bound for Liverpool, where we were told we would be in 48 hours at the most! 48 *days*, methinks! We are aboard an armoured cargo boat, the *Smolensk*, a Wilson Liner – a very comfy little tub. Our skipper, Captain Young, is one of the best, so we are in good hands. Unfortunately for us, our cargo is of value – 600 tons of zinc-spelter for munitions – so the Boches know our movements! We dashed across here under cover of darkness, made a record run, and were outside the bay by Sunday afternoon (18th).

Fortunately for us we had a thick fog all the way across. We were signalled outside the harbour to put in here, so as you can imagine our wrath is great, and we're really becoming dangerous! We hear rumours of a revolution in Petrograd, and that the Tsar and Tsarina have been deposed – we're longing to hear more. *It had to come.* Strikes me we just got away in time.

The weather outside is terrific, and no escorts are willing to take us out, so I suppose there is nothing for it but to await our souls in patience till the storm abates.

I will give this to one of the officers to take ashore to post. To think of us *looking* at Scotland, and can't get ashore! It's just d—able! It's a beautiful day, and Lerwick is looking at its best. The bay is full of all sorts of craft, Norwegian, Dutch and English boats, and dominating all, our grey mistress of the deep, keeping guard.

Petrograd to Aberdeen

Bowerman *Diary Saturday 24 March*

Got up at 5 a.m. to station – very chilly. People at that hour already standing in long queues outside bread shops. Train left 7.40 – very comfy.

Sunday 25 March Torneo

Arrived at Torneo, Finnish frontier 12 noon. Drove in sleigh over river to Customs House. Big luggage not come from Petrograd – Birkbeck, Turner and Mackenzie-Edwards staying here the night for it. We go on.

Wednesday 28 March Christiania

Arrived Christiania – stayed at Grand Hospits – awful place. Difficult to get meals there – horror of the maid when I asked for coffee in the evening!

Thursday 29 March Christiania to Bergen

Left at 7.35 a.m. Birkbeck and Co. arrived with luggage night before – just got it from them in time to take it on with us. General agitation about keys, etc. at station. Journey through mountains and fjords all day.

*Monday 2 April **SS Vulture**, Bergen to Aberdeen.*

Went on board *Vulture* 3 p.m. Lovely sail up fjord into the sunset. German Consul and his wife drove down to the quay to see us off. Sailed 5 p.m.

Tuesday 3 April Aberdeen

Coast of Scotland in distance. Two destroyers met and escorted us for a few hours. Four submarines – patrol boat stopped us in Moray Firth – allowed to proceed. Reached Aberdeen harbour midnight.

Belfast to Edinburgh

Moir *Saturday 31 March* **SS Smolensk**

It's 'Ireland for ever' this time *and* I don't think! I wonder if we will ever reach home? I hae ma doots! Well, we 'looked' at Lerwick for a week; at last the storm subsided, and we put to sea again, escorted by two gallant little minesweepers who took us as far as the west coast of Scotland. There they left us, unable to weather the storm which we encountered going through the Minch.[16] We got a terrible tossing; the good old *Smolensk* did her best, but nevertheless she rolled and tossed and heaved! When going down the west coast of Scotland we sighted a German sub and enjoyed a little game of hide and seek with her, dodging about among the Islands, Rum, Eigg, Coll, etc., and through the Mull Sound. I'm sure we must have gone round all the islands on the west coast, both Inner and Outer! Finally we made a dash for the north coast of Ireland, reached Rathlin Island, and were met there by a patrol boat, and were told to make for Belfast Lough, as we would not be able to get in to Liverpool owing to the Boche subs. So into Belfast Lough we went – that was yesterday – and here we are 'interned' once again, this time admiring Belfast from afar! It's a most beautiful day, calm and peaceful – more than can be said of our tempers! Fourteen days exactly since we left Bergen!

Sunday April 1 N B Hotel Edinburgh

Three cheers for 'Auld Reekie'! We arrived here this morning – OK and in the very best of tempers. We four 'Scittish Widows' were transhipped in all haste at midday yesterday – we took a tender farewell of the *Smolensk*, our gallant captain and kind crew, and crossed to Ardrossan last night. We arrived in Glasgow at a late hour (Sunday morning, practically) yesterday. This being the Sabbath Day, no trains are running (in war time!), so there was nothing for it but to board a 'Theatrical Special' which was going through to Edinburgh. That we did, and arrived here at 12 o'clock. Back to Blighty, Scotland, and home once again! We just feel as if someone had played a 1st of April trick on us – we simply can't believe that we are really back in Scotland! Our excitement is beyond words. Good old Scotland! So long! Cheers!! (from four Scittish Widows').

CHAPTER 11
Under Suspicion

(See map 5)

On 6 April 1917, chiefly as a consequence of Germany's unrestricted submarine warfare, the United States declared war on Germany. There is a strange silence on this topic in the extant diaries and letters of the Scottish Women, even those of the most politically aware. Normally the women kept abreast of events on the western front, and some had friends or brothers serving there, but news of its limited movement was seldom dramatic, and no doubt the advent of a new combatant (unable to supply fighting forces for at least a year) must have seemed to hold consequences both remote and dubious. Important as it turned out to be, the coming American intervention seems to have been eclipsed as a topic of conversation by the more pressing matters of the revolution and its sequels.

Even the revolution, at first, was not expected to make much difference to life in the hospitals. Dr Inglis continued to insist on strict hospital routine, and there was little resistance from either the patients or the Russian orderlies. It was assumed that Russia's relations with her allies would remain unchanged. Milyukov, Foreign Minister in the new Provisional Government, had assured the French and British ambassadors that Russia would stand by the secret treaties with her allies (awarding her Constantinople and the Straits in the event of victory), and he promised an early offensive. The hospitals' earliest indication that there was trouble in the local regiments came with the influx of lightly wounded, 'mostly hands', on 27 March. This was the first time the Scottish Women had come across self-inflicted wounds, although the practice was not uncommon in the Russian Army, which was composed largely of conscripts: Florence Farmborough comments on the same phenomenon on the Galician front in April 1915[1], and it no doubt happened in other armies, if less frequently. But by March 1917 such a ruse was not strictly necessary in Russia; the death penalty for disobedience had fallen away on 14 March with the issuing of Order No 1 by the Petrograd Soviet of Workers' and Soldiers' Deputies. This order had in effect transferred authority from the officers to the soldiers' committees 'elected from the lowest ranks of the military units',[2] and since it also placed all arms under the control of these committees, their authority was more persuasive than that of the officers. Although the order also stipulated that during the

233

performance of their duties soldiers must observe the strictest military discipline, the realisation that non-compliance would not be punished meant that with the resumption of military action in the spring, many soldiers refused to advance when ordered. What they most wanted to be liberated from was the war.

Returning in April from his exile in Switzerland, Lenin maintained that it was in the interests of the Bolsheviks to promote peace with Germany, in spite of the fact that Germany was another imperial power. He argued that a successful revolution in Russia would be followed by socialist revolutions in the rest of Europe,[3] and his peace programme undoubtedly increased the popularity of his party. For Germany, too, a temporary alliance with the Bolsheviks was expedient, because another revolution would put Russia out of the war. If this could be brought about before the United States could mobilise a trained army, Germany would be free to concentrate on breaking the stalemate on the western front.

For this reason Lenin and other exiles had been allowed to travel through Germany on their return to Russia, and had been given every consideration and assistance.[4] Secret funds, perhaps without Lenin's knowledge, had since 1915 been channelled into Russia, and into Bolshevist coffers.[5] In part, these funds were used to support a propaganda campaign, designed to persuade the Russian soldiers that this was England's and France's war, paid for in Russian lives. Mrs Milne had come across this view in January on her visits to the physiotherapist in Odessa,[6] and by April it was indeed true that Britain and France were doing their utmost to keep Russia in the war, in spite of her internal difficulties. And although losses to all the Allies had been unprecedentedly high, particularly in 1916, the Russian losses of three million in that year exceeded even those of Britain and France together.[7] There was real cause for discontent in the Russian army, and the intensified propaganda campaign now made good use of it, with severe consequences to all British and French citizens in Russia.

In early April, however, the suspicions of the policemen at Barlad and of the newly-formed Soldiers' Committee at Reni seem to have been aroused not because the Scottish Women were British warmongers, but because they were foreigners thought to be in league with the enemy. Dr Chesney and Rendel, as strangers in strange uniforms, understood the hostility of the Roumanian policemen who apprehended them in Barlad, but the arrests at Reni of Murphy on 10 April, and of Broadbent the next day, came as a great shock to everyone in Hospital A; they had grown accustomed to being welcomed and cheered and treated as friends. As in all wars, the soldiers were quick to credit accurate firing not to the observation of the reconnaissance planes or the skill of the enemy gunners, but to the betrayal of their positions by local spies. In retrospect it is easy to see how it happened that the women came under suspicion. Their hospital was so positioned that they could not ride or walk far without crossing the Russian trenches behind them, while their turreted and curtainless billet commanded a magnificent view over the Danube marshes and river to the Bulgar-held Dobrudga mountains in the distance. Enchanted with the Bessarabian spring, they walked and rode whenever they had the time, often coming upon gun emplacements, and sometimes losing themselves among the trenches; as Fawcett's diary records, she and Murphy had been riding and had lost themselves in the maze of trenches on the evening of 9 April, the day before the soldiers' investigation. Added to these suspicious circumstances was the newly-acquired power and responsibility of the Russian rank and file, and their difficulty in distinguishing between 'foreign' and 'German': other writers record meeting with the frequent assumption that the two were synonymous.[8] Probably only the reputation of the hospital and the loyalty and affection of their patients saved the women from the summary punishment meted out to spies on that front,[9] or at best from an ignominious transfer to some quieter and saner area. The arrests of Murphy and Broadbent were, as Mrs Milne saw, a warning of the unreliability of Russian feelings towards their British allies, and evidence of the insecurity of the Hospitals' position.

Hospital A Reni

Fitzroy *Letter Monday 26 March*
A very cold spell lately, but today again floods of sunshine. We have seen the wild geese heading north, and we have seen the storks beginning to nest. We have looted irises for our garden, and we have planted sunflowers. We are, in fact, happy and comfortable, and therefore expect to be forced to leave Reni before we are very much older!

Providence has provided a postman in the shape of an Armoured Car officer bound for Odessa. The BAC are, by the way, in a rather pessimistic frame of mind, as the enemy are using a new bullet which goes straight through their armoured cars – poor dears!

The hospital is fast filling up again.

Fawcett *Diary Tuesday 27 March*
Mr Henderson to lunch today. He is sending jam and marmalade. Lieutenant Hunter has sent Sister Walker-Brown and Sister Hopkin a German revolver each – also some shells for Holme.

Another aeroplane this morning – no bombs. Nineteen new wounded in this afternoon – mostly hands. We have practically the whole of the men out of doors today; the sun is simply glorious. Today's news – the German lines have been broken at Riga, and 125,000 prisoners taken. The Bulgars are being driven back here, and burning the villages as they go – we can see the fires just this side of the mountains.

Twenty [more] wounded in – the bad cases will be following soon. All these are very slight, mostly hands. They come from beyond Galatz.[10]

Friday 30 March

Nine operations this afternoon – all quite small. We are to evacuate thirty-four tomorrow. Off duty in the evening – went for a walk alone over the steppe, finishing up by the quay. I came across some Roumanian sailors dancing – their dancing is quite different from that of the Russian soldiers. About fifteen dance in a ring – there was no elaborate step, but the rhythm was very charming. It reminded me of the Serbian National Dance – the Kola – that we once joined in at Ismail. I also met an English-speaking Roumanian officer.

Nikolai – the bladder case – is still extremely trying. He cries for cigarettes every time anyone passes his bed.

Saturday 31 March Train Reni to Bolgrad

This morning a dead man was brought into hospital. The regiment was on its way to the front and this man dropped behind and shot himself. One of the officers rode back and came to our house as the nearest, and asked if we could help, so we sent out two Austrians to bring him in.

I am now in a sanitary train preparatory to going to Bolgrad to get money – while there I am to have my teeth attended to. I am quite looking forward to the adventure alone, but would have preferred it had Murphy or Fitzroy been coming too.

Milne *Diary Friday 30 March*

Nothing much doing. The weather is perfectly glorious. I go for walks on the steppe with Dr Laird as often as I can, and we have found heaps of lovely bulbs. The steppes will be a mass of bloom very soon – what a joy it all is. I told Dr Inglis yesterday that I would stay till the end of October, and she was very pleased. I am going to get a decent salary perhaps, also good fun.

Wednesday 4 April

On the night of the 3rd we were awakened by tremendous cannonading – the largest guns we have heard yet. They went on from 1.30 till after 3 o'clock. The windows and doors shook – I thought that Reni must be being bombarded – but as our house still remained standing, I decided it must still be poor old Galatz – and in the morning we heard that the enemy beyond Braila were trying to break through the Russian line. They have been dropping hundreds of bombs about, and enormous shells have been falling – so I rather hope we are spared that.

I have been for marvellous walks, and last night Dr Laird and I lifted lots of grape hyacinths and Star of Bethlehem bulbs to dry and send home... I think the steppes are the most wonderful joy I have ever met – miles and miles of rolling grass plains, quaint villages and orchards – one goes for miles without seeing a soul – and the Danube is a perfect dream.

Hospital B Barlad to Tecuci

Chesney *Report 31 March Barlad*[11]

Miss Inglis directed me to send you a report of the movements of this unit, and as this is the last opportunity that we may have for some time of sending any letters, I write to inform you that our present orders are to go to Tecuci tomorrow or the next day, and start a fever hospital there for typhus, recurrent and typhoid fever, and any other medical cases which may be sent in. I hear that Tecuci is quite a small place and therefore we shall probably have the patients in tents, and possibly have to live in tents ourselves. The weather today is fine and warm, but we had a snow-storm last Friday and the mud is fearful; but (if the weather keeps warm) living in tents will be quite practicable and pleasant in a week or so. When the present epidemics die down, which they will probably do rapidly with the onset of warm weather, we shall probably be formed into a field hospital and go up to the front.

We are very short of stores in the way of food (beyond bread and meat there is nothing to be had here) and invalid foods; there is no milk to be got in Roumania, and of course nothing in the way of tinned milk or foods. I hope that the stores Miss Henderson was bringing out will arrive soon and if Miss Inglis lets us have any of them I will send to Odessa for them, and for further hospital supplies.

We have now been twelve days in the train, doing a journey of about four hundred miles. We are to be sent on to Tecuci today, and are to put up our tents. The difficulty is the beds; we have none and of course did not bring them, as, with an allowance of 20 waggons, it would be quite impossible to carry even stretcher beds about. Straw they say is very scarce, and unless we can persuade the Russians to give us camp beds, it will be impossible to open the hospital. However, as they say the hospital is really very much needed, the beds will probably be forthcoming; the Russians, though they are extremely loth to part with anything for the use of English hospitals, generally contrive to find all they want for their own hospitals, and will supply us when they really want our hospitals.[12]

I am glad to report that the health of the unit up to now has been very good, and in spite of a long, tedious, tiring journey everyone has been very cheerful.

Rendel *Letter Saturday 31 March Barlad*

We are still in the train. This has been the worst journey we have had so far... We arrived here yesterday morning. In the afternoon Dr C and I went for a walk. We were strolling along the outskirts of the town when we found that we were surrounded by armed policemen. They were polite but firm. They could only speak Roumanian, but we gathered that they thought we were spies. They kept on pointing to our short hair.[13] In vain I produced my passport. They insisted on marching us to the police station where we were interviewed by their superior officer. We were soon able to persuade him of our innocence and our guards looked very foolish when they saw him shaking hands with us and smiling on us.

Diary Monday 2 April Tecuci

Went to interview officials with Dr Chesney, Mr Rothe, and Miss Corbett. Unsatisfactory. Told to go to Hospital 14 lately evacuated by Russians; a filthy hole. Found a house close to hospital with enough ground for camp. Overrun by horses and covered with manure heaps. Settled to take it.

Tuesday 3 April

Mr Berry appeared and wanted to be put up. He drove over from Barlad in search of a suitable hospital building.

Friday 6 April

Started to clean the hospital in the afternoon; the dirt indescribable. Rubbish of every kind on the floor; stoves filled with old dressings, black beetles hopping about. Yard full of old bones, dressings and scrap iron. Dust and refuse inches deep.

Hospital A Reni

Fawcett *Diary Sunday 1 April Bolgrad*

Arrived here this afternoon at 1.15 p.m. – we did not leave Reni till about 9 or 10. I came along from Traianoval in a soldier's cart – the roads are getting too exciting. Our horses shied twice at motors, and we had several collisions when we got into the street.

General Krupensky is away at Galatz, but his deputy – who alas, speaks only Russian – has let me have the money, which was the chief reason for my coming. I have also had my tooth dressed. I go once more tomorrow, and then I get it finished in Reni.

The scenery along the Danube was glorious today; the river is speckled with wild fowl. At one place where we stopped, I watched hundreds of frogs jumping into the water. There are still a few snowdrifts left in ditches and on the mountains.

Tuesday 3 April
I got back from Bolgrad at 12 midnight. Quite safe and sound, also 80 lbs of soap, and 8,000 roubles, which I kept in the leg of my knickers. The hospital is practically full again, with slight cases.

Letter Wednesday 4 April
The Danube looks quite blue today. I only wish it looked as inviting when it came up here for us to use – it really makes the most filthy tea. The weather is glorious – not too hot yet, with plenty of air going. The peasants have started their ploughing, and work hard all day long. The other day from the place where I was standing, I could see nineteen teams.

There is an awfully nice cultivated valley, parallel to the Danube, just over the hill behind the hospital. It is nicknamed 'The Happy Valley'. We spend a great deal of our time there when we are free. Most of the land is planted with maize or wheat, but there are several vineyards. There are lots of storks' nests in the village now. The mother stork looks so sweet sitting on her nest, and very often the father bird stands beside her to keep her company. They mostly build on outhouses that have roofs made of reeds.

A sweet thing happened this morning. One of the men, a Cossack, had a most beautiful curl over his ear, and as all the men in the hospital have to have their hair cut, I had to insist on the beautiful curl coming off. After it was all over, Fitzroy came along and pretended to be cross with me, and took her scissors to cut off one of my curls. This was too much for the poor boy, who hopped out of bed to hold her hand.

Thursday 5 April
Evacuated twenty-five men this morning. I heard some of them telling some Russian officers at the Evacuation Hospital that the Shotlandsky Lazaret was a *khoroshy* lazaret.[14] Went for a walk to the Happy Valley and picked grape hyacinths and sweet violets.

Inglis *Report*[15]
One of the appendix cases is a very fine-looking young Cossack, about

6' 3" without boots. He came to the Outpatients' Department with a thick crop of curly hair, and was very depressed when I insisted upon him having it all cropped off. I was sorry, but when all heads have to be cropped for fear of lice, one cannot well make an exception in any one case. After all he has forgiven us, and the other day he told Sister Kolesnikov that he was very happy in hospital. He added that he did not know why he was so happy. But I think I can answer that question: he came in not only with appendicitis but suffering from overstrained nerves, and the long rest and quiet have done him a great deal of good.

Fitzroy *Letter Saturday 7 April*

A delirious, a positively delirious mail this morning. To perfect matters, Fawcett, with the energy that distinguishes her, pointed out to the authorities that we evacuated half the patients yesterday, that our day off had been promised ages ago, and that we had better have it at once. So it came about that the mail surprised us having scrambled eggs for breakfast in the turret, where we spent a blissful morning. Now she and Murphy and I are away in a dip of the steppe which we have christened The Happy Valley, with luncheon, tea and supper in our knapsacks. The Happy Valley is partially cultivated, and full of little fruit trees not yet in blossom, and of little queer flowers that are. There is a vineyard further up, and flocks of sheep led by minute and altogether delightful shepherd children. In a little while we will shoulder our belongings and strike out over the steppe to a little village about four miles away that clings to a bare brown hill above two distracting little blue lakes. Then back after sunset to the Danube and the hills. *Some* day off, I assure you – but without a mail it could never have been so harmonious.

Sunday 8 April

We did about ten miles after I wrote this yesterday. The village was too fascinating for anything. The willows were turning a soft very young green, and large black and white storks balanced themselves in pools for our especial benefit.

Milne *Sunday 8 April Easter Day*

I have had several jolly little gifts from the Austrian prisoners which I prize very much – four Artillery buttons, which I shall make into studs – Luschke gave these to me – also two *abzeichen* – 1st Franz Joseph, the Austrian hat badge, and Franz Joseph 1st, the Hungarian badge. Very interesting to have, as they will never be made again. Then the joiner made me the dearest little riding whip out of cherry, with bits of shrapnel to decorate it and Reni 1917 on it. I love that.

Dr Scott came yesterday to see us on his way to Galatz – he is a perfect dear – I wish he was here. He is going to give me some empty 3-pound shell cases for flower vases.

Monday 9 April

Reni was shelled this evening by the Bulgars across the Danube. We hear the church was damaged, but how much we do not know. Four or five shells fell. I suppose we will be the next target – I am not a bit keen on that sort of thing. General Krupensky's son had supper with us tonight, and he was very depressing, more about the revolution than about the war. No workmen will do any work, and they will not be able to get ammunition enough, so the war will be much hampered by it, instead of helped on.

Inglis Report[16]

Since my last report there has been very little work on this front. Most of our cases have been accidents or ordinary operations, and a few medical cases. The only hospitals which have been full here have been the medical hospital and the infectious diseases hospital. I offered to take in medical cases, and they asked if I would also take in infectious cases. We have a small room with three beds in it which I had intended to be used for officers; so I answered that we would have it ready for infectious cases, and, if necessary, another ward which is on the corridor away from the main ward, and which has twelve beds. So far, however, we have only had one case of enteric.

Fawcett Diary Monday 9 April

Went for a lovely ride with Murphy over the steppe, and lost ourselves amongst the trenches on the way back. Reni was shelled this evening; one shell hit the church.

Tuesday 10 April

Visited the dentist and saw the hole in the church made by the shell. One house was absolutely ruined.

10.40 p.m. We have just had a thrill. First the house was surrounded; then two officers and about eight soldiers invaded the turret and went up to Murphy's room. They say that they have seen blue and red lights on our roof. Luckily I had just finished my bath. We were very annoyed, as they were so rude. We were just settling down for the night when another lot arrived, this time from the Expedition[17] – the others were from the Division. This lot we did not mind, as they were charming. They searched the roof and tapped all the walls. I suppose they thought we signal to the Germans, or else have a wireless apparatus. Murphy has had to go down to the Expedition to answer some questions. We are sitting up waiting for her return.

One rather sad thing is that they have taken away all our Austrian orderlies, and are going to send us fifteen Russians to replace them. Thirty would have been more use.

Wednesday 11 April

Further developments – it seems an age since last night. Dr Inglis went down with Murphy to the Expedition – also Sammy, bless him, and they were kept all night. That of course is all right; one can't blame the army for being careful. In the meantime, they sealed up Murphy's part of the turret, and we had an armed sentry there all night, which changed every two hours, and of course woke us every time they went up or came down. It seems that they have been watching the house carefully for some time; but why didn't they come straight to Dr Inglis if they had any suspicions? It was simply treating us as enemies instead of friends. Then again, they refused to allow Dr Inglis to wire to the British Consul. The crowning point of the insult was this morning, when they produced a paper which we all had to sign, saying that we believed in Murphy's fidelity. When they got this, they let Dr Inglis and Murphy come up (about 11.30 a.m.). Dr Inglis has sent along to General Krupensky telling him that we have been accused of espionage; will he come at once. Dr Inglis says that Murphy is not to sleep right up in the turret, so she is coming down with us.

12 midnight. General Krupensky arrived about 10.30, and is furious about the whole thing. He is going down to see the colonel of the regiment and arrange everything. He thinks that an apology will be forthcoming, otherwise we shall have to move on. He will not let us stay unless he can persuade the soldiers that we are not spies. The front is simply riddled with spies; they [the soldiers] seem to think that everyone else is a spy.

Milne *Wednesday 11 April*

The Austrians were released and are now back at their work, and very thankful we were to see them, and the dear things were glad to see us. They were very nastily treated by the Russians – they said the three men who worked in the house had been helping the sisters to work the lights.

Fawcett *Diary Thursday 12 April*

General Krupensky came back from visiting the colonel. The colonel had nothing to do with the actual arrest of Murphy; he simply ordered the house to be watched, as the men had complained of lights. This morning General Krupensky brought the colonel of the regiment up, and they went round asking the men if they liked us – of course they all said 'Yes, very much', and Nikolai made a long speech. They apologised abjectly to Murphy, and we congratulated ourselves that the matter had ended so satisfactorily.

General Krupensky wants us to move on rather than stay here and be shelled. Ten shells fell in Reni today. The hospitals and my dentist have been told that they may have to evacuate at any time.

Coming off duty this evening I was greeted with the news that Broadbent had been taken prisoner, and Murphy, Fitzroy and Dr Inglis had gone down with her to the commandant's. It seems that she was walking over the steppe, miles away from the trenches, carrying her diary and Russian Grammar, when she was arrested by two ordinary soldiers, and her books taken away from her. On their way along they were met by Fitzroy and Murphy, who insisted on the soldiers walking in front, and so they walked to the commandant of the town. There the soldiers' tale was listened to – first – and fully reported on, and our people were allowed to speak afterwards. How can they ever expect discipline, revolution or not, if they allow their soldiers to do this sort of thing? They all came back at about 10.30, but the books were kept and sealed up. If Broadbent gets them back without being opened she will have two Russian seals.

Milne *Thursday 12 April*

Last night General Krupensky came... the apology was all right, but it turns out that the soldiers are all against us here and think we are spies, and the authorities are afraid for our safety; also the place will be shelled tomorrow, perhaps. The general says it is unsafe for us to be here, but he does not wish us to go just at this moment in case it looks as if we were being sent away and gives truth to the men's suspicions – but he says he can't delay for more than a day or so as it is unsafe. The enemy is getting quite close, and the town was shelled this morning, and many killed; but Dr Inglis laughs and says we don't want to move unless it is absolutely necessary. I think it is the limit that she can want to stay and work for people who insult us...

Friday 13 April

Dr Inglis made a speech at roll call. I was not there, but most of the girls are furious about it; then she was in my room for nearly an hour, talking over the situation with me. I did not agree with her, I am afraid. She seems to think we are going to teach Russia what England stands for – she says it is the chance of our lives, and perhaps Russians will say, I have met a Scottish Woman, so I know what England is like.

Fawcett *Diary Saturday 14 April*

Two Russian Tommies came into the hospital this morning to ask if they might see over it. I sent for Matron to interview them, as I thought they probably wanted to say something. After they had finished, they apologised for the soldiers' behaviour to us and said that now they realised we were English, it would be all right. We are to have official passes which we are always to have on us.

Much shelling tonight.

Sunday 15 April [Russian Easter]

A priceless Easter Sunday in the hospital! First thing this morning a telegram came from General Surikov, the head of all the cavalry on this front, conveying his humblest apologies to Miss Murphy, one of the best workers of the Allies.

When we got into hospital, everyone greeted us with *'Khristos voskrese'* – Christ is risen; and all the soldiers were kissing each other. For breakfast they had coloured eggs. All the morning the men were charming – they presented Dr Inglis with a letter – most beautifully written. In the afternoon the colonel of one of the neighbouring regiments was carried into the hospital and kissed the men three times each. At five o'clock the sanitars danced outside the hospital. We soon collected a crowd of soldiers and several of them danced. Fitzroy and I also joined in, much to the joy of the men. We have both lost our heart to the same man – which is likely to cause complications.

The Armoured Car people (Mr Henderson and Dr King) say that probably Galatz is to be abandoned.

Wednesday 18 April

It is all nonsense about Galatz. Thank goodness! If Reni is shelled and we have to move on, we are to go to a charming little village on the banks of the Pruth.

Our little Cossack sergeant, aged 15, was in hospital this morning. He has four medals. He was picked up by the Cossack regiment when he was a baby and was brought up by them. He is a very nice boy.

Fitzroy *Letter Sunday 15 April*

We are enjoying our Russian Easter *so* much. I have just been down to the wards. They were full of sailors up from the quay laden with bowls of white bread, coloured eggs, Easter cake and bottles of wine. The men were delightful and made us all partake, and their greeting *'Khristos voskrese', 'voistinu voskrese'*[18] is perfect. The friendship for us heretics was I thought very pleasant, and I am so glad to be spending Russia's greatest feast here, though every green thing that grows makes us dream of our English Spring!

Hospital B Tecuci

Rendel *Letter Tuesday 24 April*

Our hospital now looks very fine. It is comparatively clean and all the most obvious dead cats and dogs have been buried or burned. I have two wards to myself and a sister. Unfortunately they are not using us for typhus after all. The typhus epidemic is almost limited to the Roumanians, and the Russians who are running us don't care a damn what happens to the Roumanians. I went over five typhus hospitals the other day – all Roumanian, and I saw patients in every stage, some at the beginning of the illness, some at the crisis, some dying, and others convalescent. Poor wretches! They are fed on tea and soup. Many were lying on the ground. The hospitals are all dirty, smelly and crowded. The doctor who took us round, a Roumanian, was very kind and showed us all the best cases and let us examine them. It was very interesting but depressing. It has been a bad epidemic, but worse at Jassi than here. Here the mortality has not been so high. The doctor in charge said he thought the death rate was less here because of *les petits soins* the patients receive. But you can hardly imagine anyone receiving less attention. They have taken no steps to stop the spread of infection. The patients are brought in here from the surrounding villages and dumped down in the first house that comes handy. They are all filthy dirty and covered with lice. The chief, or possibly the only, method of infection is from lice so you can imagine the condition of things is not hopeful.

Wednesday 25 April

Drove to the Berry Hospital in the afternoon with Dr C and Miss C... On return found a telegram from Miss Henderson saying that she is in Odessa with stores and is going to Reni. Miss Little is to go to Odessa at once to fetch them.

Hospital A Reni

Fitzroy *Letter 15 April*

I do hope you got away for Easter, and that some of our constant sunshine is yours. The moon shines on our faces all night and the sun all day. I don't pretend our complexions are the better for it – but our minds and bodies most certainly are! We wonder sometimes whether your, and particularly our mamas', natural pleasure in our return will survive the beholding of our freckles? (And remember this is only April.) So this is in the nature of preparation.

The front is getting very much alive, and my latest acquisition is a beautiful Russian shell-head...

The cherry blossom is out and the peach not far behind. It is very pleasant to go for a walk on the steppe and come suddenly to these most delicious valleys. Quite soon I am going to collect bulbs and growing things wherewith to adorn our water-garden – that is, if there exists anything brave enough to survive incarceration in a kit-bag.

I feel very uninteresting, and that this letter is most unsuitable – but after all the spring is new and the war – it seems – very very old!

CHAPTER 12
Struggles with Red Tape

After the initial spy scares the Scottish Women's Hospitals seem to have weathered revolutionary indiscipline relatively well. Officers who visited the hospital at Reni brought tales of insubordination, of orderlies refusing to work, patients refusing treatment, and soldiers refusing to advance. In all this turmoil, the hospital at Reni remained surprisingly peaceful and happy, held together by Dr Inglis's strength and by the affection and respect both staff and patients felt for her.

There were, however, other factors which seriously hampered their work. Their future, always dependent on the movements of the volatile eastern front, was now also affected by the progress of the revolution, and, more directly, by the opinion of the British Foreign Office about the interaction between these two factors. Doubts about Russia's ability to continue fighting and fears for the safety of British subjects in Russia made decisions difficult for those at home, while replacing staff became a serious problem for those on the spot. April 1917 marked the start of a struggle over personnel between Inglis (usually, though not always, supported by the SWH committees) and the various authorities responsible for granting permission to travel.

Before Christmas she had telegraphed from Galatz asking the London Committee to send out replacements for the few orderlies and nurses who had gone home in November, and for those due to leave in February. Even before the uncertainties occasioned by the February revolution, the committee was in some difficulty about meeting this request, for trained nurses, in particular, were in short supply. The employment of women had expanded so successfully that at the end of 1916 the War Office had reversed its earlier policy, and had begun using them in hospitals and base camps in France as well as at home; and early in 1917 the Women's Army Auxiliary Corps was formed, to be followed by the Women's Royal Naval Service and the Women's Royal Air Force.[1] Trained women of every kind, and medical women especially, were at a premium.

Since any person wishing to travel abroad had to obtain permission from the Foreign Office, the London Committee accordingly made a routine application on behalf of the nurses and orderlies needed by Inglis. Instead of the expected permission, they received, on 23 April, a letter relaying the War Office's instructions that no more medical women were to leave Britain, since they were wanted at home. At the same meeting the committee heard that the British Red Cross, at the behest of Mr Kimens, their commissioner in Petrograd, had stopped sending hospital staff to Russia and Roumania, and advised the SWH to do the same. Travel inside Russia was becoming increasingly difficult, and as all returning travellers reported, Petrograd was crowded with foreigners waiting to get away.

A few days later the difficulties of the committee were compounded by another letter from the Foreign Office to say that the Consul at Odessa had cabled, with the concurrence of Marx and Miss Henderson, that conditions in Russia were so uncertain that it was inadvisable to send women drivers, and he recommended that the SWH engage men locally, or use Serb drivers, some of whom had already been taught to drive by the women.[2] This was treachery indeed on the part of Miss Henderson and Marx, and Dr Inglis was very angry when she heard later of their intervention. Meanwhile she cabled from Odessa on 8 May:

> Have your telegram saying orderlies required in January have not yet started. One matron, one cook, sixteen sisters, besides these orderlies, clerk and sanitary inspector required on July the fifteenth, therefore should leave England on June fifteenth; also two doctors. British Red Cross arranged with War Office that these hospitals should be kept up to original strength, ask Mr Stanley, showed me letter. Unless reliefs arrive July sixteenth must close hospital in middle of summer campaign.[3]

The Honourable Arthur Stanley, in charge of the British Red Cross in London, had indeed made such an arrangement with the War Office; he now reminded the commissioner in Petrograd of it, but his intercession merely provoked a sharp reply from the overtaxed Kimens:

> Your telegram May 12th respecting Scottish Women party. As Englishwomen continue to come to Russia contrary to my advice I have submitted matter to His Majesty's Ambassador who is absolutely against it and considers conditions at present quite unfit for Englishwomen to work in Russia. If they nevertheless insist on coming they must do it on their own responsibility.[4]

After their record in the Dobrudga retreat, the assumption that Englishwomen (or Scottish ones) required special conditions was both an insult and an anachronism, but this was no time to protest. 'On their own responsibility' left a narrow loophole, and dismayed, but not defeated, the London Committee went on struggling with bureaucracy. The orderlies 'required in January' to replace Bowerman and the other six-monthers were allowed to leave some time in mid-May, but the twelve-month contracts of the rest of the unit would soon expire, and so far no travel permits had been granted for their substitutes. The secretary, Miss Palliser, personally visited Lord Robert Cecil, Under-secretary for Foreign Affairs, who agreed to write to the relevant authorities, and who suggested that the Serbian Foreign Minister might write too. Cecil recognised the diplomatic importance of the work of the Scottish Women, and now began using this argument in his communications with the War Office.

So the long process of negotiation continued, a process involving a succession of anxious telegrams and visits to people with influence in high places. In a letter to the Foreign Office on 26 May, Miss Palliser explained that the sixteen orderlies for whom permits were requested were being sent to Russia to replace *trained*[5] nurses now returning to Britain. Although there was no national register of trained nurses until 1919, and definitions of training varied considerably, the Joint War Committee of the British Red Cross and St John's Ambulance Societies had drawn up their own list of requirements for sisters, which specified three years of training in a general hospital of not fewer than fifty beds, those with shorter training being accepted as staff nurses at a lower salary.[6] By this standard no members of the SWH party in question, except Dr Ward, fell into the prohibited category of 'medical women', although the intention was certainly to employ most of them as nurses.

By 7 June there had been no response from the Foreign Office, and Dr Inglis's deadline of 15 June was very close. Miss Palliser wrote urgently to Lord Robert, who had still not heard from the War Office; after he had prodded them, authorisation for the journey was at last given on 11 June,[7] and the first party of four was able to leave. The rest left at intervals in small groups, Butler's and Hedges' parties in mid-July and August being the last. Women drivers were again refused permits, which probably explains why Birkbeck and others of the Transport joined other organisations instead of returning to Russia as they had intended, and why Hedges, one of Mrs Haverfield's original drivers, was officially designated 'laundry superintendent' for her second spell of duty.

Given the late arrival of the new staff, it was fortunate that neither of the hospitals was very busy in the spring of 1917. The Galatz front had been quiet since early January, with little aggression from the Russian side, except for some heavy firing by a detachment of the British Armoured Cars – an exercise resented by the Russian soldiers, because it provoked retaliatory shelling.[8] The Provisional Government, initially dominated by Constitutional Democrats (Kadets)[9] found itself helpless in the face of the soviets, especially the soldiers' committees, and many of its cabinet ministers resigned in mid-May. They were replaced by a coalition of Kadets and moderate socialists who, like their predecessors, intended to keep Russia in the war, and to defer the redistribution of land and other reforms until victory had been won. In the cabinet reshuffle, Aleksander Kerensky became Minister of War, and immediately planned an offensive, using his considerable rhetorical powers in an attempt to instil new spirit into the Russian army. The Allied ambassadors and military attachés began to hope for an effective Russian diversion to relieve pressure on the western front, where their own forces were in some disarray.[10]

Dr Inglis's telegram of 8 May[11] mentions an impending summer campaign, and the coming offensive, soon to be known as the 'Kerensky Offensive', was talked of all through May and June. The hospitals were repeatedly told to prepare for it, but it was repeatedly postponed. So inactive were all sections of the eastern front that the British Red Cross seriously considered withdrawing their units under Drs Berry and Clemow. As they talked to their patients, to visiting officers, and to the Armoured Car men stationed in Galatz, the Scottish Women could see that the Russian army was in no spirit to continue the war, and some began to think that the Hospitals might be better employed elsewhere. Yet the many unknown factors made it impossible to foresee how the eastern front might develop, and Dr Inglis's primary commitment was to the Serbian Division, which had agreed to recall her hospitals when they were needed. In this climate of uncertainty, the best thing to do was to keep the hospitals up to strength, and she continued to press for more staff.

Hospital A Reni

Fitzroy *Letter Sunday 29 April*
We are hourly expecting Miss Henderson with not only parcels but mails and all the news – so you may imagine the unit to be all of a flutter. She reported herself at Odessa some while back, so every night we go to bed mourning her absence and every morning we rejoice that there is still something to look forward to.

I am the proud possessor of one entire tent to myself. I wonder if you can realise what a godsend that is after a minimum of four in a room? Relations between Fawcett, Murphy and I and our M.A. laundry superintendent became the merest shade strained and we three leapt at the opportunity of moving. As most of the unit are still in the house, that leaves us the proud possessors of a tent apiece. We moved yesterday and our tempers are becoming momentarily more angelic. To wake up in the morning and to find yourself lord of a kingdom 8' x 10' is real bliss. The weather is uncertain and prone to sudden violent storms of wind and rain, so I trust the kingdom won't collapse. The art of keeping warm in bed I have brought to perfection.

Letter continued 3 May

Dr Inglis is becoming very restless as the fighting on this front seems ever delayed, and believes, I think, that the First Serb Division will soon be reformed and require us, but whether to work on this front or to follow them to Salonica seems particularly hazy. Of news from Petrograd we have none, and Miss Henderson still delays.

I went for a ride with my chief the other night. We came in for the May-day celebrations in the village. It is very incongruous to hear the Marseillaise sung by these soldiers – their own national anthem having for the moment been dropped as it contains some reference to the Tsar. And it's funny how they miss the rhythms thereof – it's wholly unsuitable, besides they have other things as fine of their own.

Saturday 5 May[12]

Matron was stopped by some soldiers on her way into the village this morning, who asked her if we had everything we wanted – for if not, *they* would see that we got it! And Nikolai distinguished himself by telling four Russian doctors who were paying us a state visit that no Russian hospital he'd ever seen was anything like as good as ours!

Hospital B Tecuci

Rendel *Diary Tuesday 1 May*

Woken up at 5.30 a.m. by aeroplanes (enemy) dropping bombs. 8 a.m. sent for to hospital. Two victims brought in. Both leg cases. Amputation necessary. I gave the anaesthetic for both. Very bad cases. Nervous work. Dr C's patient died soon after operation.

Friday 4 May

Mrs Berry[13] returned. She says that Miss H is still in Odessa and the stores are in Petrograd!

Monday 7 May

Woken up by aeroplanes. Fierce attack. A great many bombs fell. 7 a.m. sent for to hospital. Man brought in with smashed legs and haemorrhage. Sent for Dr C to put on tourniquet; gave a saline. Dr C amputated at once. Busy morning.

From 9th to 19th no firing heard. All kinds of rumours. Some people say the Russians are going to advance. We had orders to evacuate everyone and prepare for a big battle. Nearly all patients were sent off as soon as possible; meantime not a gun was heard. Rumours say that the Russians and Germans are picnicking in each other's trenches. Everyone says there is complete disorganisation. Many people say that a separate peace is imminent. There is a good deal of anti-English feeling.

Saturday 12 May

Miss Little returned with the stores and a mail. Except for winter vests, everything was very welcome... The commissariat men are very hopeful. They say there will be an advance.

Hospital A Reni

Milne *'Some Months in Bessarabia'*[14]

Spring slipped imperceptibly into summer, and the Danube was blue again. The willows across the river came into leaf; the miles of marsh-land which stretched beyond were covered with a yellow weed, which looked like gold in the sunshine; and in the background was the range of beautiful Roumanian mountains, at the foot of which the Bulgarians were camped. And so from week to week we waited for the great advance. We were told to be ready for hundreds of wounded, and always the date was changed, and still we waited, but there was no advance. It was a glorious summer. We saw the beauties of the steppe in every season: first miles and miles of dazzling spotless snow; for a short spell the dry withered grass, which after the first spring rain seemed to turn green in a single night. Then came the spring flowers. Carpets of sweet violets, flowering bulbs in endless variety, and the dainty scarlet windflower everywhere. Orchards of apricot and almond trees, with their dark stems and glorious pink blossoms; hillsides white with the cherry. No wonder the Russian loves his beautiful country, and the simple peasant, who has only the vaguest idea what the war is all about, longs to be back in his vineyards and his maize-fields.

Fawcett *Letter Sunday 6 May*

Yesterday Murphy, Fitzroy, and I went for a picnic – our object was to get to the Pruth valley, where there is a splendid view of the Pruth and Danube valleys and of Galatz and Braila. This we did quite easily, but coming home by moonlight, walking as we thought parallel to the Danube, we got too far inland and went about six miles beyond Reni, and had to come all the way back. Altogether we must have gone about twenty miles.

We were told the other day by one of our patients that the Russian sisters were pretty but not good, and the English sisters were good but not pretty.

Diary Tuesday 8 May

Miss Henderson arrived at eleven last night, with Mr French, a Church of England parson.[15] They brought mails, and all sorts of stores.

Fitzroy *Letter Saturday 8 May*

The mail – the mail! Late last night Miss H arrived, and now Captain Henderson of the Armoured Cars has arrived to take *our* post with him to Odessa. So there is no time to thank or answer you properly... The big parcel from the Army and Navy Stores arrived; the new officials are much more honest!

Fawcett *Diary Thursday 10 May*

We had Holy Communion this morning in a marquee.

Such a blow! Fitzroy is going home almost at once. Miss Henderson tells her that her mother has had an attack of appendicitis, and although she is all right now, is to have the operation when Fitzroy gets home. Naturally she feels that she should go at once. I shall miss her horribly, especially if Murphy decides to go too.

Inglis *Letter 11 May*[16]

Miss Fitzroy has had disquieting news brought to her by Miss Henderson about her mother's health, so I am letting her go home at once, as the new orderlies are so close at hand. I should like the committee to know that she has done splendidly, a real asset to the unit, hard-working and conscientious and good-tempered, and as cheery and plucky as they are made. A first-rate girl to have in any unit...

Your telegram about the salaries has arrived. Miss Fawcett is quite happy. (She will miss Miss Fitzroy very much. They had become great chums.) Many thanks from myself for the doctors. Personally I am more than content, – but I cannot help thinking that if you want to keep the supply you would be wiser to put the remuneration on the War Office basis. Apart from anything, we are a Women's Society. It was one thing to give an honorarium, and a very generous honorarium too. It is another to give a smaller salary, – for it is much too big now to be an honorarium.

Fawcett *Diary Saturday 12 May*

Murphy and I went to see Fitzroy and Sisters Walker-Brown and Susie[17] off to Odessa. Mr French came with us to get the tickets. He is quite a good sort. I think Broadbent is rather disappointed that he is not more pi.

Inglis *Report 27 May*[18]

The Out Patients' Department is a thing which has 'growed of itself'.

There were at one time three regiments which had no doctors, and the men used to come up for treatment. Now we have three or four regiments, also recruits and men from the Expedition, and the department flourishes exceedingly. It is very monotonous work, but I am glad to have it, as it brings us in touch with the ordinary Russian soldier; also, some of the men are really ill, and require hospital treatment; e.g. the appendix case. Further, it is a splendid barometer of outside feeling. For a few days at the time of the spy incident hardly a man came near us. But since then the number of patients has steadily increased...

The little burst of feeling aroused by the spy scare has quite died down, and has given place to very friendly relations. I had a very delightful postcard from one of the men who went to Odessa, and we have also had letters from some of the patients which I shall get translated and send to you some time. One day when Matron went to Reni to see about something, she found a group of Russian soldiers round her horse when she came out. The men asked her if she had got what she wanted, and she answered that he had promised to see about it; whereupon the men said, 'The commandant must be told that the Scottish Women's Hospital is the best hospital on this front, and it must have everything that it wants. That is the opinion of the Russian soldier.'

Miss Henderson has now gone to Barlad to see Dr Chesney's hospital, and intends to go from there to Jassi to rescue the stores which I asked for in October, and which have not yet arrived. She will then go to Odessa and bring on a few things that are required here. Miss Henderson very kindly says that if the committee agree, she will be willing to come back again about September and bring with her winter supplies. I hope the committee will agree, because it is obvious from our experience with the stores that have now gone to Jassi that unless accompanied by someone, it is almost impossible to get them.

Dr Chesney's hospital is, I understand, at Barlad. But there is evidently some little doubt as to this. I had a letter from her sent in by a Serbian soldier, but with no address. She said that they were getting a fair amount of work, but the building they were in was dirty and dark, and nothing would ever make it look nice. They were asked to work as an infectious diseases hospital, but were doing surgery.

Hospital B Tecuci

Rendel *Letter Wednesday 9 May*
We are really very busy now as our hospital is full of patients. Several of them are poor wretches who have been bombed by German aeroplanes.

Since I wrote last we have had two bad visitations. They came about 5.30 each morning and stayed for half an hour. About 30 bombs were dropped in the town and the noise was terrific. It is such a very small place, hardly more than a village, so you can imagine it is not very pleasant to have eight or nine enemy aeroplanes just overhead. Last time they came there was a furious battle in the air and at last they were driven off by four French planes. Mr Rothe our commissariat man has now insisted on having a dug-out built for us and our Serbs. It will hold 75 people when it is finished and according to him will be bomb proof. At present it is hardly a foot deep.

Diary Tuesday 15 May

The Russian Red Cross general came round. We asked him if the Russians would advance. He said that it was impossible. The disorganisation is too great. He said that it was slightly better than it had been, but that fighting was out of the question. But he was evidently very anti the new regime.

Hospital A Reni

Milne '*Some Months in Bessarabia*'[19]

'Off-duty time' was looked forward to by everyone. Some took tea with them, others supper, just as their free time allowed; then away to the 'Happy Valley', as we called it, among the flowers and the bluebirds, either on foot or on horseback. There were twenty horses for the hospital transport, six of which we rode, on extraordinary saddles, padded like the arm of a Chesterfield sofa, but quite comfortable when one got used to them. What glorious rides we had, over the steppe, through the maize-fields (the maize standing above our heads on horseback), down to the water-meadows, where we let the horses graze while we sat beneath the apricot trees to eat our supper and watch the storks go to roost on the pollard-willows by the edge of the lake.

I would not like it to be thought that our life was all 'off-duty time', joy-riding and flowers – far from it; but these are the times one loves to remember. Though no wounded were coming into the hospital, the doctors saw dozens of outpatients every day, soldiers belonging to the various regiments stationed in Reni. There were many operations among them which kept the hospital staff busy. As far as my own department was concerned, whether the work in hospital was heavy or light, the appetites of the staff were fairly healthy. Sometimes, with the heat and the flies in the kitchen, life was hardly worth living. The fly we had to contend with was not the mild English fly, but a much smaller brand, and very venomous. We had periodical 'fly strafes', but after working like slaves to clear them from the mess room, next day they would be as bad as ever. Then the dogs were sent to try us, thirty to forty wild steppe dogs; they got into our tents by day, lay under the beds to keep cool, and covered everything with fleas; they fought and howled all night. Some of them were savage brutes, and we never knew when they would attack us.

Fawcett *Diary Tuesday 15 May*
An English Tommy came into hospital yesterday – a nasty wound in the right shoulder. He seems a very nice boy, named Vaughan. Mr Edwards and Mr Henderson came to bridge last night. Mr Henderson came without his Sam Browne, and he looked as if he hadn't brushed his hair for a month.

Friday 18 May
Ecroyd, the second Armoured Car casualty,[20] arrived in the night – he has a wound in the chest and pleurisy. He seems awfully seedy. The BAC are ready to leave Galatz at a minute's notice, as the Russian War Minister has had to resign and it is very probable that there will be a separate peace. I can't quite see the idea, but I suppose it is to get out of the country quickly before we have a chance to declare war on Russia. If this happened, of course Japan and China would step in against Russia. I suppose we should be sent home.

   We have Vaughan and Ecroyd in our ward, much to the disgust of the sisters in the other ward.

Monday 21 May
Telegram this morning saying that the new orderlies and the administrator have left Petrograd.

Hospital B Tecuci

Rendel *Diary Saturday 19 May*
Miss H and her tame parson Mr French arrived.

Letter Wednesday 23 May
Two days ago an English general inspecting the front came along and paid us a visit. General Powel or Pool, I'm not sure which.[21] He came out with Lord Milner and was left behind in Petrograd. He was very pleasant and admired our funk-hole very much. He said it was quite the latest pattern, except for one omission. It ought to have a layer of stones to act as a breaker. He said it was quite right to have one as we are within range of German guns. They did shell the aerodrome the other day. He was more

hopeful about the situation here than some others. Opinions vary very much. Some people say we shall have an offensive here in a week or two.

We have some fine English anti-aircraft guns here now in armoured cars. But they will be moving off soon. Two days ago we had three enemy aeroplane attacks in one day. Thanks to our guns they didn't last long.

Hospital A Reni

Milne *Friday 3 June*
The new orderlies arrived in the night of the 1st. My kitchen orderly is very good and will be a great help to me – Haviland is her name. They are all nice girls and will be a great addition – but they brought no letters or photographs, which was a terrible disappointment.

Inglis *Letter Tuesday 5 June*[22]
The party under Miss Genge has arrived and I like them all very much. Miss Genge is not exactly my idea of an administrator! But she will probably do all right... In my report I have told you that Miss Marx wants men drivers – and as she cannot have them has resigned. It would be absurd after the extraordinary success the Transport has made, to climb down and fall back on men. When Miss Marx wrote to me, I explained that our first object was to care for the wounded – but our second to do it through a women's organisation. That is the case, isn't it? And now that the Transport is to be closely attached to the hospital, there is no reason whatsoever for changing. Miss Marx seems to have got very panicky about the condition of things in Russia – but if she were right (which she isn't) it would be a reason for giving up the hospitals, *not* for having men drivers for the cars!

Fawcett *Letter Friday 8 June*
We have quite a plague of dogs in the camp – they are great big beasts of all descriptions, but all with a touch of the wolf about them. They hang about the camp all day, and bark all night. The other day we thought we would drive them away, but they resented it bitterly, and have been snappy ever since. They also bring a plague of fleas with them, which get into our beds and devour us.

Russian news seems awfully black, and things seem as bad as they did before the revolution. The first days after the revolution were the brightest at the front – then they put the best men into power, and things flourished for a bit. Now the real leaders are just throwing up their position because they can do nothing with their men. The whole army now is being run by the soldiers' committees, and if they decide that they don't want to fight, they just go home. As far as we can see, there is nothing to stop them deserting.

An officer, who used to be our administrator, and is now in charge of the ASC[23] or something of the sort at Galatz, was sitting at his desk the other day when two soldiers came in. They said that they would see to the day's business, so they took his pen and signed all his papers. There was a case in Odessa the other day when they flogged a spy through the streets.

Letter Saturday 16 June Reni

Dr Inglis is going to Odessa tomorrow to find out if the Serbs want us. If they are still doing nothing and so do not need us, she will demand to be sent to some more exciting place where there is more work to be done. We really aren't doing much good here – just a few sick men from the neighbouring regiments.

We have a good many Roumanian soldiers who come to the hospital as outpatients. Poor dears – they look quite worn out and fit for nothing but bed. They wear sort of sandal things on their feet. This morning out of twenty men who came to the hospital only one had a pair of boots. Their uniforms are of powder blue, often with red revers, and are most frightfully shabby.

SWH Committee London

Clearly by mid-June the Scottish Women's initial euphoria about the revolution had worn off, and they were worried about their future. Both hospitals had been 'lent' to the Russians while the Serbian Division was in reserve, and although they dutifully repaired the scores of Russian left hands that came their way, this was not what they had come to Russia to do. At home, too, there was anxiety, and even while Dr Inglis was on her way to Odessa to negotiate a return to the Serbs, the committee in London met to discuss the withdrawal of the unit. On 18 June Miss Palliser went to see Mr Sawyer, of the British Red Cross; he showed her a letter from Kimens in Petrograd reiterating the conviction expressed in his earlier telegram, and told her of the plan to withdraw the Berry and Clemow units.[24] Before the committee meeting that afternoon, however, she received the following letter from Mrs Laurie, the treasurer in Edinburgh.

Sunday 17 June

I have just heard you are having a special meeting tomorrow to discuss the future of the Russian units, and that this may possibly mean a proposal to withdraw them. It seems to me that the SWH are now so much a part of international politics that we would have to look at the position of the hospitals from a wider point of view than merely that of the number of patients they might for the moment have in their care. There is no doubt that the Russians have been a source of usefulness as allies in the past, and we must hope they will be as valuable in the future... Do not let us push them over into the arms of the German sympathisers, who are there in their myriads to get them detached from their allies by every manner of means.

If Dr Inglis cannot get wounded patients to look after, that does not hinder our work from going forward. From our first appeal to the public, we have always put forward the plea that whether it was fever or cholera, whether it was wounded or sick, we were ready to help in every way we were wanted. We have in Corsica a striking instance of this in our care of the refugees of the Serbian population who got asylum there...

I would not have written to you at all had I not felt that the policy of withdrawing would be fatal.[25]

Probably this encouragement tipped the balance, for there was no decision to withdraw the hospitals.

Hospital B Tecuci

Rendel *Letter Monday 18 June*
I was stretched on a bed of sickness for a week but I am now quite well again. Dr C was very kind and looked after me very well. It was just like my luck that the Queen of Roumania[26] came to Tecuci whilst I was ill and asked to see some of the Scottish Women. She went to the Berry hospital, which is three miles from here, and Dr C, Miss Corbett, and the matron drove over there to be presented to her. They said she was very beautiful although very much made up, and she was dressed from head to foot in flowing white draperies swathed round her face like a nun.

The Russians have given us for the use of the unit an elegant carriage drawn by two horses. In this we drive about when off duty and see the country. The other day we drove off towards the front. We went on and on till we were within a mile of the position. On our way home just as we had turned round we heard a loud explosion, looked back, and saw a column of dust and dirt in the air. It was about 200 yards away, so we couldn't see what had happened, but we hoped that it was an enemy shell.

Letter to Ray Monday 18 June
We are having rather a dull time of it here waiting for the Russians to make a move. Every now and then a stray shell or mine explodes in a trench and we are very busy for a day or two. Then for long intervals we get nothing but patients who have been kicked by horses they were

probably ill-treating or who are tired of fighting and say they have got pains in their insides. Periodically we get a notice to evacuate all possible patients and to prepare for a rush of severe cases. We obey orders, our hospital is empty for a day and then they send us the same old rubbish as before. We are almost empty now and everyone says that something is going to happen at last but it is all very doubtful and extremely irritating. The Provisional Government seems to be chiefly occupied with altering the alphabet and the calendar. One of the latest rules that the soldiers' committee has made is that a soldier may if he likes be an officer's servant but it is to be a purely voluntary arrangement.

Letter Monday 25 June
Dr C got a letter from Miss Inglis yesterday saying that Lady Decies[27] was on her way out and was to be sent here as 'house superintendent'. We haven't got a house and the only thing there will be for her to superintend is the laundry-tent in which two thieving, idle and very dirty old Roumanian women wash the clothes for us and for the hospital. I suppose Lady D is hoping for some adventures at the front.

Hospital A Reni

Inglis *Letter 24 June*[28]
I have had a long talk to Miss Marx, and she has quite come back to her bearings, so... I am keeping her on as Transport Officer.

Fawcett *Letter Friday 6 July*
Poor Dr Inglis has Hunpox. She is awfully seedy with gastritis as well.

There are thousands and thousands of flies in the house – when you go into the kitchen at night and disturb them, they make as much noise as half a dozen kettles boiling.

We have been at Reni for nearly seven months now, so I am beginning to think we should get a move on. Of course we don't want any more retreats, but would like the Russians to buck up and do something. They have hardly done anything on this part of the front since we have been here. We occasionally hear the enemy shelling Braila or Galatz, and once or twice there have been shells on Reni; once they landed on the battery quite close to us, but that is all. Of course we often get enemy aircraft over, but they don't seem to have any grudge against us. The other day one of the sisters picked up quite a big piece of shrapnel just behind the house.

Foreign Office London

In London, in response to a request on 3 July from the Royal Serbian Legation, the Foreign Office made the first half-hearted move to have the

Serbian Divisions transferred to the Salonica front, 'if the Russian Government allows them to go'. Conditions inside Russia appeared so inimical to a successful campaign that there was a general desire amongst the Serbs in Russia to join the Serbian army, now refitted after the 1915 retreat and stationed at Salonica. Comments pencilled on the minute circulating with the Serbian Legate's letter read:

> 1) The Serbs are evidently afraid of the demoralising effect of the Russian anarchy, but it is a very serious proposition to transport these men the whole way round to Salonica, and I doubt whether it is feasible.
>
> 2) We should do this if at all possible, which I doubt – we might support the idea.[29]

A week later the Army Council wrote to the Admiralty saying that this transfer of the Serbian Divisions was very desirable, and asking for ships to transport them.[30] Clarity on the future of the Divisions would provide clarity on that of the Hospitals, and Dr Inglis began to plan for Salonica.

Hospital A London to Petrograd

Also about this time, four newly-engaged nurses were on their way to Reni, under the guardianship of Elsie Butler. A graduate in Modern Languages, and accepted because of her linguistic skills and experience of foreign travel, Miss Butler is designated in the official list simply as 'orderly'. Like many of the other orderlies, she clearly had the talent and initiative that Dr Inglis was looking for when wrote on 8 January, 'Does the committee think it would be possible to send five or six more strong orderlies at once over and above the six I have already asked for – the sort of girl I have here is very suitable.'[31]

Butler[32]

...It was much the same story with the capers cut by Russian diminutives. They could do almost anything with a noun: toss it up and down, turn it inside out, make it look sweet or funny, or silly or grotesque, as their fancy dictated. I can still see Jane Harrison at her desk, her black head-dress sweeping round her shoulders, a dedicated and sibylline expression on her face, as she expounded the difference between the perfective and imperfective aspects of the verb and dawn began to glimmer over the Slavonic mind.

'Yes, I know Russian,' I boldly declared to the London Committee of the Scottish Women's Hospitals, who wanted nurses for Russia. I had got as far as an interview, but was not making much headway. My VAD experience was lamentably slight, it was felt; and a university education was not likely to be much of an asset in a field hospital. My usefulness to Dr Inglis, if they sent me out, seemed highly problematical. On the other hand, they needed someone to shepherd a party of four nursing sisters through Norway, Sweden, Finland and Russia right down to Bessarabia in the south. None of the four had ever been abroad, none of them spoke any language but their own. Someone was needed to act as courier and wrestle with foreign currencies. I said I knew Russian, and so I was sent.

I doubt if we should ever have reached our destination, had it not been for those two remarkable women, Jane Harrison and Dr Inglis, who seemed to be guiding me from afar. I did not know the latter then; but I later realised the extraordinary power over persons and events which she exercised even from a distance. All I knew about her when I left England was that she needed the four nurses urgently; and that to fail her in the slightest particular was regarded by the London Committee as tantamount to high treason. So that my consternation was great when, having struggled as far as Petrograd through obstacles innumerable, I was nearly prevented by the Red Cross commissioner [Kimens]. He had no real jurisdiction over me; but we were travelling under the auspices of the Red Cross and he flatly refused to give me the necessary vouchers. There was only one train a week to Odessa, he told me, and that was a troop train which took four days to get there. He could not countenance such a journey. The soldiers had taken complete control since the revolution, and they were in a dangerous mood. We should certainly be raped, and probably murdered. It was the height of folly to have come out at all at the present juncture, and the only thing to do now was to go straight back home. He held most of the cards, for he held the vouchers and also the funds; but I had the ace of trumps up my sleeve. 'Has Dr Inglis cancelled my orders?' I asked. 'They were to the effect that I was to get the nurses down to Reni at all costs and at top speed.' He crumpled up, being obviously far more frightened of what Dr Inglis would say to him than of anything the Russians could do to us. 'Lily-livered,' I chanted happily to myself, vouchers and money in my pocket, as I walked back to the hotel where the sisters were safely immured.

The Kerensky Offensive Galicia
Kerensky himself was present on the Galician front when his offensive opened on 1 July. Knowing that it would be something of a gamble, he followed the expedient of 'stiffening' his armies with troops who could be trusted to obey their officers. The Cossacks were, on the whole, willing to fight: fighting was their profession, and was the agreed price for ancient privileges, which they hoped the Provisional Government would continue

to allow them. But apart from the Cossacks and the volunteer Battalions of Death,[33] the other reliable troops were foreigners: some Polish regiments, who had agreed to fight for the Tsar in return for a measure of independence; Czechs and Slovaks who, like the Austrian Slavs, had 'gone over' to the Russians; a detachment of Belgian machine gunners, some French airmen, and those old friends of the Scottish Women, the British Armoured Cars, recently transferred from Galatz and Tiraspol.[34]

Surgeon W.H. King of the BAC, describing the first day's fighting in Galicia, tells how some regiments advanced and did well, but were forced back because they were unsupported, either on their flanks or by the reserves who should have followed them. In others, officers who had pleaded in vain with their men eventually advanced alone to become certain casualties.[35] Although further south there was more apparent success, much of this was due to the surrender of more bands of discontented Austrian Slavs; and it was soon clear that the offensive had failed. For a few weeks the front returned to its quietly endemic trench warfare, while the hospitals did their best for the wounded.

Also at work in Galicia were some of the ex-members of the SWH Transport unit, among them Hodges and Donisthorpe. These were working, some as drivers, some as nurses, with Dr King-Atkinson's Millicent Fawcett Unit, which had become a military hospital attached to the Russian army.[36] When the fierce German counter-attack came on 20 July, the Russians left suddenly without providing transport for the British hospital. Luckily Staff-Surgeon Scott was there helping Dr Atkinson, and he commandeered a BAC lorry to take the staff to safety; once again, the Armoured Cars had come to the rescue of their compatriots.[37]

News of the failure in Galicia was quick to reach Southern Russia and Roumania, and the Scottish Women were downcast. Rendel and Milne (and the sisters whose contracts were finishing) began to fear that they might never get away, while Butler, newly arrived and full of a refreshing romantic excitement, was afraid that she would arrive too late. All longed to be doing some really useful work.

Hospital B Camp near Tecuci

Rendel *Letter Monday 2 July*

The game is up here and I am coming home as fast as possible. But at the best it will be a slow process. The Russian offensive, after beginning well, failed hopelessly in Galicia owing to want of discipline. Some of the regiments refused to fight, and while their delegates were discussing the matter, the Germans advanced. The result is that the offensive has come to an end all along the line. The fact is the Russian soldiers have had enough of it. All the officers say the same thing – there is absolutely no discipline, everyone does exactly what he likes.

They moved us here two days ago. The main party came by night as the road isn't safe by day, especially for a long trail of cars. We thought our camp here was very safe from German shells, as it is just under a cliff over which the shells come, aimed at some Russian batteries just opposite. Below is a map of our position.

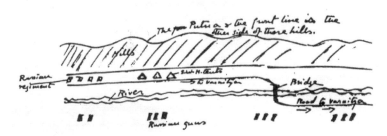

The very first morning we were here we were rather startled when a Russian shell lodged in our midsts. Instead of going over the hills it fell in the middle of our camp. Luckily it didn't burst or it would have killed two or three of our Serbs who were sitting less than two feet away.

Except for very desultory shelling and aeroplanes there is no fighting. Dr Chesney saw the general today and he said there was no hope of anything happening. Dr C is motoring to Reni tomorrow to see Dr Inglis and as soon as we can get our equipment away, we shall go.

I am sick of Russia and of Russians.

Diary 5 or 6 July

Mr Retkin came and told us to prepare for a big battle. Dr C told him the sisters were all going home on the 17 July and that no more were coming out. Mr R said it was impossible they should go. He came again and begged them to stay. All but three refused to stay. Sisters Henderson, Mundie, and Atkinson stayed.

Hospital A Reni and Petrograd

Fawcett *Letter Sunday 8 July*

What do you think about Russia now? We are frightfully sick of the whole thing. Individually I like the Russians awfully; even the peasants – who collectively are causing all the fuss in Petrograd – are charming when they come into hospital. The other day we had a Russian doctor through the hospital. At first he did not want to come in, as he said the men in his hospital had been so unbearable. However, we persuaded him, and he was struck with the peaceful atmosphere of the place.

Butler *Petrograd*[38]

Next morning we were at the station hours before the train was due; but a surging mob of soldiers was there before us; and when it came in five hours late we couldn't get anywhere near it. Those soldiers at least were not pulling out of the war. Determined to get to the front, they took the train by storm, pouring into the compartments, overflowing into the corridors, clambering up on to the roofs, crowding into the engine driver's cab and clinging on to the running boards, while hundreds left on the platform with us roared in rage and dismay. A whistle sounded, and the tumult died down. From the roof of one of the waggons a soldier called out something which I recognised as a double diminutive signifying 'poor little sisters'. Jane had impressed upon me that diminutives of compassion were very potent. I stood on tiptoe, wrung my hands, wailed like a lost soul, and generally speaking, 'created'; whilst the cry 'poor little sisters' was taken up behind, above, around and in front of us. Jane would have called it 'a holophrastic howl', for, being interpreted, it meant, 'We cannot leave them behind'. Five men came tumbling out of the train, we were dragged in and our kit-bags hurled after us just as it began to move.

As they had begun, so those soldiers went on. Rape and murder were far from their thoughts. They saw to it that we had our full share of sitting down in the daytime and lying down in shifts at night. They cleared the way for us when we had to struggle down the corridor to the appalling lavatory at the end. They filled our drinking bottles for us from the huge station urns, and they shared their bread with us. They patted us occasionally and smiled and said, 'Poor little sisters'; and poor little sisters we were; suffocated, nauseated, exhausted, and filthily dirty before the end. Three of us at least would have gone to pieces completely had it not been for the matter-of-fact brotherliness surrounding and protecting us. As it was, practically in a coma and crawling with lice, we found ourselves joining in the Volga Boat Song, though none of us knew the words, and we were an integral part of the Russian army when the train steamed into Odessa at last.

Elsie Inglis and Nursing Staff at Reni
(Roger and Patrick Cahill)

CHAPTER 13
The War Moves South Again

(See map 5)

By July 1917 there was widespread disenchantment with the war, and not only on the eastern front. As Fitzroy had written to her father in April, the war seemed very very old; and still it showed no signs of ending. Britain's naval blockade of Germany and the retaliatory German submarine blockade had succeeded in causing hardship and death to thousands of civilians; yet neither side had achieved any decisive victory. President Wilson's attempt to get the belligerent nations to state their war aims – the achievement of which would satisfy their conditions for making peace – had resulted only in a proliferation of claims which suggested that the territorial demands of both the Entente and the Central Powers were unnegotiable, and that both were committed to absolute victory. Soldiers and civilians on both sides and all fronts, even where there had not been a February revolution, were dispirited. The British enthusiasm for heroic patriotic sacrifice, reflected in much of the early war poetry, had perished at Gallipoli and on the Somme, as had two of its best champions, Rupert Brooke and Julian Grenfell. A new and bitter kind of poetry, unpublishable until after the war, was being written in the trenches by Wilfred Owen, Robert Graves, Siegfried Sassoon, Isaac Rosenberg and others; expressing the pity and horror evoked by the large-scale carnage and the wastage of young lives, this unquestionably spoke for a much larger constituency than the class of young officers to which its authors belonged.

At a less intellectual level, criticism was expressed in other ways. On the western front in May there were mutinies in fifty-six French regiments, successfully hushed up at the time, but effectively neutralising France's military strength for months to come.[1] German troops, too, were rebellious: in July there was a mutiny in the German High Seas Fleet,[2] and by the end of 1917 tens of thousands of army deserters had fled to Holland and other neutral countries.[3] In Russia, as the Scottish Women well knew, many regiments were refusing to fight, while others in the reserve trenches disbanded and went home. The Bolshevik slogan of 'Peace without annexations and indemnities', though often only half-understood, was almost irresistible to soldiers who had endured so much for so long, as was the promise of 'bread, land, and freedom'; and many who left the front did so in order not to miss the expected division of land amongst the peasants.

Nevertheless, feeling within the army was by no means undivided, and in spite of much Bolshevik activity and German propaganda, there were still strong waves of patriotic emotion among ordinary Russian soldiers, as Butler's troop train experience attests. Even in Galicia, some regiments had gone forward at the beginning of July, and it was only after the German counter-attack on 16 July that the line was completely broken.[4] After this the activity moved south to the Roumanian front on the lower Sereth, where Chesney's hospital was posted, justifying both Inglis's insistence on keeping her hospitals up to strength and the pressure of the committees at home for their withdrawal.

Inglis's visits to the Serbian headquarters in Odessa, emanating at first from a desire to be doing more useful work, soon gave her a new mission. Her letters to the London Committee are clouded by the spectre of spies peering into the diplomatic bag, and it is difficult to know when she became clearly aware of the dangers facing the unit. It is probable that she had a good idea of what she was risking when she decided to add her now considerable influence to General Zhivkovic's efforts to get the Serbian Divisions removed from Russia.

Their time in reserve at Voznesensk since the Dobrudga withdrawal had not been all rest and recuperation, and from the beginning there had been difficulties which the women had not heard about, and which had been only hinted at in Inglis's previous conversations with Zhivkovic. As early as October 1916, even while the Hospitals and the remnants of the First Division were still moving out of the Dobrudga, there had been trouble in the garrison at Odessa where the Second Division was in the process of being formed. To make up the heavy losses of the First Division in the battles of September 1916, just before the Scottish Women arrived, and following the example of Britain's recently-introduced conscription, the Russians had attempted a forcible recruitment of South Slav prisoners of war. This was a different matter from accepting volunteers, and the tales told by the thousands of wounded First Division men as they reached Odessa resulted in a mutiny in the barracks, and in the desertion or withdrawal of 44 per cent of the Second Division.[5] Although over the months volunteers continued to come in, the Second Division never gained full strength; it became a pool from which the First Division was replenished, and was never employed inside Russia.[6]

A further problem was that the political and sectarian differences which were later to destroy Yugoslavia were already making themselves felt in the so-called Serbian Divisions; although Serbs were in a considerable majority,[7] many of the prisoners of war who volunteered were Croats and Slovenes who espoused the ideal of a united Yugoslavia, while the Serbian officers who had come from Corfu on the *Huntspill* were more interested in a Serbian-dominated federation, a policy which Colonel Hadjic had been ordered to pursue. Attempts to have the Divisions renamed 'South Slav' instead of 'Serbian' were resisted by the commanders, discussion of the topic was strictly forbidden, and dissidents were severely punished, a procedure which caused much resentment.[8] After the February revolution and under pressure from the Russians, some concessions were made: the official name became 'The Volunteer Corps of the Serbs, Croats and Slovenes' (thus avoiding mention of the tendentious term 'Yugoslav', but evidently not much used by Inglis or the officers whom she met); soldiers' councils were introduced; and Stavka, the Russian High Command, agreed to permit the on-demand transfer of South Slav dissidents to other divisions in the Russian army, thus providing a more attractive alternative to a return to prisoner-of-war status. Anxious about the Bolshevik influence on the discipline of his men after the formation of the soldiers' councils, General Zhivkovic ordered that dissidents should be expelled from the Volunteer Corps: 149 officers (three-quarters of them Croats and Slovenes) and 12,740 soldiers were transferred to Russian regiments, leaving about two-thirds of the Serb soldiers, almost all the Serb officers, and better military discipline, if less democracy.[9]

Thus, by the time Inglis went to see Zhivkovic in July 1917, the Serbian First Division was in fact largely Serbian, and comprised men who wanted to remain in it, who could be trusted to obey their officers, and who were for the most part antagonistic to Bolshevism. As the revolution progressed, their future as part of the Russian army became more and more problematic; their existence, like that of the Czech Battalions, was an obstacle to the popular Bolshevik plans for a separate peace, and they were in continual danger of being disbanded and left without means of subsistence or travel, and with every chance of being handed over to the invading Austro-Hungarian army from which they had deserted. They had lost faith in either the will or the ability of Russia – Serbia's traditional protector – to fight on; and as we know, they had asked to be sent to the Salonica front. This request evidently expressed a well-matured hope, for Fitzroy's letter of 14 February (before the first revolution) mentions the possibility as 'a rumour which has been afloat [in Odessa] for some time'.[10] Now the changed circumstances made the move imperative.

Having agreed in principle to this transfer when it was supported by the British War Office in early July, Stavka began to have second thoughts. The reputation which the Serbs had gained in the Dobrudga made them strong candidates for inclusion in the stiffening force of foreign units to be sent to

Galicia to open the Kerensky Offensive, and it is not clear why they were not employed there at the beginning of July. The most likely explanation is that their internal difficulties had not been sufficiently settled, and that the soldiers' committees were doing their best to get them disbanded. At any rate, in early July the Second Division was severely under strength, and the First still in reserve near Odessa, awaiting the reply to its request for a transfer, but fearing that it would be sent to the Galician front. If that were to happen, the Scottish Women intended to go too.[11]

The anxiety of the Divisions to get away from Russia is understandable. Both officers and men knew enough about the morale of the Russian soldiers to be certain that their small force would simply be sacrificed, and so many Serbian men and boys had already perished in the 1915 retreat over the Albanian mountains that the very survival of the nation was threatened. Nevertheless, it is probable that they would have fought on the Galician front if required; what they objected to most intensely was the subsequent plan, hatched some time in mid-July, to send them to the Roumanian front. They had neither forgotten nor forgiven the way the Roumanian divisions alongside them had abandoned them in the Dobrudja. In addition, there had been the recent publication of the secret treaty promising Roumania the Banat province of Austria-Hungary as part of her reward for entering the war; containing a large Slav population, the Banat was coveted both by Serbia and by the fledgling Yugoslav movement as a legitimate extension to their territory. The men of the First Serbian Division made it known to their commander that they unanimously refused to fight for Roumania.[12]

The Russians were still hesitating about whether to let them go to Salonica when Inglis went to Odessa to arrange for her unit to rejoin the First Division. The hospitals had, after all, been only lent to the Russian army, on the understanding that they would return to the Serbs when required; now they would certainly be required, whether at Salonica, in Galicia, or back in Roumania.

Ironically, just as this arrangement was being concluded, the idle days of the hospital at Reni came to an end. The Roumanian front, which since the fall of Bucharest had become a more defendable line stretching north-north-west from Galatz along the Sereth, became very active towards the end of July, when the Russians and Roumanians attacked at a weak spot in the German line, initially driving the Germans back up the Susitza and Putna valleys, with Chesney's dressing station in tow. Mackensen quickly brought up reinforcements, and it was his successful counter-attack on 6 August which filled the hospital at Reni a few days later. Even while Inglis was conferring with Zhivkovic in Odessa, the first big convoy of wounded reached Reni, serious cases this time, and not just left hands. Fortunately Butler and her four nurses arrived in time to help, and to find that their uncomfortable journey had been justified; Rendel and Chesney, whose dressing station had followed the retreating army, and whose contracts expired at the end of August, happened to be at Reni with their three remaining sisters; and soon afterwards they were joined by a new doctor, Gladys Ward. Even so the hospital was frantically busy, and for several weeks every available person was needed.

Elsewhere other forces were at work. Alarming reports of the situation in South Russia were reaching the committees at home, and Onslow, who returned to Odessa as Transport Officer in mid-July, appears to have been charged with urgent and secret messages to Dr Inglis. At the same time, Inglis learned from Zhivkovic that the commander-in-chief on the Roumanian front was insisting on having the Serbs transferred there instead of to Salonica. Zhivkovic appealed to Inglis for British intervention, and she became an unofficial liaison officer between him and the British War Office. Getting the Divisions transferred from an increasingly hostile environment became her chief anxiety, and in spite of rapidly deteriorating health she worked indefatigably at it, visiting Odessa, cabling the Foreign Office and her committee at home, and in desperation at the constraints of censorship, sending verbal messages with some of those going home. In this matter, no one else had quite her power, for no one else held her trump card: her hospital would remain with the Serbian Divisions, wherever they were sent. If those in high office at home wanted the Scottish Women out of Russia, the Serbs must be rescued too. Since the War Office had refused her help at the outset of the war, neither they nor the Red Cross had the power to recall her. Her staff became in effect hostages, at risk until the Divisions were safe.[13]

Hospital A Reni

Milne *Friday 13 July*

We have been asked to be ready to take up to 400 wounded, as they expect a great rush when the big battle comes off on Sunday. Will it really come off, and shall we leave just as there is something doing on this front?

Saturday 14 July

There is a tremendous noise going on at this moment – an enemy is overhead, and is being shot at from two sides. This is the sisters' last day – I wonder if they will really leave, or will wounded come and they stay on? Life is becoming more interesting. Lady Decies is a perfect fool – it is a great mistake to bring a woman like that out to make a fool of one.

Fawcett *Letter Monday 16 July*

I have just started my month's night duty. Lady Decies is in charge, and I am the second. We have had quite a busy time; if it is like this all the time, we shall not be dull. To start with, five sisters arrived from 'B' Hospital and had to be fed. They were all very bad-tempered, as they had had to walk from the station.

Now we have had something far more exciting – a soldier walked in with his arm in a sling and looking like a ghost. He was so ill that I fetched Dr Laird. After she had come, I took the bandages off his arm, and found that more than half his arm had been blown away. He had been shot by a sentry. His arm is to be amputated directly after roll-call in the morning.

Dr Inglis is in Odessa trying to arrange matters with the Serbs. It is possible that we shall go to the Galician front.

Afternoon, Tuesday 17 July

When I finished my letter last night our adventures were by no means over. After the poor boy had been in bed for about an hour he started to haemorrhage. I fetched Dr Laird, and she said that she would amputate at once, so I fetched the theatre sister and Murphy for the anaesthetic, and the operation took place at 4 a.m. It was my first op, and I thoroughly enjoyed it.

It is just too difficult for words, sleeping in the daytime, because of the heat.

Hospital B Tecuci and Varnitza

Rendel *Letter Sunday 15 July*

There is no news here except that it is impossible to get away decently. They expect a big battle in a few days, our sisters, except three, all insist on leaving because their year is up, and the Russians are in despair for want of hospitals. We have volunteered to form a field dressing station; we can't run a hospital with only three sisters.

Mary Atkinson, Sister. *15 July*[14]

At two in the afternoon we were startled by a loud report, which we took to be bombs. As the reports got louder, we all went to our funk hole, which was one of the best in the neighbourhood, and was built by our admirable administrator, Mr Rothe. The reports did not cease, and as smoke was issuing in great clouds from quite close to our hospital, we all left the funk hole and went to the hospital, where Dr Chesney and Sister Mundie were. The explosions had blown several windows out, and some of the ceilings had fallen. Fortunately the patients had all but one been evacuated the previous day. Then it was we found out what had happened. The enemy had tried to shell the station, with the result of the first shell hitting the ammunition train, which of course set the whole train on fire and was the cause of all the heavy explosions we heard. In less than twelve hours the station was burned down and miles of army stores which held food and clothes for the troops at the front were also burned out.

Monday 16 July

The following day the enemy had stopped shelling, but the explosions still went on in the ammunition train. At six in the evening the two sisters and myself went down to the station to see the damage. Hundreds of soldiers were busy trying to save food and clothes from the wreck. We crossed the lines and were very busy picking up shrapnel and stray bullets, when quite suddenly we were startled by something coming over our heads. The soldiers with one accord dropped everything and ran in the direction the shell was coming. When the men began to run, we also ran, not knowing where we were running or why; quite suddenly the men lay flat down on the earth and so did we. It was really too comical for words to describe, as we caught each other peeping to see what the others were doing. After the shell burst we all ran again and in about two seconds another came over, and the same performance was gone over. When we got home arrangements were being made with the Red Cross director about sending us to the Carpathians as a field hospital dressing station; at this news we were all delighted.

Rendel *Letter 18 July Varnitza*

I am very glad that we have left Tecuci. It was a horrible place. Two nights before we left the Germans shelled it. They only sent five shells, but the second one destroyed a train full of food and ammunition. There was an enormous fire and Russian shells kept on exploding for two days afterwards. They destroyed food supplies for 20,000 men. The Russians just managed to get away a trainload of dynamite. They backed it out of the station down the line. The Roumanians who were guarding the station and nominally in charge of course lost their heads and promptly ran away. The shells all fell close to the station and only fifty casualties were reported.

Diary Wednesday 18 July

Got up at 3 a.m. Took down the tents.

5.30 a.m. Started. 19 waggons, 55 Serbs, Mr Rothe on horseback, Dr C, Miss Corbett, Miss Robinson[15] and myself in carriage. Drove or walked until 11.30. Unhitched the horses and rested for 3 hours.

2.30 Went on through Panciu and got to Varnitza, our goal, at 9 p.m. Last part of journey was done in storm of rain and over very bad roads. Lovely hilly and well-wooded country. Panciu 10 miles in our rear completely deserted and in ruins from shells.

Atkinson[16] *Wednesday 18 July*

At five we were off trekking to the Carpathians; the journey was a very beautiful one, and the wild flowers were growing in abundance. As we got near the Carpathians, we passed through villages without an inhabitant left, just the cottages, as the people had fled and left everything. Practically none of the houses had any windows left in, and a tremendous number of hungry cats abounded. The mountains are too beautiful for me to describe; the colouring is gorgeous, and with the evening sun on them they are superb.

About ten at night seven weary but cheerful Scottish Women arrived at their destination, and tried to put a few emergency tents up for the night. It rained very heavily all through the performance, but did not stop us from eating a good many sandwiches when the work was finished.

The following day was a very busy one. A very pretty place was chosen for our tents, and our dressing tents we placed in the valley. Two large tents were filled with stretcher beds so that the men could have rest and refreshment after being dressed and before being sent to another hospital.

Rendel *Letter 18 July*

I really think we shall get some good work here. In any case it is extremely interesting. The only drawback is that Dr Chesney speaks no Russian and is very much of an autocrat, and has quite failed to realise the difference the revolution has made. Even our Serbian soldiers are affected by it. For the moment there is practically no discipline and the soldiers can say and do what they like. If they choose to be impertinent or worse no one can prevent them and very few officers would have the courage to stand up to them. Dr Chesney ignores this completely, and if they annoy her or interfere or disobey regulations or don't stand up when she speaks to them she goes for them and gives them a most severe dressing down.

Hospital A Reni

Milne *Wednesday 18 July*

Dr Inglis is back, but we still have no definite news of where we shall go. The Serbs are to let us know in a few days; it may be the Galician front, but if it is Salonica we shall all stop in England for ten days and join up at Southampton again. That would be perfectly splendid, but we must wait to hear what is doing. I should love to go home, even for a short time, and the journey to Salonica would be grand. There is much activity on this front now, and we are expecting a convoy any day. We are awfully shorthanded, so it will be all hands to the plough if they do come.

Fawcett *Diary 19 July*

Dr Inglis, recovered from German measles, has gone to Tecuci. There was a great deal of firing this morning. There are rumours of another revolution in Petrograd,[17] and an attempt to proclaim the Tsarevich as tsar with Nikolai Nikolaievich as regent.

Milne *Friday 20 July*

Had a perfectly glorious ride with Murphy last night – I rode White Stocking, quite the best ride I have had here. She went beautifully. We were out for four hours, a wonderful ride through maize fields and water meadows in the valley. This morning the Bulgars have been shelling us, and more damage has been done at a little distance. There is a big battle raging – the Bulgars and the Russians are both trying to take Braila.

Tuesday 24 July

Onslow is here – perfectly grand having her back – I do wish she was staying with us. And in October I go over to the Transport. I shall be working with her. Rode at 5 this morning – had a beastly horse. Lots of strafing going – battles quite near. The guns are making an awful noise – the Russians are said to have advanced, but is it true?

Fawcett *Letter Wednesday 25 July*

The firing at the front has been going on steadily for the last three days and nights. We can distinctly see the flashing from the bursting shells after dark.

Our two Armoured Car men will be leaving us soon – we shall be awfully sorry to lose them, as they are both very nice boys. We hear that their people have had a good many casualties lately.[18]

Hospital B Varnitza

Rendel *Letter Wednesday 25 July*

On Sunday Mr Retkin told us that we must dig ourselves a 'blindage' for shells and prepare at once for a big battle. On Monday they sent an instructor to show us how to dig, and some men. All the hospital and transport people were feverishly digging as we expected the valley to be shelled any minute. The guns were getting very noisy and as they are behind us and at the side of us and just in front of us, the echoes in the hills were tremendous. During that night the noise became louder and louder, and for two hours there was a continuous roar. Of course this is child's play compared to real business, but still it was quite impressive. In the early hours of the morning the wounded began to come in.

Then we heard that the Germans were retiring in haste and that we had captured an important spur of hill. The Germans had made hardly any artillery reply. No shells came to our valley. They simply ran as hard as they could go. Since then nothing has happened. We expect every hour to be sent forward again but there is some hitch and grave fears that the Russians won't advance. The news from Galicia is bad too. A very large percentage of our wounded were wounded in the left hand!

Atkinson[19]

Air raids were very frequent and usually occurred while we were having our meals; as we dined in the open we had the advantage of sitting watching the fight. These air fights were of daily occurrence, yet not one of us or our men was ever hit. About two days after our arrival in the valley, we were heavily shelled, and at times had to take shelter under the cover of the trees on the sides of the mountain. This terrible bombardment went on unceasingly for about two days and two nights, and was just like a continuous roar of thunder with occasional flashes of lightning.

Our patients came to us straight from the trenches, and generally reached us about three in the morning, continuing to come in batches for the rest of the day. Some of the cases were very serious ones, but the majority were hand cases. The Russian soldier is very patient, and bears pain well. His food, however, is very poor compared to that of our own boys, and comforts in hospital are very scarce. We used to watch the divisions go through the valley every night on their way to the trenches; they had their tents in the valley just a little further through than ours, and used to come to rest after being relieved in the trenches.

As far as I can remember we stayed about a fortnight in this beautiful spot, then we trekked a few miles further on, starting at dusk so that the enemy would have less chance of spotting us. We all arrived safely, but felt great disappointment at the sight of our camping ground after the beauty of the last place.

Foreign Office London

On 26 July the Serbs' hopes of a transfer to Salonica were dashed: they were ordered to the Roumanian front, and Inglis was called to Odessa to consult with Zhivkovic. Fearing that her letters and cables might not get through, she entrusted Marx, who was going home, with the task of conveying to the

War Committee the seriousness of the situation of the Serbian Divisions and her impression of the morale of the Russian soldiers. She also sent, on 28 July, a message in cipher through the British Consul, requesting that it be given to Robert Seton Watson, the historian and a prominent member of the committee of the Serbian Relief Fund; to Mrs Kinnell, an influential member of the NUWSS committee; and to Lady Selborne, the sister of Lord Robert Cecil.

> Serbian Division has been ordered to front. After seven months intimate acquaintance with and personal observation of officers and men it is clear to me that Russian army cannot fight now. Fear repetition of what took place in the Dobrudga. It is a waste of splendid men to leave Serbian Division in Russia. It is imperative to get them removed to France or Salonica as quickly as possible but action must be taken immediately as they are ordered to go at once to the Roumanian front. Do not think it will meet point to recall Hospitals. If Serbian Division goes to Roumanian front Hospitals should go also and do their best. But if possible Division should be prevented from going and probably wiped out as in Dobrudga. Could not transports be sent to Archangel immediately? Ends[20]

Since the message dealt with troop movements and with the inadequacies of an ally, the Foreign Office was in some doubt about whether to pass it on, as pencilled comments on the accompanying minute show. Most of the Foreign Affairs Committee were against acting without permission from the War Office, who after some delay refused it. One of the comments, however, reads:

> Dr Inglis has, of course, very intimate knowledge of the morale of the Serbian troops, and her own good work entitles her to much consideration. I submit therefore that we should pass on this message, sending a copy to the Director of Military Intelligence.

A far cry from the 1914 response of 'Go home and sit still', this signalled the growth of a process by which Inglis's opinion was to be taken more and more seriously by both the Foreign Office and the War Office. After pencilling a note to the effect that the movement of troops was not the proper concern of Dr Inglis, and that in any case the order for Roumania had already been cancelled, someone at the War Office wrote a hasty postscript, and a fuller letter the same day: a further cable had just arrived from General Barter, British military attaché in Petrograd, to the effect that the cancellation had been rescinded, and that the Serbian Military Representative once more appealed for British intervention.[21] Although Inglis was told that her cable could not be delivered, the implicit reprimand about her 'proper concern' was not sent. The cable had, however, been read and marked by the War Committee, who on 9 August at a conference called to determine shipping priorities from Archangel, gave top priority to the Serbian Divisions, arranging for 210 officers and 2,900 men to leave about 9 September, and for the remainder to follow as soon as possible.[22] Barter was cabled about this.

In response to British pressure, the first group was allowed to leave in early September, but since it comprised only what was left of the Second Division after the First had been made up to strength, the fate of the remaining 15,000 hung in the balance, while the Russian generals wavered, and convoys of troopships came and went, filling up with other passengers.

Hospital A Reni

Milne *Sunday 29 July*
We hear we are off to the Roumanian front almost at once – base hospital for 200 beds – I wonder when and where.

Wednesday 1 August
Still no word of Dr Inglis returning to us, so we do not know where or when we are going. She is fixing up the affairs of the Serbian army. Of course wherever we go to will be a retreat – the Germans are only waiting for the harvest to be gathered in, and then they will go for it and make a sweep over the country, as they did in Roumania.

Monday 6 August
I don't believe that the Serbs will ever do anything, and we will just wait here doing nothing till Mackensen comes along.

Hospital B Varnitza

Mackensen was indeed coming along, and on 6 August, even as Mrs Milne wrote, the Germans were counter-attacking, storming the Russian and Roumanian positions north of Focsani, very near to Varnitza, and only forty miles from Galatz. They reached the Susitza River on 8 August,[23] the day Hospital B packed up; there were substantial grounds for Rendel's fear that the German soldiers might swarm over the hill. On the same day the Russo-Roumanian forces in the area retreated to their earlier positions east of the Sereth, blowing up the bridge behind them a few days later.[24]

Atkinson[25]

There is little more to tell you of our last three weeks in Roumania. Unless one has actually been under shell fire, it is impossible to expect a person to understand from a description what it is like. Every day we were shelled; the enemy found the positions of our guns by aeroplanes, and the result was a continual rain of shell. We became very interested watching the shells burst in the air: first we heard them coming, then watched for them to burst first, then go on and burst again when they reached the desired goal. We were in constant danger of shrapnel – indeed, it was dropping all around us.

Rendel *Letter 10 August*

Since I last wrote we have had many adventures. The Germans suddenly started an offensive and for two days they shelled us in our river bed.

On the 7th an artillery officer took Dr Chesney and me up to the first line trenches. We rode for a mile up the hill at the back of our camp. Then we dismounted, left our horses with the officer's servant, and walked with him for another half mile towards the Putna. We had to jump across a maze of trenches and wind about and finally we dropped into the first line trench. It was about 10 feet deep. I dare not describe them any more for fear of the censor. Our officer was really taking us to the observation post but when we were in the trenches they told him it had been moved two miles further off, and as it was then 6 p.m. he said it would be too dark for us to see anything. But even as it was, we had a splendid view of the lines.

That evening the German offensive began. Next day they shelled our valley continuously. The shells fell on the slopes of the hill opposite us and on the road running under the hill. The day after that the shells came much nearer to us. Just to our left and to our right they came one after the other quite close to our cliff. It was impossible to move from our tents, and finally we decided to skip. There were no wounded coming along, and we had already given notice that we were shutting up shop, so there was nothing to keep us. The regiment had been moved from the valley, we had no news as to how the battle was going, and we felt that at any moment German soldiers might swarm over the hill on to our tents. At 10 p.m. we set off in our carts. We crawled along with no lights under the shelter of our hill and hoped for the best. At a certain point we had to cross the valley and go up a road leading over the opposite hill to Panciu and from there to Tecuci. Luckily for us the Germans got tired of shelling and had a rest and we arrived safely here at 9 a.m. the next morning.

Hospital A Reni

Fawcett *Letter Tuesday 7 August*

I am still on night duty, and am getting rather tired. It is too hot to sleep in my tent this evening, so I am lying outside in my pyjamas trying to get cool. My night duty is nearly over. Matron, who is an awful idiot, will try and persuade me to go on with it as I know the work. That is the sort of reason she gives for everything she does. On the whole I have quite enjoyed my time, although days when they operate at five in the morning – the only cool part of the day, and just at my busiest time – are not nice. They are operating tomorrow morning – bother them.

We are still waiting for orders from the Serbs. They may be coming down to this front.

Yesterday we had the biggest thunderstorm we have had at all. Murphy and I were down by the Danube. For a long time we sat under a willow tree hoping that the torrents of rain would stop, and getting wetter and colder every minute. Finally we decided to make a bolt for it. By the time we got to the hospital we looked as though we had fallen into the Danube. As we came back the water was tearing down the hill in mighty torrents. We have always wondered what made the huge gorges that are all along the steppe and lead into the valleys – we imagined it must be the thaw after the snow. However, when we saw the thaw it was quite gentle, and not nearly enough to cut gorges – but now we see that it is the thunderstorms that cause the damage.

Hospital B Tecuci

Rendel *Letter 10 August*
The battle is still going on and the news is vague. Some people say that Jassi is being evacuated[26] but no one knows what is happening. Tomorrow evening we are going by cart to Reni and from there Dr C and I shall go to Odessa and so home. Dr C is bound to stay at Reni until 1 September and I shall wait to come with her.

Atkinson[27]
We left this place under cover of the darkness, starting about eleven at night, and dividing our carts by good distances between them. The villages we passed had all been previously evacuated. The journey that night is one that will not easily be forgotten. We were held up several times for ambulances to pass, also whole divisions of soldiers going up to reinforce. We arrived at Tecuci the following morning at eight o'clock, very tired after a very exhausting night. A few days later we joined Dr Inglis and party at Reni prior to leaving for home.

Hospital A Reni

Convoys of wounded from the German counter-offensive now began to reach Reni, and the hospital was again very busy. Elsie Butler and her contingent of nurses arrived, to find that any help they could give was badly needed. There were very few experienced sisters left, and the four who had come with Butler were a disappointment to Dr Inglis because they had had no surgical training, and needed more instruction than she had time to give them. Murphy and Fawcett, the two orderlies who had been with the hospitals from the beginning, had by now had a rigorous practical training and carried a large share of responsibility, working sometimes with the new sisters, and sometimes with only the recently-arrived orderlies and no trained sister on the ward at all. Butler, fortified by her degree in Modern Languages, was immediately initiated into the practical domesticities of ward work.

Milne *Friday 10 August*

Still no word of leaving, or of the Serbs. A big convoy of wounded came in yesterday, so that keeps them busy. I expect we shall stay till we are driven away by the Germans coming for the harvest. Oh well, it is very pleasant here. The work is hard, as we have seven of our staff down, and a lot of extra hospital cooking, but the riding makes up for it. Three of us go tomorrow at 5, before it is light, and we watch the sun rise away over the steppe, and then gallop back across the stubble field in time for breakfast.

Tuesday 14 August

Dr Inglis has gone off to Odessa again to try and work up the Serbs – how tiresome they are. We hear we are to go to Galatz now – perfectly absurd. We have an enormous unit now: staff of fifty, and we can't get the food to feed them. It isn't like old times a bit.

Wednesday 15 August

What a day. We were up most of last night feeding the tired staff as it came in for a few minutes rest; then I was up at 4.30, and hard at it all day. The wounded have been pouring in from early morning, and the doctors haven't a minute off. It is terribly hard work – awful wounds, poor souls. It is terrible to hear them.

Thursday 16 August

Still streams of wounded coming in. All the tents are full, and the hospital is crammed. Terrible wounds – it makes me miserable – I can't think how the girls are so brave, and the doctors are wonderful. There is a battle raging not far off – the guns are going hard.

Butler [28]

That was the prelude to those four or five months in Russia which were the happiest time of my life. To begin with, there was the release from the fearful strain of living under a cloud of war as a useless civilian. However terrible the sights, however dreadful the situations, however intolerable the pity wringing one's heart, that cloud at least had lifted. Then too, being in a strange land among a strange people gave a saving sense of remoteness from reality; yet everything one did was vital, urgent and exacting. There was tremendous pressure on the spirit, tremendous demands on the flesh; for when at last I got down to Reni on the Danube with my nurses, the last great Russian offensive was in full swing, the wounded were pouring into the hospital in hundreds, and even the most ignorant and inefficient were needed. As for me, I was put straight on to night duty to fetch and carry for the sister in charge, and was literally run off my legs. At least twice every night it was my duty to collect all the bed-pans in the hospital and empty them into so-called sanitary pails and stagger with them for about a quarter of a mile across the steppe to the so-called sanitary trench. It was noisome work, and frightening too, for I was nearly always accompanied by a savage pack of pariah dogs snapping and snarling at my heels. On the way back, I used to pause, drink in great gulps of air, and look up at the stars. I would then become conscious of a sound never heard in the daytime. It was as if the steppe were sighing, softly, hopelessly, uncomplainingly. It was in fact the subdued chorus of the wounded men, hundreds of them, moaning in the night. They were heroically silent under suffering by day; but nature spoke at nightfall. I lost my heart to the Russians then; I felt that I could never do enough for them, and indeed so did everyone else. We also felt much the same about Dr Inglis, although our devotion to her was mixed with fear.

Fawcett *Letter Friday 17 August*
There is no time for a long letter today, as we are in the midst of an immense rush of work – there are two hundred and twenty cases in hospital, all badly wounded, and every precious minute off duty has to be spent in sleep. Wright[29] and I are in charge of the dressing room, a very strenuous but very interesting job. The first day of the rush, the day after I came off night duty, we did sixteen hours, with barely time for meals. Now things are settling down a bit and people are getting used to working in double quick time, we have arranged to divide our work into shifts so things will not be so strenuous. The cases are by far the worst we have had since we have been here, and we get a huge percentage of deaths. This is very depressing, but is due to the fact that the majority of cases are men who are too ill to be sent on – those who are not so seriously ill are sent on to Odessa. On an average since the rush we have evacuated about twenty slight cases per day and admitted as many serious ones. You can

imagine how the number of bad dressings to be done every day accumulates. We have all four of our doctors here, so dressings go on all the time. Whilst the 'B' Hospital doctors operate, our own do dressings, and vice versa.

My last letters from you were dated February and March. This you will observe was the time of the first revolution.[30] We were told at the time that they were keeping our letters in Petrograd so they needn't censor them.

Milne *Sunday 19 August*

Dr I not back yet, so we do not know what is to happen to us yet. The patients are not coming in quite so quickly today, but the hospital is as full as it can take. Braila has been retaken, so perhaps things may look up. The Serbs are not in action yet, so there may be time for them to leave the country before they are cut up.

Hospital B Reni

Rendel *Letter Monday 20 August*

We came here a week ago, by night in our carts. We took 26 hours to come with four hours rest in the middle of the day. Dr Inglis has her hospital here and they are very busy. We have been working very hard since we came here and I have had quite good cases. But it is a horrible place and I shall be glad to see the last of it.

Foreign Office London

In London there was now serious concern about the safety of the Hospitals, but anxious communications between the War Office and the Foreign Office, and between the Foreign Office and the British Red Cross, merely established that the Scottish Women's Hospitals were entirely independent of all three, and could be withdrawn only by their own headquarters. All that the Foreign Office could do was enquire whether the SWH Headquarters Committee had been persuaded to accept the advice of the Red Cross to withdraw their Russian Unit.[31] The reply from Edinburgh was reassuring: although the letter advising withdrawal had just missed a committee meeting, those members who had been shown it were agreed that the unit should be recalled. The formal concurrence of the committee, it was thought, would doubtless be forthcoming after their next meeting.

Meanwhile, in Odessa again on 20 August, Inglis responded to the news that her message of 28 July could not be delivered by sending much the same message direct to Lord Robert Cecil at the Foreign Office; he had, of course, already noted the earlier one. This time she spelt out more clearly what she had hinted at before:

40% to 50% of wounds are self-inflicted in left hand. His [the Russian general's] troops are completely disorganised. Perhaps several army corps might stiffen them. One division of Serbians will only be sacrificed. Russian Government are sheltering behind hope that transports cannot be given. Our hospitals accompany division and will stand by and save as many as possible.[32]

It was arranged that the hospital – for with Dr Chesney's departure there could now be only one – would join the men at Hadji Abdul, where they were to assemble until they went into action. Sent in the diplomatic bag from Odessa, Inglis's last report, dated 20 August, is written as if she assumed that the hospital would continue in Russia or Roumania, and gives instructions about the personnel and equipment required.

But she had not given up attempts to get the Divisions moved. Understandably doubtful about the efficacy of telegrams in conveying the complexities of the political and military situation, as well as about their security, she had already sent one urgent message by Marx, who had not yet reached home; and now that another group was about to leave Russia, she arranged for Frances Robinson and Vera Holme to memorise and deliver to the London Committee a long memorandum from Dr Jambrisak, a member of the Yugoslav Committee then in Odessa. In substance it was much the same as Marx's message, but the uncharacteristic cloak-and-dagger methods reveal Inglis's anxious recognition of the delicacy and danger of her negotiations.

Hospital A Reni

Milne *Monday 20 August*
Dr Inglis has come back, and brings the news that we are going to join the Serbs in five days at a small place fifteen *versts* from here. Then we wait there till the Serbs receive orders – and go on to the front with them. So that is what all the talk of Salonica, etc. has come to. It seems a pity to leave all the work we are doing here, a full hospital, etc., just to sit in a village and do nothing for weeks perhaps. However, we are under orders, so there is nothing for it. I suppose it will be pandemonium from now onwards.

Inglis *Report 20 August* [33]
Our work is now drawing to a close, as we have been ordered to rejoin the Serbian Division.

The work during the last fortnight has been very difficult, owing to the fact that all our trained sisters have now left, and the women who have been sent to us have none of them had surgical training. You can imagine how this has added to the anxiety and difficulty of the work. I had hoped to have had time to give them a few elementary lectures on the use of antiseptics, etc., but the rush began before I was able to do it. The orderlies are worth their weight in gold; they have done splendidly and their training in military hospitals has stood them in good stead. It was most fortunate that Sister Sturt, who had been working with the Anglo-Russian Hospital, applied to us, otherwise I should not even have had a properly trained sister for the theatre and general sterilising for the dressings, and I don't know what we should have done.

I should like the committee to remember the names of the sisters who stayed to help us, not knowing when the reliefs were coming out, because they felt they were wanted. There were six. Sisters Florence Jenkins, Wilcox, Atkinson, Henderson, Mundie, and McElhone. Some of them stayed on at great personal inconvenience.

Of the parties from home all have safely arrived, including the last four sisters who travelled with the orderly Butler. Everybody has in fact arrived except Hedges and Arbuthnot. Miss Palliser's telegram came while I was in Odessa asking whether they should come on from Norway and bring the equipment. As it is quite indefinite as to how long we shall have to stay here and what work we shall have to do, I have wired saying send them on to Petrograd. We may need all the equipment and all the help we can get.

Four times since my last report I have been in Odessa over the question of our future, and I am sorry that it is impossible to give details of the conversations I have had with people in authority there in this report. The final result, however, is that we are going back to our original work, and I greatly fear that the work will take on its original intensity.

Dr Laird, now that Miss Ward has come, feels that she is no longer justified in staying. I cannot speak too warmly of the comfort she has been since she came out... Dr Chesney, who always said she could not have another winter out here, now tells me that she meant she must be home in England by the winter. She will therefore leave us when the hospitals leave Reni, and Miss Rendel will go with her. Miss Rendel is of course bound to go, as she ought to finish her medical course.

We shall therefore be left with three doctors, only two of us surgeons. I am very glad to hear that Miss Florence Inglis is coming out, and I should like a senior surgeon, if possible.

Miss Robinson and Miss Holme, whose agreement ended some time ago and who stayed on to help us, are now going home, and I hope the Committee will make a special point of seeing them.

285

As soon as our new work develops I shall let the Committee know. At present the idea is that we shall form a camp hospital of 200 beds and be prepared to send forward a dressing station. If I had more doctors I should try to send forward two dressing stations. However that is impossible at the moment.

Milne *Saturday 25 August*

Still no word of our leaving... The Hun is crouching about Jassi and going to take all Bessarabia, come quietly down on us here, and lock us into this corner. That is what we shall get for staying with the Russians.

Fawcett *Letter Sunday 26 August*

At last there is a lull in the work. For the last fortnight we have been rushed to death with as many as two hundred wounded in at a time. This meant that, besides the usual hundred beds in the hospital, we had eight big marquees full. Then we were evacuating every day, so that there were more than two hundred dressings to be done every day. Dr Laird and Dr Ward were simply splendid, and ripping to work for; they worked all day and much of the night. For about a week this was their programme:

8.00 – 10.00	Dressings
10.00 – 12.00	Operations
12.00 – 12.30	Lunch
12.30 – 4.30	Dressings
6.00 – 7.30	Operations

Then after supper they dressed all the new cases that came in. The new patients hardly ever started to arrive till after supper when we were supposed to have finished work. This meant all the bathing and everything had to be done that night.

One night the day sanitars refused to stay on and help with the bathing and stretcher bearing; and as there were only perhaps half a dozen night sanitars for the whole hospital, we set to and did all the bathing ourselves. For stretcher bearers we had to rely on an ex-patient named Andrea, who often helped us, a Russian Jew who was our accountant at the time, and two of the Austrian prisoners, who came on without a murmur.

I had to take a day off duty in the middle of the rush with malaria; it was particularly unfortunate as all the sisters were new. At one time seven of the sisters were ill, and as we already had a Russian sister with typhoid – which meant someone for day duty and someone for night duty for the staff alone – the hospital work was fairly heavy. Whenever we had a minute off duty we cut up thousands of dressings.

The Germans in hospital have been most troublesome – they treat us like dirt under their feet. The only decent one amongst them died.

Inglis *Letter to Onslow [in Odessa] Sunday 26 August*[34]

Our orders at last. We are to go to Hadji Abdul as soon as possible. We are evacuating the hospital tomorrow and then we start packing. Will you bring down the Transport as soon as possible? Miss Genge with a girl orderly will leave here on Tuesday morning (by car if we can get petrol, but you had better meet the Wednesday night train) to take over the store from you.

Dr Chesney is taking this for me. She is going home. I am going over to Hadji Abdul tomorrow to see the camping ground. We'll have everything ready for you when you come.

Milne *Tuesday 28 August*

Great excitement – I am to be allowed to go to Odessa with Dr Laird tomorrow. I am so glad, as I am tired of cooking, and we have looked forward to a little holiday together. I come back with Onslow when she goes – I am going to get my new uniform, so I am busy packing.

Friday 31 August Train to Odessa

A year today since we left England, and I am in the train again on my way to Odessa with Dr Laird for a little frisk. I am in great form – awfully pleased at getting out of the removal to the new camp. The unit leaves today for Hadji Abdul – oh, the fuss there will be...

We have just been to Benderi market – simply lovely with fruit, but we may not eat grapes, and they are the loveliest things I have seen. But we gorge on melons.

SWH Committee and Foreign Office London

23 August – 3 September

In London the plight of the Serbian Divisions in Russia was by this time being taken very seriously. Towards the end of August, and following hard upon Dr Inglis's urgent telegram to Lord Robert Cecil, came Marx, entrusted with a verbal report to the committee, to be passed on to the Foreign Office. She set out in a memorandum what she had to tell about the situation in south Russia; it was no longer news to the Foreign Office, but combined with anxiety about the safety of the unit, it no doubt contributed to a recognition of the urgency of the matter. She also brought a letter to Mrs Kinnell, written a month earlier at the time of the undelivered telegram. Copies of both these, accompanied by a tactful covering note from the secretary, were sent to the Foreign Office, and to Lloyd George himself.[35]

Mindful of the bearer's safety, Dr Inglis had carefully omitted from her letter any direct reference to wounded hands; but it expressed clearly enough her desperate anxiety, and her reliance on the good sense of the committee and on its power to pull strings.

> This is to introduce Miss Marx to you. She has been recalled for special work by the Women's Volunteer Reserve, and I have asked her specially to see you, about the question of the Serb Division being used on the Roumanian Front.
>
> I sent you a telegram yesterday.[36] You once said to me that if I wanted anything to come straight to you, and I have taken you literally at your word. You'll know who to go to and what to do, so I shifted the trouble on to you. For I am miserable about it. You know how the Serb Division were left high and dry in the Dobrudga, held on for 24 hours without support, and came out of action having lost 11,000 out of 15,000. Well, that will simply happen again now. Miss Marx will tell you why...
>
> General Zhivkovic said to me yesterday, 'The men want to fight; they are not cowards. But it goes to my heart to send them like this to their death for nothing.' They are such a splendid body of men. It is such wicked wicked waste from *every* point of view. I am up here to see what I can do to get this miserable tangle about the Division undone. They want the Division to go on to the Front to 'encourage' the Russians. Miss Marx will tell you.
>
> Goodbye, dear Mrs Kinnell. It is such a comfort to know you are there.

Marx's arrival was well timed. On 1 September the War Office received a cable from General Barter confirming the most recent orders for Roumania, and on the same day the Foreign Office passed on to the London Committee a somewhat scrambled telegram from Dr Inglis, who had just received one from them advising withdrawal, but finally leaving the decision to her:

> Thanks for leaving decision in my hands. Will join division on Friday.[37]

There was now no doubt in the minds of either the War Office or the Foreign Office about what they meant to do. But the reluctance of Stavka to let the Serbs go, and the tardiness of the British authorities about insisting, meant that they might now be too late. The Germans had entered the northern tip of Bessarabia at the beginning of August, the Russian line near Focsani broke on 28 August, and in the north, where the Russians had withdrawn in disorder, Riga fell on 3 September, putting Petrograd itself in danger. The

Russian army was hopelessly dispirited, and as those on the spot could see, capitulation was only a matter of time.

The Scottish Women joined the First Serbian Division at Hadji Abdul, and went on preparing for the front.

Nurses at Tea *(Roger and Patrick Cahill)*

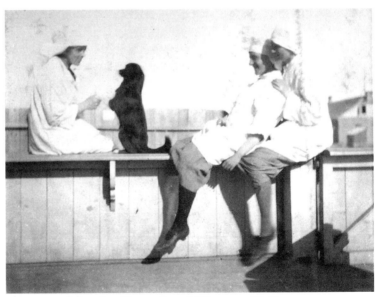

Murphy, Fawcett and Fitzroy with Sammy
(Roger and Patrick Cahill)

Dr Corbett, Dr Inglis and Onslow
(Mitchell Library)

Marx in Odessa
(John Orr)

Laundry Orderly *(Edinburgh Central Library)*

Murphy and Fawcett
with Camp Followers
(Edinburgh Central Library)

CHAPTER 14
On Standby

(See maps 2 & 5)

At Hadji Abdul the Hospital, now entirely under canvas, pitched its tents in a wooded valley near the encampment of the First Serbian Division, and began to enjoy relative leisure after the intensive work. There were about forty patients, mostly sick, with a few recovering from operations or long-term wounds.[1] Mrs Milne and Fawcett, who had both been ill, were allowed to take a short holiday in Odessa, where the hospital supplies were being stored, and where the Transport and its repair shop were based. Onslow was now Transport Officer in place of Marx, and Hedges had recently returned to join her, having evaded the ban on women drivers by signing on as 'laundry superintendent'. While letters and telegrams could be sent to Britain through the Consul at Odessa as before, there does not seem to have been any reliable telephonic or postal communication between Hadji Abdul and Odessa. All the surviving letters between these two places were carried by personal messenger, and there was occasional motoring to and from Odessa, as Inglis continued to press for a change in the orders. At the same time she proceeded with arrangements to assemble all her resources at Hadji Abdul so that she would be ready to move quickly if the Division should go into action.

At the beginning of September the last orders for Galatz still stood, but the Consulate in Odessa was a source of early information about the intentions of the British War Office. Onslow, in frequent contact with Mr Bagge, was able to report on the latest telegrams and directives concerning the Serbian Divisions. However, directives from a distance had limited influence over the generals of Stavka, who in any case had other anxieties by October 1917; and requests from Britain were not readily translated into decisive orders. A telegram to the War Office announcing that the First Division would 'for the present' be retained in reserve, and would 'not be available for embarkation before the beginning of November', while it gave rise to some optimism, gave no unequivocal assurance that even November would bring the release of the Division.[2] It was now 15,000 strong, and if it were really to go into action on the Roumanian front, there would not be much hope of its being ready for embarkation before Archangel became ice-bound in mid-November, nor could sufficient ships be made available to convey such a large number at one time. There was so much hesitation and vacillation on the part of the Russian High Command that the Scottish Women found it impossible to make plans. Even at those times when the orders were for Salonica rather than the front, the position of their present encampment, so close to Galatz, was a reminder that the Serbians were being kept on stand-by. The fate of the Scottish Women's Hospital was contingent on theirs.

Hadji Abdul

Fawcett *Letter 6 September*

We have left Reni at last. The Serbs have moved down to Bessarabia and are at present with the SWH at Hadji Abdul, a place two stations nearer Odessa than Reni, waiting for orders to proceed to the front...

We had an awful bother getting away from Reni. Perssé and I were to go by train with the equipment, and Dr Inglis and two others were to go by road; then we were to put the tents up and the rest of the unit would come two days after. Perssé and I got into the train on the Wednesday morning, and after fussing around and running backwards and forwards to the house for meals, we finally started at four o'clock on Thursday afternoon and arrived at Hadji Abdul at eight o'clock. We travelled in the truck with the luggage. You can have no idea what the heat of that truck was like; as it was, my temperature was 105°F, and I didn't feel at all happy. There was nothing to drink but lukewarm water, and nothing to eat except hard-boiled eggs and black bread and butter.

Inglis *Letter*[3]

We came here from Reni. It is a little village – which clearly shows its Turkish origin in its name, doesn't it? It lies in a wide wooded valley. The Headquarters are in the village, and we have a perfectly lovely camping ground among the trees. The Division is hidden away peacefully under the trees, and at first they were awfully loth to let us pitch our big tents that could not be so thoroughly hidden – but I was bent on letting them see what a nice hospital you had sent out, and they are so pleased with us. They bring everybody – Russian generals and Roumanian military attachés and ministers to see it. And they are quite content because our painted canvas looks like the roofs of ordinary houses; and from the hill opposite we look like a little village among the trees, and I have no doubt the same to aeroplanes.

The hospital tents stand in two rows, and our own personal tents below them; and the kitchen and the mess tent and office at the top facing the hospital. The three black spots are our flag poles: on the single one the

Red Cross, and on the other two the Union Jack and the Serbian flag; but the red of the last two showed up too strongly against the green, so they are only run up when generals and great people come to see us.

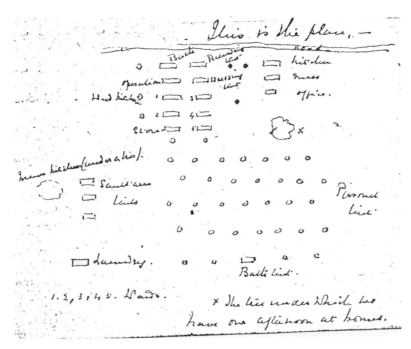

Odessa

Milne *Sunday 2 September*

Here we are, and how perfectly lovely the sea is. I have been paddling this morning. Yesterday we shopped – I got some treasures in the Jews' Market. I am glad to see Onslow again.

Tuesday 4 September

Dr Laird left last night for Kiev. We hear the war news is very bad – Riga has been taken, so they say. I dare say we shall leave in a jolly hurry, chased by the Hun, when it comes to the point.

Hadji Abdul

Geraldine Hedges, Driver. *Letter 2 September*[4]

Onslow has been quite seedy, and has had two days in bed, so I have been carrying on and consequently haven't drawn breath from morn till night, as Dr Inglis wanted the lorries down and certain things in a hurry, so a petrol bidon had to be found where none was, so to speak...

Onslow, having important despatches for Dr Inglis, commissioned me to carry them and to lay certain things before the CMO, so Elizabeth [Arbuthnot], Percy [Cowland] and I motored to Hadji Abdul, 250 *versts* across the steppe, quite lovely, but bumpy. We left at 8 a.m., and went on till 7.30 p.m., slept, and arrived Saturday morning to find the new camp being erected.

Sunday was a big lunch at the sub-headquarters, to which Dr Inglis, Dr Corbett, Lady Decies, one sister, one orderly and I went, and very nice too. We ate from 1.30 until nearly four; there was a delightful orchestra, and they played all the nice Serbian tunes I know. After tea Perssé and I went for a walk and lay on our backs, then service at 6.30. After supper we waited for Dr I's letters and finally went to bed about 11.30, only to be woken at 3 a.m. as we had to start back at 4 in order to get there in one day. E stayed, of course, and Fawcett came with us for a little change.

Inglis *Letter to Onslow Monday 3 September*[5]

I have thought it all out and decided the Transport must come down. We cannot sell, in any case, for three weeks or more until the Division really moves. And it is essential that we have the lorries here. Also it is essential that we have a real mechanic, and a garage for repairs. I am at the present moment without a car, as a spring is broken. I must go to Bolgrad about money and accounts. I am firmly rooted in this camp! There is a good supply of wood, which simply cannot be got here, lying at the Pruth with two Serbs guarding it, and we have nothing to bring it up in.

These are the immediate reasons for bringing up the whole Transport, and making a proper repair shop here, under Day.

The wider reasons are that no one really knows what the Russian Government means or will do. I don't think the last explanation of how the last order for Archangel came to be altered improves things at all. It shows there is no settled policy, but that they are swayed by the last opinion. Such a wave may carry us right into Roumania – and I want *this* hospital at any rate to be ready. It has always been my policy to be ready, and then one often gets a chance of helping one would otherwise lose.

Colonel Milotinovic knew nothing of your news.[6] Fortunately I put it to him simply that you 'had heard'. I explained to him how the question was complicated by the possibility of selling the cars at a good price and starting elsewhere with a beautiful new Transport. And he said, 'Well, wait – three weeks.' But the more I realised how absolutely necessary the lorries and repair shops are here, the more I saw it would be wiser for the cars to wait here than in Odessa. We are right away from anywhere, and food and everything has to be brought from a distance.

The only argument of any weight on the other side is that we may damage the cars by bringing them here, and lessen their market value. But I must take the responsibility of that risk! You have fully warned me – and Hedges. The lorries are our great asset, and they are necessary *now*. Hedges has a plan of getting a new driver. Certainly get him. And the bidons. We can always sell them at any rate.

As soon as I can get a car to go in I shall go to Galatz to fix up about petrol. But bring as much as you can possibly get. We can always sell that too. Come as soon as you can. And bring my cool uniform please!

We have a lovely camping ground here, and I am going to get the camp absolutely right, so that we may know exactly how to do it next time. It is awfully nice being back with the Serbs. We had lunch at the Headquarters today – six of us – a kind of official welcome to the unit.

Thank you awfully much, my dear, for writing so fully and clearly – I felt that I had all the facts before me.

Odessa

Fawcett *Letter 6 September*
I am staying with the Harrises for a little while, as I had malaria again and need a change. I came along here with Hedges and Percy in one of the run-abouts. We had a splendid ride which took us about fourteen hours, which is a record. For part of the way we came on a ferry across the estuary of the Dniester. The end of the journey was frightfully dusty, and by the time we arrived we were covered with dust and looked like scarecrows.

Here it is just heavenly, and I'm enjoying it thoroughly. I spend the daytime at the unit's *dacha*, which overlooks the Black Sea, and return to the Harrises' for dinner and bed at night.

The cigarettes you sent have been very much appreciated. There were two English dining with the Harrises last night, and as it has been almost impossible to get cigarettes of any sort, you can imagine how they enjoyed the English ones.

We have just heard of the fall of Riga.

Milne *Saturday 8 September*
Still in Odessa. I should be back at work, I know, but I haven't been fit, and am not specially keen on going back. The war news is bad. If Petrograd falls we shall be in a trap down here and our only way out will be by Siberia and Japan.

Hedges *Letter Saturday 8 September*[7]
We are all leaving here next week for Hadji Abdul, where Dr I is installed;

there is no work at all, but the aforesaid Dr I wants to have the entire unit about her (by the way, she made me an officer); so that if there is another retreat we shall be well in for it, especially if it rains, as we are dependent on mud tracks, now good. But never worry – our usual luck will, I'm sure, remain with us. Last night, for instance, both Curtis and Tindall[8] ought to have been killed, but they were only bruised; a tram ran into their car (my car, as it happened) and simply smashed it to bits. A Sub came up to tell us of it, but although rumour had it that two sisters were in a hospital, search how I might I could not discover which, for the simple reason that they were not hurt, but contrariwise had gone to the police station!

Petrograd *9-14 September*

Not only had the fall of Riga put Petrograd in a dangerously vulnerable position, but severe internal trouble, with serious repercussions for British subjects, was brewing between Kerensky, who was by then Prime Minister in the Provisional Government, and Kornilov, commander-in-chief of the Russian army. Kornilov had recently proposed strong disciplinary measures, including the establishment of martial law in Petrograd, the enforcement of the death penalty, and its extension to troops behind the lines. Alarmed by the publication of such inflammatory measures in a situation of domestic instability and military vulnerability, Kerensky ordered Kornilov to send troops to Petrograd to defend the government. The Third Cavalry Corps, under General Krymov, was already nearing Petrograd when Kerensky changed his mind: apparently distrusting Kornilov, and interpreting (or perhaps misinterpreting) his written proposals as an ultimatum, he cancelled his earlier orders for troops, and relieved Kornilov of his position as commander-in-chief. Kornilov refused to accept his dismissal, and allowed his troops to continue advancing on the capital, expecting that they would have popular support.[9]

The immediate consequence of this action was to unite Mensheviks, Bolsheviks and the Provisional Government for the purposes of defeating what appeared to be a right-wing coup. The Bolshevik Red Guard, which had been disbanded during the July Days, was re-armed, and emerged as a Workers' Militia 25,000 strong. A force of 100,000 armed men was deployed in and around Petrograd to repel Krymov's force; railway and telegraph officials refused to co-operate with him, and his own troops deserted when met by the Petrograd workers and soldiers.[10] Nothing could have been more advantageous for the Bolsheviks, whose following increased dramatically, who were now legitimately re-armed, and who very soon had control of both the Petrograd and Moscow Soviets.[11]

Nor could anything have been much worse for British prestige in Russia. Since the British military attachés, Generals Knox and Barter, were known to favour Kornilov's strong-arm tactics and traditional military discipline, and were suspected of having intended to aid his coup, British subjects were more unpopular than ever, and positively endangered. The Armoured Cars had indeed been summoned by Kornilov, without the British Ambassador's knowledge; but they were stopped by revolutionaries who had got wind of their destination.[12] They hastily entrained, and set off for Archangel, remaining in their trucks as their train passed through Petrograd. The version put out in an unpublished article written by C. J. Smith, a BAC officer, is that *en route* to Archangel, they found their train unexpectedly diverted to Petrograd, and discovered that their presence there was to be used to give colour to the rumour that Britain had sent troops in support of Kornilov. Although such support seems to have been far from the minds of the War Office and the Ambassador, the rumour was not such a distortion of the truth as Smith implies. He tells how, as the Petrograd liaison officer for the Armoured Cars, he recognised the danger, and kept the men in the train while arrangements were made to reroute it by the newly-completed Murmansk line. His comment gives some idea of the prevailing hostility towards British subjects:

> Had we appeared on the streets of Petrograd we would have been slaughtered to a man, shot down like dogs, in fact; and not only so, but every British civilian resident in Petrograd would have shared the same fate.[13]

Remaining in Petrograd himself, Smith was later arrested and imprisoned.

Odessa

Fawcett *Letter Monday 10 September*

There is civil war in Petrograd. I imagine it will be worse than the war. Two of our sisters left for there on Saturday – it is a great pity that they started; Dr Inglis will be very angry when she knows, as one of them has been very ill for a long time.

I don't think I shall be home at the end of my contract, which is 15 October, as there seems every prospect of the whole unit going home almost immediately. How can Russia be at war and have a civil war as well? The soldiers tell us quite frankly that the revolution is of far more importance than the war, and so they all just want to drop it.

Odessa is in a filthy condition. In former times each house had a sort of porter person, called a *dvornik*, who was responsible for the pavement outside his house, and in those days the town was noted for its cleanliness;

we remarked it when we arrived a year ago. Now things are very different – at the beginning of the revolution the householders went on strike about it, so that now it is no one's business to clean the streets, with the result that they are in a filthy condition. It would be the people's own fault if they had an epidemic of cholera.

We watched the Reni train start this morning – it was simply a free fight to get on it at all. I was thankful that I hadn't to go back to Hadji by train. They always have an armed soldier at the door of each carriage before the train comes into the station, to keep the people off until the train stops at the platform. Otherwise they would walk right down the line to meet it.

Milne *Tuesday 11 September*

Great excitement in these circles. There is talk of civil war; Kornilov, the Cossack general and Kerensky, the Minister in Petrograd, have come to loggerheads, so there may be some fun ahead of us. I go back to the front today.

SWH Committees and Foreign Office London

In Edinburgh and London anxiety intensified. The Edinburgh Committee was so worried that it sent a deputation to the meeting of the London Committee on 10 September, urging it to insist on withdrawal. Its delegates reported to their London colleagues that since their arrival they had visited the headquarters of the British Red Cross and been given confidential information of such a nature as to make them feel that the responsibility of leaving the unit exposed to such unusual danger was too great. They were not free to say what this information was. It may have concerned Kornilov's march on Petrograd, and the suspicion that the Serbian Division, as 'politically reliable', was taking part in this civil strife; on the other hand, perhaps the Red Cross had been told of General Alekseev's report that the Germans' next target would be Odessa, in order to paralyse the Black Sea Fleet.[14] At any rate, whatever the Edinburgh Committee's private information, there were certainly sufficient grounds for concern.

The London Committee had recently received Inglis's telegram thanking it for leaving the decision in her hands. While the members shared the anxiety of their Edinburgh colleagues, they responded by showing them the Foreign Office's reply to Marx's memorandum, which reassured them that it was in direct communication with Dr Inglis and aware of the difficult position of the Serbian Division. The London Committee argued that this implied Foreign Office sanction of the situation: if it were really dangerous, the Foreign Office would order the unit's withdrawal. Neither committee appears to have understood that the Foreign Office believed itself to be powerless to do this. In any case, the reassurance referred not to the safety of the Hospitals, but to efforts to transfer the Serbian Division, and might have been differently worded had it been addressing a different question. Nobody recalled the unit, but it was agreed that the committees would communicate their joint fears to Dr Inglis by cable, and ask for news.[15] The secretary also wrote to the Foreign Office, asking, 'Can rumour that Division is in action be either confirmed or denied?'

The Foreign Office sent another vague and reassuring reply, saying that the Division was being held in reserve, but that everything possible was being done to secure its transfer. Again, the comments on the minute show an increased respect for the responsibility and good sense of the SWH, and a willingness to take their opinions seriously. Recommending that the London Committee be told the contents of General Barter's secret military reports, one comment concedes a recognition that much of the information on the situation of the Serbian Divisions derived in the first place from members of Scottish Women's Hospitals. The Foreign Office's interpretation of the position was that the Russians had 'promised' to release the First Division by the beginning of November.[16] But Russia was a divided nation, and the promises of Stavka could be no more than half-hearted intentions; the Scottish Women at Hadji Abdul and their committees at home were to know many more weeks of uncertainty.

Hadji Abdul

In September and October there was a good deal of illness among the hospital staff, the chief afflictions being malaria and dysentery. In her letters Fawcett commented frequently on Dr Inglis's poor health: German measles, gastritis, general tiredness; but no one yet realised the seriousness of her condition. Photographs taken in the summer of 1917 show her looking emaciated and drawn, in contrast to her plump, healthy appearance in a photograph of the previous year. In fact she had not been well since her return from Occupied Serbia, and may have known when she set out for Russia that her disease was malignant.[17] By mid-September she must have realised that she was seriously ill, and it is all the more remarkable that she pursued the matter of the Division's release so vigorously. An additional anxiety was the absence of potential commanding officers in the unit; after Dr Chesney's departure there was no other senior doctor, and neither the administrator nor the matron had much capacity for leadership.[18] Among the older women on the staff Mrs Milne was the one person whose department had always run smoothly, and who was generally popular and tactful – much more tactful than her private diary might suggest. On 24 September, Dr Inglis raised her to the rank of officer, and from this time, it is clear, Milne

301

undertook a good deal of the responsibility for organising the unit's departure, ordered once again, though still not finally, on 28 September.

Milne *Tuesday 18 September*
I arrived yesterday in Hadji Abdul, a perfectly lovely spot; I am sorry I was not here long ago.

Saturday 22 September
The Transport has arrived – I am glad to see them – they got jolly well strafed on arrival...

Monday 24 September
I am tied up in bed. Dr Inglis is looking after my heart, which has gone off a bit – after the three weeks of dysentery, I suppose... There is some talk of our going to Roumania – I do wish that might be the case. It would be nice to do something to help them. They are fighting splendidly now, they say.

I am being made an officer – rather thrilling – I am glad Dr Inglis thinks I deserve the honour. I am to be the officer in charge of the kitchen, so I shall wear thistles on my coat and sit at high table – not but that I shall miss being among the girls and having fun.

26 September 'Some Months in Bessarabia' [19]
Soon after our arrival in Hadji Abdul, Dr Inglis began to be ill. She had been unwell on and off for some time past at Reni; but her extraordinary will-power prevented anyone from knowing how ill she really was. On 26 September she was unable to leave her tent, and from then onwards she was more or less ill all the time. Some days she was well enough to sit outside her tent in the sunshine; but whether in her tent or outside, she directed all the work of the hospital even to the last. She was the pivot on which the unit turned, and without her nothing seemed to be very much worthwhile.

Friday 28 September
Tremendous joy – we have just had official news that we leave for Archangel in a few days, *en route* for France and Salonica; but of course we shall go home first – fancy getting home – too wonderful. I suppose I shall be going out with them again – I do hope nothing stops our getting away – I couldn't bear that – I just pine for a sight of the housie and the garden.

Inglis *Letter Monday 1 October* [20]
I must send you a line from this lovely place – even though we may be home ourselves before you get this letter. Think of it! Isn't it joyful?

We got the Transport down with difficulty! But we did get it down eventually. There were prospects at that time of our having to go on to Roumania. It goes back today to Odessa, where we hope to sell it. All explanations on this point when I see you!

We have been very happy here, and have been most kindly and hospitably treated by the Serbs. Colonel Milotinovic gave an official lunch here just after we arrived, and asked six of us. After that we had a joint evening picnic, and later nine of the staff came to dinner, and the rest afterwards. The girls got up quite a clever cinema play, and then there was dancing. And there have been soldiers' sports, and rides; and you will see that I have drawn into the plan a special big tree where every afternoon we have what Mr Glacier, a Frenchman here, calls a 'reunion'.

Fawcett *Letter Tuesday 2 October*

At last we have got our marching orders, which are to go home. The Serbs have orders to go to Salonica via England. We are to travel with the Serbian staff and probably land in England. Then I believe the unit will re-equip and follow them to Salonica. I shall not go out again with them, I expect. Dr Inglis still hopes to take them out although she is still very ill. I don't think she will ever be well enough to go out again.

Odessa

Much of October Dr Inglis spent in bed, or sitting outside her tent, but her efforts on behalf of the Serbs did not slacken. Unable to go to Odessa herself, she delegated tasks – including consultations with the Consul and cables to the Foreign Office – to Onslow and Hedges, who were back in Odessa arranging the sale of the cars. The order for Archangel stood for another three weeks, and on 7 October when Inglis wrote to Onslow about arrangements to leave in Odessa a patient too ill to travel, she seems to have been confident of their imminent departure. But the departure was inexplicably delayed, and as the winter approached, both the men and the women began to lose heart. Archangel would soon be icebound.

Butler[21]

Doing my bit in the stores was much more to my liking, especially when it came to transporting part of the equipment to Odessa and housing it in the spacious warehouse assigned to our hospital there. This necessitated several lorry drives over the steppe, partly by day, and partly by night, and how can I ever forget them? I had already succumbed to the language and the people; I now succumbed to the country, to the vast dreaming spaces, the wide white roads, the little pink and blue villages, the fields upon fields of sunflowers; and brooding over them all, the 'limitless melancholy of the steppe' evoked by Chekov. It was indescribably romantic, too, dossing down in a desolate little summerhouse on the shores of the Black Sea which had been allotted to Dr Inglis for official visits to Odessa. Her chief of Transport and one or two drivers were camping there and negotiating for the sale of our cars; for the fighting was now coming to an end, the country was dangerously unsettled, and the Foreign Office had ordered the unit home. I was at that *dacha* sometimes for three or four days, sometimes for a week on end whilst the summer waned and the autumn waxed, and it began to look as if my prayers would be granted, and we should remain where we were. For I loved Russia more than enough.

Hadji Abdul

Milne *Sunday 7 October*
Not away yet, and I don't think it seems as if we would ever go. The first train is said to be going today, but I don't think it will, and we are on the sixth.

Inglis *Letter to Onslow 7 October*
As I am not well, Gwynn is taking down from my dictation. There are two or three things I want to write about.

As to Joe,[22] there are apparently no sanitary trains running just now, but he is getting on splendidly and my present plan is to bring him up to Razdelnaya[23] where you will join us with your contingent and the three waggons. Will you please have there to meet Joe two sanitars and somebody in charge of them to take him back by car or train, whichever you find most convenient, and to see him safely into the Evangelical Hospital. I shall send with him a full account of his illness and operation.

The second thing is that Colonel Chorlac Antic and a good many of the officers here are anxious that the Division should pass through England on its way. They think it would do the men a great deal of good. One of my officers said to me, 'These men have been taught to think that Russia is the greatest power in Europe, and they find things like this, and it is difficult to make them believe that things are different in England and France.' I am writing a letter to the Consul, which I enclose. If you can persuade him to send a telegram home about it, that of course will be first-rate. I think as it is worded there is no danger of its giving away military secrets.

Fawcett *Letter Tuesday 9 October*

We are still here doing nothing at all – there are, I think, two men in hospital, but as I have done only one night's duty since we left Reni, I really don't know much about it. Dr Inglis is still very ill – she has been a good deal worse lately.

Today we hear that at the eleventh hour the Russians are stopping the Serbs from leaving the country. They, poor dears, are feeling most depressed about it. I don't wonder. We, of course, are furious. The English transports are supposed to be waiting for us at Archangel. We have been here for nearly six weeks, and now we get this news at the end of it. Of course I'd love to go and nurse the poor Roumanians, but as that is impossible, we might as well go home.

Today Murphy and I are doing the cooking for the unit, and are thoroughly enjoying ourselves. For breakfast they had fried eggs, for dinner boiled mutton, pumpkin, mashed potato, and sponge cake pudding with apricot sauce. For tea they had scones and for supper, soup, Russian cutlets, potatoes in their jackets, and pancakes.

Milne *Wednesday 10 October*

Still not away, and no sign of it. There is said to be a railway strike somewhere in the north of Russia, so that is making a delay; but if we do not get off soon it will be too late for Archangel. As it is the cold of the Arctic Ocean will be impossible.

Inglis *Letter to Onslow 10 October*

There seems to be another hitch! Why or wherefore one cannot see. The railway trucks for the first *eshelon* ought to have been here five days ago. They haven't come. And now there is a story of a railway strike in the north. It may or may not be true, but as the trucks ought to have left Petrograd at least ten days or a fortnight ago, it is *not* the reason for their not being here. In the meantime the men have had all their ammunition taken away from them, except six rounds each man. And *nothing whatever* is being done about winter clothes.

The Russians must be made to do something or other. As things are going at present the Serbs will fall between two stools. But what can we do? Will you see the Consul? And talk it all over? I am writing to him. Send the man who takes this back with your news, and a mail bag!

Glorious weather here for the moment, but it will get cold soon. Please bring every coat you can find in the store – black or white – for it will be bitterly cold on the voyage. Could Butler let me know exactly how many there are?

London and Jassi

There was indeed another hitch, and the rumour recorded by Fawcett on 9 October was close to the truth. The only section of the eastern front still offering resistance to the Germans was the stretch on the Sereth north of Galatz, where the formerly despised Roumanian army, now retrained by French officers under General Berthelot, was 'fighting splendidly', as Mrs Milne noted. Now it was the Roumanians' turn to be doubtful of the divisions on their flanks, and they were the ones insisting on reliable allies. They enlisted the support of Sir George Barclay, the British Consul in Jassi, and on 7 October he cabled the Foreign Office that General Berthelot was objecting to the transfer of the 13,000 Serbian troops from the Galatz front – where they had not as yet been employed – to Salonica. The French Ambassador supported Berthelot, as did Barclay himself. He added that the Russian commander was postponing his decision for the moment. The next day he cabled again, saying that the King of Roumania had urged him to do his utmost to bring about the retention of the troops in question. The women were kept in the dark about this for another fortnight, but it was a hitch of royal proportions.[24]

Hadji Abdul

Milne *Sunday 14 October*

This has been a great day – I had to take the service this morning – it was simply too awful; but all I can say is that I did not stick – but I was thankful when it was over.

The Colonel came to see about getting our medals[25] – I do hope we get them before we leave; but when do we go? It was to have been this week for sure – it may be still – but the time gets on – and Archangel may be closed if we do not hurry up.

Tuesday 16 October

We hear that we are to leave on Saturday or Sunday first – perhaps even before – for Archangel. I shall be quite sorry to leave here – it is so perfectly lovely, and I am feeling so well again. I got one jolly long rug and a strip of carpet yesterday, from the Roumanian peasants in Hadji Abdul. I now have several carpets for William's bungalow – I hope I get them home safely. I am going again with a bundle of clothes to see what I can get for them. They will not sell for money – only exchange.

Inglis *Letter 17 October*[26]

I wonder if this is my last letter from Russia! We hope to be off in a very few days now. We have had a very pleasant time in this place with its Turkish name. It shows how far north Turkey once came. We are with the Division, and were given this perfectly beautiful camping-ground, with trees, and a slope towards the east. The question was whether we were going to Roumania or elsewhere.

It is nice being back with these nice people. They have been most kind and friendly, and we have picnics and rides and dances and dinners; and till this turmoil of the move began we had an afternoon reception every day under the walnut trees! Now we are packed up and ready to go, and I mean to walk in on you one morning. It does not stand thinking of!

We shall have about two months to refit, but one of those is my due as a holiday, *which I am going to take.* I'll see you all soon.

Odessa

Onslow *Letter to Inglis Monday 15 October*[27]

I have delayed the messenger in the hopes of being able to send you some definite news, but unfortunately there is none. Mr Bagge has forwarded your suggestion, which he endorsed, to the Home authorities, and he has also wired to Petrograd to know the reason for the delay. I mentioned the subject of the Serbs visiting England to Colonel Milotinovic; he was most enthusiastic, and spoke of it with great feeling.

We go every day to the railway office to get information as to the date of our departure, but so far there is none. Mr Bagge cannot account for the delay – it may be the shipping transport is not quite ready and they prefer keeping us waiting here rather than up north – or – the Russians or Roumanians are making another effort to keep the Serbs; but if it is that our transport is being held up, Mr Bagge says the British Government will have something to say on the subject.

I sold the cars last Friday for 140,000 roubles to the Zemskii Soyuz;[28] the Roumanians were most unsatisfactory and offered much less. The equipment was all loaded and sent off two days after our arrival here. Mr Dobrinovic advised our getting it off as soon as possible – it is now at Razdelnaya under the charge of four Serbs awaiting the sixth *eshelon* to which it is to be attached.

We were all sorry to hear how seedy you have been. I do hope you are better now and that we may soon be *en route* for England; that at present seems to be the cure for all ills.

Hedges sends love and good wishes to you for a speedy recovery.

Hadji Abdul

Milne 'Some Months in Bessarabia '[29]

It seemed too wonderful to be true that we were perhaps going home. Days passed, however, and there was no more news. For several reasons this uncertainty was rather agitating. Hadji Abdul, although a Turkish village before it became Russian, was entirely inhabited by Roumanians, many of them refugees; and these peasants had stores of beautiful rugs and carpets which we coveted very much, but all our offers of roubles were refused. We were given to understand that they would be willing to exchange some of them for clothing, and especially boots, as such things were not to be had for love or money. Of this plan we heartily approved, being only too pleased to make room in our kit-bags for the treasures we had gradually collected.

Inglis Letter to Onslow 19 October [30]

There really does seem to be a prospect of our getting off soon! But there are several things I want to write to you about, so I am sending up another man...

Would you spend 25 roubles for me on paperbacked English novels to keep the unit going on the train and transport? I found one shop with a really splendid collection, at a rouble each.

We have had absolutely no news here for days and days – so we are longing to see you for *many* reasons. By the way, only 6,000 of the Division are going with this first lot – will you tell the Consul – as transports for 6,000 only have been sent. The rest of the 15,000 are to follow. I cannot help wishing that the Headquarters Staff and we were staying to see them out ahead of us.

P.S. Your letter arrived last night – very many thanks. You *have* done well with the cars! The Committee will be stricken dumb – you wonderful businesswoman. I don't suppose we can know exactly what it means in English money till we get home and exchange it – or can you do that here?

By the way will you make quite sure that our accounts are quite straight with the Consulate? They had better keep some money in hand to pay things that may turn up later – for instance there is a letter today from Mr Kimens about an account from Trondheim for the equipment which Lady Decies brought out!

Milne Sunday October 21

A terrible shock – it is said that we are not going home after all – the Roumanians are keeping the Serbs to fight with them – it is too awful after we were all ready to go; and the disappointment of it – I feel I can't settle to the idea. I was so longing for home. The cold in the tents is simply awful – and cooking out of doors is beyond a joke – so different from the heat of last October. It is a year today since we retreated from Medgidia – it seems like three.

Dr Inglis is still very ill – she certainly can't do anything – she should be home – so should we all.

'Some Months in Bessarabia'[31]

As the days passed, and we had no more definite news about leaving, our agitation increased. We had parted with nearly all our warm clothing, and the weather was beginning to be very cold. We had expected to be off in six days at the latest; so when making up our bundles had calculated to leave ourselves one change only for the journey, and part with everything else. On October 21st it was almost more than we could bear. We got news that, after all, the Serbs were going to join the Roumanians, proceed at once to Akermann – a town on the Black Sea near Odessa – there to re-equip during the winter, and in spring in all probability go to Ismail; and we, of course, would go with them.

I went to see Dr Inglis in her tent that afternoon, and she told me it was the first time in her life she had ever been homesick. She had written to her people, saying it was the last letter from Russia, and now we were not going after all. She then proceeded to tell me how she would arrange the hospital; who would be sent home, and who would remain, mentioning that Dr Corbett and Matron must go home first; then in spring, when Dr Corbett returned, she herself would go home and have a rest. It was perfectly wonderful. Ill as she was, all the details were arranged in her mind, and we had only heard of the change of plan that morning. I was very miserable when I left her. She was so obviously unfit to stay on, yet she would not give in.

Inglis *Letter to Onslow October 22*[32]

Thanks for your letter about the Roumanian rumour. I am afraid it is more than a rumour and that there is a determined effort on the part of the Roumanian Minister at Jassi and various other people, naturally the Roumanians among them, to keep the Serbs here. The day before yesterday a telegram came saying our departure was again postponed. Colonel Milotinovic has gone to Mogilev, the Russian Headquarters, to see about it all.

Now it may end all right, but what I am writing about is this. Would it be worth while for you to go at once to Petrograd and see the Ambassador? If I were not tied by the leg to bed, I should certainly go myself, and, though I should like you to go and have a talk with the Consul about it, I cannot help feeling that you might do the trick by going up now. Explain to him that these men have not got their winter clothing, have had all their ammunition except six rounds taken away from them, that last winter they were short of fuel and clothing and food, that he will have one difficulty after another if he lets them stay in this country, and that the only thing is to get them out. And impress upon him that the whole division must go together. The idea of sending one brigade and the General Staff and then the second brigade simply means that the second brigade would never go.

Now if this plan is worth carrying out it must be done at once, so that the Ambassador can wire to the authorities at Russian General Headquarters immediately. I cannot understand how they imagine that England is going to send transports to Archangel while they play these irresponsible games at this end; but if the transports have been sent and are there, it seems to me that the Ambassador is in a very strong position.

If you think it necessary, take Hedges with you and send the other girls back here, or if Hedges' back is still bad, take Butler. I do wish I could go with you; it is just like our luck that I should be laid on my back at this point. I believe you and I together might do something with the Ambassador...

London

While the unit waited for news, the drama on the home front had continued. On 8 October, the day that Barclay telegraphed the special plea from the King of Roumania, Robinson and Holme, newly arrived from Russia, attended a meeting of the London Committee of the SWH. They reported that Dr Inglis had urged them to impress on the authorities the urgency of withdrawing the Serbian Division, and they reiterated her intention to remain with it in Roumania if it were not transferred to another front. They had been charged to deliver to the Foreign Office a private report which they had not dared to bring with them; instead, Robinson had committed it to memory, writing only the briefest of notes on a piece of paper the size of a postage stamp, which Holme had carried with her in a packet of needles.[33] There were ten headings, outlining the history of the Serbian Divisions, the causes of discontent with their situation in Russia, the presence of Austrian spies in their midst, internal troubles with the Soldiers' and Workmen's Committees, and the repeated and deliberate frustration of their desire to leave Russia. The memorandum itself, written by Dr Jambrisak, a member of the Yugoslav Committee then in Odessa, runs to 2,273 words; and this

Robinson subsequently dictated for transcription and delivery to the Foreign Office, where it was immediately circulated, together with Marx's earlier memorandum and Barclay's recent cables, before being sent on to the War Office.[34]

Even in those quarters, it was now realised that time was running out, and Dr Jambrisak's memorandum made it clear that there were other agents besides the Russian generals who were determinedly obstructing the transfer. British ships had at the beginning of September transported only 3,148 Serbian soldiers, the depleted Second Division, who had had great difficulty in leaving. Their commandant and chief of staff had been arrested by the Soldiers' and Workers' Soviet at Aleksandrovsk, near Murmansk; only the intervention of Sir George Buchanan and Mr Bagge had secured their release and authorisation for the Division to leave.[35] A second convoy had subsequently been sent to Archangel for the First Division, who were not there to embark, so that their places had been filled with 'Czechs, Italian prisoners, Alsatians, and civilians of various nationalities' wanting to get away from Russia.[36] In the meantime the pleas from Barclay and the King of Roumania had encouraged the Russian Headquarters Staff to 'postpone' yet again the Division's departure.

Now the War Office insisted that the earlier arrangements should stand, cabling to Barclay on 23 October:

> War Office do not consider that any fresh developments have arisen which call for reconsideration of decision to transfer First Serbian Division to Salonica. This division has been exposed to exceptional strain on the eastern front, and I do not consider it would be fair to cancel their transfer, especially in view of the fact that their arrival at Salonica will have vital effect upon morale as well as manpower of Serbian army.[37]

This was really the final word and there was no more arguing; but it came very late. The Germans were already in northern Bessarabia, and another, more thorough-going revolution was brewing in the cities. Transport in south Russia was inadequate and disorganised, with roads, railways and rolling-stock in disrepair, and there was no possibility of moving all 15,000 men of the First Division either before winter or before the Russian front collapsed. The trap which Mrs Milne had foreseen was closing fast.

Dr Inglis and Staff at Hadji Abdul

(Roger and Patrick Cahill)

CHAPTER 15
Recalled At Last

The combination, in the last week of October, of the visit of Colonel Milotinovic to the Russian Headquarters, the orders from London to Roumania, and the intervention of the British diplomats in Petrograd and Odessa, succeeded where these forces separately had failed. At last Stavka took the point. Orders for the Division to move to Archangel came through yet again, and miraculously this time there were trains available to transport them. There was not time to move all 15,000 men before the port closed, but ships were waiting to transport the first 6,000, and it was promised that the rest would follow in the spring. Had Inglis been in command she would undoubtedly have insisted on the staff and the hospital staying to see the last man out, but arrangements were no longer in her hands. Trains filled up and left at the rate of two a day, the women and the Divisional Headquarters staff leaving on the sixth, which picked up Onslow and Hedges at Razdelnaya, where they were waiting with their two waggons of equipment.

Few written records survive about the journey: the Scottish Women were on their way home, and there was no point in writing letters or reports that would arrive after them. Besides, they were separated from the lifeline of the diplomatic bag, and what they had to tell would not have passed the censors of the postal services, either Russian or British. Only Milne went on scribbling regularly, her almost daily diary and her subsequent *Blackwoods* articles serving to reclaim the month-long journey from oblivion.

Neither could the women hear much of what was going on elsewhere in Russia. Without Onslow and Hedges to be their eyes and ears in Odessa, they lost their link with the dependable news from the Consulate, and with the anxious rumours and informed speculations of the English colony. Suspended between the anxiety of the past months and the risks of the Arctic voyage ahead, they adapted to the train as they had done many times before. They made themselves comfortable, enjoyed their meals, continued their Serbian lessons, and entertained themselves and one another. They rode on the engine, walked in the woods when the driver stopped to gather fuel, and ran beside the toiling locomotive for exercise. Their train became a little world on its own, its insular life breached only by their expeditions into the markets of the towns where it was sometimes detained, and which supplied them with fresh provisions but little fresh news.[1]

The main anxiety was Dr Inglis's condition. Dr Ward, who attended her, wrote afterwards of her desperation at finding that the local chemists could offer nothing to alleviate her patient's pain: while there was an abundance of fresh food in the country, there was an acute shortage of even the most basic drugs. Inglis languished uncomplainingly in the second-class half-compartment which she shared with the matron, who was also ill, while those around her worried about her suffering, able to give her only the good nursing that had always been a feature of her hospitals.

Had the travellers had any metropolitan news, their journey would have been much more fraught. In the last ten days of October, while the Roumanians and British wrangled over the future of the Serbian Division, a storm had been brewing in Petrograd, with even wider implications than those of the previous disturbances. On 20 October Lenin returned from his Finnish exile in disguise, contending that the time was ripe for a Bolshevik rising. Two days later the Petrograd Soviet formed a Military Revolutionary Committee, and adopted his resolution in favour of an immediate insurrection. This was widely rumoured to be timed for 7 November,[2] the opening day of Second Council of Soviets, as General Knox noted in his diary on 1 November.[3] On 3 November, General Poole (the optimistic General Poole whom Rendel had met at Tecuci) wrote to a member of his staff in London that the worst feature of all was the growth of anti-Allied and pro-German feeling. One of his officers reported that robberies with violence were becoming common in the capital, with gangs of hooligans holding up women and girls to rob them of their footwear and purses, while in the country houses and estates were being burned and pillaged.[4] It was just as well that Onslow and Hedges had not tried to go to Petrograd to see the ambassador; a troop train with a friendly armed guard was probably the safest place to be.

Hadji Abdul

Milne *Saturday 27 October*

Glorious – it is to be home after all. The Colonel sent up to tell us yesterday morning. The first *eshelon* is to leave Etulia today. We are on the 6th with the staff, so it is expected we leave Monday or Tuesday... I hope we stop in Moscow long enough to see things. Archangel will be awfully cold, and the sea journey simply hideous.

'Some Months in Bessarabia'[5]

Dr Inglis was rather better and able to sit out in the sunshine, and when at last the great day of departure arrived she even inspected the row of very portly kit-bags and bed bundles, turning a lenient eye upon their dimensions, for were we not after all sharing an entire train and a boat with friends, not merely a few coaches and cabins? So our kit was allowed to pass. On the evening of Monday the 29th we said good-bye to Hadji Abdul; it had never looked more beautiful, and our feelings were mixed on leaving it all behind.

Train Reni to Kharkov

Milne *Thursday 1 November*

We are now on the train en route for home – perfectly wonderful. We started on Monday evening (29th) from Hadji Abdul, and were very sorry to leave. Oh, what a time we had packing up. But it was fine weather, and that made all the difference. I am in charge of all the feeding on the train; it is a great business, but great fun all the same, and my girls are very astute – but there is talk of a frost among the sisters, as they have been changed into the Transport carriage – and they are not looked after at all. We are to be sixteen days on the train – but we stop at Moscow for a little breather I am glad to say.

'Some Months in Bessarabia'[6]

There were two fourth-class carriages set apart for our use, long waggons fitted with wooden shelves in three tiers – to be used as beds by night and seats by day. At first it looked rather hopeless, but when each had claimed a shelf, unpacked the blankets, and spread some of the gay rugs over them, it was not so bad; and so we settled down to a journey of from ten days to a fortnight across Russia. There were seventeen of us in our waggon, not including the four pets – three dear Russian pussies – and Sammy, the faithful mascot, a 'thoroughbred Roumanian dog'. A section of the compartment nearest the door we used as a kitchen. In it there was a small iron stove for heating the carriage, and on this we cooked our breakfast and prepared the invalid diets. Before leaving Hadji Abdul we were told that everything in the way of food we required for the journey must be taken with us, as nothing could be procured on the way. We could get nothing that would last any length of time in Hadji Abdul, and everything cost a ransom, so it seemed rather a black look-out. We arranged that at midday we would share the soldiers' soup, and the evening meal was cooked for us in the officers' kitchen. All we had to do was to provide the materials to cook with. So whenever the train stopped for any length of time at a town of any size, the secretary and I made journeys to the market. It was most interesting. And we were surprised at the quantity there was of everything – beautiful bread nearly white, meat, fowls, fruit, eggs, and milk in plenty.

Saturday 3 November

Yesterday we had a long stop at Kremenchug. I had a great time buying food to keep us till Archangel. Everything very cheap, but there was a little revolution going on in the town: twenty people had been shot in the morning, and there were lots of soldiers tearing about with fixed bayonets and others blazing away at large – just hitting anything and anyone they could. We didn't come in for anything, I am glad to say, but it was quite exciting to be in it. The journey is progressing well – we have done over 1,000 *versts*, and we are very cosy and happy. We play bridge a lot, and overeat too much. Dr Inglis is still far from well.

Sunday 4 November

Had a jolly time in Kharkov. We stopped for several hours, so we took cabs and flew to the old market and bought things. I got a beautiful old icon – I had longed for one – I only paid 18 roubles for it. We get to Moscow tomorrow night – how long shall we have, I wonder? I hope we can see things. We are very happy in the train, and the time simply flies.

Fawcett *Letter*[7] *29 October – 4 November*

We finally left Hadji Abdul on 29 October, so that it has taken us a month to do the whole journey. The train part from Hadji to Archangel was most enjoyable. We had fourth class railway carriages, which were quite comfortable as we had lots of bed clothes with us, the chief objection to them, as a rule, being that the berths are so hard. The weather on the whole was quite good; rather cold at times, and once we had a wet day, but nothing to grumble at. At Kharkov, one of the towns we stopped at, where we had three hours, there had been a riot. The soldiers had broken into the vodka factories and had got very drunk. We met one or two of them; in fact one of them invited Murphy and me to sit down on a doorstep with him.

London and Petrograd

On 5 or 6 November, in answer to another complaint about the delay in transferring the Serbian Division, the Foreign Office received the following telegram from Buchanan in Petrograd:

> Minister for Foreign Affairs in expressing concurrence said that delay in despatch of Serbian troops had been due to action of General Berthelot and Roumanian Government who had wished them to serve on Roumanian front. They were now, he believed, on the way to Archangel.[8]

In the light of the events of the next few days, this can scarcely have been reassuring to those at home. The Serbian staff, with 6,000 men and the

Scottish Women, were indeed on their way to Archangel, expecting to spend 6 November and perhaps the 7th in Moscow, and hoping to have a little more time to see the Kremlin than they had had on their outward journey. But by the time they reached the outskirts of the city, there was fighting in the streets, and on 7 November the October revolution began in earnest. In Petrograd, Sir George Buchanan and his wife watched from the Embassy as Bolshevik forces fired on the Winter Palace, to which the Ministers of the Provisional Government had retreated, guarded only by the Women's Battalion and a detachment of military cadets.[9] Cruisers and gunboats of the Baltic Fleet were brought up the Neva and opened fire upon the palace, which fell the next day; most members of the government were arrested, Kerensky himself having escaped on 7 November disguised as a sailor, to return a few days later to attempt an unsuccessful counter-attack. By 12 November the Bolsheviks were in control of Petrograd, and Kerensky once again escaped.[10] Resistance was rather stronger in Moscow, where fighting continued until 15 November, when it became clear that the Bolsheviks had triumphed there too.

Train Kharkov to Archangel

Milne *'Some Months in Bessarabia'*[11]

What we were really living for was Moscow. We had been promised a few days there, so instead of exchanging our roubles or getting rid of them, we treasured them up to spend. This time we meant really to see all there was to be seen. Meaning to lose nothing, we arranged to go to the opera as soon as we got there. So we made ourselves as smart as circumstances permitted, and waited, and waited – and so did the train, outside Moscow again.

Wednesday 7 November

What a frost – we did not stay in Moscow after all. During the night we went on, and in the morning were far away. We were told no troops of any sort were allowed in Moscow – and the Serbs would have picked a scrap with a Russian over nothing, knowing they were leaving the country. We are very angry and disappointed. Then yesterday we hoped to see the Volga, and came to Yaroslavl in the night, so that came to nothing. It is a big place, and we would have loved seeing it all by day – jolly bad luck. I rode a long way on the engine yesterday – it was lovely. The country is simply charming, and today we have got into snow – real Russian look about things. We get to Vologda today – I hope in the day time, and that we stay there some time. We all long to buy things, and it makes a nice break to get out and walk. I am fed to the teeth with cooking on the train;

we have so many invalids I have to be at it all day long. Well, home will be simply lovely.

Archangel

Milne *'Some Months in Bessarabia'*[12] *10 November*

Archangel lies on the opposite side of the river from the station. On crossing in the boat we spoke to some English sailors, who, to say the least of it, were not very reassuring. They told us the last convoy which left for England had been lost; in fact, all outward-bound boats were torpedoed, and they generally gave us to understand that we were doomed.

Fawcett *Letter Saturday 10 November*

At Archangel our boat, the *Porto Lisboa*, a Portuguese German prize with an English crew,[13] was exactly opposite the town of Archangel, so it was quite easy to get across on the ferry.

Sammy, our dog, has been a continual anxiety to us all the way along. At Archangel we had to get permission from the head of the Transport there, Commodore Bevan, who interviewed the captain before we were allowed to take him on board at all.

Butler[14] *10-11 November*

The train crawled northwards, whilst Kerensky was falling and Lenin was marching on Moscow. I was almost suffocated with grief at leaving Russia. In a sense I am suffocated still, irrational though that sounds. And how irrational my feeling for Russia was and yet how powerful became apparent to me in Archangel where, being in charge of the equipment, it was my duty to see it loaded on to the *Porto Lisboa*, which was taking us home. The vans had been uncoupled a good mile from the quay and would have to be shifted before the Serbian soldiers could carry the cases and bales to the ship's side, where the Chinese labour on board would handle them. It was towards the end of November and already bitterly cold, with a good deal of snow on the ground and very little daylight. But I had three clear days before me and never doubted that I could get the forty tons safely stowed on board within twenty-four hours. However, I went straight off to the station master, who spoke fluent French, and asked him to have the vans moved immediately. He replied that it should be done at once. I wasn't too much surprised next morning to find that he hadn't kept his word; but I got very uneasy when I found his office locked and the station itself completely deserted. There wasn't a soul to be seen as I ploughed backwards and forwards through the snow all that day between his office and the ship; and I was getting quite desperate when I finally ran him to earth at nine o'clock in the evening. He looked rather desperate too, and dog-tired into the bargain. He hadn't been able to do anything about the vans, he told me, because he had been attending meetings all day; and he wouldn't be able to do anything about them tomorrow either, for a general national strike had been declared, and all work of any kind had been prohibited until further notice. I was dumbfounded. 'Those are my orders,' he kept on saying, and I gathered that it had something to do with the revolution, now in its third stage.

Very much perturbed, I went back to the ship to report the matter to Dr Inglis. She was lying exhausted on her bunk, and seemed to be in great pain. But she opened eyes which looked enormous in her small, white, freckled face, and whispered: 'You must either get the equipment on board before we sail, or stay behind to guard it. Your duty is to the equipment.' Then she closed her eyes. I now had *my* orders, and my reaction at first was perfectly natural. Surely, I thought, this is going rather too far? The equipment I knew had cost a mint of money; it was urgently needed in Macedonia and would undoubtedly be stolen if left behind unguarded. But what about me? I had heard that the port might be blocked up with ice any day now; and was I to stay behind alone in Archangel, guarding it till the spring? And then suddenly it dawned on me that I was being given my heart's desire; and that what I had longed to do was now my bounden duty. Ecstasy flooded over me at this discovery; for surely even Dr Inglis couldn't expect me to break that strike?

Milne *Saturday 10 November*
We have a jolly cabin – Fooks, Gwynn, and I – Oh, how comfortable compared with the train. But I could wish we were safely home. We may not start for a few days yet, but it will be good to have the voyage behind us. Tomorrow Gwynn, Dr Inglis and I lunch with the commodore. I am so glad I am asked – how good it is to see a man of our own nation again – I am sick of the Serbs – I have little use for them. I do hope we have a decent passage. I don't expect so, and I wonder if we land in England or France. The war news is not very good – Kerensky is said to have escaped from Petrograd, and a three-months truce with Germany has been signed; a separate peace and an alliance are also said to be in the wind. We are well out of it now – or will be when the time comes.

Sunday 11 November
What a lovely Sunday – I haven't enjoyed myself so much for a long time. We lunched with the commodore and his staff at their flat in Archangel – the Admiralty launch fetched us all at 12.30 – two of the officers came

for us – Dr Ward, Hedges, Gwynn and I went, and we had a perfectly lovely time. Captain Bevan is a perfect darling – and I simply loved talking to him. He comes from Devon and knows Chagford and all the moors. He took me in to lunch.

Monday 12 November

This evening I enjoyed myself to the full – the five officers came to dinner. Major Frost and the commodore were my chief joys. I had a delightful time with the commodore – we talked of all sorts of things. He has promised me a naval duffel coat to keep me warm in the Arctic Ocean. I hope I shall see him again.

Butler[15]*Monday 12 November*

...surely even Dr Inglis couldn't expect me to break that strike? No; but I ought to try by every possible means to get the equipment on board. And wasn't it just barely possible that a posse of Serbian soldiers *could* get it to the ship's side in time tomorrow? Forty ton? More than a mile? Through all that snow? Ought I to consult one of the officers? Need I? This conflict raged in my mind all night, one of the fiercest I have ever fought; and I lost it in the morning, deciding without consulting anyone that of course the Serbian soldiers could never accomplish such a feat in time, and salving my conscience by staging (for that was what it amounted to) a last appeal to the station-master. He was having tea in his office when I got there after breakfast, and far from pleased to see me. 'As I told you yesterday,' he protested; and as I listened, trying to look distracted, I heard two other sounds simultaneously: 'Get the equipment on board,' a thread of a whisper in Dr Inglis's voice, and the whistling of an engine just outside the office. '*He's* working,' I gasped. 'No,' sighed the station master, 'he's putting the engine away. Ask him yourself if you like.' He signalled to the driver to stop, and I clambered up into the cab...

In my halting Russian, supplemented by gestures, I explained what I wanted. He shook his head, and I breathed a sigh of relief; but a will far stronger than my own forced me to go on. In much more fluent Russian than I have ever commanded, I told him what lay in store for me if those vans weren't shifted immediately; and to my horror and dismay I found myself pulling out the *vox humana* stop. That did it. Without a word said on his side, the engine was driven up to the vans, coupled to them, and driven up to the quay. 'Get the equipment on board,' said Dr Inglis, and broke a nation-wide strike, breaking my heart in the process. Far from being left behind in Russia, I left Russia behind me for ever, and the Russia I left behind me vanished away.

London and Petrograd

The last news the Scottish Women's Hospitals committees at home had received of their Russian Unit had been Buchanan's disquieting cable of 5 November, saying that the Serbian Division was on its way to Archangel; now an anxious fortnight followed. It was impossible even for those in Petrograd to discover exactly what was happening, and in the outside world rumour was rife. As the telegraph office at Tsarskoe Selo was fought over and changed hands, and as the subsequent general strike took effect, conflicting reports reached London. The fighting in the capital and in Moscow had been announced on 8 November, but after that all was confusion. Bulletins proclaiming that Kerensky had routed the Bolsheviks and was in control of Petrograd alternated, often on the same day, with announcements that he had been defeated or arrested, or had fled. 'Don't believe anything you hear,' the women's letters had long insisted, and now it was evident that even the printed word was false.

The War Cabinet in London, having heard nothing reliable since 11 November, ascertained on the 16th – not from Russia but from Teheran – that Odessa and the Black Sea Fleet were in Bolshevik hands, and that there was anarchy in south Russia, where estates were being seized and houses plundered.[16] Only then did the newspapers admit that previous reports had been based on rumours emanating from unconfirmed travellers' tales gathered on the Finnish-Swedish frontier; and that even the Russian Embassy in London had been without news for many days. A stack of accumulated official telegrams from Reuters' correspondent in Petrograd arrived on 18 November, recounting the tides and currents of the previous week, and adding to the alarm of the committees and the few score of English families who had a personal interest in the Russian crisis.

At last, on 20 November, a further cable arrived, having been dictated by Inglis in Archangel just before the convoy left on 12 November. Even then, there remained some doubt as to whether the unit had actually embarked and set sail, for as Butler had discovered, the revolution, with its attendant strike and civil chaos, had reached the northern fringes of Russia almost at the same time as their train. This cable just hinted at Inglis's illness: 'On our way home, everything satisfactory and all well except me...' In the relief of receiving some real news at last, this hint was not taken very seriously.[17]

White Sea and Arctic Ocean

Milne *13-14 November*

We left Archangel today at 9.30, but only as far as the bar; and we may lie till tomorrow when we start our homeward journey – and they say it will only take us seven to eight days to Scotland, where we disembark, if we have good going. The commodore sent the coat by a special messenger on the Admiralty launch, and a nice little note. I am so glad I have met him, and I hope I shall see him again.

We had a quiet night, and are now heading out to sea, where the other transport ships are lying – we cross the bar soon and then lie there for a bit before we really start. *Porto* [sic] – *Dvinsk* – *Tsar* – *Tsarina* – *Vindictive* (Escort).

Friday 16 November

12.30 Have just left Ukansky harbour, where we have been at anchor all night. Our destroyer, or rather our light cruiser, the *Vindictive*, has just passed, and we are all following. Yesterday till we came to this harbour, we had minesweepers with us, but we have left them behind. The coast of Lapland is perfectly lovely – I should like to land and have a look at the country. It is Russian Lapland; I am awfully glad to have seen it all. We are promised heavy weather, and the ship is busy bumping about even now. I should like to be home.

Saturday 17 November

What a night we have had – a storm such as I never want to meet again. The ship sat up on its hind legs, and came down again, till I thought we were done for. All the crockery in the ship seemed to break at once. Two of the boats were torn loose, but they got them again. In the morning we found we had lost our escort, but she found us later on, and the day was much calmer.

Sunday 18 November

I thought Saturday night was bad, but it was child's play to this last night. It was too awful – we all lay waiting for anything to happen, but thank goodness nothing did happen. But we lost our escort and the rest of the transports in the storm, and are now alone. At the time I write the captain has told us that within 100 miles he has no idea where he is. We have passed the North Cape, but when, he does not know. We are not likely to pick up our escort again, so must get on as best we can alone. We have been anchored for four hours, as the pumps have gone wrong – and there is seven feet of water in the engine room – so it is not a very cheery look out. Last Sunday we were all so happy lunching with the commodore – we are not quite so happy today.

'Some Months in Bessarabia' [18]

Later we were told that we owed our safety to the two engineers, who had said they would not let us drown so near home after all we had come through, if they could help it. They were recommended for Serbian decorations as a small token of gratitude for what they did. The thought of having to take to the boats in the awful cold of the Arctic regions was petrifying. It was quite bad enough to struggle out every night in the darkness to practise finding our lifeboats, so as to be prepared should the whistle be blown during the night.

Tuesday 20 November
We puffed along by ourselves all yesterday, not knowing where we were; we got into communication with our escort, but as we did not know where we were it was not easy to explain where we were to be found. We were to pick it up at two in the morning, but that did not come off. We are some way behind, they say. We had another wild night of tossing – I hate the nights...

Arctic Ocean and North Sea

Losing their escort and the rest of the convoy was no light matter. The first four months of unrestricted submarine warfare had resulted in such huge losses that the convoy system had been introduced at the end of May, bringing much greater safety to travellers by sea. U-boat commanders were wary of groups of ships, and particularly of the easily-manoeuvrable destroyers; but alone, the *Porto Lisboa*, described by Milne as 'a jolly big boat', was a vulnerable target. Fortunately the rough weather which broke up the convoy probably also deterred the U-boats; none appeared, although by then Germany had an average of forty-seven at sea each month,[19] and the convoy was on the main supply route to the eastern front.

Milne *Wednesday 21 November*
Oh, what an awful night. The ship got up on its hind legs and begged – I nearly went mad in the night. I am not a coward really, but this continual strain is terrible. I know that what is to be will be – still, I do love living, and on all hands we are warned of the dangers we are facing. And still we have not picked up our escort. We passed the Faroe Isles at three this afternoon; we were told we had passed them in the night, but no two people tell one the same story, and the captain is most alarming in the things he tells us. We must hope for the best; but this ten days has been the most trying of the fifteen months I have spent with the Scottish Women.

Thursday 22 November
Joy – we have been in sight of land nearly all day. We saw the Orkney

Islands, and came up close to them. We expected to be going into Kirkwall Harbour, but a destroyer, the *Tenacious*, came tearing out to meet us, and gave us orders (we suppose) we were not to go into Kirkwall, but right on to our destination, at present to all of us unknown. The *Tenacious* is with us, to guide us to safety – we hope so, at least. Still we have no news of our other transport and escort – I wonder where they are...

Newcastle on Tyne

Milne *Friday 23 November*

Safe at last! We had a very interesting time getting into the Tyne. We had destroyers and minesweepers to escort us along a narrow path of mine-free sea till we got to the Tyne; then we sailed quietly up ourselves looking at all the big boats lying there, and feeling really safe home at last – a glorious sunset, and we were so happy. We sang after dinner till we were tired, then went happily to bed. Our poor sailor boy who was so ill died at the ebbing of the tide.[20] How sad to bring him so far to die. Dr Inglis is also very ill, I think.

Fawcett *Letter*

At last after a vile trip we have arrived safely in the Tyne. We didn't see any submarines or anything of that sort.

We have had a beastly voyage; we were most of us very ill. I think I only went on deck two days since we started. It has also been a bad voyage from the captain's point of view. To start with we ran right into a blizzard outside the White Sea; then we lost our escort and the rest of the convoy the first day. Another trouble was that with the rough seas the valves let the water through. They had evidently all been loosened before the Germans left the boat. The engineer tells us that one night there were seven feet of water in the engine room, and it was only because of the cold and the rough sea that we did not all take to the boats.

Dr Inglis is still very ill, although on the whole she has stood the journey well. She means to spend a night or two in the hotel at Newcastle, and then go on to London.

Milne *Saturday 24 November*

We have been getting the soldiers off all morning – poor chaps, they will be glad to get on dry land. The Division is being sent to Farnham and Winchester; trains are waiting to take them off at once. The wind is rising and the river is getting very rough.

What a day it has been – it was too wild for us to be landed – our ship went adrift and we nearly had two very bad accidents – we had to get salvage tugs to come to our aid. We had to stay on board all night again – I was terrified; they said it was far more dangerous than at sea, with so many ships in the river.

Fawcett *Letter Saturday 24 November*

Our adventures were by no means over when I wrote last night. To start with, it was so rough in the Tyne that our boat broke her moorings, and we drifted nearly a mile downstream. All the morning we had various launches buzzing around making us fast again. They finally got us fixed, and after lunch a small passenger launch came to take us up to Newcastle. As we had not heard anything from the Customs people we decided to smuggle Sammy on shore, so we put him in a wire paper-basket and covered him with Murphy's rug, and took him with us. When about nine of the unit and our luggage had got safely on to the launch, she broke away from the *Lisboa*, and as it was so rough they could not get her back again. After trying for about an hour, orders came from the ship's captain that we were to proceed without them, and that Dr Inglis and the rest of the unit would follow tomorrow.

When we got to the landing stage we had to wait whilst the naval authorities came to receive Colonel Milotinovic and his staff, who had come with us. Of course this was frightfully annoying for us, as we wanted to get through quickly with the dog. None of our luggage was to be inspected, so that when we did start we had only to have our passports stamped.

Whilst Murphy and I were waiting to have our passports looked at, there was a slight block and we had to put the dog on the floor. Of course we felt sure he would whine. However, he must have known that it was a critical moment, for he didn't make a sound. Now he is safely on English soil.

Milne *Sunday 25 November*

At last we got away this morning – it was grand to get away from the ship. Sailing up the Tyne was quite interesting – we saw all the new ships building, and the new submarines, etc. Everyone was so nice to us when we landed – policemen and soldiers and officers. We had our passports stamped, then got into a motor lorry and drove to our hotel. We had a lovely lunch – looked at everyone, and everyone looked at us. Did luggage all afternoon, and went to church in the evening – the Cathedral – it was delightful. Dinner, then bed; we start at 9.30 for Edinburgh. The London girls left tonight. Dr Inglis is very ill, I'm afraid.

'Some Months in Bessarabia'[21]

Dr Inglis was brought ashore in the afternoon. The last few days of the voyage she had been very ill, though just the day before she dressed fully, wearing all her decorations, and stood for nearly twenty minutes while the entire Serbian staff said good-bye to her. When on Monday morning I went to say good-bye to her, she thanked me for all I had done, told me to take the Scots girls as far as Edinburgh, and see the committee there. And she added, 'In a few days come and see me in Edinburgh.'

Edinburgh

Milne *Monday 26 November*

Here I am in the N.B. Hotel, back in Edinburgh. I brought the Scotch girls back; then I went to Dr Inglis' sister to tell her how ill she is – I am afraid she is dying. Then I went to the committee, and was well received – they were very nice – and I had to tell them everything – am to go back tomorrow and perhaps see reporters – and come in on Friday to a committee meeting. I went to get some clothes; then had my hair cut, and back to the hotel for dinner. Have written to William since – home tomorrow – perfectly splendid.

Tuesday 27 November

Home at last, and how lovely and peaceful it is – if only William had been here to meet me. Poor Dr Inglis died last night. What a sad ending to our trip. But she accomplished what she had before her – she got the Serbs out of Russia, and died knowing she had won.

London

Fawcett *Letter Tuesday 27 November The Wilton Hotel*

We heard last night that Dr Inglis was very dangerously ill, and now this morning there is a telegram to say that she died last evening. Isn't it a sad ending to our unit?

Butler[22]

Dr Inglis lived a bare twenty-four hours after reaching Newcastle. When the Serbs who had travelled with her regained their own people, they found her name already figuring in their epic songs; and an Englishman working with the Yugoslav partisans in the last war[23] heard the Inglis verses sung to the *gusla*. What she had done in Serbia, and what she had done for Serbia, is part of their history now.

CHAPTER 16
Sequels

The immediate sequel to Inglis's death was a ceremonial recognition of her work. There was a lying-in-state in St Giles's Cathedral in Edinburgh, and a full military funeral. This was followed by a memorial service in St Margaret's, Westminster, attended by royalty, by the Serbian Legation, and by members of the diplomatic corps and of government departments.[1] No longer was there any question in official circles about the value of women's work, for great numbers of women had been successfully employed in a variety of ways since 1916, but these ceremonies marked a spectacularly dramatic acknowledgment of their achievement, and made the exploits of the Scottish Women's Hospitals widely known. Elsie Inglis had wanted desperately to go on living, and had made detailed plans for the next unit in Salonica; but had she been able to determine the date of her own death, she could not have staged a more telling exit.

Of the reflected glory shed on the Scottish Women's Hospitals in general, much was focussed on the Russian Unit in particular. The submarine danger was such that the unit's departure from Archangel would have been kept secret even if the Foreign Office had had reliable knowledge of it; but now with its safe arrival there was no need for caution, and in the publicity resulting from Inglis's many obituary tributes, the women's former perils were made known, and the narrowness of their escapes relished. When in February the following year the re-equipped London Unit, now named the Elsie Inglis Unit, mustered for its passage to Salonica, it was inspected by the King and Queen, whose questions showed them to be well acquainted with its past adventures.[2] As Inglis had predicted, 'they' had indeed seen 'every bit of this', and her refusal to sit still was publicly vindicated.

What was not publicised was the presence of the Serbian Division in England, and their morale-raising visit to the army camps at Farnham and Winchester. Their arrival was unannounced, and those in Newcastle who saw them disembark wondered at the appearance of a large body of ragged soldiers whose feet were bound in hessian, who carried balalaikas instead of rifles, and who sang in a strange tongue as they marched through the streets.[3] The women were asked not to speak about their fellow-travellers until they were safely in Macedonia, and the silent drama of Inglis's part in their transfer was not made public. From correspondence afterwards, and from the recognition accorded Inglis in Serbian legend and song,[4] it is clear that many Serbs regarded the transfer of the Divisions as entirely due to her, and as a triumph greater even than the introduction of clean water and anti-typhus measures for which the British hospitals were already renowned. Instead of perishing vainly in defence of Roumania or becoming embroiled in Russia's civil war, the 6,000 who had travelled with the Hospital were transported through France and the Mediterranean to Salonica, which the 3,000-strong Second Division had already reached.[5] Drafted into what was left of the Serbian Army, they found themselves close to the border of their own land.

As Inglis had warned, the remaining 9,000 men of the First Division had the greatest difficulty in leaving Russia. Soldiers' committees obstructed them, interviewing them individually to check that the transfer was their own choice, and not imposed by their officers. Archangel was by then closed, and in the icy mid-winter they travelled by the Trans-Siberian and the Manchurian railways to Port Arthur, from where the Japanese government arranged for their transportation to Salonica, via the China Seas, the Indian Ocean, the Red Sea and the Suez Canal.[6] It was a very long way round, but by mid-April all were there. Their advent more than doubled the Serbian component of the malaria-stricken Allied Armies of the Orient, so long and so thoroughly dug in that the French Prime Minister had scornfully dubbed them the Gardeners of Salonica.[7] Some of the newcomers were drafted to the existing Serbian divisions to bring them up to strength, but a whole new division, now known as the Yugoslav Division, was added to the Serbian Army, which was entrenched high up in the Moglena Mountains. And at the beginning of April the Elsie Inglis Unit under Dr Annette Benson, with Hedges in command of the Transport, set up its field hospital at Verbliani, some miles behind the Yugoslav section of the line.[8]

The excitement of the Division at being so near home was quite the reverse of the prevailing depression of the rest of the Armies of the Orient, which had thought and spoken of themselves as forgotten by the Westerners, and had indeed been badly neglected in the matter of arms and reinforcements. After the hopelessness of the Roumanian front, to be so close to the Serbian border seemed to the Yugoslavs almost as good as victory, and their excitement was infectious. On the Serbian troops already in Macedonia, and indeed on many of the other forces there, their effect was as dynamic as the War Office could have hoped. The fact that the Yugoslavs had insisted on travelling half-way round the world in order to join them, and that they believed in the possibility not only of victory, but of victory on the Macedonian front, lifted the spirit of the forgotten armies, and gave them new hope.[9]

A more material result of the addition of these substantial reinforcements was the possibility of a new offensive on the hitherto stagnant front. General Franchet d'Espérey, who took over the command in Macedonia in June 1918, agreed to a bold plan to attack in the most unlikely and apparently impregnable part of the mountains in front of the Serbian sector, instead of through the easier Vardar valley as expected by the Bulgars. This plan, which had been devised in 1917 by the Serbian chief of staff, became feasible now that the Serbian force was so much stronger. In September the whole Serbian army, reinforced by two French divisions, attacked the enemy strongholds in the high peaks facing their positions, while the British made a feint attack farther to the east where the Bulgars were expecting it.[10] After costly fighting the Bulgars retreated, and with incredible speed the Serbs advanced far ahead of their supplies,[11] leaving the Elsie Inglis Unit facing the novel problem of being unable to keep up with an advance.[12] These men, as they entered Belgrade in triumph, must have felt that they were winning the war. Only the hardy Serbs could have succeeded in that rugged and almost trackless terrain, and their breakthrough led to the speedy collapse of Bulgaria, one of the key factors in persuading the German High Command to sue for peace.[13]

Of the women who had returned from Russia in 1917, all had undertaken to do 'war work', but even without this obligation, they were not the kind to sit still, and all were busy in some way. Twenty-one had joined the Elsie Inglis Unit for Macedonia, among them Gwynn, who was appointed administrator, Drs Chesney and Ward, and, in November 1918 when she had qualified, Dr Elinor Rendel. Robinson and Onslow served as officers with Hedges in the Transport, and Butler, though still listed as 'orderly', continued to exercise her customary initiative. Murphy was again anaesthetist, and Moir a nurse. Moir kept another detailed diary, as innocent of censorship as her 1916 one had been, but this time without any pretence that it was a letter-book.

Some of the older women took on positions of particular responsibility. Mary Milne, the first-class cook, went as housekeeper to the Sallanche Unit of the SWH, which had formed a hospital to care for tubercular Serbian boys. Marx was employed by the War Office, and spent much of 1918 and 1919 in France tracing war graves and prisoners of war, while Bowerman (whose enthusiasm for the February revolution had been simply that of a Constitutional Democrat) worked with Emmeline Pankhurst and the Women's Social and Political Union, persuading miners and trades unionists to resist pacifism and industrial disputes.[14] Evelina Haverfield returned to Serbia to establish mobile canteens for the Serbian Army, remaining there to run a home for orphaned and tubercular children. She died in 1920, having been invested with Serbia's highest order, the Order of the White Eagle.[15]

Many of the younger Russian Unit veterans joined other women's organisations, of which there were by then a good number. Glubb and Livesay became junior officers in the Motor Transport Division of the new Women's Royal Air Force,[16] while Walker, and probably Grant and Fitzroy, nursed in army hospitals in Britain. Fawcett became an officer in the Women's Army Auxiliary Corps, and served in France, spending much of her time in an office well behind the lines censoring the women's letters home. It must have been a dull job: the first page of her next diary is headed 'Rouen 1918', and the rest are quite blank.

Most of the drivers, on the other hand, were able to continue their venturesome exploits, either with the Elsie Inglis Unit in the Macedonian mountains, or with other ambulance units in France and Flanders. Birkbeck and Plimsoll were among those working with the First Aid and Nursing Yeomanry, their unit having been incorporated into the Belgian Army in 1917 to evade withdrawal by the War Office.[17] Birkbeck was awarded the Croix de Guerre, with Bronze Star,[18] while Plimsoll also received a French decoration.[19] Hodges earned the Croix de Guerre for her work in the Hackett-Lowther Unit, another private ambulance unit, which she joined with Donisthorpe and several others on their return from Russia. Like the FANY, they were able to continue working at the front by becoming attached to an Allied army, in this case the French.[20]

The war had been so traumatic an experience for those directly involved that many women, as well as most of the men, found it difficult to settle down afterwards. To be desperately needed, and to have an urgent and vital task in hand is a very rewarding experience, and probably many of our diarists perceived their peacetime futures as a considerable anticlimax after the uncertainties and excitements they had been through. Butler found the adjustment so difficult that she wrote a novelette about it,[21] and her analysis probably holds true for many of the others. They must at first have missed the sense of immediate purpose which their work had given them, and wondered what their role in the new world could be, until they found other purposes and other causes. The vote, the great objective of the Suffrage Societies which had engendered the Hospitals, paled into insignificance beside the new freedoms women had discovered, and the new struggles which disclosed themselves. The franchise[22] did not automatically dispense justice or equality of opportunity, and the limitations of its power are all too evident even in our own society. But many took full advantage of the opportunities opened to women, and their confidence in their own capacities, combined with a well-ingrained habit of taking responsibility when there was no one else to do so, ensured that in any crisis, they were likely to be front-line workers.

By the end of the war marriage had become much less important as a measure of success in life, and many of the women continued their interrupted careers as teachers, nurses or secretaries; or they trained for new ones. Even Yvonne Fitzroy, who did not need to earn her own living, but who had enjoyed her nursing experience, worked for some years as private secretary to Lady Reading, the Vicereine of India.[23] Among the most noteworthy professions was that of Elsie Bowerman, who studied law as soon as the gender disqualification was removed, and became the first woman barrister to appear at the Old Bailey.[24] Elsie Butler, too, had a distinguished academic career, continuing her study of Modern Languages, and being appointed to the chair of German at Manchester in 1936, and a few years later to the same position at Cambridge.[25] Of the doctors, Lilian Chesney, whose sciatica had grown worse during the Macedonian campaign, opened a practice in Majorca, while Elinor Rendel became a clinical consultant at the Great Ormond Street Hospital for Sick Children and the Hospital for Diseases of the Heart.[26] She also set up in private practice, numbering among her patients Virginia Woolf and others of the Bloomsbury set.[27]

Those who married included several whose sons and daughters or other younger relatives inherited and preserved the records which have contributed to this history. I have not been able to trace the family of Lilias Grant, whose married name was Dyson, but her diary was carefully typed out and safely housed, together with Ethel Moir's, in an Edinburgh archive, for which posterity must be grateful. Lois Turner married her Petrograd friend Blake, and for many years lived in Wales, where she was instrumental in reviving Welsh folk dancing, becoming the first president of the Welsh Folk Dance Society on its formation in 1953. Her daughter Felicity has been a collaborator in the gathering of information for this book.

After her adventurous war, Katherine Hodges married Peter North, an army officer who became a distinguished photographer. She drove an ambulance again in the London blitz, and then worked for the Red Cross until 1968. The typescript of her memoirs was lodged with the Imperial War Museum. Patricia Walker, one of the original Transport drivers, met and married Jack Orr in Moffat, Dumfries, where he was recovering from a wound and where she was nursing in a military hospital. She maintained her friendship with Margaret Marx and Frances Robinson, and in later life was given Marx's meticulously-labelled photograph album; this, now in the care of her son John Orr, has helped in the matching of names and faces. Ysabel

Birkbeck lived in the Sudan for some years, where her husband was a District Officer 'on the educational side'; before she died she gave her lively illustrated diary to her young friends, Margaret and the late Douglas Baxter, who must have spent many months producing a legible typescript from her difficult handwriting. Margaret Fawcett took a teaching contract in Natal in 1922, where she met and married Walter Cahill, a country station master, returning to the teaching she loved as soon as her children were old enough. When she died in 1987, her diaries and letter-book were among the few items she had taken with her to the hospital. They were in a brown paper packet tied up with wool, and labelled 'Important'.

The probability that theirs was a positive and maturing experience has already been discussed in the introduction, but these diarists did not talk much to their families about their war service; even less easily than for those who had served in Western Europe could the women's Russian service be related to their subsequent lives. Considering that, with a few exceptions, they seem to have lost touch with one another after the war,[28] and considering that their memories were overlaid by very different and busy lives, it is surprising that their war records came to survive and to assume the importance that they did. Perhaps the very events which conspired against any continuity with their ensuing experience marked the venture as being of more than personal interest. For one thing, it was unrepeatable: as Butler put it, the Russia they left behind them had vanished away; it could never be revisited, nor its impressions qualified by a sentimental return. What they had written, in diaries and letters, was distinct, discrete, isolated.

It was also complete, for the experience had fortuitously been given a significant form. For most servicemen and women, 1918 and 1919 were to tail off into the anticlimax of lingering piecemeal demobilisation, as the Elsie Inglis Unit discovered.[29] But in 1917 the combination of Inglis's death and the October revolution emphatically marked for the Russian Unit the end of a chapter, rather as the February revolution had done for those who returned home in March. The disconnected diary entries, made in response to events of the passing moment, and the individual letters written originally for other purposes, were given a greater significance by the end towards which they could subsequently be seen to point. Probably only Butler and Bowerman would have been able to analyse this; but Fawcett, Moir, and Milne were at least intuitively aware of it, and made use of it in deciding where to close their diaries and letter-books. Life, in imitation of art, had provided a conclusion that transformed the indeterminate contours of the personal records into a coherent and unified structure, and gave them an enduring form.

NOTES

The locations of the core manuscripts and the positions of articles and chapters within larger works are given in full in the bibliography. Page numbers are not given for *The Times Diary and Index of the War*, as entries in this are both alphabetical and chronological.

Introduction

1. Lawrence, *Shadow of Swords* (1971), p 98. 'Lawrence (1971)' in subsequent entries refers to this book, and not to Lawrence's article, which also appeared in 1971.
2. For detailed histories of the organisation, see Leneman, *In the Service of Life* (1994); and McLaren (ed.) *A History of the Scottish Women's Hospitals*. For a biography of Elsie Inglis, see Margot Lawrence, *Shadow of Swords*.
3. Lawrence (1971), p 81.
4. These belonged to the older, non-militant movement, not the Women's Social and Political Union. The Federation was formed in 1909. Leneman (1994), p 2.
5. Strachey, *The Cause*, p 338.
6. So successful was this venture that in 1915 the War Office revised its policy on women doctors, and asked Anderson and Murray to take charge of a military hospital of 520 beds in Endell Street in London, where they remained until the end of the war. Strachey, p 347.
7. McLaren, pp 4-5; Lawrence, (1971), pp 99-100; Leneman (1994), p 2.
8. Letter to Millicent Fawcett, 9 October 1914. NUWSS Collection, Fawcett Library.
9. Leneman (1994), p ix.
10. Elsie Inglis to Millicent Garrett Fawcett, 13 October 1914. NUWSS Collection, Fawcett Library.
11. Lawrence (1971), p 117; Leneman (1994), p 21.
12. Lawrence (1971), pp 169-172; Leneman (1994), p 48.
13. Lawrence, 'The Serbian Divisions in Russia, 1916-1917', *Journal of Contemporary History*, Vol 6, no 4, 1971; Banac, 'South Slav Prisoners of War in Revolutionary Russia,' in Williamson and Pastor.
14. Inglis, Letters to Muriel Craigie, 22 July 1916 and Dr Beatrice Russell, 23 July 1916. Mitchell Library; Lawrence, (1971), p 180.
15. The hospitals funded by the Serbian Relief Fund were in the charge of Dr Clemow and Dr James Berry, and became known to the Scottish Women in Russia as 'the British Red Cross'.
16. Leneman (1994), p 62.
17. The construction of the Trans-Siberian Railway, begun in 1891, had just been completed in 1916.
18. Turner, John. *British Politics and the Great War*, pp 59, 66, 174.
19. Strachey, pp 344-5.
20. Terraine, *The First World War 1914-1918*, p 116.
21. Gilbert, *First World War*, p 282; Stone, *The Eastern Front 1914-1917*, p 273.
22. Stone, pp 273-4.
23. These two German cruisers had been in the Mediterranean when war was declared, and had sought refuge in the Black Sea. In order to comply with the ruling of the 1878 Berlin Congress barring the Dardanelles to warships of all nations, the German Ambassador in Constantinople immediately transferred the ships to the Turkish Navy. Von Rintelen, *The Dark Invader*, pp 24-5.
24. Stone, p 274; Cruttwell, p 295.
25. Lawrence (1971), pp 199-200.

Chapter 1 Getting Acquainted

1. Birkbeck, Diary, Sunday 27 August 1916.
2. Report 1. All Inglis's reports are in the SWH Collection, Fawcett Library.
3. Lawrence (1971), p 180.
4. *Times Diary and Index of the War*, Appendix V, p 187.
5. Memoirs, pp 1-3.
6. Letter to Amy Simpson, 6 September 1916. Quoted from Balfour, *Dr Elsie Inglis*, pp 197-201.
7. To 'C'.
8. After an inspection by the US naval authorities, the *Deutschland* was declared a merchant U-boat. It returned to Germany on 1 August 1916, and was back in the US by 1 October. *Times Diary and Index of the War*.
9. Sir Almeric Fitzroy was Clerk to the Privy Council.
10. Letter to Amy Simpson. Balfour, pp 197-201.
11. Letter to Betty, her sister. Where not otherwise stated, passages quoted are from Rendel's letters to her mother. All Rendel's letters, excepting those to Ray, are in the Imperial War Museum.
12. The Women's Sick and Wounded Convoy Corps was founded in 1909 by Mrs St Clair Stobart and Lady Ernestine Hunt. Its members were trained in first aid, military drill, and horsemanship; the intention was that they should carry wounded men from the battlefields to the dressing stations and hospitals. Summers, *Angels and Citizens*, p 25.
13. Unless otherwise specified, Milne's entries are from her diary.
14. Unless otherwise stated, Fawcett's diary entries are from her original diary.
15. Letter to Amy Simpson. Balfour, pp 201-3.
16. Dated 20 September.
17. This was the unit funded by the Serbian Relief Fund, and administered by the British Red Cross. See Introduction.
18. At this reception, the Crown Prince decorated Dr Inglis with the Order of the White Eagle, the highest Serbian decoration. Lady Cowdray was then Treasurer of the London Committee of the SWH. Lawrence (1971), pp 174 and 110.
19. Memoirs, p 9.
20. To her sister Betty.
21. To Ray Strachey. Rendel's letters to Ray are in private hands.
22. Memoirs, p 12.
23. Memoirs, p 13.
24. Memoirs, p 14.
25. Mrs Stobart's Women's Sick and Wounded Convoy Corps which served in Bulgaria in the First Balkan War was run by women, and it was certainly a field hospital.

Chapter 2 The First Wounded

1. *The Times History of the War*, Vol XI, p 219.
2. Pares, *Day by Day with the Russian Army*, p 113.
3. Report 3, 26 October 1916.
4. Report 3.
5. For confirmation of the respect of the Germans for the Serbian Division, see Ludendorff, *My War Memories*, Vol 1, p 286.
6. Undated report, SWH Collection, Fawcett Library.
7. Memoirs, p 15.
8. *With the Scottish Nurses in Roumania*, pp 33-4. (Abbreviated to *Scottish Nurses* in subsequent entries.)
9. The order of paragraphs has been slightly changed.
10. 'Three Months on the Eastern Front', p 119, *The Englishwoman*, Vol 33 (1917).
11. The Transport cooks.
12. *Scottish Nurses*, pp 37-8.
13. Memoirs, p 23.
14. Memoirs, pp 23-4. The sentences in the last paragraph have been slightly rearranged.

15. SWH Collection, Fawcett Library.
16. *Scottish Nurses*, pp 46-7.
17. In a diary entry made on 3 December Petty Officer George Martin observes of the same regiment, 'They are a poor lot of men they are the Siberian Regts, some without boots on their feet, and look as if they have had no food for a week, very young and old men.' The women were very soon to learn the difference a few weeks fighting could make to a man's appearance and bearing.
18. Memoirs, p 25.
19. This and the following four sentences are quoted verbatim (without acknowledgement) from pp 182-4 of Hugh Walpole's *The Dark Forest*, one of the books which some of the women mention having read on their long train journey. The borrowing indicates Moir's tendency, noticeable elsewhere in her writing, to perceive her experience in terms of literary or conventional modes.

Chapter 3 Sticking to the Equipment

1. 'The Roumanian Campaign of 1916: To Fall of Bucharest', *The Times History of the War*, XI, pp 433-72. These contemporary histories are useful for the details of the military positions and for their maps of the Roumanian Campaign, but considerable allowance has to be made for the Allied bias and for the constraints of censorship and propaganda.
2. *Scottish Nurses*, pp 47-8.
3. *Scottish Nurses*, pp 48-50.
4. 'The Dobruja Retreat', pp 343-4, *Blackwoods*, March 1918.
5. *Scottish Nurses*, pp 50-1.
6. 'Three Months on the Eastern Front', pp 125-6.
7. 'The Dobruja Retreat', pp 344-7.
8. Turkish for 'hurry'.
9. Milne's article identifies this village as 'Toxof', but this seems an unlikely name, and I have not been able to check it.
10. *Scottish Nurses*, pp 51-4.
11. 'The Dobruja Retreat', pp 347-8.
12. Black bread baked or dried hard, to last for years.
13. Red Cross nurses; literally, 'women who have exchanged crosses'. I am indebted to Richard Davies for this explanation.
14. Bowerman and Brown were not as mistaken as they supposed: General Popovic was the Inspector-General of the Roumanian cavalry, and no doubt his name would have elicited the response they wanted.
15. *Scottish Nurses,* pp 54-6.

Chapter 4 The Field Hospitals and the Transport Retreat

1. Rendel, Letter to Betty, 20 November 1916.
2. Stone, pp 278-9.
3. e.g. *The Illustrated London News* of 16 December 1916 reads: 'The Germans... are accomplishing only a strategic manoevre in Roumania. The Roumanian army, elusive and strong as ever, is awaiting a favourable opportunity to strike back with Russian support. Territorial losses mean little in the present war, provided that the armed forces subsist to win them back.'
4. Memoirs, pp 25-6.
5. Undated Report, SWH Collection, Fawcett Library.
6. This and Rendel's other accounts of the retreat are quoted in a letter to her sister Betty, 20 November 1916, and also occur in her article 'Fragments from a Diary of the First Retreat in the Dobrudja'. Although they are dated and written as a diary, there is no diary for 1916 with her papers in the Imperial War Museum.
7. Memoirs, pp 26-7; p 31; p 36.
8. 'NUWSS. Scottish Women's Hospitals: Work in Roumania', *The Common Cause*, 5 January 1917.
9. Memoirs, pp 31 and 36.
10. 'NUWSS. Scottish Women's Hospitals: Work in Roumania'.
11. Memoirs, p 28; pp 29-30.

12. 'NUWSS. Scottish Women's Hospitals: Work in Roumania'.
13. Memoirs, pp 31-3.
14. This last sentence is from the Retrospective Diary, which adds, 'especially as he disappeared later on when we were at Ismail.'

Chapter 5 The Hospitals Reassemble

1. W.H.King, 'Ten Months with the Russian Army', p 10.
2. See James Berry and others, *The Story of a Red Cross Unit in Serbia*.
3. The official British Red Cross report says that 'political reasons' prevented this Second Division from being sent to the front. These were indeed serious: an attempt to make up for the September losses in the Dobrudga by forcing prisoners of war to join the 'Voluntary' Division culminated in a mutiny in the Odessa garrison, and in large numbers leaving the division. Ivo Banac, in Williamson and Pastor, p 127.
4. Letter to Dr Beatrice Russell, 23 July 1916. Mitchell Library.
5. *Scottish Nurses*, p 57.
6. Rumour was wrong, in both cases: on 26 October Hospital B was by no means safe, and Dr Inglis had already left Hirsova, and was working at Braila.
7. This was Sammy, who was to become the unit's mascot. He was possibly the dog offered by the Roumanian woman to the driver who picked her up on the retreat.
8. Clare Murphy.
9. 'Three Months on the Eastern Front', pp 127-8.
10. *Scottish Nurses*, pp 58-9.
11. Memoirs, pp 33-5.
12. In fact, Miss Henderson had been ordered back by Dr Inglis, who wanted the equipment where it would be useful. See Inglis, Report 3, and Lawrence (1971), p 196.
13. Agnes Mackenzie, not the ambulance driver, but a hospital orderly.
14. Memoirs, pp 37-9.
15. Bernard Pares, who spent some months with the Russian Army in Galicia, comments on the reaction of an Austrian Slav, who when asked whether he had been taken prisoner, replied indignantly, 'I was not taken prisoner at all; I have come over.' Pares adds, 'In our interrogations we were later instructed, in the case of Czechs, Serbs, and other Slavs, always to mark this difference, and to begin by asking: "Did you surrender, or did you come over?"' *My Russian Memoirs*, p 293.
16. 'Three Months on the Eastern Front', pp 127-8.
17. *In War and Peace: Songs of a Scotswoman*, p 12.
18. Hebrews 11 v 37.
19. *Scottish Nurses*, p 62.
20. Letter to Betty, 20 November 1916.
21. Memoirs, pp 40-1.
22. Fawcett was mistaken about Tulcea; it did not fall until 24 December.
23. Dr Frances May Dickinson Berry, of the British Red Cross Hospital.
24. Probably the Berrys' Hospital, sponsored by the Serbian Relief Fund.

Chapter 6 The Work Continues

1. A third bridge was constructed at Galatz just before Christmas.
2. Stone, pp 287-8.
3. Hodges, Memoirs, p 22.
4. Lawrence (1971), p 200.
5. Lawrence (1971), p 200.
6. The Mitchell Library collection of lantern slides was obviously put together for such fund-raising talks.
7. Perrett and Lord, *The Czar's British Squadron*, p 80.
8. *Times History of the War*, Vol XII, p 124.
9. These trenches would have been constructed in 1915 or in the spring of 1916, when Roumania was hesitating about which side to join.

10. *Scottish Nurses,* p 67.
11. Memoirs, pp 41 and 42.
12. Almost all the diarists note the careful grooming and the powder and paint of the Roumanian officers, even during the retreat. In *The Eastern Front* Stone comments that 'among the first prescriptions, on mobilisation, was a decree that only officers above the rank of major had the right to use make-up.' p 265.
13. The Roumanians were understandably reluctant to implement the scorched-earth policy of their allies, and Colonel Norton Griffiths had been sent to carry it out. Stone, p 280; Perrett and Lord, pp 94-5.
14. Memoirs, pp 42-3.
15. 9 December.
16. Greece was at this time a divided country, with the pro-Entente followers of Venizelos in rebellion against the pro-German King Constantine. Venizelists controlled Salonica, where the Entente had a considerable force. On 1 December the commander-in-chief of the French Mediterranean Fleet had attempted to take from Athens by force some batteries and equipment as compensation for a key fortress which the Greeks had handed over to the Bulgarians. Their landing parties had met with resistance, and it was news of this fighting which reached Ismail on 10 December. Constantine was deposed in June 1917, and Greece then joined the Entente. *Times Diary and Index of the War,* entries for December 1916 and June 1917; Schmitt and Vedeler, *The World in Crucible,* pp 156-7.
17. *Scottish Nurses,* pp 34-5.
18. Lloyd George as War Minister had warned Asquith in September of the vulnerability of Roumania, but the Prime Minister had ignored his warnings. When Bucharest fell, Lloyd George resigned as War Minister, and the resignation of Asquith followed. Lloyd George became Prime Minister, and set up a small War Cabinet with almost dictatorial powers. Cruttwell, pp 298, 390, and 394.
19. Stürmer, the ousted Prime Minister had been appointed in February 1916 at the instigation of Rasputin and the Tsaritsa. He was the target of a fiery denunciation by Milyukov in the November Duma, a denunciation which also set in motion the conspiracy to assassinate Rasputin.

Chapter 7 Retreating Again

1. Perrett and Lord, *The Czar's British Squadron,* p 88.
2. Lawrence (1971), p 216.
3. Perrett and Lord, p 19.
4. Perrett and Lord, p 36.
5. Perrett and Lord, p 21.
6. Perrett and Lord, p 87.
7. See Turner's entry for 18 December.
8. *Scottish Nurses,* pp 85-6.
9. Memoirs, pp 45-7.
10. This was not a railway train, but a convoy of vehicles.
11. Spelled Alebei Chioi in Gregory's report.
12. Unpublished article (untitled), Typescript, pp 21-2.
13. Locker Lampson Papers, Imperial War Museum; Perrett and Lord, pp 88-9.
14. The Armoured Car men referred to all the Scottish Women, even the drivers, as 'nurses'. There were no trained nurses with the Transport.
15. The captured Armoured Car men were the crew first reported as Scottish Women taken captive.
16. Locker Lampson had left for Britain on 13 October to fetch more equipment, and so missed all the fighting in the Dobrudga. Perrett and Lord, p 75.
17. This was the party with the equipment, which had come by steamer down the Danube and through the Black Sea to Odessa.
18. The officer in question was Lieut. Ingle, wounded in action at Pantilimon Ustin on 1 December. See Perrett and Lord, p 85-6.
19. Memoirs, pp 47-52. A few sentences have been slightly rearranged.
20. Memoirs, pp 52-3, including insert in typescript.

21. *Scottish Nurses*, p 90.
22. *Scottish Nurses*, pp 91-2.

Chapter 8 New Quarters

1. *The Times Diary and Index of the War.*
2. Perrett and Lord, pp 98 and 104.
3. See Rendel's letter of 13 October, Ch 2 above.
4. See Leneman (1994), p 85, for a discussion of the suggestion that Mrs Haverfield may have had a nervous breakdown. I think the change in her behaviour is sufficiently accounted for by the spiral of conflict with the members of her unit.
5. The list of those who left at the end of December or before is in the back of Birkbeck's diary.
6. London Committee Minutes, 2 February 1917. Wooden box, Mitchell Library.
7. Wooden box, Mitchell Library.
8. The men wore khaki military-style uniforms, with the SWH tartan and insignia.
9. Memoirs, pp 53-4.
10. Report 7, 8 January 1917.
11. Report to Commander Gregory, Locker Lampson Papers, Imperial War Museum.
12. Maitland Scott was the Staff Surgeon's brother.
13. Report 7.
14. 'Some Months in Bessarabia', p 633, *Blackwoods Magazine*, May 1918.
15. *Scottish Nurses*, p 101.
16. *Scottish Nurses*, p 104.
17. Memoirs, pp 63-5.
18. This hospital, at Zaleschiki, was run by Dr King-Atkinson, and was one of the Millicent Fawcett Units, another project of the National Union of Women's Suffrage Societies. Originally sent to help civilian refugees after the German advances of 1915, these had switched to army medical work in 1916. *The Common Cause*, 9 February 1917.
19. This extract has been slightly reordered.
20. Report 8, 24 January 1917.
21. The Expedition was the detachment of 20,000 Russian troops sent by sea to Constanza in accordance with a secret military convention signed by the Entente eleven days ahead of Roumania's declaration of war in August 1916. Its purpose was to defend the Dobrudga from a Bulgarian attack. I am indebted to Alan Palmer for this explanation.
22. *Scottish Nurses*, pp 108 and 110.
23. This line had been completed since the women's arrival in the Dobrudga. Constructed hurriedly at the end of 1916, it was badly laid and subject to flooding.
24. This entry has been slightly rearranged.

Chapter 9 An Eventful Spring

1. In fact there was very little fighting on any part of the eastern front that winter, the armies of both sides being worn out and in need of rest and re-equipment. Ludendorff, *My War Memories 1914-1919*, p 303.
2. Kerensky, in *The Crucifixion of Liberty*, p 160, makes it clear that by 1916 rumours of various plans for the replacement and even the assassination of the Tsar were widely current.
3. 16 December, Old Style (Julian Calendar). Youssoupoff, *Rasputin*, pp 171-82; Kerensky, p 190.
4. See Ch 7, entries for 19 and 20 December.
5. Yousoupoff, pp 69 and 76.
6. Service, *The Russian Revolution 1900-1927*, p 15. In subsequent entries 'Service (1986, 1991)' refers to the second edition of this book, and not to *Lenin: A Political Life*, also published in 1991.
7. Service (1986, 1991), p 8.
8. Fitzroy, *Scottish Nurses*, p 153.
9. Service (1986, 1991), p 21.
10. *Scottish Nurses*, pp 112-13.
11. The severance of relations between the United States and Germany, on 3 February, was the consequence, not the cause, of Germany's policy of unrestricted U-boat warfare. Schmitt and

Vedeler, *The World in Crucible*, p 237.

12. There were five excellent photographs on the front page of the *Sunday Pictorial* of 14 January. The one Fitzroy refers to is probably the one captioned 'Dr Elsie Inglis (seated) with her staff at their headquarters.'
13. *With the Scottish Women in Roumania*, pp 117-18.
14. This was her account of the First Dobrudga Retreat. See Ch 5.
15. Letter to Miss Palliser, SWH Collection, Fawcett Library.
16. Report 11, 6 March 1917.
17. Report 11.
18. The yacht was *Prince Ferdinand of Roumania*, which was being used to ferry supplies to the Armoured Car detachment at Galatz. Perrett and Lord, *The Czar's British Squadron*, p 100.
19. *With the Scottish Women in Roumania*, pp 129-31.

Chapter 10 Upheaval in Petrograd

1. This decision was not as unreasonable as it might appear. Since the end of 1914 the British Navy had been making use of 'Q-ships', decoy ships fitted with concealed guns and appearing to be ordinary merchant ships, often flying a neutral flag. When a submarine approached in order to identify them, they would open fire. *The Times Diary and Index of the War*, entry for 29 November 1914; Schmitt and Vedeler, *The World in Crucible*, p 239.
2. Those in Petrograd in early March were Clare Murphy; Moir, Grant, Sedgwick, Kent and Brand; Birkbeck, Mackenzie-Edwards and Turner; Bowerman, Brown, Hedges and Walker; an unidentified four whose arrival on 24 January Grant mentions in her diary; and Miss Henderson, travelling in the opposite direction.
3. Clare Murphy was taken on as a nurse aide at the Anglo-Russian Hospital.
4. 23 February, Old Style (Julian Calendar). Dates given in this chapter are New Style (Gregorian Calendar).
5. Carmichael, *A Short History of the Russian Revolution*, p 49.
6. Mstislavskii, *Five Days which Transformed Russia*, pp 32-46.
7. Started in 1916 by Lady Muriel Paget as a gesture of goodwill towards the Russians, the Anglo-Russian Hospital was for other ranks only. It was housed in the palace of the Grand Duke Dmitri Pavlovich, the chief accomplice of Prince Yusupov in the assassination of Rasputin. Blunt, *Lady Muriel*, pp 61-6.
8. Fitzroy, leaving Russia at the end of May, gives a more impartial assessment of the Tsaritsa, speculating that she worked unconsciously in Germany's interests, owing partly to her submission to German influences at court and partly to her fear of democracy. *Scottish Nurses*, p 158.
9. 'The Firm' was what Mackenzie-Edwards, Birkbeck and Turner called themselves.
10. The nickname 'Skittish Widows' had been in use much earlier in Serbia. Leneman (1994), p 32.
11. Blake and Bennet were two naval engineers hurrying home from their assignment in China to join the armed forces.
12. By nightfall on 12 March most regiments of the Reserve Guards had mutinied and joined the Revolution.
13. British Red Cross commissioner in Petrograd.
14. Many officers (including Commander Locker Lampson of the BAC) were quartered at the fashionable Astoria. Perrett and Lord, *The Czar's British Squadron*, pp 106-10.
15. To Stella Gadense, or Gadeuse.
16. The Minch is the strait between Lewis and Sutherland.

Chapter 11 Under Suspicion

1. *Nurse at the Russian Front: a Diary 1914-1918*, p 45.
2. Vernadsky, *A Source Book for Russian History from Early Times to 1917*, Vol 3, p 882.
3. Service (1986, 1991), p 40.
4. Zeman, *Germany and the Revolution in Russia 1915-1918: Documents from the archives of the German Foreign Ministry*, Documents 14-21 (pp 25-30), documents 24-53, (pp 33-53).
5. Zeman, Document 57, pp 54-6; Kettle, *The Allies and the Russian Collapse*, pp 25-33, 46-8; Service, *Lenin: A Political Life*, Vol 2, pp 248-9.

6. 'Some Months in Bessarabia', pp 633-4.
7. There are no accurate statistics of Russian losses, but Stone quotes 'a sober Soviet investigation' estimating between 7,000,000 and 7,500,000 losses of all categories to December 1917. Three million of these occurred in 1916, and the bulk of the rest in 1914-15. *The Eastern Front 1914-1917*, p 215.
8. Perrett and Lord, *The Czar's British Squadron*, p 115; Fitzroy Maclean, *Holy Russia*, p 62.
9. See Fawcett's entry for 8 June.
10. General Surikov, Commander of the 6th Army, had made Galatz his headquarters for the winter, and throughout February, March and April a squadron of British Armoured Cars held a section of the line along the Sereth. Perrett and Lord, pp 98 and 104.
11. Letter to Miss Chapman, Dr Chesney's 'Personnel' file, Tin 35, Mitchell Library.
12. Dr Chesney adds a list of the staff accompanying her. They were Corbett, Rendel (both listed as doctors), Fox (matron), Little (secretary), Ford (cook), Ulph, Edwards, Kinnaird, Jackson, Henderson, Mundie, Atkinson and Bangham (sisters); and the quartermaster, Mr E. Rothe, supplied by the Russian Government.
13. Dr Joan Rose, who served with an SWH unit at Ostrovo in Serbia, described Dr Chesney as follows: 'Sharp featured face, hair cut like a man's, dress v. like a man, voice v. like a man — witty and seems capable.' Diary of Joan Rose, Imperial War Museum; Leneman (1994), p 27.
14. A good hospital.
15. Report 12, 16 April 1917.
16. Report 12.
17. 'The Expedition' had been fighting in the Dobrudga in late 1916, and Dr Inglis's hospital was known to them; the Division had recently arrived from another front.
18. 'Christ is risen.' 'He is risen indeed.'

Chapter 12 Struggles with Red Tape

1. Strachey, p 345.
2. Foreign Office Papers, FO 371/2993/83817/17.
3. Miscellaneous Letters, Tin 5, Mitchell Library.
4. FO 371/2993/100068.
5. Palliser's emphasis.
6. McGann, *The Battle of the Nurses*, pp 168-80.
7. FO 371/2993/106487.
8. Perrett and Lord, *The Czar's British Squadron*, p 105.
9. So called from the initials, KD, of their party name.
10. See introduction to Chapter 13.
11. See Ch 11.
12. *Scottish Nurses*, p 147.
13. The Berry Unit of the British Red Cross had also established a hospital in Tecuci.
14. pp 638-9.
15. One of the English chaplains at Petrograd, Mr French was spending his leave doing Red Cross work. He had travelled with Miss Henderson partly to help her shepherd the equipment through safely, and partly to pay a pastoral visit to the British hospitals at the front.
16. Letter to London Committee, SWH Collection, Fawcett Library.
17. Susie was Sister Susan Jenkins, distinguished thus from Sister Florence Jenkins, who was also at Reni.
18. Report 13, 27 May 1917.
19. pp 639-40.
20. In early May the Galatz squadron of the British Armoured Cars was recalled to the base at Tiraspol, prior to their deployment on the Galician front in July. The two seriously wounded men were therefore moved from Dr King's small hospital at Galatz to Inglis's at Reni. King, 'Ten Months with the Russian Army', pp 14-15.
21. Brigadier-General Poole was at this time in charge of the British Mission in Petrograd. He is described by Michael Kettle as displaying 'a cheerful and bustling optimism'. *The Allies and the Russian Collapse*, p 43.

22. Letter to Miss Palliser, SWH Collection, Fawcett Library.
23. Army Service Corps. The officer must have been Captain Bergman.
24. In fact these hospitals did not leave until much later. Dr Berry closed his hospital on 18 August, and the unit returned to London, arriving on 8 October. Dr Clemow was sent to the Roumanian front in mid-September, but found on arrival that there was no longer any prospect of fighting, and he too left for Britain. *Reports by the Joint War Committee of the British Red Cross and the Order of St John of Jerusalem* Part XXIII, Russia and Roumania, pp 457-60.
25. Wooden box, Mitchell Library.
26. Queen Marie of Roumania was a granddaughter of Queen Victoria, and cousin to Tsar Nicholas II.
27. Lady Decies was Commandant of the Westminster Detachment of the British Red Cross. Minutes of London Committee of SWH, 26 March 1917, Wooden box, Mitchell Library.
28. Letter to London Committee, SWH Collection, Fawcett Library.
29. FO 371/2889/133164.
30. FO 371/2889/139550.
31. Report 7.
32. *Paper Boats*, pp 64-5.
33. These had pledged themselves to fight to the death.
34. Perrett and Lord, p 113.
35. King, p 19.
36. King, p 19; *The Common Cause*, 21 September, p 275; Hodges, Memoirs, pp 83-97.
37. King, pp 21-2.
38. *Paper Boats*, p 67-8.

Chapter 13 The War Moves South Again

1. Terraine, *The First World War 1914-18*, p 143; Cruttwell, pp 413-15.
2. Cruttwell, p 336.
3. Ludendorff, *My War Memories 1914-1919*, Vol 2, p 585.
4. Perrett and Lord, *The Czar's British Squadron*, pp 119 and 126.
5. Banac, in Williamson and Pastor, pp 126-7.
6. Miss Palliser's interview with Mr Sawyer, 18 June 1917. Wooden box, Mitchell Library.
7. Banac, in Williamson and Pastor, p 125.
8. Banac, in Williamson and Pastor, p 126.
9. Banac, in Williamson and Pastor, pp 126-31; Dr Jambrisak, 'Statement to Illustrate the Difficult and Dangerous Position of the Serb Army on the Rumanian Front', FO 371/2889;
10. See above, ch 9.
11. Fawcett, 16 July; Milne, 18 July.
12. Banac, in Williamson and Pastor, pp 131-2; Marx's memorandum to Foreign Office, 23 August, FO 371/2889/165539.
13. Apart from Milne's diary and the official minutes and letters of the SWH, a few early histories hint at Inglis's intervention over the withdrawal of the Serbian Divisions: see McLaren, pp 215-20; Butler, *Paper Boats*, p 73; and Strachey, p 348. The first detailed account is to be found in Lawrence (1971), pp 249-71, to which I am indebted for the references which helped me to locate and collate the relevant Foreign Office records.
14. Letter to Mrs Laurie, written on 15 October 1917 after Atkinson's return to Britain, and giving an account of Hospital B's last few weeks in Roumania. Tin 35, Mitchell Library.
15. One of the few original Transport members who had remained with the unit, Robinson was acting as secretary for Hospital B.
16. Letter to Mrs Laurie.
17. This was the abortive Bolshevik rising now known as 'the July Days'. It was put down by the Provisional Government: Trotsky was arrested, and Lenin escaped to Finland, to return at the start of the October Revolution. Service (1986, 1991), p 41; Kettle, p 51; Pares, *A History of Russia*, pp 534-5.
18. The Armoured Car Division was fighting in Galicia, as one of Kerensky's stiffening units. Perrett and Lord, p 113.

19. Letter to Mrs Laurie.
20. FO 371/2993/1492501.
21. FO 371/2993/154909.
22. Minutes of Proceedings of Conference, FO 371/2889/157367.
23. *Times Diary and Index of the War.*
24. Report of Unit Z [the Berry Unit], *Reports of the British Red Cross Society and the Order of St John of Jerusalem*, p 460.
25. Letter to Mrs Laurie.
26. The Roumanian Royal Family left Jassi on 11 August. *The Times Diary and Index of the War.*
27. Letter to Mrs Laurie.
28. *Paper Boats*, p 68.
29. Margaret Wright had arrived with Miss Genge at the beginning of June.
30. See Fawcett's diary entry for July 19, in which she refers to 'the July days' as 'another revolution'.
31. FO 371/2993/161161.
32. Comments on the minute circulated at the Foreign Office with this telegram show that her point had been taken:

    1) I submit that Dr Inglis and her unit, who have done admirable work, merit every consideration.

    2) While I endorse fully the view expressed by Mr Nicolson regarding Mrs Inglis [sic], I submit the matter is one for decision by the military alone...

    3) It is not only a question of transport: we have also to get the Russians to let them go. Gen Barter has not replied to the tel in 257367, and I think we should ask the W.O. to stir him up, as otherwise the Serbs will be engaged in the front, and, as Dr Inglis says, only sacrificed. FO 371/2889/165429.
33. Report 15, SWH Collection, Fawcett Library.
34. SWH Collection, Fawcett Library.
35. FO 371/2889/169949.
36. This was the telegram that 'could not be delivered'.
37. Wooden box, Mitchell Library.

Chapter 14 On Standby

1. Balfour, *Dr Elsie Inglis*, quoting Elizabeth Arbuthnot, p 238.
2. Telegram of 1 September, 1917, from General Barter, GHQ, Russia, to CIGS. FO 371/2889/172869.
3. Letter to Edith Palliser, 1 October 1917. SWH Collection, Fawcett Library.
4. Letter to D Wilkes, 8 September 1917. SWH Collection, Fawcett Library.
5. SWH Collection, Fawcett Library.
6. This news seems to have been an unconfirmed report that the move to Salonica was again in prospect.
7. Letter to D Wilkes, 8 September 1917. SWH Collection, Fawcett Library.
8. There were at this time five women drivers with the SWH: Geraldine Hedges, Alexandrina Onslow, both now officers; Dora Curtis, who had left Britain before the April ban on women drivers; and Dorothy Cockshott and Madge Tindall, who had presumably signed on, as Hedges and Onslow did for their return, in another capacity. Vera Holme and Frances Robinson, who had been with the unit from the beginning, were on their way to England with Dr Jambrisak's memorandum.
9. Service, (1986, 1991), pp 42-3; Service, *Lenin: A Political Life*, p 210; Katkov, *Russia 1917: The Kornilov Affair*, pp 79-97; Kettle, pp 76-94.
10. Kettle, pp 83-4.
11. Carmichael, p 135; Lenin, in a letter to the Central Committee, quoted by Kerensky, p 328.
12. Kettle, p 88.
13. C.J. Smith, Untitled Article, typescript, p 29. Locker Lampson Papers, Imperial War Museum.

14. Kettle, p 73.
15. Minutes of Executive Committee of London Committee of SWH, 10 September 1917. Wooden box, Mitchell Library.
16. FO 371/2889/177536.
17. Leneman (1994), p 137; Lawrence (1971), p 182; Interview with Mrs McLaren and Mrs Simson, 8 June 1918. SWH Records, Imperial War Museum.
18. Lawrence (1971), p 266.
19. p 641.
20. Letter to Miss Palliser, SWH Collection, Fawcett Library.
21. *Paper Boats*, p 70.
22. Joe was a Serbian chauffeur on whom Dr Inglis had recently performed a gastro-enterotomy. Lawrence (1971), p 265, quoting private information from Hedges and Arbuthnot.
23. Razdelnaya was the junction at which the line from Reni joined the Odessa - Moscow line.
24. FO 371/2889/193370.
25. These were Russian Medals for Meritorious Service. They appear to have been awarded for service in the Dobrudga Campaign of 1916, since the lists include all those who had gone home early in 1917, but none of the recent arrivals. The doctors were listed as having been awarded the St Anne's Medal, First Class; Miss Henderson, Mrs Haverfield, and the trained nurses, clerk, and sanitary inspector qualified for the St Anne's Medal, Second Class, while orderlies and chauffeurs were awarded the Medal of St Stanislav, Second Class. Owing to the October revolution the actual medals were never received, but the women were sent certificates confirming the awards. BRC 24³/21, Imperial War Museum; and private information, Margaret Cahill and John Orr.
26. Balfour, p 233. The letter is to a niece, but Balfour gives no references.
27. SWH Collection, Fawcett Library.
28. The Zemskii Soyuz, or Union of Zemstva, was a large non-governmental organisation running schools and hospitals in the countryside, and providing medical services for the troops. See Hodges' entry for end of January in Chapter 8.
29. p 642.
30. SWH Collection, Fawcett Library.
31. p 643.
32. SWH Collection, Fawcett Library.
33. McLaren, p 215 and frontispiece; Lawrence (1971), p 261.
34. FO 371/2889/198581.
35. Dr Jambrisak's Memorandum, FO 371/2889/198581.
36. Secret minute from the Admiralty to the War Office insisting that Serbs have priority over these others. FO 371/2889/207047.
37. FO 371/2889/198581.

Chapter 15 Recalled at Last

1. Milne, 'Some Months in Bessarabia', p 646.
2. 25 October, by the Julian Calendar.
3. Kettle, p 103.
4. Letters from General Poole and Captain Pindar to Colonel Byrne. Kettle, p 103.
5. p 644.
6. pp 644-5.
7. Written on November 23 at Tynemouth aboard the *Porto Lisboa*. All Fawcett's entries in this chapter are from the same letter.
8. Telegram No 1750, FO 371/2889/211788.
9. Kettle, p 106.
10. Kettle, pp 107-8.
11. pp 645-6.
12. p 646.
13. The *Porto Lisboa* was an Austrian ship recently captured by the Portuguese; the captain and officers were English, the seamen Chinese.

14. *Paper Boats*, pp 74-5.
15. *Paper Boats*, pp 75-6.
16. Kettle, pp 117-8.
17. Lawrence (1971), p 275.
18. p 647.
19. Entry for July 31, 1917, *Times Diary and Index of the War*.
20. Commodore Bevan had arranged for the Scottish Women to take charge of a sick naval officer who was being invalided home.
21. p 648.
22. *Paper Boats*, pp 73-4.
23. The Second World War.

Chapter 16: Sequels

1. Lawrence (1971), pp 279-81.
2. Moir, Diary, 18 February 1918; Leneman (1994), p 144.
3. Lawrence (1971), p 277n, quoting Arthur Johnson of Newcastle in a letter to *The Guardian* (10 December 69).
4. Lawrence (1971), p 29; Butler, *Daylight in a Dream*, p 35; Butler, *Paper Boats*, pp 73-4.
5. These figures are from Lawrence (1971), p 270, and Foreign Office Records FO 371/2889/ 222192 and FO 371/2889/ 233191.
6. FO 371/2889/237687; FO 371/2889/240698; FO 371/2889/243580; Lawrence (1971), p 270n; Palmer, *The Gardeners of Salonica*, pp 173-4.
7. Palmer, p 70.
8. Moir, Diary entry for 2 April; Leneman (1994), p 161.
9. Falls, *Official History of the War: Military Operations, Macedonia*, Vol 2, pp 68-9; Palmer, p 174.
10. Palmer, Chapters 11 and 12; Brooke-Shepherd, *November 1918*, pp 126-37.
11. Brooke-Shepherd, p 139; Palmer, p 217.
12. Butler, *Paper Boats*, pp 122-3.
13. For a discussion of the factors leading to Ludendorff's decision to ask for peace terms, see Brooke-Shepherd, pp 64-5 and 212.
14. Undated photo-copy of Elsie Bowerman's obituary from the Wycombe Abbey School Gazette, Elsie Bowerman Collection, Fawcett Library.
15. Krippner, pp 207, 210; Leneman (1994), p 203.
16. David Mitchell, *Women on the Warpath*, pp 236-41.
17. Ward, Irene. *F.A.N.Y. Invicta*, p 55.
18. Information from Douglas Gordon Baxter.
19. Photograph Q107973 in the Imperial war Museum Collection identifies Plimsoll among other F.A.N.Y. members being decorated.
20. Hodges, Memoirs; *Times* obituary, 'Mrs Katherine North', 9 December 1982.
21. *Daylight in a Dream*.
22. In February 1918 the Representation of the People Act gave voting rights to women over 30; some of the Scottish Women would have to wait another three or four years for it, although they would have been eligible to stand for Parliament at 21 if they had wished. Strachey, pp 366-8.
23. Yvonne Fitzroy's scrapbook, LHB8/12/8, Lothian Health Services Archive.
24. Obituary, Wycombe Abbey School Gazette.
25. Information from her Memoirs, *Paper Boats*.
26. Leneman (1994), p 211.
27. *The Diary of Virginia Woolf*, entry for 27 November 1925, p 46.
28. A note at the end of Grant's diary directing attention to Moir's letter-book suggests some collusion between the two. The other exceptions were those who served in Macedonia, and were able to join the Salonica Society after demobilisation.
29. Leneman (1994), pp 188-9.

MAPS

Maps

(Marise Bauer and Diana Matheson)

Map 1 Main Battle Fronts in World War 1
    (for Introduction)

Map 2 The Eastern Front 1914-1917
    (for Introduction and Chapter 14)

Map 3 The Dobrudga Front September-October 1916
    (for Chapter 2)

Map 4 Retreat Routes October-December 1916
    (for Chapters 3-8)

Map 5 The Roumanian Front in 1917
    (for Chapters 8, 11, 13 and 14)

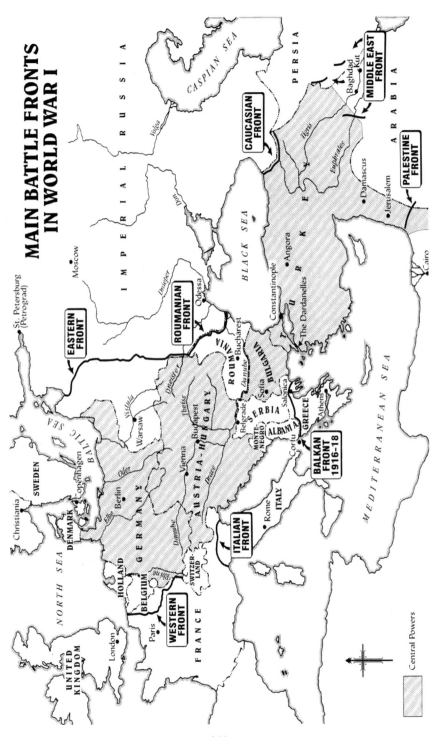

MAIN BATTLE FRONTS IN WORLD WAR I

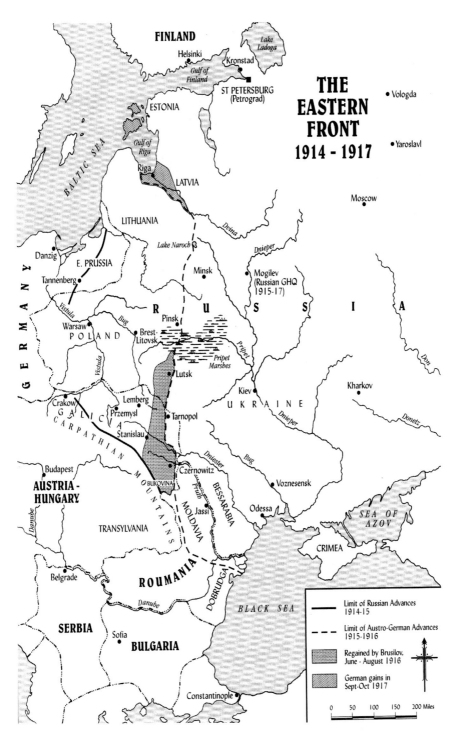

THE
EASTERN
FRONT
1914 - 1917

FINLAND
Helsinki
Lake
Ladoga
Kronstad
Gulf of
Finland
ST PETERSBURG
(Petrograd)
• Vologda

ESTONIA
• Yaroslavl

BALTIC SEA
Gulf of
Riga
Riga
LATVIA

Moscow
•

LITHUANIA
Dvina

Danzig
E. PRUSSIA
Lake Naroch
Dnieper

Tannenberg
Minsk
Mogilev
(Russian GHQ
1915-17)

Vistula
Bug
R   U   S   S   I   A

Pinsk
Warsaw
POLAND
Brest-
Litovsk
Pripet
Pripet
Marshes
Don

Vistula
Lutsk
Kiev
Kharkov

Crakow
Lemberg
UKRAINE
Dnieper
Donetz

GALICIA
Przemysl
Tarnopol
CARPATHIAN
Stanislau

Budapest
Dniester
Bug
Czernowitz
BUKOVINA
Voznesensk

AUSTRIA -
HUNGARY
MOUNTAINS
Pruth
BESSARABIA
Odessa
SEA OF
AZOV

TRANSYLVANIA
MOLDAVIA
Jassi
CRIMEA

Belgrade
ROUMANIA
DOBRUDGA
BLACK SEA

Danube

SERBIA
Sofia
BULGARIA

Constantinople

	Limit of Russian Advances 1914-15
	Limit of Austro-German Advances 1915-1916
	Regained by Brusilov. June - August 1916
	German gains in Sept-Oct 1917

0   50   100   150   200 Miles

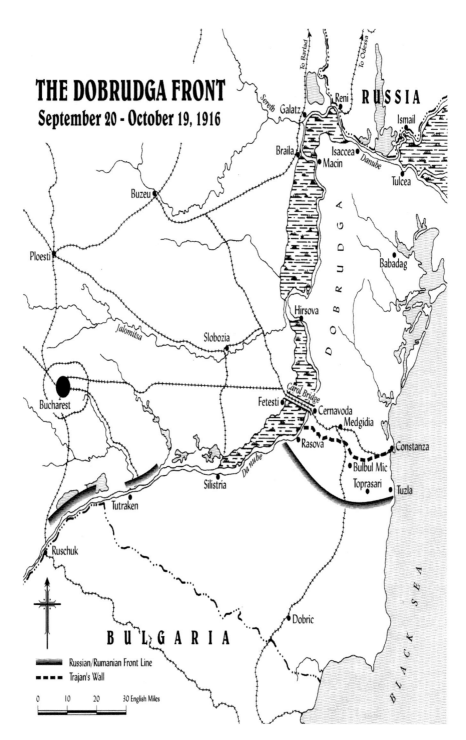

THE DOBRUDGA FRONT
September 20 - October 19, 1916

To Barlad

To Odessa

Sereth

Galatz

Reni

RUSSIA

Ismail

Braila

Isaccea

Macin

Danube

Tulcea

Buzeu

D
O
B
R
U
D
G
A

Babadag

Ploesti

Hirsova

Jalomitsa

Slobozia

Carol Bridge

Bucharest

Fetesti

Cernavoda

Medgidia

Rasova

Constanza

Bulbul Mic

Danube

Silistria

Toprasari

Tuzla

Tutraken

Ruschuk

B
L
A
C
K

S
E
A

Dobric

BULGARIA

Russian/Rumanian Front Line

Trajan's Wall

0   10   20   30 English Miles

348

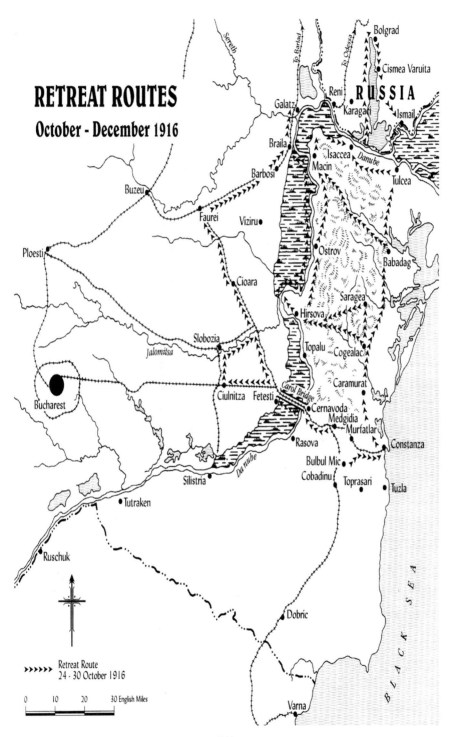

RETREAT ROUTES

October - December 1916

>>>>>> Retreat Route
24 - 30 October 1916

0   10   20   30 English Miles

349

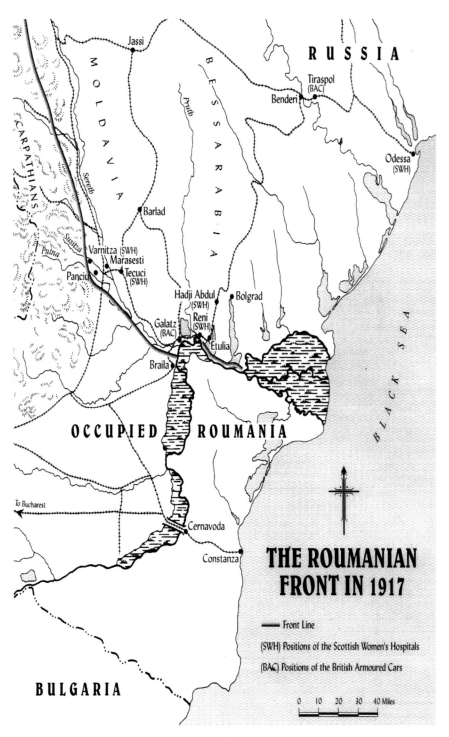

RUSSIA

Jassi

MOLDAVIA

CARPATHIANS

Sereth

Seretu

BESSARABIA

Pruth

Tiraspol
(BAC)

Benderi

Odessa
(SWH)

Barlad

Susitea

Putna

Varnitza (SWH)
Marasesti
Panciu
Tecuci
(SWH)

Hadji Abdul
(SWH)

Bolgrad

Galatz
(BAC)

Reni
(SWH)

Etulia

Braila

BLACK SEA

OCCUPIED   ROUMANIA

To Bucharest

Cernavoda

Constanza

**THE ROUMANIAN
FRONT IN 1917**

Front Line

(SWH) Positions of the Scottish Women's Hospitals

(BAC) Positions of the British Armoured Cars

BULGARIA

0   10   20   30   40 Miles

350

APPENDIX

Members of the London Unit Serving in Roumania and Russia

From lists held by the Mitchell Library and the Fawcett Library. The 1918 dates indicate those members who went on to serve with the Elsie Inglis Unit in Macedonia.

Arbuthnot, Elizabeth G.	Orderly. July-Nov 1917, Feb 1918-Jan 1919
Atkinson, Mary.	Nurse. Aug 1916-Oct 1917
Bangham, Katie E.	Nurse. Aug 1916-Aug 1917
Bell, Angela M.	Orderly. Aug-Nov 1916
Birkbeck, Ysabel	Chauffeur. Aug 1916-April 1917
Bowerman, Elsie E.	Orderly. Aug 1916-March 1917
Brand, Hester	Orderly. Aug 1916-April 1917
Broadbent, Ellenor L.	Laundry Supt. Aug 1916-July 1917
Brown, Lilian J.	Orderly. Aug 1916-March 1917
Butler, Elsie M.	Orderly. July-Nov 1917, Feb-Dec 1918
Carlyon, Charlotte	Chauffeur. Aug 1916-Jan 1917
Chapple, Margaret E.	Sanitary Inspector. July-Nov 1917, Feb-Sept 1918
Chesney, Lilian M.	Doctor. Aug 1916-Sept 1917, Feb 1918-Mar 1919
Clack, Kate D.	Laundry Supt. Aug 1916-Feb 1917
Clibborn, Dorothy M.	Chauffeur. Aug-Nov 1916
Cliver, Mary E.	Nurse. Aug 1916-Oct 1917
Cockshott, Dorothy B.	Chauffeur. July-Nov 1917
Collins, Edith D.	Nurse. July-Nov 1917
Corbett, Catherine L.	Doctor. Aug 1916-Nov 1917
Cowan, Elizabeth B.	Nurse. July-Nov 1917
Cowland, Percy A.	Mechanic. Nov 1916-Nov 1917
Cunningham, Arminella L.	Chauffeur. Aug 1916-Mar 1917
Currie, Agnes	Orderly. Aug-Dec 1916
Curtis, Dora	Chauffeur. April-Nov 1917
Day, George H.	Mechanic. Nov 1916-Nov 1917
Decies, Gertrude	House Supt. May-Oct 1917
Donisthorpe, Francis E.	Chauffeur. Aug 1916-Jan 1917
Douglas, Cecilia M.	Orderly. April-Nov 1917, Feb-Dec 1918
Edwards, Edith M.	Nurse. Aug 1916-Aug 1917

Ellis, Winifred	Chauffeur. Aug 1916-Mar 1917
Faithfull, Edith O.	Chauffeur. Aug 1916-Jan 1917
Fawcett, Margaret	Orderly. Aug 1916-Nov 1917
Fitzroy, Yvonne	Orderly. Aug 1916-June 1917
Fooks, Idaberga	Orderly. April-Nov 1917, Feb 1918-Jan 1919
Ford, Maud R.	Cook. Aug 1916-Nov 1917
Fox, Marion	Matron. Aug 1916-Oct 1917
Gartlan, Eveleen	Chauffeur. Aug 1916-Mar 1917
Genge, Elizabeth M.	Administrator. April-Oct 1917
Gilchrist, Emily L.	Nurse. Aug 1916-Aug 1917
Glubb, Gwenda M.	Chauffeur. Aug 1916-Jan 1917
Grant, Lilias M.	Orderly. Aug 1916-Mar 1917
Gunn, Isabella M.	Cook. July-Nov 1917, Feb-Sept 1918
Gwynn, Margaret K.	Secretary. July-Nov 1917, Feb-Sept 1918
Hanmer, Helen C.	Asst. cook. Aug-Dec 1916
Haverfield, Evelina	Transport officer. Aug 1916-Mar 1917
Haviland, Louise	Orderly. April-Nov 1917, Mar-Sept 1918
Haviland, Maud D.	Orderly. May-Nov 1917
Hedges, Geraldine	Chauffeur. Aug 1916-April 1917
	Laundry Supt. July-Nov 1917
	Transport officer. Feb-Nov 1918
Henderson, Margaret	Nurse. Aug 1916-Aug 1917
Henderson, Mary	Administrator. Aug 1916-July 1917
Higgs, Eveline	Nurse. July-Nov 1917
Hodges, Katherine M.	Chauffeur. Aug 1916-Mar 1917
Holme, Vera	Chauffeur. Aug 1916-Oct 1917
Hopkin, Rowena	Nurse. Aug 1916-Aug 1917
Inglis, Elsie M.	Chief Medical Officer. Aug 1916-Nov 1917
Jackson, Martha	Nurse. Aug 1916-Aug 1917
Jenkins, Florence	Nurse. Aug 1916-Nov 1917
Jenkins, Susannah G.	Nurse. Aug 1916—Aug 1917
Jensen, Gladys Sophie	Chauffeur. Aug-Dec 1916
Johnson, Sybil	Orderly. Aug 1916-Jan 1917
Jones, Elizabeth M.	Nurse. July-Nov 1917
Kent, F. Ruby	Orderly. Aug 1916-Mar 1917
Kinnaird, Margaret W.	Nurse. Aug 1916-Aug 1917
Laird, Janet	Doctor. Dec 1916-Sept 1917
Lewis, Isobel	Orderly. Aug 1916-Nov 1917, Feb-Sept 1918
Little, Winifred E.	Orderly. Aug 1916-Oct 1917
Livesay, Dorothy B.	Chauffeur. Aug 1916-Jan 1917
MacDougall, Mattie J.	Chauffeur. Aug 1916-Mar 1917
MacGuire, Mary E.	Chauffeur. Aug 1916-Jan 1917

Mackenzie, Agnes (Biddy)	Orderly. Aug-Nov 1916
Mackenzie, Catherine I.	Nurse. July-Nov 1917
Mackenzie, Edith M.	Chauffeur. Aug-Dec 1916
Mackenzie-Edwards, Hester	Chauffeur. Aug 1916-April 1917
Marx, C. Margaret	Chauffeur. Nov 1916-Aug 1917
Matheson, Katherine	Nurse. July-Nov 1917
McElhone, Mary A.	Nurse. Aug 1916-Oct 1917
Miller, Catherine C.	Nurse. July-Nov 1917
Milne, Mary L.	Cook. Aug 1916-Nov 1917
Moir, Ethel M.	Orderly. Aug 1916-Feb 1917, Feb 1918-Jan 1919
Monfries, Helen	Chauffeur. Aug-Nov 1916
Mundie, Christine G.	Nurse. Aug 1916-Oct 1917
Murphy, Clare M.	Chauffeur. Aug 1916-Mar 1917
Murphy, M. Agnes	Med. student Aug 1916-Nov 1917, Feb-Dec 1918
Onslow, Alexandrina	Chauffeur. Aug 1916-Mar 1917, June-Nov 1917
Perssé, Daphne G.	Orderly. April-Nov 1917, Feb 1918-Jan 1919
Pleister, E. Margaret	Sanitary Inspector. Aug 1916-Aug 1917
Plimsoll, Ruth W.	Chauffeur. Aug 1916-Mar 1917
Plunket, Irene A.	Orderly. April-Nov 1917
Potter, Lena M.	Doctor. Aug 1916-Mar 1917
Reaney, Mabel J.	Chauffeur. Aug 1916-Jan 1917
Rendel, F. Elinor	Medical student. Aug 1916-Oct 1917
	Doctor. Aug 1918-Mar 1919
Riddoch, Helen C.	Nurse. July-Nov 1917
Robinson, E. Francis	Chauffeur/clerk. Aug 1916-Oct 1917
	Transport officer. Mar 1918-Mar 1919
Robinson, Esther L.	Cook. April-Oct 1917
Sedgwick, Mary K.	Orderly. Aug 1916-Mar 1917
Stewart, Isabella T.	Nurse. July-Nov 1917
Sturt, Winifred	Nurse. July-Nov 1917, Feb 1918-Jan 1919
Suche, Geraldine K.	Cook. Aug 1916-Jan 1917
Tindall, Madge	Chauffeur. July-Nov 1917, Feb 1918-Jan 1919
Turner, Lois	Orderly. Aug 1916-April 1917
Ulph, Laura H.	Nurse. Aug 1916-Aug 1917
Vizard, Mary	Matron. Aug 1916-Nov 1917
Walker, Patricia	Chauffeur. Aug 1916-April 1917
Walker-Brown, Helen	Nurse. Aug 1916-Aug 1917
Ward, Gladys	Doctor. June-Nov 1917, Mar 1918-April 1919
Wilcox, Eva	Nurse. Aug 1916-Oct 1917
Wotherspoon, Elizabeth L.	Clerk. Aug 1916-Aug 1917
Wright, Margaret	Orderly. April-Nov 1917, Mar 1918-Mar 1919

GLOSSARY

ASC	Army Service Corps
BAC	British Armoured Cars
BRC	British Red Cross
CMO	Chief Medical Officer
CO	Commanding Officer
FANY	First Aid and Nursing Yeomanry
GHQ	General Headquarters
GOC	General Officer Commanding
NCO	Non-Commissioned Officer
NUWSS	National Union of Women's Suffrage Societies
OC	Officer Commanding
RAMC	Royal Army Medical Corps
RNAS	Royal Naval Air Service
RNVR	Royal Naval Volunteer Reserve
SWH	Scottish Women's Hospitals
VAD	Voluntary Aid Detachment
WAAC	Women's Army Auxiliary Corps
WRAF	Women's Royal Air Force
WSPU	Women's Social and Political Union

Anglichane	Englishmen
bashlyk	Caucasian hood
blindage	An armoured shelter
Boche	French slang for German
Bolsheviks	The left wing of the Social Democrats
Central Powers	Alliance initially of Germany and Austria-Hungary
chef-de-gare	Station master
chai	Black tea
cojoc (Roum.)	Sheepskin coat
Constitutional Democrats	Reform party espousing democracy under a tsar
dacha	Summer house
droshki	Horse-drawn cab
dugout	Trench shelter; retired officer recalled for service
dvornik	Yard-man
Entente	Informal alliance initially of Russia, France and Britain

eshelon	Military train
Expedition	The Russian Expeditionary Force serving in the Dobrudga
Gregorian calendar	A calendar devised by Pope Gregory XIII in 1582, to correct the inaccuracies of the Julian calendar
gusla	Ancient one-stringed instrument played with a bow
intendantstvo	Supply store
Julian calendar	A calendar devised by Julius Caesar, and followed by Eastern Church and by Russia until 1918
Kadets, KDs	Constitutional Democrats
kasha	Porridge
lazaret	Military hospital
Mensheviks	The right wing of the Social Democrats
nevazhno	It doesn't matter
otryad	Detachment
Privia Lista	Surgical dressing room
sanitar	Ambulance or hospital orderly
sanitary train	Hospital train, often endowed by an aristocrat
sanki	Sleigh
sestra	Sister
sestritsa	Little sister
Social Democrats	Russian Marxist party
Social Revolutionaries	A populist party to the right of the Social Democrats
slava	Anniversary of a Serbian family's conversion to Christianity
Stavka	General Headquarters of the Russian Army
strafe	To bombard; to reprimand (from Ger. *strafen*, to punish)
sukharki	Rye bread rusks
tsar	Emperor
tsarevich	Eldest son of a tsar
tsarina	(Anglicised form of tsaritsa)
tsaritsa	Empress
verst	Just over a kilometre
Zemskii soyuz	Union of rural zemstva and their urban counterparts
zemstvo (pl. zemstva)	Provincial body responsible for rural social services

BIBLIOGRAPHY

Primary Sources: Books

Butler, Elsie *Paper Boats* (Collins, London, 1959).

Fawcett, Margaret *The First World War Papers of Margaret Fawcett* ed. Audrey Fawcett Cahill (Wyllie Desktop Publishing, Pietermaritzburg, 1993).

Fitzroy, Yvonne *With the Scottish Nurses in Roumania* (John Murray, London, 1918).

Henderson, Mary *In War and Peace: Songs of a Scotswoman* (Erskine Macdonald, Edinburgh, 1918).

Primary Sources: Articles

A Member of the Scottish Women's Hospitals [Mary Lee Milne] 'The Dobruja Retreat', *Blackwoods,* March 1918, 335-55.

A Member of the Scottish Women's Hospitals [Mary Lee Milne] 'A Few Weeks in Galatz', *Blackwoods,* April 1918, 477-90.

A Member of the Scottish Women's Hospitals [Mary Lee Milne] 'Some Months in Bessarabia', *Blackwoods,* May 1918, 633-48.

Henderson, Mary 'N.U.W.S.S.: Work in Roumania', *The Common Cause,* 5 January 1917.

Inglis, Elsie Maud 'Three Months on the Eastern Front', *The Englishwoman*, Vol 33 (1917), 113-29.

'L.E.' [Frances Elinor Rendel] 'Fragments from a Diary of the First Retreat in the Dobrudja', *The Englishwoman*, Vol 29 (1916), 65-8.

Primary Sources: Manuscripts and other unpublished material

Atkinson, Mary. Letter to Mrs Laurie (Mitchell Library, Glasgow).

Birkbeck, Ysabel. Diary. In private hands.

Bowerman, Elsie. Diary (Elsie Bowerman Collection, Fawcett Library).

Bowerman, Elsie. Letters (Elsie Bowerman Collection, Fawcett Library).

Bowerman, Elsie. Photograph album (Elsie Bowerman Collection, Fawcett Library).

Brown, L. Jay. Letter to Mrs Summerson (Hawkesley Collection, Imperial War Museum).

Chesney, Lilian. Letter to Miss Chapman (Mitchell Library, Glasgow).

Fawcett, Margaret. Letter-book (Imperial War Museum).

Fawcett, Margaret. Original Diary (Imperial War Museum).

Fawcett, Margaret. Photograph album. In private hands.

Fawcett, Margaret. Retrospective Diary (Imperial War Museum).

Fitzroy, Yvonne. Letters (Lothian Health Services Archive, Edinburgh).

Foreign Office Papers, 1917 (Public Record Office).

Grant, Lilias M. Uncensored Diary (Edinburgh Central Library).

Gregory, Reginald. Reports and Orders (Locker Lampson Collection, Imperial War Museum).

Hedges, Geraldine. Letter to D. Wilkes (SWH Collection, Fawcett Library).

Hodges, Katherine. The Memoirs of Katherine North (née Hodges) (Imperial War Museum and Leeds Russian Archive).

Inglis, Elsie. Excerpts from letters (SWH Collection, Fawcett Library).

Inglis, Elsie. Reports and letters to the London Committee (SWH Collection, Fawcett Library).

Jambrisak, – [Dr] 'Statement to Illustrate the Difficult and Dangerous Position of the Serb Army on the Russian Front' (FO 371/2889/198581, Public Record Office).

Jensen, Gladys. Diary (SWH Collection, Fawcett Library).

Jensen, Gladys. Letter (SWH Collection, Fawcett Library).

King, W.H. 'Ten Months with the Russian Army' (Locker Lampson Collection, Imperial War Museum).

Martin, George. Diary (Locker Lampson Collection, Imperial War Museum).

Marx, C. Margaret. Memorandum on the Situation of the Serbian Divisions in Russia (FO 371/2889/165539, Public Record Office).

Marx, C. Margaret. Photograph album. In private hands.

Marx, C. Margaret. Report (Mitchell Library, Glasgow).

Milne, Mary. Journals of Mary Lee Milne (National Library of Scotland).

Moir, Ethel M. Uncensored Letters (Edinburgh Central Library).

Moir, Ethel M. Diary (1918) (Edinburgh Central Library).

Moir, Ethel M. Photograph album (Edinburgh Central Library).

Onslow, Alexandrina. Letter to Dr Inglis (SWH Collection, Fawcett Library).

Personnel Files of 5th Serbian Unit (Mitchell Library, Glasgow).

Rendel, F.E. Correspondence for 1916 (Imperial War Museum).

Rendel, F.E. Correspondence for 1917 (Imperial War Museum).

Rendel, F.E. Diary (Imperial War Museum).

Rendel, F.E. Letters to Ray Strachey. In private hands.

Scott, G.B. Reports and Orders (Locker Lampson Collection, Imperial War Museum).

Scottish Women's Hospitals Collection. Business books, correspondence, papers, personnel files, press cuttings, and lantern slides (Mitchell Library, Glasgow).

Scottish Women's Hospitals Collection. Reports, records, and correspondence relating to the London Units (SWH Collection, Fawcett Library).

Smith, C.J. Untitled Article (Locker Lampson Collection, Imperial War Museum).

Turner, Lois. Diary. In private hands.

Vizard, Mary. Extracts from letters (Mitchell Library, Glasgow).

Secondary Sources: Women's History; Medical Work; the Scottish Women's Hospitals

Alberti, Johanna *Beyond Suffrage: Feminists in War and Peace, 1914-28* (Macmillan, London, 1989).

Balfour, Lady Frances *Dr Elsie Inglis* (Hodder and Stoughton, London, 1918).

Berry, James, Frances May Dickinson Berry, W. Lyon Blease, and other members of the unit *The Story of a Red Cross Unit in Serbia* (Churchill, London, 1916).

Blunt, Wilfred *Lady Muriel* (Methuen, London, 1962).

Braybon, Gail *Women Workers in the First World War: the British Experience* (Croom Helm, London, 1981).

Braybon, Gail and Penny Summerfield *Out of the Cage* (Pandora, London, 1987).

Butler, Elsie *Daylight in a Dream* (Hogarth Press, London 1951).

The Common Cause Weekly Journal of the NUWSS, 1914-1917 (Fawcett Library).

Condell, Diana and Jean Liddiard *Working for Victory? Images of Women in the First World War 1914-1918* (Routledge and Kegan Paul, London, 1987).

Crofton, Eileen *The Women of Royaumont* (Tuckwell Press, East Linton, 1997).

Dixon, Jess (ed.) *Little Grey Partridge* (University Press, Aberdeen, 1988).

Farmborough, Florence. F.R.G.S. *Nurse at the Russian Front: A Diary 1914-1918* (Constable, London, 1974).

Krippner, Monica *The Quality of Mercy* (David and Charles, London, 1980).

Lawrence, Margot *Shadow of Swords: A Biography of Elsie Inglis* (Michael Joseph, London, 1971).

Leneman, Leah *A Guid Cause* (Aberdeen University Press, 1991).

Leneman, Leah *In the Service of Life* (Mercat Press, Edinburgh, 1994).

Macdonald, Lyn *The Roses of No Man's Land* (Michael Joseph, 1980; Papermac, 1984).

Marwick, Arthur *Women at War 1914-1918* (Fontana, Glasgow, 1977).

McGann, Susan *The Battle of the Nurses* (Scutari Press, London, 1992).

McLaren, Eva Shaw *A History of the Scottish Women's Hospitals* (Hodder and Stoughton, London, 1919).

Mitchell, David *Women on the Warpath* (Jonathan Cape, London, 1966).

Popham, Hugh *F.A.N.Y. 1907-1984* (Lee Cooper, London, 1984).

Strachey, Ray *The Cause: A Short History of the Women's Movement in Great Britain* (Bell and Sons, 1928; Virago, London, 1978, 1989).

Summers, Anne *Angels and Citizens* (Routledge and Kegan Paul, 1988).

Thurstan, Violetta *Field Hospital and Flying Column* (Putnam's Sons, London and New York, 1915).

Ward, Irene *F.A.N.Y. Invicta* (London, Hutchinson, 1955).

Secondary Sources: The War; Russian History and Politics

Banac, Ivo 'South Slav Prisoners of War in Revolutionary Russia', Williamson and Pastor (eds.), 119-48.

Brooke-Shepherd, Gordon *November 1918: The Last Act of the Great War* (Collins, London, 1981).

Buchanan, Sir George *My Mission to Russia and other Diplomatic Memories* (Little, Brown, Boston, 1923).

Buchanan, Meriel *Ambassador's Daughter* (Cassell, London, 1958).

Buitenhuis, Peter *The Great War of Words* (Batsford, London, 1989).

Carmichael, Joel *A Short History of the Russian Revolution* (Sphere, London, 1966).

Cecil, Hugh and Peter H. Liddle (eds) *Facing Armageddon: The First World War Experienced* (Leo Cooper, London, 1996).

Cruttwell, C.R. *A History of the Great War, 1914-1918* (Clarendon, Oxford, 1934, 1936).

Falls, Cyril *The First World War* (Longmans, London, 1960).

Falls, Cyril *Official History of the War: Military Operations, Macedonia*, Vol 2 (London, 1933).

Gilbert, Martin *First World War* (Weidenfeld and Nicolson, London, 1994).

Gilbert, Martin *First World War Atlas* (Weidenfeld and Nicolson, London, 1970).

Griess, Thomas E. *Atlas for the Great War, 1914-1918* (Avery Publishing Group, New Jersey, 1986).

Hart, B.H. Liddell *History of the First World War* (Cassell, London, 1930, 1970).

Haythornthwaite, Philip J. *The World War One Source Book.* (Arms and Armour, 1996).

Katkov, George *Russia 1917: The Kornilov Affair* (Longmans, London, 1980).

Kerensky, Alexander *The Crucifixion of Liberty*. Trans. G. Kerensky (Arthur Barker, London, 1934).

Kettle, Michael *The Allies and the Russian Collapse*: Vol I 1917-1918 (Andre Deutsch, 1981).

Lawrence, Margot 'The Serbian Divisions in Russia, 1916-1917', *Journal of Contemporary History,* Vol 6, no 4, 1971.

Lockhart, Bruce *Memoirs of a British Agent* (Putnam, London and New York, 1932).

Ludendorff, E. *My War Memories 1914-1919*, 2 vols (Hutchinson, London, 1920).

Macdonald, Lyn *1914* (Michael Joseph, London, 1987).

Maclean, Fitzroy *Holy Russia* (Weidenfeld and Nicolson, London 1978).

Mstislavskii, Sergei *Five Days which Transformed Russia*. Translated by Elizabeth K. Zelensky (Hutchinson, London, 1988).

Palmer, Alan *The Gardeners of Salonica* (Andre Deutsch, London, 1965).

Pares, Bernard *Day by Day with the Russian Army* (Constable, London, 1915).

Pares, Bernard, *The Fall of the Russian Monarchy* (Jonathan Cape, London, 1939).

Pares, Bernard *A History of Russia* (Jonathan Cape, London, 1926, 1949).

Pares, Bernard *My Russian Memoirs* (Jonathan Cape, London, 1931).

Perrett, Bryan and Anthony Lord *The Czar's British Squadron* (William Kimber, London, 1981).

Reed, John *Ten Days that Shook the World* (Boni and Liveright, 1919; Penguin, Harmondsworth, 1966).

Reports by the Joint War Committee and the Joint Finance Committee of the British Red Cross Society and the Order of St John of Jerusalem in England on Voluntary Aid Rendered to the Sick and Wounded at Home and Abroad and to British Prisoners of War, 1914-1919 (HM Stationery Office, London, 1921).

Robbins, Keith *The First World War* (Oxford University Press, 1984; OUP Paperback, 1985, 1993).

Schmitt, Bernadotte E. and Harold C. Vedeler *The World in Crucible* (Harper and Row, New York, 1984).

Service, Robert *Lenin: A Political Life*, Vol 2 (Macmillan, London, 1991).

Service, Robert *The Russian Revolution 1900-1927* (Macmillan, London, 1986, 1991).

Stone, Norman *The Eastern Front 1914-1917* (Hodder and Stoughton, London, 1975).

Terraine, John *The First World War 1914-18* (Macmillan, 1965; Papermac, London, 1984).

The Times Diary and Index of the War, 1914-1918 (Hodder and Stoughton, for *The Times*, London, N.D.).

The Times History of the War, Vols. IX-XIII. (*The Times*, London, 1916-1917).

Tuchman, Barbara *August 1914* (Constable, London, 1962).

Turner, John *British Politics and the Great War: Coalition and Conflict 1915-1918* (Yale University Press, New Haven, and London, 1992).

Vansittart, Peter *Voices from the Great War* (Jonathan Cape, London, 1981).

Vernadsky, George and others (eds.) *A Source Book for Russian History from Early Times to 1917,* Vol. 3. Compiled by Sergei Pushkarev (Yale University Press, New Haven and London, 1972).

Von Mohrenschildt, Dimitri (ed.) *The Russian Revolution of 1917: Contemporary Accounts* (Oxford University Press, New York, London and Toronto, 1971).

Von Rintelen, Franz *The Dark Invader* (Lovat Dickson, London, 1933).

Walpole, Hugh *The Dark Forest* (Nelson, London, 1916).

Williamson, Jr, Samuel R. and Peter Pastor (eds.) *Essays on World War 1: Origins and Prisoners of War* (Social Science Monographs, Brooklyn College Press, New York, 1983).

Wilson, H.W. and J.A. Hammerton *The Great War,* Vols 7-9 (The Amalgamated Press, London, 1916-1917).

Wiltsher, Anne *Most Dangerous Women: Feminist Peace Campaigns of the Great War* (Pandora, London, 1985).

Winter, J.M. *The Great War and the British People* (Macmillan, London, 1986).

Youssoupoff, Prince [Felix Yusupov] *Rasputin* Translated Oswald Rayner (Jonathan Cape, 1927; Florin Books, 1934).

Zeman, Z.A.B. *A Diplomatic History of the First World War* (Weidenfeld and Nicolson, London, 1971).

Zeman, Z.A.B. (eds.) *Germany and the Revolution in Russia 1915-1918: Documents from the Archives of the German Foreign Ministry* (Oxford University Press, London, 1958).

INDEX

'Scottish Women's Hospitals Russian Unit' refers to the whole unit; the three sections of the unit are indexed under 'Hospital A', 'Hospital B' and 'Transport'. Entries in bold refer to **chapters** in which there are substantial narratives concerning those groups, or more than two diary or letter extracts by the writer indexed.